212973634

THE LONG WORK HOURS CULTURE:
CAUSES, CONSEQUENCES AND CHOICES

THE LONG WORK HOURS CULTURE: CAUSES, CONSEQUENCES AND CHOICES

EDITED BY

RONALD J. BURKE

Schulich School of Business,
York University,
Toronto, Canada

CARY L. COOPER

Lancaster University Management School,
Lancaster University,
Lancaster, UK

United Kingdom • North America • Japan
India • Malaysia • China

Emerald Group Publishing Limited
Howard House, Wagon Lane, Bingley BD16 1WA, UK

First edition 2008

Copyright © 2008 Emerald Group Publishing Limited

Reprints and permission service
Contact: booksandseries@emeraldinsight.com

British Library Cataloguing in Publication Data
A catalogue record for this book is available from the British Library

ISBN: 978-1-84855-038-4

Printed and bound by MPG Books Ltd, Bodmin, Cornwall

Awarded in recognition of
Emerald's production
department's adherence to
quality systems and processes
when preparing scholarly
journals for print

INVESTOR IN PEOPLE

Contents

List of Contributors

Morris Altman	Department of Economics, University of Saskatchewan, Canada
Arnold B. Bakker	Department of Work and Organizational Psychology, Erasmus University, The Netherlands
Carmen Binnewies	Department of Psychology, University of Konstanz, Germany
Ronald J. Burke	Schulich School of Business, York University, Canada
Rebecca Burwell	Lecturer, Consestoga College, Canada
Charles P. Chen	Ontario Institute for Studies in Education, University of Toronto, Canada
Lisa Fiksenbaum	Department of Psychology, York University, Canada
Lonnie Golden	Department of Economics and Labor Studies, Pennsylvania State University, PA, USA
Francis Green	Department of Economics, University of Kent, UK
Constance Noonan Hadley	John F. Kennedy School of Government, Harvard University, MA, USA
Anne Laure Humbert	Middlesex University Business School, Middlesex, UK
Jerry A. Jacobs	Department of Sociology, University of Pennsylvania, PA, USA
Suzan Lewis	Middlesex University Business School, Middlesex, UK

Lynley H. W. McMillan	Simply Strategic, Tauranga, New Zealand
Carla Medalia	Department of Sociology, University of Pennsylvania, PA, USA
Jason M. Moore	Department of Criminal Justice, Washington State University, WA, USA
Michael P. O'Driscoll	Department of Psychology, University of Waikato, New Zealand
Jamie L. Perry	Department of Psychology, Rutgers University, NJ, USA
Gayle Porter	School of Business, Rutgers University-Camden, NJ, USA
Wilmar B. Schaufeli	Department of Social and Organizational Psychology, Utrecht University, The Netherlands
Sabine Sonnentag	Department of Psychology, University of Konstanz, Germany
Toon W. Taris	Department of Work and Organizational Psychology, Radboud University, The Netherlands
Bryan Vila	Department of Criminal Justice, Washington State University, WA, USA

Preface ☆

Congress reduces work-week to 135 hours.
> — *The Onion*, Tuesday, May 20, 1902

In a move that resounded like thunder throughout our great Republic, a congress made up of influential Progressive Republicans has voted 'Yea' on legislation that would cut the work-week to a scant 135 hours and hobble fair Dame Industry with many other insidious and crippling reforms.
> — *The Onion*, 1999, Running Press Book Publishers

This tongue-in-cheek newspaper story has some truth to it. Consider the following vignettes, obviously not a random or representative sample of people's experiences at work. The first two were taken from do Rosario (1991) and the third from the *Globe and Mail*, a Canadian newspaper. They illustrate, first, death from overwork, and second, the extent to which some people overwork.

Shinji Masami, 37, a design engineer at Hino Motors, a large subsidiary of Toyota that produces trucks, had to design parts that fit together in final assembly. The job was intense and had pressing deadlines. From 1980 through 1986, Masami worked an average of 2600 h, about 25% more than the average Japanese. Days before his death he complained of severe headaches and abdominal pains. Yet he forced himself to go to work until his last day. He died of brain hemorrhage while at work in the office.

Jun Ishii, 47, a manager of Mitsui's Soviet division, collapsed and died at a business hotel after having spent his last five days escorting Russian visitors to local machine manufacturers. During the 10 months preceding his death, Ishii had made many business trips, totally 103 days, to the Soviet Union, with little time for rest in between.

The *Globe and Mail*'s Report on Business (January 2008, pp. 24–33) had a profile of Tony Merchant, a Canadian lawyer. Merchant wakes up at 2:00 am and is in his office at 4:00 am. He reportedly billed 5300 h in 2005, when most lawyers consider

☆ Preparation of this manuscript was supported in part by York University.

2000 h a demanding workload; 14.5 h a day, 365 days a year, leaving 9 h a day for everything else. He apparently has few hobbies and rarely takes time to eat and is married with grown children. Not surprisingly, his law firm has staff answering the phone from 7:00 am to midnight.

This volume examines the long hours work culture that exists in many organizations and in many professions. It considers why people work long hours and the risks and rewards of working long hours. Should organizations care about the number of hours their employees work? Should long work hours be a concern if organizations are to be effective and truly socially responsible?

Imagine this scenario. An organization is able to have their employees work incredibly long hours and not have to pay them any wages. Although this is obviously unrealistic in most countries, it has recently come to light (November 2007) that some organizations in China had boys and girls working long hours for no pay, being kept as virtual slaves. Children as young as 9 working in filth up to 15 h a day, sleeping on the floor in the room in which they worked all day. A more recent story in the *National Post* reported a study by Human Rights Watch indicating that migrant workers in China are working 17 h a day in order to get Beijing ready for the Summer Olympics and are underpaid and mistreated without insurance to cover workplace injuries. Apparently six migrant workers had already died while working on these construction sites. Migrant workers get paid about $200 a month with many working for considerably less.

But now imagine that some organizations are able to have some employees work extra hours, typically overtime beyond the contracted for hours, and not have to pay their employees for these extra hours. This scenario does exist today. For years many organizations have had employees work unpaid overtime hours. Employees, however, are increasingly unwilling to work these unpaid hours and are successfully taking their employers to court to receive back payment (Orey, 2007) consider the following:

- IBM paid $65 million to 32,000 technical and support workers (November 2006).
- Citigroup/Solomon Smith Barney paid $98 million to 20,000 current and former stockbrokers (June 2006).
- UPS paid $87 million to 23,000 drivers (October 2006).
- Cases pending include FedEx, Wal-mart, Intel, Sprint Nextell, and CIBC among others.
- KPMG, in an attempt to circumvent a class-action lawsuit, has admitted that it withheld $10 million in overtime pay from some employees. KPMG said it would pay employees who should have been paid overtime over the last eight years and apologized for not paying them. The original suit was for $50 million in unpaid overtime. KPMG has also develop an "overtime redress policy" to be administered by an outside firm.

Some occupations have historically been exempt from overtime including executives, professionals, creatives, administrators, and outside sales people. Other occupations fall into ill-defined categories: store managers, accountants, and sales representatives.

An employee working for Oprah Winfrey, however, filed for more than US $39,000 in overtime pay having worked 800 h of overtime (112–113 working hours, 7 days a week, January through April 2007). Unlike the employees of those other organizations mentioned above that are currently suing their employers for overtime, she received the money — but no free car!

Work hours has become a "hot topic" in the past few years (Bunting, 2004; Philipson, 2002). Some government and business leaders have stated that employees need to work more hours (e.g., Canada, France) if their countries are to remain competitive. The evidence in the developed, industrialized, and wealthier countries has shown that blue-collar workers are now working fewer hours than earlier while their professional and managerial colleagues are working more hours. Several factors are likely at work here. More organizations operate on a 24/7 basis; there is more competitive pressure on organizations; downsizings and cost containment initiatives have either increased the work load, reduced staff or both; new technology makes it possible to work from anywhere at any time; increasing competition for fewer promotions as hierarchies flatten, higher organizational performance expectations; peer pressure, potential rewards, and in a small number of instances, work life has been reported to be more satisfying than home life (Hochschild, 1997). It is certain that more organizations will have facilities across the world to reduce turnaround time by working around the clock based on a 24 h productivity model. A project will be started in one part of the world, passed on to a second, and then to a third, where it will be completed.

There also exist wide country differences in average yearly hours work; the US and UK are high, France and Germany are low. Managers in the UK work the longest hours in Europe, 42% working more than 60 h a week against an average 34% of all European managers. Spanish managers were the lowest (28%), followed by Italians (29%), and French (30%). More than half the survey respondents, however, stated that they worked more hours now (2007) than in 2000.

There is also some evidence that work intensity (e.g., pace, level of responsibility) has also increased during this time with a corresponding increase in levels of reported workplace stress. Not surprisingly, there have also been signs of decreasing job satisfaction in some quarters during this same time period. Thus although many companies may want their employees to work more hours, most employees actually want to work fewer hours.

Work hours have also become problematic because of the changing demographics of the workforce. There are more women in the workforce, and many of these women have home and family responsibilities making working long hours difficult. Forty percent of 124 working mothers in the US surveyed by Careerbuilder.com said they would take a pay cut if it bought them more time with their children. Twenty-three percent of US working mothers missed three of more significant events in their children's lives in the past year, and 28% said their jobs negatively affected their relationship with their children. There are also more dual-earner families with children. In addition, the younger generation of employees seems to be more interested in integrating both their work and personal lives than were the present generation of managers and professionals. Most workers would prefer to work fewer hours (Babbar & Aspelin, 1998).

In the past few months, several writers in Canada (primarily economists) have suggested that we Canadians are not working enough hours resulting in lower levels of productivity and a lower standard of living (less per capita income) than other countries or US states where women and men work more hours. Economists refer to this as a "prosperity gap". It seems that Ontarians (citizens of the province in which I live) work three and a half weeks less per year than do our US counterparts. Ontarians are more like the French in this regard. It seems that highly educated and well-paid Ontarians in particular are less interested in working more hours to become wealthier. It is also not clear that working more hours equates with working harder or smarter. This raises the intriguing question of whether working more hours per year represents real prosperity. Although women and men in the UK are now working long and longer hours, when this trend began, they referred to it as "the American disease". Nicholas Sarkozy won the Presidency of France in 2007, a key part of his campaign was a call to end the 35 h workweek. In order to increase their standard of living and levels of pay, citizens of France will apparently have to work more hours and be more productive.

In addition to longer working hours for some, there is also evidence that work intensity has increased for many during the past decade or two. More than 60% of workers in the UK claimed that the pace of work and the effort they had to put into their job had increased during the past five years. Both work intensification and job insecurity were associated with poor general health and tense family relationships. About 60% stated that the speed of work had also increased during this period. Major causes of work intensification include organizational and technological changes, high involvement work organizations, downsizing of staff, increasing job insecurity, declining union membership, and increased computerization and automation (Burchall, Lapido, & Wilkinson, 2002; Green, 2001).

What do we know about long work hours, work intensification, and work addiction? There is research support for the following observations.

The Japanese have coined a term, "karoshi", to refer to death from overwork and have specified the number of hours of consecutive and total hours needed to qualify as such a death.

The International Labor Organization (ILO), a United Nation's agency, based on a study of working trends in 50 countries reported that one in five people, more than 600 million worldwide, worked excessively long hours based on a maximum 48 h work week, the ILO standard developed almost 100 years ago. Peruvians worked the longest hours, with the British highest among the developed richer countries. The ILO concluded that shorter working hours benefits employee's health and family lives, lowers accidents and errors in the workplace, and increases employee efficiency and productivity.

Managers and professionals often choose to work long hours as they believe this shows senior managers that they are committed to the organization and willing to put work ahead of all else. Working long hours seems to be essential in some professions if one is to advance (Wallace, 1997). There is also evidence of a relationship between hours worked and objective indicators of career success such as income and career advancement. Duckworth Peterson, Matthews, and Kelly (2007) have shown, in a series of studies, that grit — defined as perseverance and striving for long-term goals — was associated with objective indicators of success. Should it then be surprising that ambitious women and men work long hours? Some senior managers, however, may view employees working long hours, non-stop, in a stressed-out way as signs that they are not capable of taking on more responsibility.

In Japan, dozing in a meeting is permitted. It is called "inemuri" and is defined as to be asleep while present, and is viewed as exhaustion from working hard and sacrificing sleep at night. Many employees then fake sleep while in meetings to look committed to their jobs.

In addition are managers and professions ever really "free"? Donnelly (2006) examined flexibility available to knowledge workers, consultants in this case. These well-educated and highly paid individuals were unable to control their work arrangements being restricted by the needs of their employers, clients," profession-alism", network relations, and personal career ambitions.

Long work hours and overtime work have been found to be associated with adverse psychological and physical health difficulties.

Time, like money, is a finite resource. There are only 24 h a day and 365 days in a year. Like money, time is saved, spent, and wasted. Time is needed to participate in activities that make people happy and improve their well-being. Time is also needed to support personal growth, close relationships, and community involvement (Kasser, 2002; Myers, 2000; Van Boven & Gilovich, 2003). A shortage of time, time poverty, can reduce experiences of joy and spontaneity and increase feelings of pressure and overload.

Long work hours and overtime work have been shown to be associated with negative family functioning. Most children want their parents to work fewer hours and would trade off material benefits for more time with their parents (Galinsky, 1999; Taylor, 2003).

Taylor (2003) found that children want more time with friends and family not more "stuff". Ninety percent of children ages 9–14 said that friends and family were "way more important" than things that money could buy. Time starvation emerged as a major concern for these children; about one quarter indicated that their parents were too busy working to spend time with them. Less than one in three children said they spent a lot of time with their parents. Nearly two-thirds said they wished their parents had a job that gave them more time to do things together.

When individuals work long hours it provides new workforce entrants with negative images of the costs of success.

Women more than men have difficulties working long hours because of family and home responsibilities. It is possible that this is one explanation for the "glass ceiling", the relatively small number of women at senior levels of large organizations. Women in law firms are so concerned about appearing unproductive they sometimes conceal cancer or heart attacks to avoid being judged weak. One lawyer had a heart attack but returned claiming he had been on a vacation.

Long work hours also impose costs to society as a whole. Working women and men are less able to participate as citizens, and consequences of working long hours impose a drain on the health care and social welfare systems.

Some employees feel guilty about their work hours and how these affect their personal and family lives (Hochwarter, Perrewe, Meurs, & Kacmar, 2007).

Managers and professionals are often unable or unwilling to use all of their vacation time. There are even "how to" suggestions on managing your work while on vacations (e.g., have technology always available to capture your thoughts, give staff your number where you can be reached). Not surprisingly, the benefits of vacations on levels of employee stress tend to be short-lived; within a few weeks it is "business as usual" (Westman & Eden, 1997). But taking vacations have health benefits regardless of their duration. Men and women taking their vacations have fewer heart attacks and deaths from a variety of causes.

About half of managers and professionals work during their lunchtime. It has been shown that managers that take a complete break from work during lunchtime are more productive. Useful things to do during one's lunch instead of working include napping or resting without interruption, socializing with colleagues over lunch, having lunch with a friend, reading a good book, or going for a walk (Mednick & Ehrwan, 2006).

Sirota Survey Intelligence in a press release titled "Bored employees are more disgruntled than overworked ones" found that people would rather have too much work rather than too little work. They acknowledge however the downside of work overload.

William Strange and Stuart Rosenthal, in a recent article published in the *Review of Economics and Statistics*, compared hours of work in three large and three small US cites and found that employees in the same professions (e.g., lawyers, accountants, investment bankers) worked more hours in the larger cities than in the smaller ones. They attribute this, in part, to having workplace rivals — a kind of urban rat race.

Long work hours and overtime work are associated with fewer hours of sleep. Sleep deprivation is associated with increased on-the-job accidents, increased off-the-job accidents, and reduced job performance. Medical interns working long hours have actually fallen asleep during surgery and during patient interviews. In addition, medical interns working long hours report more car accidents and near misses after work. A study of 350 medical trainees intern (physicians) and other health care workers in Canada and the US, recently published in Infection Control and Hospital Epidemiology, who had sought help for sharp object injury found that the average intern had worked almost 70 h in the previous week and almost 40% reported fatigue at the time of the injury.

Czeisler and his colleagues found that overworked interns made 36% more serious medical errors and five times as many diagnostic mistakes during a typical work shift than did their better rested colleagues. Duty hours of interns have been limited to 80 h per week but interns can still work for continuous stretches of 30 h at a time. Interns working five marathon shifts (24 consecutive hours or more in a week) in a month were seven times more likely to report significant medical errors than interns working no marathon shifts. Interns working more than five marathon shifts a month (24–30 h in length) were involved in 300% more fatal errors and were more likely to fall asleep during surgery, while examining patients in hospital rounds, and during lectures and seminars. You might ask your intern how much sleep she/he had during the past month before going under!

Going without sleep or sleeping as little as 4–5 h daily for a week produces the same level of cognitive impairment as is if the person were legally drunk with a blood alcohol level of 1.0 (Czeisler, 2006). Organizations would never reward employees who came to work drunk yet they praise individuals who go without sleep so they can work more.

Besides tired physicians, Vila (1996) suggests we should also be concerned about tired cops. Tired cops are more likely to make errors, sometimes involving the excessive use of force. Police officers in high crime areas often work 20 h of overtime a week. Interestingly, most police departments had no policies limiting hours worked in a week or a month.

Sleep loss has been found to play a role in heavy truck driver traffic fatalities, the Challenger explosion, Three Mile Island, Chernobyl, and the Exxon Valdez disasters (Mitler, Carskadon, Czeisler, & Diment, 1988). Drivers in some countries have been convicted of vehicular homicide for driving while impaired by sleeplessness.

The most productive time of the regular workday is 10:30 am. People lose focus after 3:30 pm and start thinking about what they plan to do after work. A recent study in the UK sponsored by the large pharmacy chain, Boots Co. PLC, found that workers in the UK have enough energy to work only for five hours of the day.

Czeisler (2006) argues that companies should develop sleep policies that: limit scheduled work to no more than 12 h a day (16 h in exceptional circumstances), 11 consecutive hours of rest every 24 h, scheduled for 60 h a week but not more and not permitted to work more than 80 h, and for those working nights, only scheduled 4 or 5 consecutive days, taking red-eye flights should be discouraged, if traveling overnight, the individual should have the next day to adapt. Corporate education programs should address sleep, health, and safety content. Both alcohol and caffeine interfere with sleep and their use should be discouraged. Managers should receive training in sleep and fatigue management.

Some individuals report "leisure sickness", emotional and physical symptoms while on vacation or on weekends (van Heck & Vingerhoets, 2007).

A recent study reported that Americans on average spend 38 h per year stuck in traffic jams on the way to work. This figure did not include commuting time. The highest figure was 70 h per year in Los Angeles. This adds to the work hours actually spent on the job.

A newspaper article reported data on the speed people walk in various cities and how these speeds have increased over the years. This probably reflects increases in the speed that people undertake an increasing number of activities nowadays.

There has been an increase in multitasking — doing several things at once. Multitasking has been shown to decrease performance effectiveness; the "time cost" from switching from one task to another is significant. Employees are more productive if they spend time and concentrate on only one thing for an unbroken period of time. Multitasking while driving (use of cell phones, sending and receiving e-mails) increases the risk of accidents.

Middleton and Cukier (2006), based on focus groups and interviews with mobile e-mail users, found that this technology had both functional and dysfunctional characteristics. They suggest however that individuals can reduce the dysfunctional qualities of the technology and offer practical suggestions in this regard. Some individuals reported sending work-related messages on their Blackberries while driving to work. Others, thankfully, reported waiting for a stop sign before checking their e-mails.

A recent study by Solutions Research interviewed more than 3000 Canadians in 2007 and reported that 26% exhibited strong levels of disconnect anxiety. Some respondents reported taking their Blackberrys with them to the bathroom.

A new term "no-mo-phobia" was recently coined in the UK, being short for "no mobile", as more than half of the UK's cell phone users feel anxious when they lose their mobile phone, run out of battery power or credit, or have no network coverage. An online survey of 2163 people found, in response to the question of whether they would interrupt various situations to take a call on their mobile phones, the following: 58% when in bed alone; 18% when in bed with someone else; 40% when eating a meal; 80% when watching TV; 79% when shopping, 48% when spending time with family; 78% when doing gardening or yard work; and 56% when in the bathroom.

Blackberry, e-mail, and cell phones intrude into an individual's personal time and distract from one's work (Wajcman, 2008). Research has shown that employees working on a computer typically check e-mail 30–40 times an hour and one-third feel stressed by the number of e-mails they receive and the felt obligation to respond quickly. It has been estimated that these interruptions produce a drop of 10 IQ points in those being interrupted. Experts suggest the following: turn off one's automatic e-mail notification, block e-mails on which one is cc'd, and understand that receiving a lot of e-mails does not mean that one is important. Turn off one's technology; if people need to contact you in an emergency, they will phone you (Song, 2004).

A study by Alan Hedge, a Professor at Cornell University, found that individuals spending a lot of time sitting at computers are more productive and accurate if they take breaks, stand up, stretch, and assume good posture while working.

A recent global survey of 20,000 professionals indicated that 70% admitted a constant urge to check their Blackberry after hours and on weekends.

Some companies are now declaring e-mail free days, setting aside thinking time and waging war on Blackberry addiction. Some firms begin with ruling out e-mail on one day. Individuals in such firms talk more with colleagues in person and do more thinking and planning.

Other companies discourage employees from sending out e-mails between 7:00 pm and 7:00 am and on the weekends and on holidays.

Individuals feeling under the pressure of time demands can now outsource the handling of routine daily tasks. Individuals, likely to be in India, can be paid a relatively low hourly rate to take care of the mundane tasks that busy professions find they have not enough time to do. In addition, small jobs can be posted online and individuals can then bid on undertaking to do them.

Different types of workaholics have been identified, some dissatisfied with their jobs and reporting psychological distress (e.g., Work Addicts) while other types were more satisfied with their jobs and reported psychological well-being (e.g., Work Enthusiasts) though both worked the same number of hours per week. The key differences were why (motivations) and how (work behaviors) they worked hard.

There are both performance and financial costs to organizations from high levels of employee fatigue.

Most theories of work motivation taught to business students in MBA programs and executive development offerings have the effect of enhancing work hours and workaholic behaviors (Boje & Rosile, 2004).

There is evidence, however, that managers and professionals in "extreme jobs", jobs in which they worked 60–70 h a week or more, reported high levels of satisfaction, excitement, and commitment. They did, however, express some concern about the effects of these hours on their well-being and that of their families, and some hoped to work fewer hours in the near future (Hewlett & Luce, 2006). Key factors in accounting for these high levels of satisfaction were levels of challenge, rewards and perks, development opportunities, and sense of meaning and accomplishment.

Individuals get seduced by the rewards and recognition they receive from working long hours and going the extra mile. Several writers have documented the process by which organizations mold individuals to put work over everything else (e.g., Carr, 1993; Kofodimos, 1993; LaBier, 1986; Maccoby, 1980). Maccoby has observed that organizations mold the character of their employees in ways that strengthened their "head"(industrious, independent, tough, driven to succeed) and diminished their "heart" (emotional, compassionate, empathetic). In becoming valued members or their organizations, individuals gave up much of their individuality — captured by Carr (1993) by the phrase "a passion to please". Individuals came to view their identities in terms of their work context. Individual worth too often became defined by income, organization, and job status and trappings of success.

Dunn-Jensen (2007) undertook a study of the relationship between time norms in an organization, amount of face time put in (time spent at work not accomplishing tasks of significance), and work–family conflict. She found that norms supporting longer work hours were associated with more face time, and face time, in turn, was associated with higher levels of work–family conflict.

For some people, work can be more rewarding than home. A Canadian survey reported that one in four workers said that work was less demanding than home, and one quarter of Canadian workers had used work as an excuse to avoid a family function. About one-third of Canadians indicated that they looked forward to the start of the workweek. Thank God it's Monday!

Under-aged workaholics? A study released by Statistics Canada showed that teens between 15–19 spent about 7.1 h per day on unpaid or paid labor. Twenty percent of teens worked at a paid job for 5 h on the day the survey was conducted; and 16% of teens considered themselves to be workaholics.

Two studies of law students in the US found that psychological well-being decreased during the first year of their studies; these decreases were correlated with reduced levels of intrinsic motivation during their first year and increases in "appearance" values and decreases in "community" service values. These declines (intrinsic motivation, psychological well-being) continued in their second and third years of study. Why did these changes take place? The researchers identified the following: excessive workloads, stress, competition for academic superiority, status seeking placement services, hierarchical symbols of worth, emphasis on analysis and linear thinking, student-intimidating teaching practices, and abstract content in courses. Thus the teaching taking place in the legal profession thwarts growth. A common stereotype of lawyers, particularly in North America, includes shallowness, greed, and hyper-competitiveness.

Some organizations are taking actions to reduce work hours caused by pressures for "face time" and wasting hours on the job (e.g., fewer meetings, reducing unnecessary reports). Surveys have reported that the average employee reports wasting one hour a day at work and believe that their co-workers waste an hour and a half. Other organizations, while not necessarily reducing hours worked, offer employees greater flexibility in when these hours are worked, resulting in greater satisfaction and less stress.

Munck (2001), a senior executive of the Marriott hotel chain, describes why and how Marriott attempted to change their culture of "face time", the more hours worked the better! Most mangers worked over 50 h a week. Marriott found it more difficult to recruit talented people and effective managers were leaving to spend more time with their families. Their initiative, titled Management Flexibility, resulted in managers typically working five fewer hours a week. This was accomplished by eliminating redundant meetings, requiring the filing of fewer reports, having a shorter overlap time between shifts, providing more access to e-mail and better IT support, addressing inefficient procedures, and emphasizing task accomplishment rather than hours worked. It was critical that top management was on board and believed in ways consistent with the philosophy and goals of the culture change. Interestingly, manager's levels of stress were also reduced and work–personal life conflict was lowered.

Barnett and Hall (2001), building on the increasing need for balance being expressed by managers and professionals, suggest that organizations use reduced work hours to win the war for talent. Reduced work hours can bring benefits to both employees and organizations. The key is not the number of hours worked but rather the fit between employee needs and when hours are worked. They identify several benefits of reduced hours to employees (e.g., less stress, more time for family) and organizations (fewer accidents and errors, less face time, more productivity). They offer concrete actions that organizations can undertake at the individual, workplace, and organization level to make reduced hours initiatives successful. Individuals need to understand their motives and choices for reduced hours; organizations need to create supportive policies, allow flexibility, and change their cultures and career paths.

In keeping with employee preferences to work fewer hours and increased competition for talent, more law firms are moving away from a "billable hours" or hourly targets mentality —- termed the "eat what you kill" model. Instead they consider new non-partners as consultants, allowing them to choose the number of hours they want to work and offering the flexibility to set their own schedules according to their needs.

The ILO, a part of the UN headquartered in Geneva, has embarked on a promotional and action program to foster "decent work" in member countries (Boulin, Lallement, Messenger, & Michon, 2006; Ghai, 2006).

There are larger societal movements underway to reduce the time spent at work. These include the "in praise of slow" and "take back your time" initiatives.

But for some workers, particularly those holding blue-collar jobs, working overtime or holding down two or more jobs, is critical to their family survival, for them reducing work hours represents a real financial hardship.

There is also some accumulating wisdom for reducing work–personal life conflict, often based on hours worked or the intensity of one's work. These include: not trying to do it all by working harder, the result is typically more work; use supportive workplace policies; ask other family members to help out at home; get adequate sleep; limit work taken home; say no to overtime and unreasonable work expectations; train managers to be more supportive; give employees more control over their work schedules and work arrangements; and help employees meet their personal responsibilities via referrals to childcare and/or eldercare services; offering relocation help if one is transferred; and short-term leave for family reasons.

One can also enjoy vacations. Before going, plan and prepare co-workers to handle your responsibilities; let clients and customers know you will be away and who will cover for you; leave your cell phone and Blackberry in a drawer; don't check work e-mails, do a career-building activity such as reading a business management book if you must do anything work-related; keep a notepad handy if you want to record business-related ideas; choose a place to vacation that has no internet access. A holiday should allow time to recharge, reconnect with family, and pursue one's non-work interests (e.g., golf, snorkeling, skiing). An individual is more likely to return to work rested and with a fresh perspective if these tips are followed.

Sabine Sonnentag and Fritz (2007) have shown how recovery after work reduces the negative effects of work demands on psychological health. Important elements of recovery include detachment from work when at home, relaxation, mastery, and control.

Why do people choose to work long hours? For some people they have little choice; working two jobs is necessary to make ends meet. Others may in fact have a choice. Several factors are likely to play a role in answer this question. Feldman (2002) proposed a multi-level model as a starting point. His model consisted of four panels of variables: Individual factors — demographic and family status, personality; Job factors — job challenge, levels of intrinsic motivation, and satisfaction provided; visibility of one's work' Organizational factors — socialization processes, leadership, and culture; and Economic factors — competitive pressures, threat of layoffs. Ng, Sorenson, and Feldman (2007) followed up their earlier work with a model to further our understanding of workaholism. Antecedents of workaholism or work addiction consisted of personal dispositions (e.g., achievement orientation, self-esteem, obsessive compulsive behavior), socio-cultural experiences (e.g., stressful dysfunctional family, peer competition at work), and behavioral reinforcements (e.g., tangible and intangible rewards, focus on input rather than output). There are no simple or single explanation for why people work long hours or work compulsively.

Some people work hard because they love their jobs (Brett & Stroh, 2003; Hedley, 2006; Hewlett & Luce, 2006). Others work hard for the financial rewards that hard work and career advancement bring. Materialism is a defining feature of many countries, particularly North America, but increasingly in developing countries (e.g., China, India, Russia). Materialism is commonly defined as placing a high value on income and material possessions. Individuals strive to "keep up with the Joneses" or move ahead of them. I recently read the following statement "On Wall Street, these guys tie all their self-esteem to their net worth". Research findings have consistently shown that materialistic individuals score lower on happiness, life satisfaction, and both mental and physical health. Materialistic individuals are more likely to sacrifice the fulfillment of other needs associated with well-being such as autonomy, competence, and relatedness. That is, materialistic individuals fail to address core psychological needs associated with personal growth.

Deckop, Jurkiewicz, and Giacalone (2007), for example, examined the association of materialist values with work-related indicators of personal well-being. Data were collected at two points in time from 274 managers and professionals, about two-thirds being female. Materialism was found to be associated with lower levels of affective commitment, intrinsic and extrinsic satisfaction, job and career satisfaction, and higher levels of burnout.

There are several reasons then that individuals, organizations, and society as a whole should be concerned about the effects of long work hours and work addiction. These have been shown to be associated with lower levels of employee psychological and physical health, lower levels of family functioning, less effective job performance, and higher health care costs that are borne by society at large. Unfortunately many organizations believe that, in the short run at least, there are potential economic benefits from long work hours, in part because the costs of these may be difficult to measures (e.g., employee strain, fatigue) and these costs are externalized to families and the broader society. Employees working long hours are less able to participate as citizens, and represent a drain on the social welfare and health care systems.

Organizations today are increasingly realizing that employees are vital to their long-term success. Organizations need to attract, nurture, develop, and retain talent. They need to become an employer of choice. They need to use the talents of ALL employees, realizing that women are disadvantaged in long work hours cultures. Many will state that "people are our most important asset". It is time that they come to grips with the long work hours culture to act in accordance with these espoused values. Effective and high performing organizations meet the needs of their people and the needs of the business simultaneously. Healthy employees in healthy organizations are more likely to achieve peak performance.

Overview of the Contents

This collection begins with a Preface and then is divided into three parts reflecting the three words in the sub-title: causes, consequences and choices. In the Preface, Ronald Burke sets the stage for the remainder of the volume. He reviews some antecedents and consequences of working hours, work intensity and work addiction, particularly among managers and professionals. Outcome measures include indicators of job and career satisfaction, psychological and physical health, absence and work-related injury, fatigue and family balance issues. He addresses the question of why people work hard, suggesting a range of motives, some more damaging than others. Individual and organizational actions to reduce the negative effects of long hours and work addiction are described. Considerably more research is needed on the effects of long hours among less-educated individuals in the developing countries; these people often work the longest hours.

Moving to Part I, Ronald Burke and Lisa Fiksenbaum first position work hours as a factor in organizational effectiveness. Are countries in which individuals work more hours better off? Are individuals happier in countries that work more hours? Can individuals work too much? They also review the literature on antecedents and consequences of working hours, work intensity, and work addiction. The literature suggests that working long hours was associated with adverse health effects and increased safety risk. They examine the workaholism literature which shows that different types of workaholics exist, some satisfied and healthy, others are distress. They conclude that both why one works hard (the motives) and how one works hard (the behaviors) likely account for the differences. They conclude with suggestions for altering a long work hours culture and reducing one's level of work addiction.

What does it mean to love your job? Constance Hadley draws a parallel between loving your job and romantic love. Loving your job contains passion, intimacy, and commitment. Loving one's job has cognitive, emotional, and behavioral elements. She then suggests several propositions from this perspective. Thus loving one's job would be associated with feelings of closeness and connectedness (intimacy), excitement and desire (passion), and commitment to one's job (love). She draws an important distinction between loving and liking one's job. Individuals who love their jobs would be highly satisfied. She identifies both personal and job characteristics as antecedents of loving one's job. The former would include conscientiousness and self-identification with the job; the latter, the attractiveness of the job, the presence of intrinsically motivating factors, more person–job fit, a greater number of alternative jobs, and experiencing high levels of both positive and negative affect at work. She is currently examining these hypotheses in a longitudinal study of business school graduates and we look forward to her findings in this exciting new area of study. There are potential practical applications of her conceptual framework as well, if borne out in empirical research.

Lonnie Golden and Morris Altman then tackle the central question of why people overwork. We have recently witnessed increases in desired hours of work and interest in the effects of work hours on well-being. They begin by identifying those factors associated with how many hours an individual wants to work and actually works and then examine reasons why individuals might work more hours than they desired (both push and pull factors operate here), they then raise the concept of "working too much" — for the individual's own good or the good of their family. They conclude with suggestions for individual, organizational and public policy initiatives that would optimize overall well-being by reducing the levels of overwork and over-employment.

Moving to workaholism or work addiction, Lynley McMillan and Michael O'Driscoll first provide the historical context for work hours, then review various explanatory theories of workaholism. Workaholism, to them, is a personal reluctance to disengage from work that involves intense engagement in work and a strong drive to work. Workaholics tend to work or to think about work anytime and anywhere; drive and engagement emerge as the critical factors in determining workaholism. They examine several theories of workaholic: biological, behavioral, emotion-focused, cognitive, and social systems. They compare these theories on four criteria (e.g., generality of supporting data, breadth of application in the workplace). Some theories appear to be more promising (e.g., behavioral, cognitive, systems) than others but there is not enough research to date to evaluate each of the five groups of workaholism theories adequately. They conclude that it is unlikely that workaholism arises from a single event, a single theory or can be treated with one type of therapy.

Part II emphasizes the consequences of the long work hours culture and the intensification of work. In the first chapter, Francis Green reviews research evidence on work intensification or work effort and work hours. Work effort refers to the intensity of mental and/or physical exertion during working time and is distinct from hours worked. Work intensification has increased in many countries over the past 15 years while work hours have actually decreased in some countries. But there are significant country differences in both level and pattern of work intensification. Several factors might explain increases in work intensification including new technologies, consumerism, and a decline in the power of unions. Work intensification has been found to be associated with a decline in worker well-being. His data indicate that work intensification occurred in most industries and occupations. Employee well-being was most strongly influenced by the design of jobs and individual personality factors rather than industry and occupation. High at risk jobs were found to be particularly critical here, and these types of jobs had increased over the past several years.

Carla Medalia and Jerry Jacobs next consider the work hours of married couples. Time spent at work is associated with work–family conflict, gender inequality in the labor market and in the home, and levels of unemployment. They examined working time for married couples in 28 countries (North America, Eastern and Western Europe, Asia, the Middle East, Latin America). Women's labor force participation rates varied widely across these countries. Most men worked an average of 41–46 h per week; women's work hours were shorter, but countries with long work hours for men also had long work hours for women. Dual-earner couples, on average worked 82 h per week, but there was also wide variation across countries. Some couples worked more than 100 h per week. Mothers worked fewer hours than did women without children. Couple hours tended to be longer in the poorer countries.

Their findings provide an important launch pad for future studies of the marital and parental relationship of these working couples and broader aspects of their well-being.

Anne Humbert and Suzan Lewis then consider working hours among Irish entrepreneurs. They begin by noting the growing intrusion of work into people's family lives and the blurring of work–personal life boundaries for many. They identify several reasons why individuals are working more and reporting less work–life balance. The trend for work to interfere with family lives is highly gendered however; women are more heavily impacted. And, unfortunately, organizational policies and practices allowing greater flexibility do not adequately address these issues either. As a consequence women (and some men) turn to self-employment as a solution. Their data from Irish entrepreneurs indicated that self-employment rarely improves work–life balance. They conclude with a call to broaden our thinking about long work hours to include ways of enhancing the impact of work to provide benefits to society at large.

Police officers perform a vital high risk/high demand service in our society responding to unpredictable demands around the clock. Bryan Vila and Jason Moore focus on long work hours in police work. In policing, long work hours are linked to shift work, overtime, schedule disruption and stress and, in turn, long work hours interfere with sleep. Fatigue then is associated with work-related injuries, family issues, and health concerns. They identify causes of police fatigue, important consequences of fatigue, and offer suggestions to address fatigue issues. Yet changing police behavior has proven to be difficult. Both labor and management must come together to address the causes and consequences of long work hours. They identify four issues of joint concern: risk management (legal liabilities), human capital management, officer safety, and officer health. Useful interventions include education and training of officers and having officers become involved in changing public behavior in these areas.

Wilmar Schaufeli, Toon Taris and Arnold Bakker offer a two dimensional definition of workaholism — an inner drive to work excessively and work compulsively. They first describe the development of measures of these two components. They then report findings using these measures in a national Dutch database and a sample of medical residents. In the first study, men scored higher than women on both workaholism scales. Work hours were, not surprisingly, correlated positively with both scales, and entrepreneurs and managers scored highest on both. In the study of medical residents, both workaholism components were associated with similar job demands (work–home conflict, mental demands), lack of resources (less social support from colleagues), and outcomes (e.g., burnout). Medical residents scoring high on both components reported less favorable job experiences and outcomes. They suggest that underlying motivational systems likely account for the differences between individuals that work hard but are satisfied and healthy and those that work hard and are in distress.

Ronald Burke, following on the work of Schaufeli, Taris, and Bakker, examines the motivations for working hard and reports the results of three studies that examined the relationship of measures of Passion, and of Addiction, with a variety of antecedents, work outcomes, and indicators of psychological well-being. Data were collected from Canadian MBA graduates, Australian female psychologists, and Norwegian journalists using similar measures. Similar findings were observed in all three studies. First, Passion and Addiction were significantly and positively correlated (but only moderately). Second, respondents scoring higher on Passion, and on Addiction, were more heavily invested in their work. Third, respondents scoring higher on Passion also reported less obsessive job behaviors, greater work satisfactions, and higher levels of psychological well-being. Fourth, respondents scoring higher on Addiction indicated more obsessive job behaviors, lower work satisfactions, and lower levels of psychological well-being. Thus one's motivations for working hard clearly distinguished work and well-being outcomes.

Part III focuses on the fact that individuals, families, and organizations have choices in terms of actual work hours, work arrangements, and when and how hours are worked. Gayle Porter and Jamie Perry begin by identifying current trends leading to excess work including the shift to an information-based economy requiring more flexible work hours, and working with fewer resources but as many or more demands. But working long hours is a personal choice, though influenced by one's work situation. They use an animal from Orwell's *Animal Farm*, Boxer, to depict work addiction. As the challenges increased, Boxer worked harder. But work addiction has costs including sleep deprivation. JC, a character played by Diane Keaton in *Baby Boom*, was also exhibiting characteristics of work addiction. But JC opted to make change. Technology now functions as an enabler of work addiction. Work demands are now higher and there is pressure to succeed. They present disturbing statistics and stories of ways in which technology supports work addiction. They conclude by highlighting choice — individual and organizational — a choice for fulfillment and enrichment or a choice of consumption, demands and diminished well-being; all choices have upsides and downsides. Do we have the courage to choose wisely?

Carmen Binneweis and Sabine Sonnentag examine research findings on recovery after work, the question of how employees can successfully recover from a stressful workday after work. They first describe the recovery process providing indicators of recovery. Recovery processes are the opposite of stress processes; following successful recovery, functional responses return to their pre-stress levels. Job demands such as high pace and amount of work (long work hours and overtime work) increased one's need for recovery. They review three theoretical underpinnings to recovery research. The accumulating research shows that some recovery experiences have benefits for individuals. Their own research has focused on four off-the-job experiences: psychological detachment, relaxation, mastery, and control. This chapter shows how these have health and well-being benefits to employees, as well as performance benefits to organizations. Organizations can support recovery by reducing job demands (work hours, overtime) and supporting both leisure and fitness.

Rebecca Burwell and Charles Chen examine some psychological helping methods for treating workaholic symptoms with a novel emphasis on the application of positive psychology principles. They first consider antecedents of workaholism — personal, organizational, and societal — before moving to commonly proposed treatment strategies. These include individual interventions such as therapies of various kinds (e.g., marital, cognitive, behavioral change) and workplace interventions (e.g., work–life balance programs, management training to identify, and address workaholism). They conclude with an innovative application of tenets from positive psychology. Positive psychotherapy emphasizes the increase of positive emotions, engagement freedom and choice, and recreation within a client's life. Quality of life therapy focuses on increasing one's life satisfaction by bolstering self-esteem, relationships, and play. Although the use of therapeutic approaches based on principles of positive psychology need considerably more evaluation, they represent a fresh complement to the more commonly used individual change strategies.

References

Babbar, S., & Aspelin, D. J. (1998). The overtime rebellion: Symptom of a bigger problem? *Academy of Management Executive, 12*, 68–76.

Barnett, R. C., & Hall, D. T. (2001). How to use reduced fours to win the war for talent. *Organizational Dynamics, 29*, 192–210.

Boje, D. M., & Rosile, G. A. (2004). Death, terror and addiction in motivation theory. In: J. Brewis, S. Linstead, D. Boje & A. O'Shea (Eds), *Passion of organizing* (pp. 1–36). Copenhagen: Copenhagen Business School Press.

Boulin, J. Y., Lallement, M., Messenger, J. C., & Michon, F. (2006). *Decent working time: New trends, new issues.* Geneva: ILO.

Brett, J. M., & Stroh, L. K. (2003). "Working 61 plus hours a week" Why do managers do it? *Journal of Applied Psychology, 88*, 67–78.

Bunting, M. (2004). *Willing slaves.* London: Harper and Collins.

Burchall, B., Lapido, D., & Wilkinson, F. (2002). *Job insecurity and work intensification.* London: Routledge.

Carr, A. (1993). The psychostructure of work: "Bend me, shape me, any way you want me, as long as you love me, it's all right". *Journal of Managerial Psychology, 8*, 3–6.

Czeisler, C. A. (2006). Sleep deficit: The performance killer. *Harvard Business Review*, December, pp. 53–59.

Deckop, J. R., Jurkiewicz, C. L., & Giacalone, R. A. (2007). Can't get no satisfaction: The effects of materialism on work-related personal well-being. Paper presented at the 2007 meeting of the Academy of Management, Philadelphia, August.

do Rosario, L. (1991). Grim reaper's toll. *Far Eastern Economic Review*, April, pp. 25–30.

Donnelly, R. (2006). How "free" is the free worker? An investigation into the working arrangements available to knowledge workers. *Personnel Review, 35*, 78–97.

Duckworth, A. L., Peterson, C., Matthews, M. D., & Kelly, D. R. (2007). Grit: Perseverance and passion for long-term goals. *Journal of Personality and Social Psychology, 92*, 1097–1101.

Dunn-Jensen, L. M. (2007). Beyond actual work hours: Exploring the relationship between time norms and WF conflict. Paper presented at the Academy of Management, Philadelphia, August.

Feldman, D. C. (2002). Managers' propensity to work longer hours: A multi-level analysis. *Human Resources Management Review, 12,* 339–357.

Galinsky, E. (1999). *Ask the children: What American children really think about work parents.* New York: William Morrow.

Ghai, D. (2006). *Decent work :Objectives and strategies.* Geneva: ILO.

Green, F. (2001). It's been a hard day's night: The concentration and intensification of work in late 20th century Britain. *British Journal of Industrial Relations, 39,* 53–80.

Hedley, C. N. (2006). What does it mean to "love your job"? Investigating the construct. Paper presented at the 2006 meeting of the Academy of Management, Atlanta, August.

Hewlett, S. A., & Luce, C. B. (2006). Extreme jobs: The dangerous allure of the 70-hour work week. *Harvard Business Review,* December, pp. 49–59.

Hochschild, A. (1997). *The time bind.* New York: Henry Holt & Company.

Hochwarter, W. A., Perrewe, P. L., Meurs, J. A., & Kacmar, C. (2007). The interaction effects of work-induced build and ability to manage resources on job and life satisfaction. *Journal of Occupational Health Psychology, 12,* 125–135.

Kasser, T. (2002). *The high price of materialism.* Cambridge, MA: MIT Press.

Kofodimos, J. (1993). *Balancing act.* San Francisco: Jossey-Bass.

LaBier, D. (1986). *Modern madness: The emotional fallout of success.* Reading, MA: Addison-Wesley.

Maccoby, M. (1980). Work and human development. *Professional Psychology, 11,* 509–519.

Mednick, S., & Ehrwan, M. (2006). *Take a nap: Change your life.* New York: Workman Publishing.

Middleton, C. A., & Cukier, W. (2006). Is mobile email functional or dysfunctional? Two perspectives on mobile email usage. *European Journal of Information Systems, 15,* 252–260.

Mitler, M. M., Carskadon, M. A., Czeisler, C. A., & Diment, W. A. (1988). Catastrophies, sleep and public policy: Consensus report. *Sleep, 11,* 100–109.

Munck, B. (2001). Changing a culture of face time. *Harvard Business Review,* November, pp. 167–172.

Myers, D. G. (2000). *The American paradox: Spiritual hunger in a age of plenty.* New Haven, CT: Yale University Press.

Ng, T. W. H., Sorenson, K. L., & Feldman, D. C. (2007). Dimensions, antecedents and consequences of workaholism: A conceptual integration and extension. *Journal of Organizational Behavior, 28,* 111–136.

Orey, M. (2007). Does your boss owe you overtime? Wage wars. *Business Week,* October 1, pp. 50–54, 56–58, 60.

Philipson, I. (2002). *Married to the job: Why we live to work and what we can do about it.* New York: Simon & Schuster.

Song, M. (2006). *The hamster revolution: How you manage your e-mail before it manages you.* San Francisco: Berrett-Koehler.

Sonnentag, S., & Fritz, C. (2007). The recovery experience questionnaire: Development and validation of a measure for assessing recuperation and unwinding from work. *Journal of Occupational Health Psychology, 12,* 204–221.

Taylor, B. (2003). *What kids really want that money can't buy.* New York: Warner Books.

Van Boven, L., & Gilovich, T. (2003). To do or to have? That is the question. *Journal of Personality and Social Psychology, 85,* 1193–1202.

van Heck, G. K., & Vingerhoets, A. J. J. M. (2007). Leisure sickness: A bio-psychosocial perspective. *Psychological Topics, 16,* 187–200.

Vila, B. (1996). Tired cops: Probable connection between fatigue and the performance, health and safety of patrol officers. *American Journal of Police, 45,* 51–92.

Wajcman, J. (2008). "Life in the fast lane"?: Towards a sociology of technology and time. British Journal of Sociology, *59,* 59–77.

Wallace, J. E. (1997). It's about time: A study of hours worked and work spillover among law firm lawyers. *Journal of Vocational Behavior, 50,* 227–248.

Westman, M., & Eden, D. (1997). Effects of a respite from work on burnout: Vacation relief and fade-out. *Journal of Applied Psychology, 82,* 516–527.

Ronald J. Burke

Acknowledgements

Cary Cooper and I have spent much of our professional lives examining the effects of various work experiences on individual and organizational health. It is no surprise then that this collection examines work hours, work intensity and work addiction and their correlates and consequences. The last decade had witnessed both growing concern and growing research attention to this topic. Cary and I have done a lot of writing throughout our careers and friends and colleagues have likely referred to us as workaholics and surmised that we both put in long work hours. It is true that we do enjoy our work and have worked long hours on occasion. We have also both written previously on work hours and work addiction. So our collaboration on this topic here seemed to follow nicely from both our interests in and efforts to make organizations more humane and effective.

Over the years, Cary and I have developed a fruitful and satisfying collaboration. I thank him for his efforts here and elsewhere.

Gerry Wood did a superb job in liaising with both our authors and Elsevier before the handover to Emerald. Thank you Gerry. I am grateful to our international contributors as well. The staff at Elsevier, consistent with our previous experience with them, was supportive, responsive and diligent. Preparation of this volume was also supported in part by York University.

Finally, there is Max. Max is a stray cat that Susan brought home about two years ago when he was left outside an apartment complex when his owner was evicted. He is curious, affectionate and charismatic. Max is now a member of the family. I usually write on our dining room table. Max will jump on the table, plop himself down on my papers, indicate that he wants attention and begins to play with the papers, try to pick up my pen – difficult to do without fingers – and eat my pen. I always stop what I am doing, play with him a bit, then he leaves willingly or I help him leave. This bonding provides reciprocal unconditional love, meets his needs and though disruptive, gives me a short break. Thanks Max.

Ronald Burke
Toronto
Editor

PART I

CAUSES

Chapter 1

Work Hours, Work Intensity, and Work Addiction: Costs and Benefits [☆]

Ronald J. Burke and Lisa Fiksenbaum

> Life moves pretty fast. If you don't stop and look around once in awhile, you could miss it
>
> — Ferris Bueller, Ferris Bueller's Day Off

1.1. Work Hours: The Larger Context

Ontario has its share of slackers.
> — The Globe and Mail, Nov. 1, 2006, B2

Stay later at the office, Ontario has to catch up
> — The Globe and Mail, Sept. 1, 2006, B2

Bouchard attacks work ethic of Quebeckers
> — National Post, Oct 1, 2006, A2

Is Canada a case of "Don't worry, be happy? Productivity woes linked to well-being.
> — The Globe and Mail, Nov 21, 2006, B7

Bouchard furor: Do Quebeckers work enough?
> — The Globe and Mail, Oct. 18, 2006, A1

Business leaders applaud Bouchard remarks
> — The Globe and Mail, Oct. 18, 2006, A7

☆ Preparation of this chapter was supported in part by York University. Several colleagues participated in the design and conduct of the research program: Zena Burgess, Astrid Richardsen, Stig Matthiesen, and Graeme MacDermid. Louise Coutu prepared the manuscript.

I am not an economist; I am a psychologist interested in building more effective organizations. An effective organization simultaneously meets the needs of business while satisfying the needs of the women and men who work there. An effective organization is a healthy organization employing healthy women and men.

In the past few months, several writers in Canada (primarily economists) have suggested that we Canadians are not working enough hours resulting in lower levels of productivity and a lower standard of living (less per capita income) than other countries (or US states) where women and men work more hours. Economists refer to this as a "prosperity gap".

Apparently, economists agree that Canada has a productivity problem, particularly when compared to the US. This reflects an "intensity gap", the differences in labour contribution per employed person. It seems that Ontarians (citizens of the province in which I live) work three-and-a-half weeks less per year than do our US counterparts. Ontarians are more like the French in this regard, and the biggest slackers in Ontario are the highest educated and best paid. It seems that these people are less interested in working more hours to become wealthier. It is also not clear that working more hours equates with working harder (or smarter).

Compared to their US counterparts, more workers in Ontario work part time, have shorter work weeks, and have longer vacations, and while this situation may be desirable for workers, it is bad for employers as these longer vacations represent a business expense. Economists estimate the loss in GDP comes to $3700 per person per year.

This raises the intriguing question of whether working more hours represents real prosperity? It is also not clear that working more hours is translated into higher levels of efficiency, productivity, and value addition. Is the reality that Americans work more hours than Ontarians at the cost of poorer health, less satisfying home lives, and less fun?

Interestingly, a study issued recently by the Organization for Economic Co-operation and Development (OECD) authored by Jean-Philippe Cotis suggests that Canada's productivity shortfall is the result of Canadians having high levels of happiness and well-being. Canadians seem to be more satisfied with a slightly lower standard of living than their neighbors to the South.

This chapter reviews the literature on the antecedents and consequences of working hours, work intensity, and work addiction particularly among managers and professionals. The dependent variables associated with these include health-related illnesses, injuries, sleep patterns, fatigue, heart rate, and hormone level changes, as well as several work/non-work life balance issues. Motives for working long hours such as joy in work, avoiding job insecurity or negative sanctions from a superior, and employer demands, are addressed in detail, and a multitude of moderators shown to have affected the work hours and well-being relationship, are reviewed. These include reasons for working long hours, work schedule autonomy, monetary gain, and choice in working for long hours. The chapter suggests a need for more research to better understand the effects of work hours, work intensity, and workaholism, as well as provides a number of implications and organizational and societal suggestions for addressing work hour concerns.

Managerial roles in organizations of all sizes are demanding and time consuming (Brett & Stroh, 2003; Kotter, 1999). There is some evidence that managers in industrialized countries are working more hours now than previously (Greenhouse, 2001; Schor, 1991, 2003). Working long hours may in fact be a prerequisite for achieving senior leadership positions (Jacobs & Gerson, 1998; Wallace, 1997).

Porter (2004) explored the questions of how and why people work, considering work, the work ethic, and work excess. There were several reasons why people worked hard and each reason may have both desirable and undesirable consequences to the individual, the organization or both. Some people feel compelled towards excess work even when externally imposed demands are absent. Golden (1998) proposes that the actual hours worked are a function of three factors: hours desired by the worker, hours demanded by the employer, and the institutional environment in which working hour decisions are made (legal constraints, workplace norms, the larger economic environment). There are positive reasons for working long hours (more pay, self-actualization, a sense of commitment to colleagues and clients, work enjoyment) and also negative reasons (avoid sanctions, deal with employment insecurity). Working longer hours may increase one's competitiveness in the short-term but not be sustainable — and perhaps becoming counterproductive — in the longer term. Long hours may influence physical and mental health and well-being by increasing stress. Can one make a distinction between a healthy work ethic and working to excess? How much work is too much? One can work to have material possessions, to not be left behind (Reich, 2000), to confirm self-worth, and to provide for children.

The work ethic is based on viewing hard work as virtuous. But this does not address the question of when hard work becomes a problem. What determines too much work? It seems that the norm for amount of work has risen for some in the past decade. The reasons likely include economic recession, organizational downsizings, and restructurings, and levels of insecurity of those with jobs, making it easier for them to choose to work harder (Burchell, 2001; 2002). Relatively flat income may also cause some people to work longer. Schor (1998, 2003) has suggested that under the dual pressures of employers and consumerism, individuals are in a "squirrel cage", trapped by the cycle of work — and — spend (Schor, 1991, p. 176).

Although the terms workaholic and work addict encompass all the problems that addiction brings (Oates, 1971), most people believe that work is healthy, desirable, and protective of many illnesses. In support of this view, research has shown that holding multiple roles instead of a single role (e.g., homemaker) generally leads to favorable well-being outcomes among women (Barnett & Marshall, 1992).

The importance of focusing on work hours is multi-faceted. First, a large number of employees are unhappy about the number of hours they work (Clarkberg & Moen, 2001; Dembe, 2005; Jacobs & Gerson, 1998; MacInnes, 2005). Second, the amount of time demanded by work is an obvious and important way in which work affects other parts of one's life (Galinsky, 1999; Shields, 1999). Third, work hours are a widely studied structural output of employment (Adam, 1993). Fourth, the study of work hours and well-being outcomes has produced both inconsistent and complex results (Barnett, 1998).

New technology and job flexibility have facilitated working from home or outside the office, which has contributed to an increase in hours worked in North America (Golden & Figart, 2000a). These alternative work arrangements can be seen as beneficial; for example, a working mother who chooses to spend more time with her children can do so by working from home or working night shifts. In a study of 61 French hospitals, 85% of nurses employed had requested the night shift to allow more time to be spent with their young children during the day (Barton, 1994). This accommodates dual income families, presenting an arrangement to allow them to share the child rearing and family responsibilities.

With more women now working, workers are increasingly married to other workers, making the family work week longer. In addition, smaller families also allow couples to work more. It could also be that working more hours makes it more difficult to take care of a larger family. It has also been suggested that having a wife who works full time (for men) may drive men to spend more time at work to bolster the masculine identity as provider.

Because of technological advances and flexible work arrangements, it might be assumed that working time is getting progressively shorter. However, this varies from country to country and even within countries by gender, occupation, race, and time period (Figart & Golden, 1998). Beginning in the nineteenth century with the Industrial Revolution, workers fought to get policies enacted to restrict hours of work, especially for women and children (Figart & Golden, 1998). In the mid-twentieth century, the United States began to implement employment legislation that reduced the number of hours worked (Hinrichs, Rochem, & Sirianni, 1991). A new employment arrangement emerged post World War II, which provided stable and life-long employment in addition to a family wage. This was an era of stability for North American households; however this stable period and the ensuing employment arrangement have disintegrated. Economic, technological, and cultural factors have influenced working time, making it extremely variable (Figart & Golden, 1998).

People have expected an association of long working hours and adverse well-being consequences for over 100 years. These concerns were first raised during the Industrial Revolution in 1830 and in later years, and efforts were made to legislate limits in working hours to 10 h/day at that time (Golden, 2007).

Recently there has been a rise of working hours in North America. The mean hours worked has increased slightly but there are more people working more hours and more people working fewer hours. Jacobs and Gerson (1998) found that professionals and highly educated individuals have had an increase in their hours worked. In contrast, it was also found that less educated workers have seen a decline. It is believed that professionals and highly educated persons tend to have more responsibility and are under more stress with larger workloads (Lapido, Mankelow, & Burchell, 2003).

Within the United States, large portions of people employed are working very long hours, in both paid overtime and salaried positions (Figart & Golden, 1998). Overtime, which has been used as an indicator of an expanding economy and tight labour markets, has been increasing since 1970 (Glosser & Golden, 1997). In addition, it was found that those working excessive hours, described as 49 h a week or more, has also been on the rise recently, especially for higher-educated white men (Hedges, 1993). Conversely, work hours, both weekly and annually, in Western Europe have decreased (Figart & Golden, 1998). Specifically in the Netherlands, Belgium, and West German; from 1960 to 1985 there was an annual reduction of 20% of work hours (Figart & Golden, 1998). This variation could be due to a number of factors including work legislation and standards on overtime hours. There has been a slight decrease in work hours across Canada as well, which is said to be due to increased vacation time and the expansion of part-time jobs (International Labor Organization, 1995).

Employer demands and the institutionalized nature of work and employment has tended to constrain work hours in established patterns. But these patterns are changing, several contrasting factors influenced working hours in the 2000s. First, the labor union movement for shorter hours in the EEU has lead to a reduction in working hours in some European countries (Rifkin, 2004). Second, the need for organizations to provide 24/7 service has led to the creation of more flexible and non-standard work schedules (Kreitzman, 1999). Third, more employees have also undertaken flexible work schedules to meet their family responsibilities (Hochschild, 1997).

Brett and Stroh (2003) examined the question of why some managers work 61 or more hours per week. They considered four explanations: the work–leisure trade-off, social contagion, work as an emotional respite from home, and work as its own rewards. Data was collected from a sample of 595 male and 391 female MBA alumni of the same university. The males were all married with children at home and a smaller percentage of the females were married and had children. More men than women worked 61 or more hours per week (29% versus 11%). Men worked 56.4 h/week and women worked 51.5 h/week. For males, rewards of work was the only of the four hypotheses to be supported, with hours worked significantly connected with job involvement and intrinsic satisfaction. For females, the work–leisure trade-off and social contagion hypotheses were supported. However, hours worked did not correlate with job involvement, income, or job satisfaction for females.

Hewlett and Luce (2006) examined "extreme jobs", jobs in which incumbents worked 70 h a week or more were high wage earners, and had jobs having at least five characteristics of work intensity. These characteristics are listed below.

- Unpredictable flow of work
- Fast-paced work under tight deadlines
- Inordinate scope of responsibility that amounts to more than one job
- Work-related events outside regular work hours
- Availability to clients 24/7
- Responsibility for profit and loss
- Responsibility for mentoring and recruiting
- Large amount of travel
- Large number of direct reports
- Physical presence at workplace at least 10 h a day.

They carried out surveys of high wage earners in the US and high-earning managers and professionals working in large multinational organizations. In addition, they conducted focus groups and interviews to better understand the motivations for, and the effects of, working in these jobs. Their two surveys of high-earning managers and professionals revealed four characteristics that created the most intensity and pressure: unpredictability (cited by 91% of respondents), fast pace with tight deadlines (86%), work-related events outside business hours (66%), and 24/7 client demands (61%).

They concluded that managers and professionals were now working harder than ever. Of the extreme job holders, 48% said they were now working an average of 16.6 h/week more than they did five years ago. And 42% took 10 or fewer vacation days per year (less then they were entitled to) and 55% indicated that they had to cancel vacation plans regularly. Forty-four percent of their respondent's felt the pace of their work was extreme.

But extreme jobholders (66% in the US sample and 76% in the global sample) said that they loved their jobs. Several reasons were given for working these long hours: the job was stimulating and challenging (over 85%), working with high-quality colleagues (almost 50%), high pay (almost 50%), recognition (almost 40%), and power and status (almost 25%). In addition, increased competitive pressures, improved communication technologies, downsizings, and restructurings resulting in few higher level jobs, flattened organizational hierarchies, and values changes in the broader society supportive of "extremes" also played a role (Wiehert, 2002).

Individuals holding "extreme" jobs however had to let some things go. These included: home maintenance (about 70%), relationships with their children (almost 50%), relationships with their spouses/partners (over 45%), and an unsatisfying sex life (over 40%).

Extreme jobs were more likely to be held by men than women (17% versus 4% in the US sample; 30% versus 15% in the global sample). Women were more likely to be in jobs with high demands but working fewer hours. Women were not afraid of jobs having high levels of responsibility. Both women and men in extreme jobs indicated "difficulties" with their children (acting out, eating too much junk food, under-achieving in school, too little adult supervision).

Most women (57% in extreme jobs did want to continue working as hard in 5 years (US sample), 48% of men felt the same way. Only13% of women and 27% of men wanted to continue at this pace. The numbers were higher in the global survey: women, 80%, men 55%; and women, 5% and men, 17%.

Working long hours was only partly the result of a demanding capitalist system. Most incumbents of extreme jobs found their work stimulating and rewarding. Both positive and negative pressures were found to operate here. But there are some dangers, particularly on the home and family front. Women managers and professionals are potentially disadvantaged because they are unable or unwilling to work such long hours.

Burke and Fiksenbaum (2007a), in a sample of Canadian MBA graduates, compared the work and career experiences of women and men working 60 or more hours per week with those working 59 h a week or less. Their findings were generally similar to those of Hewlett and Luce (2006). Individuals working for 60 or more hours per week reported greater job and career satisfaction, scored higher on three workaholism components, and earned more money; they also indicated less extra-work satisfaction, a more demanding work environment, and more psychosomatic symptoms. Working long hours appeared to be a mixed blessing.

1.2. Work Hours and their Effects

A variety of outcome measures have been examined in connection with working long hours (van der Hulst, 2003). Most studies of long work hours have been conducted in Japan where "karoshi", sudden death due to long hours and insufficient sleep was first observed. The Japanese coined this term, to refer to deaths of individuals from overwork or working long work hours, and have actually defined such deaths (Kanai, 2006). Several hypotheses have been advanced to explain the relationship between long work hours and adverse health outcomes. Working long hours affects the cardiovascular system through chronic exposure to increases in blood pressure and heart rate (Buell & Breslow, 1960; Iwasaki, Sasaki, Oka, & Hisanaga, 1998; Uehata, 1991). Working long hours produces sleep deprivation and lack of recovery leading to chronic fatigue, poor health-related behaviors, and ill health (Ala-Mursjula, Vahtera, Kivimaki, Kevin, & Penttij, 2002; Defoe, Power, Holzman, Carpentieri, & Schulkin, 2001; Liu & Tanaka, 2002). Working long hours makes it more difficult to recover from job demands and the stress of long work hours. Finally, working long hours has been associated with more errors and accidents (Gander, Merry, Millar, & Weller, 2000; Loomis, 2005; Nachreiner, Akkermann, & Haenecke, 2000; Schuster & Rhodes, 1985).

More specifically, the literature suggests that long hours are associated with adverse health effects and increased safety risk (Harrington, 1994, 2001; Cooper, 1996; Kirkcaldy, Trimpop, & Cooper, 1997; Spurgeon, Harrington, & Cooper, 1997). Long work hours have been found to be associated with poor psychological health (Kirkcaldy, Levine, & Shephard, 2000; Sparks, Cooper, Fried, & Shirom, 1997; Borg & Kristensen, 1999), excessive fatigue (Rosa, 1995), and burnout (Barnett, Gareis & Brennan, 1999). Several studies have also reported that long working hours are associated with more work–family conflict (Crouter, Bumpus, Maguire, & McHale, 1999; Crouter, Bumpus, Head, & McHale, 2001; Galambos, Sears, Almeida, & Kolaric, 1995; Galinsky et al., 2005; Staines & Pleck, 1984), or fatigue, worrying, and irritability (Grzywicz & Marks, 2000; Kluwer, Heesink, & van den Vliert, 1996; Geurts, Rutte, & Peeters, 1999).

Dembe, Erickson, Delbos, and Banks (2005) examined the impact of overtime and extended working hours on the risk of occupational injuries and illnesses in a representative sample of working adults in the United States. They estimated the relative risk of long working hours per day, extended hours per week, long commute times, and overtime schedules on reporting a work-related injury or illness after controlling for age, gender, occupation, industry, and region. Data were collected from 10,793 workers between 1987 and 2000. After adjusting for these control factors, working in jobs with overtime schedules was associated with a 61% higher injury hazard rate compared to jobs without overtime. Working at least 12 h/day was associated with a 32% increased hazard rate and working at least 60 h/week was associated with a 23% increased hazard rate. A strong dose response effect was observed with the injury rate increasing in correspondence with the number of hours per day (or per week) in the worker's customary schedule. Job schedules with long working hours were not more risky because they are concentrated in inherently hazardous industries or occupations, or because people working long hours have more total time at risk for a work injury.

van der Hulst, van Veldenhoven, and Beckers (2006) considered overtime, work characteristics (job demands, job control), and need for recovery in a large sample ($N = 1473$) of Dutch municipal administration employees working full time. The Effort-Recovery model (Meijman & Mulder, 1998) proposes that negative consequences of long working hours for health and well-being depends on the opportunities for recovery during the work day (internal recovery) and after work (external recovery). Working overtime reduces the time available for recovery. In addition, external recovery may be poor due to the spillover of work demands to one's home life. Finally, overtime is more likely to occur in demanding jobs limiting opportunities for internal recovery. They examined four types of jobs; low strain-low demands, high control; passive-low demands, low control; active-high demands, high control; high strain-high demands, low control. Overtime was common for a majority of employees and in jobs having high demands. While there was no relationship between working overtime and need for recovery in the total sample, there was a significant and positive relationship between overtime hours and need for recovery in high strain jobs (high job demands, low control); there was also a relationship between overtime and need for recovery in active jobs (high demands, high control). Working conditions (high demand jobs) influenced the relationship between overtime and need for recovery.

Caruso, Hitchcock, Dick, Russo, and Schmitt (2004) reviewed the accumulating research evidence on the influence of overtime and extended workshifts on worker health and safety as well as worker errors, considering 52 studies in total. Overtime has increased in the United States from 1970 to 2000 (Rones, Ilg, & Gardner, 1997; Hetrick, 2000). Overtime is defined as working more than 40 h/week; extended work shifts are defined as shifts longer than 8 h. They found, in a majority of studies of general health that overtime was associated with poorer perceived general health, increased injury rate, more illness, and increased mortality. A pattern of reduced performance on psychophysiological tests and injuries while working long hours, particularly very long shifts, and when 12-hour shifts combined with over 40 h of work a week was also noted when 12-hour shifts were combined with more than 40 h of work/week, more adverse effects were evident. Haenecke, Tiedemann, Nachreiner, and Grzech Sukalo (1998), in a study of 1.2 million German workers, found that the risk of workplace accidents increased during the latter portion (after the eighth hour) of a long work shift.

van der Hulst (2003) found that long work hours was associated with adverse health, particularly cardiovascular disease, disability retirement, self-reported health, and fatigue. She concluded that working more that 11 h a day was associated with a three-fold risk of coronary heart disease and a four-fold risk of diabetes. In addition, working 60 or more hours a week was associated with a three-fold risk of disability retirement.

van der Hulst's (2003) review showed that long work hours was associated with poorer physiological recovery; working long hours was associated with fewer hours of sleep. van der Hulst (2003) suggested two possible pathways between long hours and health: insufficient recovery — a psychological recovery mechanism — and poor lifestyle behaviors —a behavioral lifestyle mechanism. Long work hours are believed to be associated with lifestyle choices such as smoking, coffee and alcohol consumption, lack of exercise, and a poor (unhealthy) diet. These unhealthy behaviors produce physiological changes (e.g., high blood pressure, high levels of cholesterol, obesity, diabetes) and higher risk of coronary heart disease and poorer health in general. One perspective on why long work hours may be associated with reduced psychological well-being is the Effort-Recovery model (Meijman & Mulder, 1998). Working long hours is associated with short-term psychological costs which are irreversible. Individuals experience recovery when the work hours stop. Excessive work hours and insufficient recovery causes these negative effects to persist for a longer period of time or even become irreversible. Long work hours reduces the time of recovery as well as prolonging persistent and psychological demands.

Rissler (1977) studied the effects of high workload and overtime on heart rate and hormone levels during the rest and work hours. High workload was associated with higher levels of adrenaline and heart rate during evenings at home (rest periods) as well as feelings of fatigue and irritation. His results also indicated an accumulation effect of overtime on adrenaline levels. That is, it takes several weeks to return to normal (resting) values following several weeks of overtime.

van der Hulst and Guerts (2001), in a study of 525 full-time employees of the Dutch Postal Service, found that working overtime was associated with negative work–home interference. Employees working overtime and reporting low rewards, indicated greater burnout, negative work–home interference, and slower recovery. Employees working overtime and experiencing a high pressure to work overtime, coupled with low rewards, had poorer recovery, more cynicism, and negative work–home interference.

Major, Klein, and Erhart (2002) in a study of 513 employees from one firm, found that hours worked per week was significantly related to work interference with family. Antecedents of hours worked included career identity, service, work overload, organizational expectations, self-reported financial needs, and non-job responsibilities (negatively). Parental demands were unrelated to hours worked; organizational rewards for time spent at work was respectively correlated (but weakly) with hours worked. Hours worked fully or partially related to the effects of many work and family characteristics on work interfering with family.

Rosa (1995) reported that overtime and fatigue were found to be associated with increases in back injuries, hospital outbreaks of bacterial infection, a three-fold increase in accidents after 26 h of work and increased risk of safety violations in nuclear power plants, showing that long work hours does not just negatively affect the worker, it puts a strain on overall workplace safety. Shimomitsu and Levi (1992) found that two-thirds of Japanese workers complain of fatigue, with "koroshi" or death from overwork, an important social concern. Moruyama, Kohno, and Morimoto (1995) found long work hours associated with poor lifestyle habits such as heavy smoking, poor diet, and lack of exercise. Sparks et al. (1997) undertook a meta-analysis of 21 samples and found small but significant correlations between hours of work and health symptoms, physiological and psychological health symptoms. Qualitative analyses of 12 other studies supported the findings of a positive relationship between hours of work and health.

1.2.1. Motives for Working Long Hours

Porter (2004) distinguishes two motivations for long hours of work, both of which could have different moderating effects. A person can work long hours because of the joy in their work. This is a constructive, highly committed achievement-oriented style. A person can also put in the long hours in a compulsive, perfectionist fashion, driven to achieve perfectionistic standards. Such individuals react to criticism with hostility and resentment, experience frustration from failing to meet superhuman standards, and express anger and competition with colleagues in the workplace. Tucker and Rutherford (2005) argued that some individuals may work longer hours because they enjoy their job and derive pleasure from succeeding at it, enjoy the associated benefits, or want to enrich their job or quality of life. This is contrasted with someone who works longer hours to avoid job insecurity or negative sanctions from a superior. Although there might be pressure on an employee to overwork, it is ultimately their choice. The first would not experience the adverse impacts of stress and burnout as the latter would.

Eastman (1998) notes the skepticism about the benefits of working long hours. The "rat race" notion captures the sense of striving for organizational advancement and material success though working long hours leads many to disappointment and frustration and limits the levels and likelihood of taking part in other more worthwhile activities. Women increasingly report that working long hours did not provide the hoped for returns. Landers, Rebitzer, and Taylor (1999) show that typical work hours are high because firms set hours above those of hard working associates to screen out associates that prefer working fewer hours. Eastman found that his respondents indicated that their work hours were a function of the hours worked by their colleagues. In addition, desired work hours were less than expected hours of work. Individuals work long hours to get an advantage over the competition, but if competitors also increase their work hours no benefit results from this investment.

Maume and Bellas (2001) considered alternative explanations for hours worked. These included employer demands (Schor, 1991), family stress and more rewards available at work than at home (Hochschild, 1997), and individual and organizational characteristics (education, organizational level, working in large firms).

Based on data from 762 respondents in Ohio, they found some support for Schor's position in that respondents worked more hours if they had a demanding supervisor, had more education and worked in larger firms, and were in managerial and professional jobs; but no support was found for Hochschild's thesis.

Wallace (1997), in a study of Canadian lawyers, distinguished between number of hours worked and work spillover — perceptions that one's work in intruding on their non-work life. Predictors of both included work salience (work commitment, professional commitment), motivators (promotional opportunity, social value of the work) pressures (profit driven, competitive, work overload) personal demographics (gender, marital status, pre-school children, in a dual career couple), and some controls (position-partner, professional tenure, level of pay, specialization, firm size). Work motivation was associated with hours worked but not work spillover; promotional opportunity social value of the work or profit driven were associated with work spillover but not hours worked; work overload was associated with both hours worked and work spillover. Thus factors predicting work hours did not necessarily predict work spillover; work overload being the only common determinant. Work hours also had a modest relationship with work spillover ($r = .29$). These results suggest a need to distinguish between hours worked and work spillover.

Lawyers worked long hours if they were highly committed to their work (internal) or had heavy work demands (external). Work spillover was associated with hours worked, motivators (promotional opportunity, social value of the work), and pressures (profit driven, work overload) all of which were work-related.

Wallace concluded that the law firms in her study used primarily coercive strategies to influence lawyer's effort and productivity (also see Wallace, 1995). Other studies have suggested that firms should use non-coercive strategies (professional commitment, promotional opportunities, competitiveness among colleagues) to develop satisfaction and loyalty.

Wallace offered some advice to both individuals and employing organizations. If professionals want to work fewer hours and have more time for non-work activities, they should work in smaller firms. Also, individuals should know that the initial career stage was the most demanding. Firms wanting long-hour employees should try to attract highly motivated people and pay them well, and place large demands on them. But it should be noted that work overload may lead to work spillover. Work spillover can be reduced by ensuring professionals that they have a future in the firm (promotions), and their work provides a value to society. Work hours may also relate to the quality of the work performance (mistakes), and fatigue or burnout which also could reduce job performance.

1.2.2. *Moderators of the Work Hours–Well-Being Relationship*

The relationship between number of hours worked and well-being is likely to be complex. That is, it is unlikely that there will be consistent findings of the relationship between hours worked and health in the research literature.

The literature has attempted to study possible moderators in the relationship between work hours and the variety or outcomes identified. Tucker and Rutherford (2005) examined the relationship of work hours and self-reported health as moderated by the reasons for working long hours (or overtime), by work schedule autonomy and by the degree of social support experienced at home and at work. They collected data from 372 train drivers in the south of England. Respondents lacking both schedule autonomy or control and social support, demonstrated positive relationships between hours worked and physical health symptoms. Negative relationships were found among drivers reporting low-schedule autonomy or control and high social support. No such interactions were found with fatigue and psychological health however.

For some samples, such as blue-collar workers, money may be a more important moderator of the hours worked and health relationship. Brett and Stroh (2003), in their sample of MBA graduates in managerial and professional jobs, found that extrinsic (financial) and intrinsic job rewards were associated with working longer hours. How many hours a person works involves weighing the costs (more fatigue, impact on family and social life) against the benefits (income, recognition). People with good social support maybe better able to deal with the costs of long work hours; rewards will be more attractive to these individuals.

Choosing to work long hours as opposed to being pressured to work long hours are important moderating considerations. One may choose to work long hours for more pay, getting the job done, proving one is committed, and positioning oneself for advancement. One can also work long hours or overtime to avoid sanctions and increase one's job security. Barnett, Gareis, and Brennan (1999) found that discrepancies between actual and desired hours are associated with negative health outcomes. In their study of 141 married physicians, the relationship between number of hours worked and burnout depended on the extent to which work schedules met the needs of the employees, his or her partner, and their children. Physicians working more or fewer hours than they and their partners preferred and whose work hours were distributed differently than they and their partner preferred, scored higher on burnout measures.

Choosing to work long hours as opposed to being pressured to work long hours is also likely to moderate this relationship (Barton, 1994). One may choose to work long hours for more pay, getting the job done, proving one is committed, and positioning oneself for advancement. One can also work long hours or overtime to avoid sanctions and increase one's job security.

The strongest relationship of work hours and adverse health outcomes would be among individuals reporting few positive reasons for working long hours and low social support (Golden, 2003).

For some samples, money may be a more important moderator of the hours worked and health relationship (among blue-collar workers). Brett and Stroh (2003), in a sample of MBA graduates in managerial and professional jobs, found that extrinsic (financial) and intrinsic job rewards were associated with working longer hours.

How many hours a person works involves weighing the costs (more fatigue, impact on family and social life) against the benefits (income, recognition). People with good social support may be better able to deal with the costs of long work hours, the rewards will be more attractive to these individuals. In addition, these individuals may also want to work more hours. They may even experience benefits from working longer hours (more money, leading to a greater financial security and improved health; or career advancement leading to more enjoyable work.

1.2.3.   Addressing Work Hours Concerns

Is working long hours really necessary? Those who work long hours are found in particular industries. These data suggest that working long hours may be consistent with face time (Brown & Benson, 2005). Can organizations reduce the need for face time among employees without affecting their identities and further career opportunities? Can one still get the same personal and psychological rewards but work fewer hours. One solution is to separate face time from performance appraisals and opportunities for more challenging work. A second is to provide models of managers that do outstanding work but work fewer hours (Munck, 2001). It is also useful to identify unproductive but time-consuming work practices. Individuals can be encouraged and supported to make small changes in hours — but enough to be noticed — and then have these rewarded. Workers' ability to exert control over work schedules has been shown to have an influence on the effects of work hours on health (Barton, 1994; Smith, Hammond, Macdonald, & Folkard, 1998).

van der Hulst and Guerts (2001) suggest that compensation may also reduce adverse effects of work hours. In addition, length of vacation and commuting time may affect the relationship of overtime and health and safety. Strategies for preventing work injuries should consider changes in scheduling practices, job redesign, and health promotion programs for people working in jobs involving overtime and extended hours (Golden & Figart, 2000b). More days of vacation allow for more rest and may lessen the impact of overtime; longer commute times may add additional job stressors to the effects of working hours (DeGraaf, 2003).

Cartwright (2000) offers these suggestions for breaking out of the long working hours culture.

1. Schedule meetings only during core hours — no breakfast meetings or meetings after 5:00 p.m.
2. Take regular breaks. Take a short walk. Do not work through lunch.
3. Take your full vacation time. Plan your work around your holidays not your holidays around your work.
4. Do not take work home on a regular basis.
5. Say no to unrealistic deadlines. It is better to under-promise but over-deliver than to over-promise but under-deliver.
6. Do not work late because others are doing so.

7. Monitor the hours you and your staff work. Use this information to make the case for more resources.

There are a number of other initiatives that could be undertaken by societies, organizations and their employees to minimize the potential adverse effects of long work hours. These include the following.

- Encourage governments to regulate the length of work schedules as is already the case in many countries in Europe (Green, 2001; Hayden, 2003).
- Changes to the work organization and job design.
- Increase worker control of their work hours.
- Utilize ergonomic job design.
- Increase worker training.
- Develop capable supervision.
- Establish a workplace culture that promotes health and safety.
- Employ more people working fewer hours.
- Use more rest breaks (Tucker, Folkard, & Macdonald, 2003).
- Redesign work to avoid the need for overtime.
- Offer health promotion counseling about the risks of long work schedules.
- Provide medical examinations for at-risk workers.

1.3.   Work Intensity

Work intensity, on the other hand, is a construct that is not well-developed in the literature (Green, 2004a, 2004b, 2005). It is generally conceptualized as an effort-related activity. In this regard, it is very similar to the "work effort" concept discussed by Green (2001, p. 56) as: "the rate of physical and/or mental input to work tasks performed during the working day … in part, effort is inversely linked to the 'porosity' of the working day, meaning those gaps between tasks during which the body or mind rests". Obviously, it would be difficult to measure such effort objectively; it can only be determined through self-reports, or extraordinarily well-controlled laboratory experiments. Burchell and Fagan (2004) used the "speed of work" to mean work intensity, and reported that Europeans were working more intensely (2000 compared to 1991). Green (2001) focused on "effort change" (respondents were asked to compare their current jobs with that of 5 years previously on items that included "how fast you work" and "the effort you have to put into your job"), and "work effort" ("How much effort do you put into your job beyond what is required?" and "My job requires that I work very hard"). He found that work effort had increased in Britain. While these are good starting points for conceptualizing work intensity, they measure only certain aspects of it. There is no research that attempts to capture a more extensive list of attributes.

Worrall and Cooper (1999), questioning over 1200 UK managers from 1997 to 1999, found that the pace of change had increased over these years. Managers now saw their jobs as more complex and fragmented. Managers in the 1999 survey had to deal with more information, to acquire a wider range of skills, and managed more staff. Seventy-six percent of these managers felt that the number of hours worked had a negative effect on their health. Clark (2005) comes to similar conclusions in a study of changes in job quality in OECD countries.

Adams and her colleagues (2000) have identified several factors leading to increased work intensification in nursing; shorter patient stays requires work to be done faster, more managerial responsibilities, need to cut costs, sicker patients, less student assistance, a slower ratio of qualified to unqualified nurses and fewer nurses, doctors working fewer hours so nurses have to fill this vacuum, and multi-skilling.

Ogbonna and Harris (2004) studied emotional labor as an element in work intensification among university lecturers. They conclude that emotional labor has increased due to heightened intensification of the academic labor process. They isolate some factors leading to the greater intensification of academic work (e.g., more students, higher workloads, increased scrutiny).

Green (2001), using various employee surveys conducted in the UK over almost a 20-year period, concluded that work effort has intensified since 1981. And between 1986 and 1997 there have been increases in the sources of pressure inducing hard work from employees. The most common sources of pressure were: one's own choice, fellow workers or colleagues, clients or customers, supervisors or bosses, pay incentives and reports and appraisals (see also George, 1997; Gallie, 2005).

Increases in work effort or intensity are represented in employees having less idle time (less time between tasks), having to work harder now, needing more skills (multi-skilling), greater use of performance goals and appraisals, use of total quality management and just-in-time processes, needing to work faster, having more deadlines, and having more responsibility (Green & McIntosh, 2001).

Messenger (2004, 2006) makes the case for "decent working time" to balance the needs of workers and employers. Decent working time is proposed to have five dimensions: working time is healthy and safe, is family-friendly, promotes gender equality, supports organizational productivity, and offers workers some choice and influence in hours of work and when they are worked.

1.4. Workaholism and Work Addiction

Workaholism and long working hours have positive connotations such as dedication, commitment, and organizational citizenship behavior as well as negative connotations such as ill health and damaged family relationships (Killinger, 1991). Number of hours worked per week, while obviously an element of workaholism, does not capture one's degree of work involvement, a psychological state or attitude. Hours worked per week, however, is a behavioral manifestation of workaholism. Although the popular press has paid considerable attention to workaholism, very little research has been undertaken to further our understanding of it (McMillan, O'Driscoll, & Burke, 2003). It should not come as a surprise that opinions, observations, and conclusions about workaholism are both varied and conflicting (McMillan, O'Driscoll, Marsh, & Brady, 2001). Some writers view workaholism positively from an organizational perspective. Machlowitz (1980) conducted a qualitative interview study of 100 workaholics and found them to be very satisfied and productive. Others view workaholism negatively (Fassel, 1990; Killinger, 1991; Oates, 1971). These writers equate workaholism with other addictions and depict workaholics as unhappy, obsessive, tragic figures who are not performing their jobs well and are creating difficulties for their co-workers (Porter, 1996). The former would advocate the encouragement of workaholism; the latter would discourage it.

McMillan and O'Driscoll (2006) see workaholism as a value system about the importance of working and achieving that typically does not meet the scientific criteria for addiction. They propose an integrated model of workaholism which includes antecedents, behaviors, and consequences. Antecedents include a reluctance to disengage from work, an obsessive style, strong enjoyment in work, and being driven by internal positive reasons. Behaviors include working more than others, thinking about work more than others, talking about work more than others, and stability in these areas over time. Consequences include working anytime and anywhere, choosing work/chores over leisure, and unclear work/relationship boundaries. Workaholism, to them, may in fact represent an approach to work (with intensity) rather than a frequency captured only by hours.

1.4.1. Definitions of Workaholism

Oates (1971), generally acknowledged as the first person to use the word workaholic, defined it as "a person whose need for work has become so excessive that it creates noticeable disturbance or interference with his bodily health, personal happiness, and interpersonal relationships, and with his smooth social functioning" (Oates, 1971). Killinger (1991) defines a workaholic as "a person who gradually becomes emotionally crippled and addicted to control and power in a compulsive drive to gain approval and success". Robinson (1998) defines workaholism "as a progressive, potentially fatal disorder, characterized by self imposed demands, compulsive overworking, inability to regulate work to the exclusion of most other life activities". Porter (1996) defines workaholism as "an excessive involvement with work evidenced by neglect in other areas of life and based on internal motives of behavior maintenance rather than requirements of the job or organization". Most writers use the terms excessive work, workaholism, and work addiction interchangeably.

Spence and Robbins (1992) define the workaholic as a person who "is highly work involved, feels compelled or driven to work because of inner pressures, and is low in enjoyment at work". Most writers view workaholism as a stable individual characteristic (Scott, Moore, & Miceli, 1997; Spence & Robbins, 1992). Most definitions of workaholism portray it in negative terms.

1.4.2. Measures of Workaholism

Two measures of workaholism have received some research attention. Robinson and his colleagues developed the Work Addiction Risk Test (WART). The WART contains 25 items drawn from symptoms (characteristics) reported by writers on workaholism (Robinson, 1998). Respondents rate items on a four-point Likert scale (1 = never true, 4 = always true) according to how well each item describes their work habits (e.g., "It's important that I see the concrete results of what I do"). Scores can range from 25 to 100. Robinson (1998) states that scores of 25–56 indicate that you are not work addicted, scores from 57 to 66, mildly work addicted, and scores from 67 to 100, highly work addicted. Scores above 65 fall greater than one standard deviation above the mean. The items on the WART, based on a review of available literature, were grouped into five categories: over-doing, self-worth, control-perfectionism, intimacy, and pre-occupation-future reference.

Spence and Robbins (1992) report the development of their workaholism measure, providing both reliability and concurrent validity information. Based on their definition of workaholism, developed from a review of the literature, they propose three workaholism components: work involvement, feeling driven to the work, and work enjoyment. They developed multi-item measures of these components, each having internal consistency reliabilities greater than .67.

1.4.3. Types of Workaholics

Some researchers have proposed the existence of different types of workaholic behavior patterns, each having potentially different antecedents and associations with job performance, work, and life outcomes (Naughton, 1987; Scott, Moore, & Miceli, 1997; Spence & Robbins, 1992). The existence of different types of workaholics might reconcile conflicting views as to whether workaholics are productive and satisfied or tragic and unfulfilled. Naughton (1987) presents a typology of workaholism based on the dimensions of career commitment and obsession-compulsion. Job-involved workaholics (high work commitment, low obsession-compulsion) are hypothesized to perform well in demanding jobs, be highly job satisfied with low interest in non-work activities. Compulsive workaholics (high work commitment, high obsession-compulsion) are hypothesized to be potentially poor performers (staff problems resulting from impatience and ritualized work habits). Non-workaholics (low work commitment and obsession-compulsion) spend more time in other than work commitments. Compulsive non-workaholics (low work commitment, high obsession-compulsion) compulsively spend time in non-work activities.

Scott et al. (1997) suggest three types of workaholic behavior patterns: compulsive-dependent, perfectionist, and achievement-oriented. They hypothesize that compulsive-dependent workaholism will be positively related to job performance and job and life satisfaction. Perfectionist workaholism will be positively related to levels of stress, physical and psychological problems, hostile interpersonal relationships, low job satisfaction and performance, and voluntary turnover and absenteeism. Finally, achievement-oriented workaholism will be positively related to physical and psychological health, job, and life satisfaction, job performance, low voluntary turnover, and pro-social behaviors.

Spence and Robbins (1992) propose three workaholic patterns based on their workaholic triad notion. The workaholic triad consists of three concepts: work involvement, feeling driven to work because of inner pressures, and work enjoyment. Data were collected in this study from 368 social workers holding academic appointments. Profile analysis resulted in the same six profiles for women and men — three workaholic types and three non-workaholic types. These profiles were: Work Addicts (WAs) score high on work involvement, high on feeling driven to work, and low on work enjoyment. Work Enthusiasts (WE) score high on work involvement, low on feeling driven to work, and high on work enjoyment. Enthusiastic Addicts (EA) score high on all three workaholism components. Unengaged Workers (UWs) score low on all three workaholism components. Relaxed Workers (RWs) score low on feeling driven to work and work involvement and high on work enjoyment. Disenchanted Workers (DWs) score high on feeling driven to work and low on work involvement and work enjoyment.

1.5. Research Findings

The following sections of the chapter will review research findings that compare the personal demographics, job behaviors, work outcomes, extra-work outcomes, and psychological health of the three types of workaholics proposed by Spence and Robbins (1992).

1.5.1. *Personal Demographic and Work Situational Characteristics*

A critical question involves potential differences between the three workaholism types on both personal demographic and work situation characteristics including hours worked per week. If the workaholism types were found to differ on these (e.g., organizational level, marital status, hours worked per week), these differences would account for any differences found on work and health outcomes.

A number of studies (Spence & Robbins, 1992; Burke, 1999a; Burke, Burgess, & Oberklaid, 2002; Bonebright, Clay, & Ankenmann, 2000) have reported essentially no differences between the three workaholism types on a variety of personal and work situation characteristics. The workaholism types work the same number of hours and extra hours per week; the workaholism types working significantly more hours per week and more extra hours per week than the non-workaholism types.

1.6. Job Behaviors

There has been considerable speculation regarding the work behaviors likely to be exhibited by workaholics (see Mudrack, 2006). This list includes hours worked per week, extra hours worked per week, job involvement, job stress, non-delegation of job responsibilities to others, high (or low) levels of job performances, high levels of interpersonal conflict, and lack of trust. There is empirical research that examines some of these hypothesized relationships.

Burke (1999a) considered these relationships in a large sample of Canadian MBA graduates. Comparisons of the three workaholism types on a number of behavioral manifestations provided considerable support for the hypothesized relationships. First, there were no differences between WAs and WEs on hours worked per week or extra hours worked per week; workaholism types working significantly more hours and extra hours per week than did the three non-workaholism types. Second, EAs devoted more time to their jobs in a psychological sense than did both WEs and WAs. Third, WAs reported greater job stress than did EAs, both reporting greater job stress than did WEs. Fourth, both EAs and WEs reported greater job involvement than did WAs. Fifth, WAs had greater inability and unwillingness to delegate than both WEs and EAs. Sixth, EAs were more perfectionistic than were WEs.

Spence and Robbins (1992) found that WAs reported higher levels of job stress, perfectionism, and unwillingness to delegate job duties to others than did WEs. Kanai, Wakabayashi, and Fling (1996), using the Spence and Robbins measures, reported that WAs and EAs scored higher than WEs on measures of job stress, perfectionism, non-delegation, and time committed to job.

In summary, WAs reported higher levels of work stress, more perfectionism and greater unwillingness or difficulty in delegating than one or both of the other workaholism types.

1.7. Antecedents of Workaholism

Four potential antecedents of workaholism have received some conceptual and research attention. Three of these, family of origin, Type A behavior, and personal beliefs and fears, are the result of socialization practices within families and society at large. The fourth, organizational support for work–personal life imbalance, represents organizational values and priorities.

1.7.1. Family of Origin

Robinson (1998) has written about work addiction as a symptom of a diseased family system. Work addiction, similarly to other addictive behaviors, is intergenerational and passed on to future generations through family processes and dynamics. In this view, work addiction is seen as a learned addictive response to a dysfunctional family of origin system.

1.7.2. Personal Beliefs and Fears

Burke (1999b) examined the relationship of personal beliefs and fears and workaholism. Beliefs and fears are a reflection of values, thoughts, and interpersonal styles. Three measures of beliefs and fears developed by Lee, Jamieson, and Earley (1996) were used: "Striving against others", "No moral principles", and "Prove yourself". Burke compared the three workaholism types on these measures of beliefs and fears. WAs scored significantly higher than WEs and EAs on measures of striving against others and no moral principles, as well as on the composite measure. In addition, WAs scored higher on the need to prove self than did WEs. Workaholism thus emerges as work behaviors in response to feelings of low self-worth and insecurity. This is best reflected in managers' feelings of being driven to work. Paradoxically, these beliefs and fears were also found to be associated with lower levels of work enjoyment.

Kaiser and Kaplan (2006) offer some observations on the well-springs of "overdoing it" at work based on their coaching and consulting work with executive. They emphasize intrapersonal issues, describing how psychological wounds sensitize managers to be anxious about being hurt again. When managers feel threatened, their behavior frequently goes to the extreme, either overdoing or underdoing. Kaiser and Kaplan propose the following sequence: first one's sensitivity becomes activated, this influences (or distorts) one's perceptions of resources and demands in their environment, precipitating feelings of threat which in turn promote compulsion — overdoing — leading to working extreme hours, striving to prove oneself, impatience with the performance of others, over-controlling, non-delegating, and micromanaging. This list reads like a template for the work addict.

Common sensitivities include feelings of intellectual inadequacy, fears of appearing weak, reluctant to depend on others, and vulnerability from being criticized.

They offer a first cut at a process and a set of techniques to help managers and professionals overcome the limiting effects of a sensitivity. They address both managing the symptoms of a sensitivity as well as suggestions as to how to outgrow a sensitivity.

Although Kaiser and Kaplan refer to overwork as one response to a sensitivity, their writing is consistent with others that focus more specifically on work addiction (Killinger, 1991; McMillan et al., 2003). Work addicts need to constantly prove themselves, tend to overcome feelings of low self-worth, and continually increase the performance ante.

1.7.3. Work Addiction versus Work Passion?

Burke and Fiksenbaum (2007b) examined correlates of two of the three Spence and Robbins workaholism components (feeling driven versus work enjoyment) controlling for the other two using partial correlation techniques. Feeling driven was our proxy for work addiction; work enjoyment served as a proxy for work passion.

Data were collected from 530 Canadian MBA graduates using anonymous questionnaires.

A generally consistent pattern of findings emerged. Respondents scoring higher on feeling driven indicated less positive work experiences, less work and extra-work satisfaction, used poorer psychological well-being. Respondents scoring higher on work enjoyment reported more positive work experiences, greater work and extra-work satisfactions, and higher levels of psychological well-being than motives for working matter.

1.8. Type A Behavior

Zhdanova, Allison, Pui, and Clark (2006) using meta-analysis, provided support for Type A behavior as an antecedent of workaholism. Type A behavior has been shown to be associated with levels of job stress, psychological distress, and coronary heart disease. Pred, Helmreich, and Spence (1987) factor analyzed the Jenkins Activity Survey, a self-report measure of Type A behavior, producing two independent factors: achievement striving (AS) which they found to be predictive of positive work attitudes and performances, and impatience-irritation (II) found to be predictive of psychological distress.

Burke, Richardsen, and Mortinussen (2004), in a study of 171 Norwegian owners and senior managers of construction companies, that WAs scored higher than WEs on impatience-irritation; EAs scored higher than WEs on achievement striving both being dimensions of Type A behavior. Impatience-irritation has been shown to be predictive of psychological distress.

1.8.1. Organizational Values

Burke (1999c) compared perceptions of organization culture values supporting work–personal life imbalance across the three workaholism types. Organizational values encouraging work–family imbalance were measured by scales developed by Kofodimos (1993). Organizational values encouraging balance was measured by nine items (e.g., "Setting limits on hours spent at work"). Organizational values supporting imbalance was measured by eight items (e.g., "Traveling to and from work destinations on weekends"). A total imbalance score was obtained by combining both scales, reversing the balance scores. WAs reported higher imbalance values than both WEs and EAs. Thus WAs see their workplaces as less supportive of work–personal life balance than the two other workaholism types.

Johnstone and Johnston (2005), using two of the three Spence and Robbins workaholism components (work enjoyment, feeling driven to work because of inner pressures), examined the relationship of these to four aspects of organizational climate: work pressures, involvement, supervisor support, and co-worker cohesion. Data were collected in two occupation groups (business services (law firms, management consulting, accounting firms) and social services (schools, social workers in government agencies, workers in a hospice). Involvement, supervisor support and co-worker cohesion were positively related to work enjoyment while work pressures was negatively related to work enjoyment. Only work pressures were significantly related (positively) to feeling driven.

Regression analyses including age, occupation type, and hours worked along with the four organizational climate measures showed that only co-worker cohesion and supervisor support predicted work enjoyment. Age, work pressures, and occupational type were significant predictors of feeling driven. Those in business services had higher levels of feeling driven and lower levels of work enjoyment.

1.9. Work Outcomes

The relationship between workaholism and indicators of job and career satisfaction and success is difficult to specify. It is likely that different types of workaholics will report varying work and career satisfactions (Scott et al., 1997).

Burke (1999d) compared levels of work and career satisfaction and success among the workaholism profiles observed by Spence and Robbins (1992). Four work outcomes, all significantly intercorrelated, were used. Intent to quit was measured by two items (e.g., "Are you currently looking for a different job in a different organization?"). Work Satisfaction was measured by a seven-item scale developed by Kofodimos (1993). An item was "I feel challenged by my work". Career satisfaction was measured by a five-item scale developed by Greenhaus, Parasuraman, and Wormley (1990). One item was "I am satisfied with the success I have achieved in my career". Future career prospect was measured by a three-item scale developed by Greenhaus et al. (1990). An item was "I expect to advance in my career to senior levels of management".

WAs scored lower than WEs and EAs on job satisfaction, career satisfaction, and future career prospects, and higher than WEs on intent to quit. It should be noted that all three workaholic profiles (WAs, EWs, WEs) worked the same number of hours per week and had the same job and organizational tenure.

1.10. Workaholism Types and Flow at Work

Csikszentmihalyi (1990) uses the term optimal experience to refer to times when individuals feel in control of their actions and masters of their own destinies. Optimal experiences commonly result from hard work and meeting challenges head on. Would the workaholism types differ in the experience of flow? In a study of 211 Norwegian journalists, Burke and Matthiesen (2004) found that journalists scoring higher on work enjoyment and lower on feeling driven to work because of internal needs indicated higher levels of flow or optimal experience at work. In this same study, Burke and Matthiesen found that WEs and EAs indicated higher levels of flow than did WAs.

1.11. Psychological Well-Being

There is considerable consensus in the workaholism literature on the association of workaholism and poorer psychological and physical well-being. In fact, some definitions of workaholism incorporate aspects of diminished health as central elements. It is not surprising that this relationship has received research attention.

Burke (1999e) compared the three workaholism types identified by Spence and Robbins (1992) on three indicators of psychological and physical well-being in a sample of 530 employed women and men MBA graduates. Psychosomatic symptoms was measured by nineteen items developed by Quinn and Shepard (1974). Respondents indicated how often they experienced each physical condition (e.g., "headaches") in the past year. Lifestyle behaviors was measured by five items developed by Kofodimos (1993). One item was "I participate in a regular exercise program". Emotional well-being was measured by six items developed by Kofodimos (1993). An item was "I actively seek to understand and improve my emotional well-being".

Once again, the comparisons of the workaholism types on the three measures of psychological and physical well-being provided considerable support for the hypothesized relationships. WAs had more psychosomatic symptoms than both WEs and EAs and poorer physical and emotional well-being than did WEs.

In a study of 171 Norwegian construction company owners and senior managers, Burke et al. (2004) found that WAs reported higher levels of emotional exhaustion than both WEs and EAs; the three workaholism types were similar on levels of cynicism and personal efficacy.

1.12. Extra-Work Satisfactions and Family Functioning

A number of writers have hypothesized that workaholism is likely to impact negatively on family functioning (Killinger, 1991; Porter, 1996; Robinson, 1998). Burke (1999f) considered the relationship of the three workaholism types identified by Spence and Robbins (1992) and extra-work satisfactions. Three aspects of life or extra-work satisfaction were included using measures developed by Kofodimos (1993). These were: family satisfaction, relationship satisfaction, relationship satisfaction and community satisfaction. The comparisons of the workaholism types on the three measures of life or extra-work satisfactions provided moderate support for the hypothesized relationships. WAs reported less satisfaction on all three extra-work satisfaction measures than did WEs and less satisfaction on one (family) than did EAs.

1.13.   Implications

Senior managers and executive work long hours, putting in more hours than managers and professionals working at lower organizational levels in many cases (Maume & Bellas, 2001). There is also compelling evidence that working extreme hours can harm psychological and physical health, productivity, and family and social relationships (Cartwright, 2000; Sparks et al., 1997; Worrall & Cooper, 1999).

This section compared the job behaviors, work and non-work outcomes, psychological well-being and personal values among three types of workaholics, all of whom work equally long hours. A generally consistent pattern of findings emerged. WAs reported job behaviors likely to be associated with reduced contribution (job delegating) in comparison with WEs and EAs. WAs also indicated lower levels of psychological health than the two other types. And WAs indicated less non-work satisfactions.

Why would three types of managers working the same hours per week at the same organizational levels, having the same family structures, the same job and organizational tenure, and earning the same incomes indicate such different work and life experiences? The findings shed some light on this. First, WAs had values and beliefs indicative of greater needs to prove themselves greater insecurity (lower self-esteem) and a less supportive and trusting environment, in general. Second, WAs described their organizational values as less supportive of work–personal life balance. Third, they scored higher on feeling driven to work because of inner needs, probably related to their beliefs and values. Fourth, they worked in ways that treated higher levels of work stress for themselves and other because of their perfectionistic, non-delegating behaviors (Porter, 1998). Thus, it was not a question of how hard they worked but why (their motivations) and how (their behaviors) they worked hard that mattered (Burke, 1999g).

Porter (2001) distinguishes two motivations for long hours at work. A person can work long hours because of joy in the work. This is a constructive, highly committed achievement-oriented style of workaholism. This expenditure of time results in achievement. A person can also put in long hours in a compulsive, perfectionistic fashion, driven to achieve perfectionistic standards. Such individuals react to criticism with hostility and resentment, experience frustration from failing to meet superhuman standards, and express anger and competition with colleagues in the workplace.

WAs are addicted to the process of work; outcomes are important only as they supply external rewards for temporarily enhancing self-esteem. WAs strive for increasing accomplishments to achieve self-worth. WAs are given to rigid thinking and perfectionism. They have difficulty delegating which limits the development of others around them — WAs are likely not effective team contributors. They are striving to be in control, in control of their work activities and other people around them. As a consequence they increased the chances of ill health, poor relationships, and diminished leadership contribution — theirs and others around them.

1.14.   Addressing Workaholism

There is a large speculative literature suggesting ways to reduce levels of work-aholism. One part of this work focuses on individual and family therapy (Killinger, 1991; Robinson, 1998); a second part emphasizes organizational and managerial interventions.

1.14.1.   Individual Counseling

Workaholics anonymous chapters have sprung up in some North American cities. These groups, patterned after alcoholics anonymous self-help groups, endorse the 12-step approach common to the treatment of a variety of addictions. Killinger (1991) and Robinson (1998) include chapters outlining actions an individual might pursue to reduce levels of workaholism; Seybold and Salomone (1994) offer suggestions on counseling approaches. Chen (2006) shows how the use of Rational Emotive Behavior Therapy (REBT) can be effective in lessening work–life balance concerns and ameliorating the effects of workaholism. Fry, Matherly, and Vitacci (2006) suggest that spiritual leadership theory may also offer a vehicle for reducing workaholism.

1.14.2.   Family Therapy

Robinson and his colleagues, consistent with their clinical and consulting perspective, focus on treatment, both individual and family. This is not surprising given the central role they give to both family of origin and current family functioning in the development maintenance and intergenerational transmission of workaholism. The treatment recommendations Robinson offers (1998) are similar to those offered to alcoholic families.

Thus, denial is common among workaholics and their family members. Family members are reluctant to complain. Workaholics define their behavior and symptoms in a favorable light (Killinger, 1991; Porter, 1996). Parental expectations of children, often unrealistic, must be addressed. Family structures need to be identified. How do family members collude with the workaholic parent? Family members need help in expressing their negative feelings to the workaholic. Families need to learn to set boundaries around the amount they work together and talk about work. Family members can set goals to improve family dynamics (e.g., communication, roles, expression of feelings).

1.14.3.   Workplace Interventions

How can employers help workaholics and workaholics help themselves? Schaef and Fassel (1988) offer the following ideas. Employers should pay attention to the performance and work habits of employees and be alert to warning signs of workaholism. They should ensure that employees take vacation time away from work. Finally, job insecurity, work overload, limited career opportunities, and lack of control can make employees feel compelled to work longer. If these factors exist, employers should try to minimize their impact on the atmosphere within the organization.

Haas (1991) also highlights the role that managers can play in assisting their workaholic employees to change. Workaholic employees should be referred to an employee assistance program or a recovery program to start treatment processes. Managers should help prioritize projects for employees as long-term and short-term assignments. Workaholics must be encouraged and helped to delegate their work. At the end of each day, the manager should meet with the employee to discuss what has been accomplished during that day and to plan (down to short intervals) for the following day. The employee should be given specific times to take breaks and to leave work. It may also be possible to reduce the negative effects of workaholism, particularly well-being and health consequences, through stress-management training.

The development of workplace values that promote new, more balanced priorities and healthier lifestyles will support those workaholism types that want to change their behaviors (Austin Knight, 1995; Messenger, 2007). More people today want a life beyond work. Employees can work more effectively if they can integrate their work, families, and personal lives in more satisfying ways. This becomes a win-win situation for all involved (Friedman, Christensen, & DeGroot, 1998).

1.14.4. Just Enough Success

Nash and Stevenson (2004a, b) noted that many high achievers were conflicted about their "successes". They identified a potential trade-off between achievement and happiness in these individuals to be at the core of this ambivalence. They studies hundreds of high achievers who felt they were successful and observed that they had an understanding of what success was really about. Nash and Stevenson found that success consisted of four components: happiness — feelings of pleasure or contentment with one's life; achievement — accomplishments that measured up to one's personal goals; significance — making a positive impact on people they cared about; and legacy — helping others achieve success through one's values and accomplishments. If any component was missing, it did not feel like success in the person's eyes. In addition, individuals who felt successful realized satisfaction in all four deliberately went after "victories" in all four areas. They saw success as encompassing all four areas and they set "goals" in each area that were realistic — not necessarily Herculean; it was also important to be successful in all areas at the same time.

They use the metaphor of a kaleidoscope to capture the four areas and the notion of achieving a well-balanced big picture. They conclude with an activity for individuals to develop their own kaleidoscope embracing these four areas. The importance of achieving "just enough" in any area serves as an antidote to the never-ending search for "more" so common among the work addicted or work passionate.

1.15. Risks and Rewards

> By working faithfully eight hours a day, you may eventually get to be boss and work twelve hours a day.
>
> – Robert Frost, US Poet

As this review has shown, working long hours was associated with both risks and rewards. The risks included lower family satisfaction, disrupted sleep patterns, and psychological distress. The rewards included work satisfaction, upward mobility, and higher incomes (Bunting, 2004)

> They lied – hard work has killed lots of people
>
> – Author unknown

There is an old saying that "hard work never killed anybody". Our research bears this out, but with a caveat. Hard work that provides feelings of accomplishment and joy, undertaken for noble, not selfish motives, is likely to enrich a manager's life. The message here is that it is not how hard one works but why and how one works hard that matters.

References

Adam, B. (1993). Within and beyond the time economy of employment relations: Conceptual issues pertinent to research on time and work. *Social Science Information, 32*, 163–184.

Adams, A., Chase, J., Arber, S., & Band, S. (2000). Skill mix changes and work intensification in nursing. *Work, Employment and Society, 14*, 541–555.

Ala-Mursjula, L., Vahtera, J., Kivimaki, M., Kevin, M. V., & Penttij, J. (2002). Employee control over working times: Associations with subjective health and sickness absences. *Journal of Epidemiology and Community Health, 56*, 272–278.

Austin Knight. (1995). *Long hour culture*. London: Austin Knight.

Barnett, R. C. (1998). Towards a review and reconceptualization of the work/family literature. *Genetic Social and General Psychology Monograph, 124*, 125–182.

Barnett, R. C., Gareis, K. C., & Brennan, R. T. (1999). Fit as a mediator of the relationship between work hours and burnout. *Journal of Occupational Health Psychology, 4*, 307–317.

Barnett, R. C., & Marshall, N. L. (1992). Worker and mother roles, spillover effects, and psychological distress. *Women & Health, 19*, 13–41.

Barton, J. (1994). Choosing to work at night: A moderating influence on individual tolerance to shift work. *Journal of Applied Psychology, 79*, 449–454.

Bonebright, C. A., Clay, D. L., & Ankenmann, R. D. (2000). The relationship of workaholism with work-life conflict, life satisfaction, and purpose in life. *Journal of Counseling Psychology*, *47*, 469–477.

Borg, V., & Kristensen, T. S. (1999). Psychosocial work environment and mental health among traveling sales people. *Work and Stress*, *13*, 132–143.

Brett, J. M., & Stroh, L. K. (2003). Working 61 plus hours a week: Why do managers do it? *Journal of Applied Psychology*, *88*, 67–78.

Brown, M., & Benson, J. (2005). Managing to overload? Work overload and performance appraisal processes. *Group & Organization Management*, *30*, 99–124.

Buell, P., & Breslow, L. (1960). Mortality from coronary heart disease in Californian men who work long hours. *Journal of Chronic Disease*, *11*, 615–626.

Bunting, M. (2004). *Willing slaves: How the overwork culture is ruling our lives*. New York: Harper Collins.

Burchell, B. (2001). *Job insecurity and work intensification*. London: Routledge.

Burchell, B., & Fagan, C. (2004). Gender and the intensification of work: Evidence from the European working conditions survey. *Eastern Economic Journal*, *30*, 627–642.

Burchell, B. J. (2002). The prevalence and redistribution of job security and work intensification. In: B. J. Burchell, D. Lapido & F. Wilkinson (Eds), *Job insecurity and work intensification* (pp. 101–127). London: Routledge.

Burke, R. J. (1999a). Workaholism in organizations: Measurement validation and replication. *International Journal of Stress Management*, *6*, 45–55.

Burke, R. J. (1999b). Workaholism in organizations: The role of personal beliefs and fears. *Anxiety, Stress and Coping*, *14*, 1–12.

Burke, R. J. (1999c). Workaholism in organizations: The role of organizational values. *Personnel Review*, *30*, 637–645.

Burke, R. J. (1999d). Are workaholics job satisfied and successful in their careers? *Career Development International.*, *26*, 149–158.

Burke, R. J. (1999e). Workaholism in organizations: Psychological and physical well-being consequences. *Stress Medicine*, *16*, 11–16.

Burke, R. J. (1999f). Workaholism and extra-work satisfactions. *International Journal of Organizational Analysis*, *7*, 352–364.

Burke, R. J. (1999g). Its not how hard you work but how you work hard: Evaluating workaholism components. *International Journal of Stress Management*, *6*, 225–239.

Burke, R. J., Burgess, Z., & Oberklaid, F. (2002). Workaholism, job and career satisfaction among Australian psychologists. *International Journal of Management Literature*, *2*, 93–103.

Burke, R. J., & Fiksenbaum, L. (2007a). The long hours work culture: A mixed blessing. Unpublished manuscript. Schulich School of Business, York University. Toronto.

Burke, R. J., & Fiksenbaum, L. (2007b). Correlates of working hours: Work addiction versus passion. Unpublished manuscript. Schulich School of Business, York University. Toronto.

Burke, R. J., & Matthiesen, S. (2004). Workaholism among Norwegian journalists: Antecedents and consequences. *Stress and Health*, *20*, 301–308.

Burke, R. J., Richardsen, A. M., & Mortinussen, M. (2004). Workaholism among Norwegian senior managers: New research directions. *International Journal of Management*, *21*, 415–426.

Cartwright, S. (2000). Taking the pulse of executive health in the UK. *Academy of Management Executive*, *14*, 16–23.

Caruso, C., Hitchcock, F., Dick, R., Russo, J., & Schmitt, J. M. (2004). Overtime and extended work shifts: Recent findings on illness, injuries and health behaviors. Publication No 2004-143. Cincinnati, OH: NIOSH Publications.

Chen, C. (2006). Improving work-life balance: REBT for workaholic treatment. In: R. J. Burke (Ed.), *Research companion to working time and work addiction* (pp. 310–329). Cheltenham, UK: Edward Elgar.

Clark, A. E. (2005). Your money or your life: Changing job quality in OECD countries. *British Journal of Industrial Relations, 43*, 377–400.

Clarkberg, M., & Moen, P. (2001). the time squeeze: Is the increase in working time due to employer demands or employee preferences? *American Behavioral Scientist, 44*, 1115–1136.

Cooper, C. L. (1996). Editorial, working hours and health. *Work and Stress, 10*, 1–4.

Crouter, A. C., Bumpus, M. F., Head, M. R., & McHale, S. M. (2001). Implications of overwork and overload for the quality of men's family relationships. *Journal of Marriage and Family, 63*, 404–416.

Crouter, A. C., Bumpus, M. F., Maguire, M. C., & McHale, S. M. (1999). Working parents, work pressures and adolescents' well-being: Insights into dynamics in dual career families. *Developmental Psychology, 25*, 1453–1461.

Csikszentmihalyi, M. (1990). *Flow: The psychology of optimal experience.* New York: Harper Collins.

Defoe, D. M., Power, M. L., Holzman, G. B., Carpentieri, A., & Schulkin, J. (2001). Long hours and little sleep: Work schedules of residents in obstetrics and gynecology. *Obstetrics and Gynecology, 97*, 1015–1018.

DeGraaf, J. (2003). *Take back your time: Fighting overwork and time poverty in America.* San Francisco, CA: Berrett-Koehler.

Dembe, A. E. (2005). Long working hours: The scientific bases for concern. *Perspectives on Work, 62*(Winter), 20–22.

Dembe, A. E., Erickson, J. B., Delbos, R. G., & Banks, S. M. (2005). The impact of overtime and long work hours on occupational injuries and illnesses: New evidence from the United States. *Occupational and Environmental Medicine, 62*, 588–597.

Eastman, W. (1998). Working for position: Women, men and managerial work hours. *Industrial Relations, 37*, 51–66.

Fassel, D. (1990). *Working ourselves to death: The high costs of workaholism, the rewards of recovery.* San Francisco, CA: Harper Collins.

Figart, D. M., & Golden, L. (1998). The social economics of work time: Introduction. *Review of Social Economy, 4*, 411–424.

Friedman, S. D., Christensen, P., & DeGroot, J. (1998). Work and life: The end of the zero-sum game. *Harvard Business Review, 76*, 119–129.

Fry, L., Matherly, L. L., & Vitacci, S. (2006). Spiritual leadership theory as a source for future theory, research and recovery for workaholism. In: R. J. Burke (Ed.), *Research companion to working time and work addiction* (pp. 330–352). Cheltenham, UK: Edward Elgar.

Galambos, N. L., Sears, H. A., Almeida, D. M., & Kolaric, G. (1995). Parents' work overload and problem behavior in young adolescents. *Journal of Research on Adolescence, 5*, 201–223.

Galinsky, E. (1999). *Ask the children: What America's children really think about working parents.* New York: William Morrow.

Galinsky, E., Bond, J. T., Kim, S. S., Bachon, L., Brownfield, E., & Sakal, K. (2005). *Overwork in America: When the way work becomes too much.* New York: Families and Work Institute.

32 Ronald J. Burke and Lisa Fiksenbaum

Gallie, D. (2005). Work pressure in Europe 1996–2001: Trends and determinants. *British Journal of Industrial Relations, 43*, 351–375.

Gander, P. H., Merry, A., Millar, M. M., & Weller, J. (2000). Hours of work and fatigue-related error: A survey of New Zealand anaesthetists. *Anaesthetic & Intensive Care, 28*, 178–183.

George, D. (1997). Working longer hours: Pressure from the boss or pressure from the marketers? *Review of Social Economy, 60*, 33–65.

Geurts, S., Rutte, C., & Peeters, M. (1999). Antecedents and consequences of work-home interference among medical residents. *Social Science and Medicine, 48*, 1135–1148.

Glosser, S. M., & Golden, L. (1997). Average work hours as a leading economic variable in US manufacturing industries. *International Journal of Forecasting, 13*, 175–195.

Golden, L. (1998). Work time and the impact of policy institutions: Reforming the overtime hours law and regulation. *Review of Social Economy, 55*, 33–65.

Golden, L. (2003). Forced overtime in the land of the free. In: J. De Graaf (Ed.), *Take back your time: Fighting overwork and time poverty in America* (pp. 28–36). San Francisco, CA: Berrett-Koehler.

Golden, L. (2007). How long? The historical economic and cultural factors behind working hours and overwork. In: R. J. Burke (Ed.), *Research companion to working time and work addiction.* Cheltenham, UK: Edward Elgar.

Golden, L., & Figart, D. M. (2000a). *Work time: International trends, theory and policy perspectives.* London: Routledge.

Golden, L., & Figart, D. (2000b). Doing something about long hours. *Challenge, 43*, 15–35.

Green, F. (2001). It's been a hard day's night: The concentration and intensification of work in late twentieth-century Britain. *British Journal of Industrial Relations, 39*, 53–80.

Green, F. (2004a). Why has work effort become more intense? *Industrial Relations, 43*, 709–741.

Green, F. (2004b). Work intensification, discretion, and the decline in well-being at work. *Eastern Economic Journal, 30*, 615–625.

Green, F. (2005). *Demanding work: The paradox of job quality in the affluent economy.* Princeton, NJ: Princeton University Press.

Green, F., & McIntosh, S. (2001). The intensification of work in Europe. *Labour Economics, 8*(May), 291–308.

Greenhaus, J. H., Parasuraman, S., & Wormley, W. (1990). Organizational experiences and career success of black and white managers. *Academy of Management Journal, 33*, 64–86.

Greenhouse, S. (2001, September 1). Report shows Americans have more "labor days" (p. A6). *New York Times.*

Grzywicz, J. G., & Marks, N. (2000). Reconceptualizing the work-family interface: An ecological perspective on the correlates of positive and negative spillover between work and family. *Journal of Occupational Health Psychology, 5*, 111–126.

Haas, R. (1991). Strategies to cope with a cultural phenomenon — workaholism. *Business and Health, 36*, 4.

Haenecke, K., Tiedemann, S., Nachreiner, F., & Grzech Sukalo, H. (1998). Accident risk as a function of hour at work and time of day as determined from accident data and exposure models for the German working population. *Scandinavian Journal of Work, Environment and Health, 24*, 43–48.

Harrington, J. M. (1994). Working long hours and health. *British Medical Journal, 308*, 1581–1582.

Harrington, J. M. (2001). Health effects of shift work and extended hours of work. *Occupational & Environmental Medicine, 58,* 68–72.

Hayden, A. (2003). Europe's work-time alternatives. In: J. de Graaf (Ed.), *Take back your time: Fighting overwork and time poverty in America* (pp. 202–210). San Francisco, CA: Berrett-Koehler.

Hedges, J. N. (1993). Worktime levels and trends: Differences across demographic groups. *Industrial Relations Research Association 45th Proceedings* (pp. 321–325).

Hetrick, R. (2000). Analyzing the recent upward surge in overtime hours. *Monthly Labor Review, 123*(2), 30–33.

Hewlett, S. A., & Luce, C. B. (2006). Extreme jobs: The dangerous allure of the 70-hour work week. *Harvard Business Review* (December), 49–59.

Hinrichs, K., Rochem, W., & Sirianni, C. (Eds). (1991). *Working time in transition: The political economy of working hours in industrial nations.* Philadelphia: Temple University Press.

Hochschild, A. (1997). *The time bind.* New York: Henry Holt & Company.

International Labor Organization (ILO). (1995). *Working time around the world, conditions of work digest, Vol. 14.* Geneva: International Labor Organization.

Iwasaki, K., Sasaki, T., Oka, T., & Hisanaga, N. (1998). Effect of working hours on biological functions related to cardiovascular system among salesmen in a machinery manufacturing company. *Industrial Health, 36,* 361–367.

Jacobs, J. A., & Gerson, K. (1998). Who are the overworked Americans? *Review of Social Economy, 56,* 442–459.

Johnstone, A., & Johnston, L. (2005). The relationship between organizational climate, occupational type and workaholism. *New Zealand Journal of Psychology, 34,* 181–188.

Kaiser, R. B., & Kaplan, R. B. (2006). The deeper world of executive development: Outgrowing sensitivities. *Learning and Education, 5,* 463–483.

Kanai, A. (2006). Economic and employment conditions, Karoshi Work to death and the trend of studies on workaholism in Japan. In: R. J. Burke (Ed.), *Research companion to working time and work addiction.* Cheltenham, UK: Edward Elgar.

Kanai, A., Wakabayashi, M., & Fling, S. (1996). Workaholism among employees in Japanese corporations: An examination based on the Japanese version of the workaholism scales. *Japanese Psychological Research, 38,* 192–203.

Killinger, B. (1991). *Workaholics: The respectable addicts.* New York: Simon & Schuster.

Kirkcaldy, B., Trimpop, R., & Cooper, C. (1997). Working hours, job stress, work satisfaction and accident rates among medical practitioners, consultants and allied personnel. *International Journal of Stress Management, 4,* 79–87.

Kirkcaldy, B. D., Levine, R., & Shephard, R. J. (2000). The impact of working hours on physical and psychological health of German managers. *European Review of Applied Psychology, 50,* 443–449.

Kluwer, E. S., Heesink, J. A. M., & van den Vliert, E. (1996). Marital conflict about the division of household labor and paid work. *Journal of Marriage and the Family, 58,* 958–969.

Kofodimos, J. (1993). *Balancing act.* San Francisco, CA: Jossey Bass.

Kotter, J. (1999). *What leaders really do.* Boston: Harvard Business School Press.

Kreitzman, L. (1999). *The 24-hour society.* London: Profile books.

Landers, R. M., Rebitzer, J. B., & Taylor, L. J. (1996). Rat race redux: Adverse selection in the determination on work hours in law firms. *American Economic Review, 86,* 329–348.

Lapido, D., Mankelow, R., & Burchell, B. J. (2003). Working like a dog, sick as a dog. In: B. J. Burchell, S. Deakin, J. Machine & J. Robery (Eds), *Systems of production: Markets, organization and performance* (pp. 162–180). London: Routledge.

Lee, C., Jamieson, L. F., & Earley, P. C. (1996). Beliefs and fears and Type A behavior: Implications for academic performance and psychiatric health disorder symptoms. *Journal of Organizational Behavior, 17*, 151–178.

Liu, Y., & Tanaka, H. (The Fukuoka Heart Study Group) (2002). Overtime work, insufficient sleep, and risk of non-fatal acute myocardial infarction in Japanese men. Occupational Environmental Medicine, 59(7), 447–451.

Loomis, D. (2005). Long work hours and occupational injuries: New evidence on upstream causes. *Occupational and Environmental Medicine, 62*, 585.

Machlowitz, M. (1980). *Workaholics: Living with them, working with them.* Reading, MA: Addison-Wesley.

MacInnes, J. (2005). Work-life balance and the demands for reduction in working hours: Evidence from the British social attitudes survey 2002. *British Journal of Industrial Relations, 43*, 273–295.

Major, V. S., Klein, K. J., & Erhart, M. G. (2002). work time, work interference with family, and psychological distress. *Journal of Applied Psychology, 87*, 427–436.

Maume, D. J., & Bellas, M. L. (2001). The overworked American or the time bind? *American Behavioral Scientists, 44*, 1137–1156.

McMillan, L. H. W., & O'Driscoll, M. P. (2006). Exploring new frontiers to generate an integrated definition of workaholism. In: R. J. Burke (Ed.), *Research companion to working hours and work addiction* (pp. 89–107). Cheltenham: Edward Elgar.

McMillan, L. H. W., O'Driscoll, M. P., & Burke, R. J. (2003). Workaholism in organizations: A review of theory, research and future directions. In: C. L. Cooper & I. T. Robertson (Eds), *International review of industrial and organizational psychology* (pp. 167–190). New York: Wiley.

McMillan, L. W. H., O'Driscoll, M. P., Marsh, N. V., & Brady, E. C. (2001). Understanding workaholism: Data synthesis, theoretical critique, and future design strategies. *International Journal of Stress Management, 8*, 69–92.

Meijman, T. F., & Mulder, G. (1998). Psychological aspects of workload. In: P. Drenth, H. Thierry & C. DeWolff (Eds), *Handbook of work and organizational psychology* (2nd ed, Vol. 2, Work psychology, pp. 5–33). Hove, UK: Psychology Press.

Messenger, J. (2007). Decent working time: Balancing the needs of workers and employers. In: R. J. Burke (Ed.), *Research companion to working time and work addiction.* Cheltenham, UK: Edward Elgar in press.

Messenger, J. C. (2004). *Working time and worker's preferences in industrialized countries: Finding the balance.* London: Routledge.

Moruyama, S., Kohno, K., & Morimoto, K. (1995). A study of preventive medicine in relation to mental health among middle-management employees. Part 2. Effects of long working hours on lifestyles, perceived stress and working-life satisfaction among white-collar middle-management employees. *Nippon Elseigaku Zasshi (Japanese Journal of Hygiene), 50*, 849–860.

Mudrack, P. (2006). Understanding workaholism: The case for behavioral tendencies. In: R. J. Burke (Ed.), *Research companion to working time and work addiction* (pp. 108–128). Cheltenham, UK: Edward Elgar.

Munck, B. (2001). Changing a culture of face time. *Harvard Business Review* (November), 3–8.

Nachreiner, F., Akkermann, S., & Haenecke, K. (2000). Fatal accident risk as a function of hours into work. In: S. Hornberger, P. Knauth, G. Costa & S. Folkard (Eds), *Shift work in the 21st century* (pp. 19–24). Frankfurt: Peter Lang.

Nash, L., & Stevenson, H. (2004a). Success that lasts. *Harvard Business Review* (February), 102–109.

Nash, L., & Stevenson, H. (2004b). *Just enough: Tools for creating success in your work and life.* New York: Wiley.

Naughton, T. J. (1987). A conceptual view of workaholism and implications for career counseling and research. *Career Development Quarterly, 14*, 180–187.

Oates, W. (1971). Confessions of a workaholic: The facts about work addiction. *New York: World of Work, Environment and Health, 24*, 43–48.

Ogbonna, E., & Harris, L. C. (2004). Work intensification and emotional labor among UK university lecturers: An exploratory study. *Organization Studies, 25*, 1185–1203.

Porter, G. (1996). Organizational impact of workaholism: Suggestions for researching the negative outcomes of excessive work. *Journal of Occupational Health Psychology, 1*, 70–84.

Porter, G. (1998). Can you trust a workaholic? How work addiction erodes trust throughout the organization. *Journal of Contemporary Business Issues, 6*, 48–57.

Porter, G. (2001). Workaholic tendencies and the high potential for stress among co-workers. *International Journal of Stress Management, 18*, 147–164.

Porter, G. (2004). Work, work ethic and work excess. *Journal of Organizational Change Management, 17*, 424–439.

Pred, R. S., Helmreich, R. L., & Spence, J. T. (1987). The development of new scales for the Jenkins activity survey measure of the TABP construct. *Social and Behavioral Science Documents, 16*, 51–52.

Quinn, R. P., & Shepard, L. J. (1974). *The 1972–73 quality of employment survey.* Ann Arbor, MI: Institute of Social Research, University of Michigan.

Reich, R. B. (2000). *The future of success.* New York: Knopf.

Rifkin, J. (2004). *The European dream.* New York: Tarcher/Penguin.

Rissler, A. (1977). Stress reactions at work and after work during a period of quantitative overload. *Ergonomics, 20*, 13–16.

Robinson, B. E. (1998). *Chained to the desk: A guidebook for workaholics, their partners and children and the clinicians who treat them.* New York: New York University Press.

Rones, P. L., Ilg, R. E., & Gardner, J. M. (1997). Trends in hours of work since the mid-1970s. *Monthly Labor Review, 120*, 3–14.

Rosa, B. R. (1995). Extended workshifts and excessive fatigue. *Journal of Sleep Research, 4*, 51–56.

Schaef, A. W., & Fassel, D. (1988). *The addictive organization.* San Francisco, CA: Harper Row.

Schor, J. (1998). *The overspent American.* New York: Basic books.

Schor, J. B. (1991). *The overworked American.* New York: Basic Books.

Schor, J. B. (2003). The (even more) overworked American. In: J. deGraaf (Ed.), *Take back your time* (pp. 6–11). San Francisco, CA: Berrett-Koehler.

Schuster, M., & Rhodes, S. (1985). The impact of overtime work on industrial accident rates. *Industrial Relations, 24*, 234–246.

Scott, K. S., Moore, K. S., & Miceli, M. P. (1997). An exploration of the meaning and consequences of workaholism. *Human Relations, 50*, 287–314.

Seybold, K. C., & Salomone, P. R. (1994). Understanding workaholism: A view of causes and counseling approaches. *Journal of Counseling and Development, 73*, 4–9.

Shields, M. (1999). Long working hours and health. *Health Reports, 11*, 33–48.

Shimomitsu, T., & Levi, L. (1992). Recent working life changes in Japan. *European Journal of Public Health, 2*, 76–96.

Smith, L., Hammond, T., Macdonald, I., & Folkard, S. (1998). 12-hr shifts are popular but are they a solution? *International Journal of Industrial Ergonomics, 21*, 323–331.

Sparks, K., Cooper, C., Fried, Y., & Shirom, A. (1997). The effects of hours of work on health: A meta-analytic review. *Journal of Occupational and Organizational Psychology, 70*, 391–409.

Spence, J. T., & Robbins, A. S. (1992). Workaholism: Definition, measurement, and preliminary results. *Journal of Personality Assessment, 58*, 160–178.

Spurgeon, A., Harrington, J. M., & Cooper, C. (1997). Health and safety problems associated with long working hours: A review of the current position. *Occupational and Environmental Medicine, 54*, 367–375.

Staines, G. L., & Pleck, J. H. (1984). Non standard work schedules and family life. *Journal of Applied Psychology, 69*, 515–523.

Tucker, P., Folkard, S., & Macdonald, I. (2003). Rest breaks reduce accident risk. *Lancet, 366*, 361–680.

Tucker, P., & Rutherford, C. (2005). Moderators of the relationship between long work hours and health. *Journal of Occupational and Health Psychology, 10*, 465–476.

Uehata, T. (1991). Long working hours and occupational stress-related cardiovascular attacks among middle aged workers in Japan. *Journal of Human Ergonomics, 20*, 147–153.

van der Hulst, M. (2003). Long work hours and health. *Scandinavian Journal of Work, Environment and Health, 2*, 171–188.

van der Hulst, M., & Guerts, S. (2001). Associations between overtime and psychological health in high and low reward jobs. *Work & Stress, 156*, 227–240.

van der Hulst, M., van Veldenhoven, M., & Beckers, D. (2006). Overtime and need for recovery in relation to job demands and job control. *Journal of Occupational Health, 48*, 11–19.

Wallace, J. E. (1995). Corporatist control and organizational commitment among professionals: The case of lawyers working in law firms. *Social Forces, 73*, 811–839.

Wallace, J. E. (1997). It's about time: A study of hours worked and work spillover among law firm lawyers. *Journal of Vocational Behavior, 50*, 227–248.

Wiehert, I. C. (2002). Job insecurity and work intensification: The effects on health and well-being. In: B. J. Burchell, D. Lapido & F. Wilkinson (Eds), *Job security and work intensification* (pp. 57–74). London: Routledge.

Worrall, L., & Cooper, C. L. (1999). *Quality of work life survey*. London: Institute of Management.

Zhdanova, L., Allison, L. K., Pui, S. Y., & Clark, M. A. (2006). *A meta-analysis of workaholism antecedents and outcomes. SIOP conference*, Dallas, Texas, May.

Chapter 2

What Does it Mean to Love a Job?: Ideas and Implications

Constance Noonan Hadley

Abstract

The current chapter presents an initial conceptualization and framework of the construct of loving a job or "job love," drawing parallels to romantic love. Loving a job is expected to contain the same three components found in Sternberg's Triangular Theory of Love (1986, 1987): passion, intimacy, and commitment. The potential manifestation of these components in an organizational context, and in regard to a job rather than a person, is described. The experience of loving a job is also compared to liking a job and being satisfied with it, and predictions are made about the nature of loving a job in terms of its core antecedents, consequences, and evolution over time. Finally, implications for research and practice are discussed.

> Every once in a while I hear from people who love their jobs. I don't mean people who are merely pleased to have a job, or relieved not to despise that job, but rather workers who are head-over-heels ecstatic about the work they do. People who would keep on working if they hit the lottery. People who jump out of bed in the morning, thrilled that it is Monday. (Belkin, 2005, p. 1)

The phrase "I love my job" is part of the everyday vernacular of the work world. Scores of books have been written on the subject, all with the goal of helping individuals find, create, and retain jobs they love (e.g., Griffiths, 2001; Simpson, 1999; Sinetar, 1987; Whiteley, 2001). Loving a job, the books promise, will bring both personal fulfillment and extrinsic success. Yet despite the attention to this construct in the practitioner community, it has not been studied in a concerted fashion within the research community. Instead, researchers have focused on other job constructs, particularly job satisfaction, as indicators of how someone feels

The Long Work Hours Culture
Copyright © 2008 by Emerald Group Publishing Limited
DOI:10.1016/B978-1-84855-038-4.00002-6

about his or her job. The goal of the current chapter is to address this gap by presenting one of the first conceptualizations and frameworks of what it means to love a job, including the cognitive, emotional, and behavioral correlates of this state of "job love."

In developing this conceptualization, I draw heavily upon the romantic love literature, especially Sternberg's (1986, 1987) Triangular Theory of Love. I do this for three reasons. First, I hypothesize that loving a job is part of a broader taxonomy of love. In a study by Fehr and Russell (1991), subjects freely associated love of people with love of work, sports, books, food, money, and country. The authors note that for the average person, love is not restricted to the "boy-meets girl variety"; instead, it is relevant to all kinds of inanimate objects (p. 435). The second reason I draw upon the romantic love literature is that there is a robust history of theory and research in this field; indeed, love is one of the oldest subjects of study (Reis & Aron, 2008). Thus, there is a rich set of ideas and data to draw upon and apply to the work domain. Finally, I have chosen to focus particularly upon Sternberg's theory because it is one of the most validated and well-known models of love (Lemieux & Hale, 2002), and also because it is a relatively simple model that can be easily adapted to other contexts. For these reasons, I base my initial conceptualization of job love on the theories and findings embedded in the romantic love literature, especially the Triangular Theory of Love.

Before moving further, it is important to establish what is meant by a "job." A job is defined here as the entire package of a particular employment position — it includes the field or line of work in which the individual works (e.g., marketing), the particular company that the person works for (e.g., Nabisco), as well as its constituents (including customers, supervisors, subordinates, and coworkers), and finally, the day-to-day roles and activities associated with the position (e.g., developing market forecasts for a particular brand of cookie). Thus, this definition of a job is both very broad in what it encompasses and very specific to the position; even two marketers at the same company would not have the same "job" because there would be at least some differences in clients, colleagues, and daily work responsibilities.

In the first section of this chapter, an initial conceptualization and framework of what it means to love a job is presented. It includes a description of how the core components of loving a job are likely to be manifested. Next, the major ways in which loving a job is likely to be related to, but distinct from, the constructs of liking a job and job satisfaction are explored. Following this, a set of potential antecedents and consequences of loving a job are presented. A set of testable propositions is delineated throughout this first section in order to build a framework of job which is presented at the end. The second section of this chapter focuses on the life course of love, including how each of the love components is likely to evolve over time and what interventions might change its course. In the third section of the chapter, a set of research ideas and implications are presented in regard to how to operationalize and investigate the construct of loving a job. In the concluding section, how the study of loving a job can benefit practitioners is briefly described.

2.1. Initial Conceptualization of the Meaning of Loving a Job

2.1.1. How Do I Love Thee?

In Sternberg's Triangular Theory of Love, all forms of love stem from three basic components: (1) intimacy: the feeling of closeness, connectedness, and bondedness; (2) passion: a drive that leads to romance, physical attraction, and sexual consummation; and (3) decision/commitment: the short-term decision that ones loves another, and the long-term commitment to maintain that love. Consummate love, in Sternberg's view, results when all three components are present in roughly equal proportions (Sternberg, 1988). In a series of studies, Aron and Westbay (1996) confirmed that adults view prototypical love as containing these components.

Intimacy is the first element of love. Sternberg and Grajek (1984) found that the experience of intimacy in a romantic relationship included 10 clusters, such as experienced happiness with the loved one and mutual understanding. Importantly, their findings indicate that intimacy is a reciprocal experience between loved ones. For example, an individual who feels intimacy with another person gains the security that comes from being able to count on the loved one in times of need, as well as the benefits that come from receiving emotional support and understanding. In return, the individual typically desires to promote the welfare of the loved one, offers emotional support and understanding back to the partner, and even shares his or her possessions with the loved one. Thus, intimacy is a highly interactive, bi-directional, process in loving relationships.

In the workplace, the experience of intimacy is also likely to include an exchange of mutual benefits and contributions between the person and the job. That is, people who love their job are likely to receive happiness from their job, and also feel that their job provides them with a sense of security and self-worth. In return, it is expected that people who love their job will value and appreciate their job and desire to enhance and preserve it. In general, intimacy in loving a job may be manifested as a deep-seated sense of bondedness and mutual engagement with a job.

This discussion suggests the following proposition:

Proposition 1. *Loving a job will be positively associated with a sense of intimacy with the job. Intimacy is defined as feelings of closeness, connectedness, and bondedness.*

Passion, in many theories, is the hallmark component of love (Reis & Aron, 2008). Sternberg (1997) describes passion as the drive to connect, physically and otherwise, with the object of love. The underlying cause of passion may of course be sexual needs, but Sternberg also asserts that needs such as self-esteem and self-actualization may also create a sense of passion. Indeed, Reis and Aron (2008) contend that the exhilaration and excitement found in passionate relationships are at least partially due to the blossoming sense of self that occurs when falling in love. However, passion is also associated with volatility in emotion, both positive and negative. As Baumeister and Bratslavsky (1999) note, when the object of passion reciprocates, passionate love can be felt as ecstasy, but if the other person fails to return the love, then emptiness, anxiety, and despair can ensue.

A sense of passion is also central to people's definition of what it means to love a job (e.g., Simpson, 1999). Indeed, "follow your passion" is typically a core part of the prescription for finding a job you love (Whiteley, 2001, p. 14). Rather than a sexual drive, this sense of passion is likely to stem from a deep-seated desire to find fulfillment and self-actualization through work. Passion is likely to manifest as intense feelings of excitement in regard to the job, as well as a strong longing to connect with it even when not working.

This discussion suggests the following proposition:

Proposition 2. *Loving a job will be positively associated with the experience of passion for the job. Passion is defined as intense feelings of excitement and desire.*

Sternberg (1997) describes the third component of interpersonal love as including both a decision and a commitment. He defines the decision as the short-term choice to love another. In addition, Sternberg asserts that love may — but may not — involve a long-term commitment to remain in the loving relationship. Archetypically, this involves marrying and staying faithful to that other person. However, in Sternberg's model, only the immediate decision that he or she loves the other person is required to qualify as being "in love"; one could decide to love another person without being committed to them in the long term. Often, there are intervening factors, such as changes in the nature or status of individuals, or changes in environmental context, that alter the path of love. Regardless, Sternberg's model attests that as long as the initial recognition of love is present, along with intimacy and passion, the authenticity of love is taken at face value.

Similarly, the experience of loving a job is likely to involve both a decision that one loves it and also, ideally, a long-term commitment to that job. It is commonplace in the lay literature to see people spontaneously state that they love their job, as evidenced by the quotation at the start of this chapter (Belkin, 2005). Indeed, loving a job seems as recognizable an experience as loving a human being. In addition, once love is found, it is likely that people will make efforts to perpetuate that love over time. However, as in the case of romantic relationships, both internal and external factors may influence the degree to which a decision to love a job turns into a lasting commitment. Nonetheless, loving a job should at least increase the chances that an enduring commitment is made.

This discussion suggests the following proposition:

Proposition 3a. *Loving a job will be positively associated with the decision to love the job. This decision is defined as an explicit acknowledgement of loving feelings (i.e., "I love my job").*

Proposition 3b. *Loving a job will be positively associated with a commitment to a job. Commitment is defined as the desire to maintain the love and relationship with the job over time.*

2.1.2. Loving and Liking

An age-old question is whether liking can ever turn into love. According to Sternberg (1987), there are two basic views of loving and liking: as two points along a common continuum and as qualitatively distinct constructs. For example, in a continuous view of loving and liking, loving represents a proportionally greater degree of interpersonal attraction (Berscheid & Walster, 1978). In general, however, romantic love researchers object to this view of loving as being merely an extreme extension of liking, and prefer to think of the two constructs as distinct (Sternberg, 1987). As Murstein (1988) wrote:

> The behavioral correlations of these [continuously] quantified attitudes may not be proportionate to the difference in scores. For example, a woman may decide that she likes but does not love Samuel Swain. She decides she loves Wolfgang Wooer. Suppose that she had a romantic love score of 85 with respect to Wolfgang and one of 80 with respect to Samuel. The difference in score is small, but the behavioral consequences of living with Wolfgang and not Samuel are considerably greater. She moves in with Wolfgang, sleeps with him, and does his shirts because being a "one-man woman," she loves Wolfgang, not Samuel. (pp. 27–28)

In a review of the literature in which loving and liking were treated as qualitatively distinct constructs, Sternberg (1987) identified three models of their relationship: (1) disjointed, (2) overlapping, and (3) subset. Many of the disjointed models, such as Hazan and Shaver (1987), focus almost exclusively on defining love and therefore implicitly assume liking is a distinct construct. Of the overlapping models, the most well known is held by Rubin (1970, 1973). He developed the Liking Scale and the Love Scale to tap each construct separately, but found moderate overlap between the two constructs in studies with adults (Rubin, 1970). Finally, Sternberg (1987) identified several theories that view liking as a subset of loving. Davis (1985) described love as liking plus the elements of passion and caring. Meanwhile, Sternberg (1987) proposes that intimacy in the absence of passion and commitment equates to liking. In summary, the nature of the difference between liking and loving remains an open issue in the romantic love literature, although the preponderance of research and theory argues that they are two qualitatively distinct constructs.

The differences between loving and liking a job may also parallel the conceptualizations of romantic love. On the one hand, loving and liking may be on a continuous scale and loving a job might simply represent a more extreme version of liking it. In this view, people who love their job would experience the same elements of intimacy, passion, and commitment as those who like their job; they would just experience them differently. The differences may be in terms of breadth, intensity, or consistency over time. In terms of breadth, people who love their jobs might simply feel a more multifaceted form of intimacy, passion, and commitment than those who like their jobs. For example, they may feel a sense of connection with their jobs on every aspect of their being, rather than in regard to just a few of their interests and skills. Or, perhaps the intensity of the feelings and experiences are what differentiate those who love their jobs from those who like them, akin to comparing a full-blown love affair to a mild attraction. Finally, loving a job may differ from liking it in the pattern of intimacy, passion, and commitment experienced over time. For example, someone who loves their job may experience more "in love" moments, full of connectedness, attraction, and dedication, than someone who likes their job, over the course of a week or a month.

This discussion suggests the following proposition:

Proposition 4. *Loving a job will involve a quantitative increase in some aspect of the dimensions of intimacy, passion, and/or decision/commitment as compared to the experience of liking a job.*

Alternatively, as in the case of romantic love, loving a job may be a qualitatively different experience from liking a job and not simply a proportional increase on some dimension. Here again, we may draw from the love literature to examine three possible models of a non-linear relationship between loving and liking a job. One possibility is that they have a disjointed relationship, in which loving and liking are composed of a discordant set of emotions, cognitions and behaviors from each other. For example, loving a job may be dependent on experiences of intimacy, passion, and commitment and liking a job may be dependent on experiences of learning, comfort, and validation. However, the body of work on romantic love supports the two alternative possibilities for the relationship between loving and liking. One is that liking and loving overlap. In this view, certain components would exist in both states, such as feelings of intimacy, but others would be distinct. So, for example, both loving and liking a job might involve intimacy, but loving is also coupled with passion while liking involves the addition of comfort and security.

The final way that loving and liking a job may be qualitatively differentiated is to characterize liking as a subset of loving. Based on Sternberg's (1987) model, liking a job is likely to involve intimacy and commitment, but not passion. Thus, someone might feel connected at their job, enjoy it, and stay in it quite a while, but not feel that spark, that ardor, of true passion. Indeed, people who like their job, but do not love them, may feel as this writer does:

> I really, really, like my job. I don't bound out of bed energized to do it, but then again, I don't bound out of bed to do much of anything — it takes a few cups of coffee to bring me up to speed. Would I keep doing this work if I won the lottery? Probably. But it would depend how large the jackpot was. (Belkin, 2005, p. 1)

As this quotation indicates, those who like their job may simply not feel as strong a sense of self-fueling, single-minded passion toward it as those who love their job.

This discussion suggests the following propositions:

Proposition 5. *Loving a job will be experienced in a qualitatively different manner from liking a job in regard to the dimensions of intimacy, passion, and commitment. There are three potential models for how loving and liking differ qualitatively:*

Proposition 5a. *According to the disjointed model of the relationship between loving and liking, liking a job will not include intimacy, passion, and commitment, but loving a job will.*

Proposition 5b. *According to the overlap model of the relationship between loving and liking, liking a job will include a subset of the dimensions of intimacy, passion, and commitment, as well as other characteristics that will not define loving a job.*

Proposition 5c. *According to the subset model of the relationship between loving and liking, liking a job will include intimacy and commitment, but not passion.*

2.1.3. Love and Satisfaction

It is also useful to consider how loving a job is similar to and different from job satisfaction, which is already one of the most widely studied measures in the field of organizational behavior (Spector, 1997). Various scales have been proposed over the years to capture both general job satisfaction and satisfaction with specific facets of the job, such as pay, supervision, coworkers, and growth opportunities (e.g., Job Descriptive Index, JDI, Smith, Kendall, & Hulin, 1969). From these scales, much has been learned about the job and individual correlates of job satisfaction, as well as some of its antecedents and consequences (see Spector, 1997, for a review).

Job satisfaction as a construct, however, has been criticized for lacking a strong emotional component (Brief, 1998; Fisher, 2000; Weiss, 2001). Brief (1998) charged that "the study of job satisfaction appears to have been dominated (unknowingly) by measures that fail to adequately gauge how people affectively evaluate their jobs" (p. 87, italics in original). For example, in an electronic events sampling study of working adults, Fisher (2000) found relatively weak correlations between affect measures (such as positive emotion) and several measures of job satisfaction. In a commentary on the state of the field, Weiss (2001) concluded, "the enormous literature on job satisfaction does little to enlighten us about true affect as it is experienced by people at work" (p. 1). Loving a job lies in contrast to job satisfaction on this dimension of affectivity because it is so inherently intertwined with notions of passion. Passion and satisfaction, while not antithetical in nature, nonetheless have strong differences in connotation. Passion involves heightened emotionality; it is essentially a subjective feeling state (Baumeister & Bratslavsky, 1999). Satisfaction, as typically conceived and measured, is primarily a cognitive assessment of a job rather than an emotional one (Brief & Weiss, 2002).

This discussion suggests the following proposition:

Proposition 6. *Loving a job will show a stronger positive relationship with the experience of passion than will job satisfaction.*

Furthermore, loving a job differs from job satisfaction in that it implies a deeper level of engagement, or intimacy, with the job. As Maslach, Schaufeli, and Leiter (2001) noted, "job satisfaction is the extent to which work is a source of need fulfillment and contentment, or a means of freeing employees from hassles or dissatisfiers; it does not encompass the person's relationship with the work itself" (p. 416). In comparison, people who love their job are likely to experience a sense of mutual interconnectedness with their job. They are not just receiving benefits and fulfillment from it, but rather are actively engaged in efforts to support and enhance their job. One consequence of this form of intimacy, as will be discussed later, is that those who love their job are likely to contribute effort and time to their job beyond their required responsibilities. In comparison, satisfaction research has found only small to moderate correlations between such organizational citizenship behaviors and job satisfaction to date (e.g., Judge, Thoresen, Bono, & Patton, 2001; Spector, 1997).

This discussion suggests the following proposition:

Proposition 7. *Loving a job will show a stronger positive relationship with the experience of intimacy with a job than will job satisfaction.*

It should be noted, however, that it is unlikely that loving a job will be orthogonal to job satisfaction in practice. Instead, love and satisfaction are likely to be inter-correlated. In the romantic love literature, for example, Berg and McQuinn (1986) showed that feelings of love predicted marital satisfaction in couples in a longitudinal study. Sternberg (1997) found correlations between his love scale's subcomponents and a measure of marital satisfaction were .86 (intimacy), .77 (passion), and .75 (commitment). He viewed these high correlations as validation of his scale's soundness, as love *should* be related to satisfaction. Another set of researchers have argued that love and satisfaction mutually influence each other, so that initial levels of love predict satisfaction, and satisfaction in turn affects the level of love felt over time (Hendrick, Hendrick, & Adler, 1988, p. 981).

This discussion suggests the following proposition:

Proposition 8. *Loving a job will be positively associated with job satisfaction.*

In summary, loving a job is theoretically distinguishable from being satisfied with a job. Love is likely to involve a higher level of passion and/or intimacy than satisfaction, and as a consequence may be associated with both different antecedents and different outcomes. However, loving a job and being satisfied with it are also likely to be correlated and may even influence one another over time. Both constructs are needed to more fully understand the affective and cognitive aspects of people's experiences at work.

2.1.4. Antecedents of Love

The search for a magic formula to create true love has been the subject of literature and philosophy for centuries (Reis & Aron, 2008). Although no one has yet discovered such a formula, researchers in romantic love have identified certain preconditions and experiences that increase the likelihood of a love match between individuals. The simplest entry point to love, as Sternberg (1986) notes, is a sense of interpersonal attraction. Physical admiration of another is enough to trigger sexual desire, and thus, passion. Furthermore, Sternberg argues, people want what is difficult to achieve, so some element of elusiveness is often a trigger of passionate pursuit. However, Walster, Walster, Piliavin, and Schmidt (1973) investigated the notion of playing "hard to get" and found that people do not necessarily want what they cannot have; instead, they want a partner whom "getting" is easy for them, but difficult for others. Finally, Sternberg (1986) states that similarity between individuals in terms of background, life attitudes, and feelings for one another increase the chances for love to develop. These aspects of compatibility enhance the development of intimacy, which allows couples to move beyond primal passion to the richer complexity of consummate love.

The antecedents of loving a job may be similar to those of loving another person. To start, there is likely to be some form of attraction, a characteristic of the job that appeals to the person on a basic level. Perhaps he or she has always wanted to work with animals, for example, and a job in a veterinary clinic allows him or her to do so. In this case, the degree to which a job is consistent with a calling to a particular vocation is likely to enhance its perceived attractiveness (Wrzesniewski, McCauley, Rozin, & Schwartz, 1997). In addition, jobs that are "hard to get," at least for the general population, are potentially more likely to trigger feelings of attraction and desirability. For example, people who love their job may feel lucky to have it, imagining that other people would be grateful to have the same job.

This discussion suggests the following proposition:

Proposition 9. *Loving a job will be positively associated with higher levels of perceived job attractiveness.*

It is also possible that certain aspects of a job are more likely to trigger feelings of love. In his well-known Motivation-Hygiene Theory, Herzberg (1966) stated that there are two main types of job factors. The first type is called hygienic because they are maintenance factors —their absence creates negative feelings about a job, but their presence does not necessarily create positive ones. Herzberg argued that the extrinsic aspects of the job, such as company policy and administration, working conditions, and pay are likely to be hygienic in nature. The second type is called motivational because their presence has the power to create motivation and positive feelings about a job. Herzberg contended that intrinsic aspects of the job, such as opportunities for growth, achievement, and recognition, are likely to be motivational. Thus, certain hygienic attributes of a job (such as providing income at a sustenance level) may be required in order to make loving it even a possibility, but other factors (such as high opportunities for personal growth) may be the factors that increase the likelihood that a given job will be loved. This concept is also consistent with research on job design and intrinsic motivation (e.g., Hackman & Oldham, 1980).

This discussion suggests the following proposition:

Proposition 10. *Loving a job will be positively associated with intrinsically motivating job factors, such as opportunities for achievement, recognition, responsibility, and personal growth.*

In terms of individual differences, researchers have found that the personality trait of conscientiousness predicts higher levels of relationship satisfaction and love among married couples (Engel, Olson, & Patrick, 2002). The researchers note that conscientiousness is associated with self-control and a sense of responsibility, and therefore conscientious people may be more likely to dutifully engage in love generating and preserving behaviors. In addition, conscientiousness is related to achievement orientation, and thus, conscientious people may be motivated to avoid relationship failure and pursue long-term commitments with their partner.

Similarly, high levels of conscientiousness may increase the likelihood that an individual feels love for his or her job, and sustains that love over time. Conscientious people may be more likely to "give it their all" at work, which is likely to increase their sense of intimacy and connection with their jobs. Fueled by a high achievement motivation, they may also be highly motivated to convince themselves that they love their job as the ultimate marker of success. In this case, the decision to love a job may be dependent upon a certain level of sensemaking and rationalization on the part of the individual (Wrzesniewski, Dutton, & Debebe, 2001). Regardless of how they come to the short-term decision that they love their job, however, conscientious people are likely to turn that declaration into a long-term commitment because of the value they place upon being reliable and honoring their obligations (Engel et al., 2002).

This discussion suggests the following proposition:

Proposition 11. *Loving a job will be positively associated with higher levels of conscientiousness.*

It is important to note, however, that a "love match" is likely to be possible for every individual, regardless of their level of conscientiousness or other individual characteristics. There is no evidence from the romantic love literature that experiencing true love is contingent upon a particular personality type, for example (Reis & Aron, 2008). Theoretically, loving a job is also universally accessible to all workers. Yet a good fit between the individual's characteristics and the job requirements is likely to facilitate the experience of loving a job. Person–job fit is defined as "the degree to which an individual's preferences, knowledge, skills, abilities (KSA), needs, and values match job requirements" (Brkich, Jeffs, & Carless, 2002). High levels of fit are likely to make attempts to connect with a job on an intimate level more successful and rewarding. Conversely, mismatches in the skills and interests of an individual and those required by a job are expected to reduce the chances of loving it because it will undermine the development of intimacy.

This discussion suggests the following proposition:

Proposition 12. *Loving a job will be positively associated with higher levels of person–job fit.*

Finally, there are likely to be contextual factors related to the number of jobs available to an individual at any given moment, as well as the number of jobs they have experienced in the past, that will influence the likelihood of experiencing love for a job. In particular, it is likely that the more choices of jobs that individuals have available to them, the easier it will be to find love. People who are faced with a limited pool of jobs that more educated, wealthy, or otherwise privileged members of society have rejected are less likely to feel that their jobs are desirable and attractive and therefore less likely to feel passion for them. Furthermore, for various reasons, individuals with few job choices may not be motivated to invest the extra time, resources, and personal growth involved in developing intimacy with a job. However, it is important to note that even "dirty jobs" that appear on the surface to be unattractive to the majority of workers can, in fact, be the target of deep levels of engagement and identification by those who hold them (Ashforth & Kreiner, 1999).

This discussion suggests the following proposition:

Proposition 13. *Loving a job is positively associated with perceived availability of job alternatives.*

People who not only have multiple jobs to choose from at any given time, but have held multiple jobs *over* time may also be more likely to find a job they love. Exploration of different types of jobs may help individuals develop an attunement to what triggers intimacy, passion, and commitment within them. In this sense, people who have "dated around" early in their careers may be more likely to find and recognize a job they love. However, there may be a peak number of jobs held beyond which the rate of finding a job one loves decreases. Having an excessive number of jobs may be correlated with some underlying issue with the individual (such as lack of self-awareness or general incompetence) or their situation (such as needing to move frequently to accommodate a spouse) that will narrow the possibility for finding passion, intimacy, and commitment with a job.

This discussion suggests the following proposition:

Proposition 14. *There is a positive curvilinear relationship between loving a job and number of previous jobs held. A moderate number of prior jobs held will be associated with the highest incidence of loving a job.*

2.1.5. Consequences of Love

Passion is the drive to create a union with another, which means that experiencing passion for an object increases the likelihood of some kind of consummation with it (Baumeister & Bratslavsky, 1999). In a work context, this consummation may materialize as a fusing of self-concept with the job. In this case, people who love their job are likely to feel that this is the "only" job for them and that no other one could suit them as well. Their sense of self-worth and identity are consequently likely to blossom in the early throes of love for a job, which can be exhilarating and intoxicating (Reis & Aron, 2008).

This discussion suggests the following proposition:

Proposition 15. *Loving a job will be positively associated with increased identification of self-concept with a job.*

While this tight connection may be fulfilling to individuals in the short run, passion for a job is also likely to make people vulnerable to pain and heartache at work. As in the case of passionate love for another person, people who love their job may experience highs and lows, depending on how much "love" they are getting back from their job. Negative affect might occur, for example, if people feel that their job does not provide enough reward and recognition for the devotion they have provided to it. Unrequited love is cause for misery and despair (Baumeister & Bratslavsky, 1999) and this experience in a work context may trigger an extremely personal sense of rejection and failure. This in turn may lead to loss of self-esteem, which could create a negative career spiral.

This discussion suggests the following proposition:

Proposition 16a. *Loving a job will be positively associated with experiencing intense positive affect at work.*

Proposition 16b. *Loving a job will be positively associated with experiencing intense negative affect at work.*

In addition, the single-minded pursuit of the object of passion may have negative implications in other areas of the individual's life, such as his or her home life. There may be a ceiling to the amount of passion one can feel at any given time, which could make feeling it for multiple objects simultaneously difficult to achieve and sustain (Baumeister & Bratslavsky, 1999). This may be particularly true for women. Rothbard (2001) found that there was typically a depleting effect of work on home life for female professionals, so that higher levels of engagement at work created a psychological and physiological drain on their ability to engage at home. Rothbard found the opposite effect for the men in her study, in that higher levels of engagement at work were associated with an enriching effect on male workers' engagement at home. Therefore, whether passion for a job is enriching or depleting in terms of engagement at home may depend on gender.

This discussion suggests the following propositions:

Proposition 17a. *Loving a job will be positively associated with lower levels of engagement at home for women.*

Proposition 17b. *Loving a job will be positively associated with higher levels of engagement at home for men.*

In general, the experience of intimacy with a job is likely to lead to behaviors that will enhance and preserve the job. In the area of romantic love, researchers have found that people show their appreciation for loved ones by making verbal and nonverbal gestures such as holding eye contact, saying kind things, and giving presents (e.g., Rubin, 1974). It is possible that people who love their jobs will demonstrate it in a similar fashion through actions such as showing enthusiasm, putting in extra hours, and making sacrifices for their job. These might broadly be classified under the heading of organizational citizenship behaviors, which are actions that go beyond the requirements and contractually rewarded aspects of the job (Organ & Ryan, 1995).

This discussion suggests the following proposition:

Proposition 18. *Loving a job will be positively associated with higher levels of organizational citizenship behaviors.*

Similar to passion, however, high levels of intimacy with a job may create a negative consequences in other areas of life. In particular, individuals who work long hours and dedicate extra resources in order to contribute back to their jobs may spend less time with family and friends and devote less attention to hobbies and other outside interests. Eventually, this conscription of time and attention may increase the work–family conflict experienced by workers. Work–family conflict is defined as "a form of interrole conflict in which the role pressures from the work and family domains are mutually incompatible in some respect" (Greenhaus & Beutell, 1985, p. 77). Greenhaus and Beutell argue that the number of hours spent at work has a direct negative impact on the hours spent at home, thereby inhibiting the ability of an individual to fulfill the requirements of another role, such as that of spouse or parent. This time-based conflict is assumed to be true of both men and women, unlike the findings related to the spillover effects of cognitive and emotional engagement described earlier.

This discussion suggests the following proposition:

Proposition 19. *Loving a job will be positively associated with higher levels of work–family conflict.*

As stated earlier, it is not necessary for people who love their job to commit to it for the long term in order to qualify as loving it. However, they are hypothesized to be more likely to make an enduring commitment to their jobs, and as such, should display certain behaviors. In particular, people who love their job are likely to engage in fewer job search behaviors as compared to others. For example, they may update their resume less frequently and decline invitations from recruiters to pursue other jobs. In this case, the experience of commitment to a job may operate similarly to that of affective commitment to an organization (e.g., Allen & Meyer, 1990). In a meta-analysis, Mathieu and Zajac (1990) found that organizational commitment was strongly and negatively correlated with plans to search for job alternatives.

This discussion suggests the following proposition:

Proposition 20. *Loving a job will be positively associated with lower levels of job search behaviors and intentions to leave.*

Loving a job may also reduce the likelihood of experiencing burnout. Burnout, which consists of exhaustion, cynicism, and inefficacy, has been associated with a host of negative consequences, including job withdrawal behaviors and stress-related health problems (Maslach et al., 2001). Maslach and Leiter (1997) view burnout as caused by an erosion of engagement with the job, and therefore, prescribe an increase in engagement as its primary antidote. Loving a job might provide this antidote, as it includes both the heightened excitement and desire of passion and the interconnectedness of intimacy with a job.

This discussion suggests the following proposition:

Proposition 21. *Loving a job will be positively associated with lower levels of job burnout.*

Finally, the experience of loving a job may indirectly support higher levels of performance by bolstering the individuals' capabilities and resources. In her "broaden-and-build" theory of positive emotions, Fredrickson (1998) argues that:

> Positive emotions broaden (rather than narrow) an individual's thought-action repertoire, with joy creating the urge to play, interest the urge to explore, contentment the urge to savor and integrate, and love a recurrent cycle of each of these urges. In turn, these broadened thought-action repertoires can have the often incidental effect of building an individual's personal resources, including physical resources, intellectual resources, and social resources. (Fredrickson, 1998, p. 315)

Loving a job is associated with many positive emotions, including feelings of excitement, closeness, and fulfillment. These positive emotions may increase the physical, psychological, and social resources available to the individual at his or her job.

This discussion suggests the following proposition:

Proposition 22. *Loving a job will be positively associated with an increase in physical, intellectual, and social resources available to apply to the job.*

2.1.6.   Summary

The preceding discussion and propositions form an initial conceptualization of what it means to love a job. Loving a job is conceived to be analogous to loving another human being in that it consists of intimacy, passion, and decision/commitment. Loving a job is related to, but distinguishable from, both liking a job and being satisfied with it. The state of job love is likely to be shaped by a set of individual- and job-related characteristics and in turn, is likely to predict a set of consequences both at work and home. An initial framework of the construct of job love is shown in Figure 2.1.

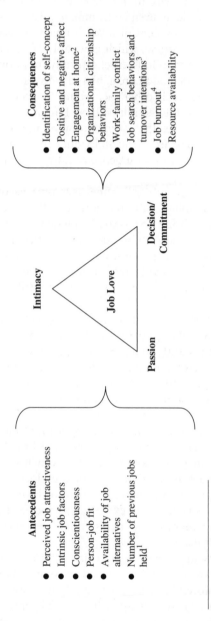

Antecedents
- Perceived job attractiveness
- Intrinsic job factors
- Conscientiousness
- Person-job fit
- Availability of job alternatives
- Number of previous jobs held[1]

Intimacy

Job Love

Passion

Decision/ Commitment

Consequences
- Identification of self-concept
- Positive and negative affect
- Engagement at home[2]
- Organizational citizenship behaviors
- Work-family conflict
- Job search behaviors and turnover intentions[3]
- Job burnout[4]
- Resource availability

---

[1] Curvilinear relationship
[2] Negative relationship for women; positive relationship for men
[3] Negative relationship
[4] Negative relationship

Figure 2.1: Proposed Antecedents and Consequences of Job Love (All Relationships are Positive Unless Otherwise Noted.)

2.2. The Life Course of Love

Another area of interest is what happens to job love over time. According to Sternberg's (1986), it is not clear that love, even consummate love, lasts indefinitely. Indeed, Sternberg argues that each component of love (intimacy, passion, decision/commitment) has a different temporal course, which inevitably affects the nature of love over time. Intimacy, at least in a manifest sense, typically dies down as greater levels of intuitive understanding and prediction are achieved between loved ones. The more couples know and understand each other, according to Sternberg, the less obviously intimate and emotional their interactions will be. Latent levels of intimacy, however, remain high. Sternberg asserts that some form of interruption in the relationship routine, such as the departure of an individual on a business trip or undertaking a joint vacation, can result in a resurgence of intimacy behaviors at the manifest level.

It is also likely that intimacy with a job will wane over time as the individual becomes more experienced and familiar with the job. On the one hand, such experience and knowledge is likely to bring deep-seated confidence and security. But over time, such connectedness may also lead to boredom and restlessness on the part of the individual, undermining his or her manifest experience of intimacy with the job. In this case, introducing novel elements to the job may be useful to rejuvenate the relationship so that the individual can connect with and contribute toward the job in new ways.

Passion, according to love researchers, is the element most vulnerable to decay over time (Reis & Aron, 2008). Sternberg (1986) asserts that passion for another individual is likely to peak almost instantly in a relationship, rather than experience the slow build found with intimacy. However, it also falls off quickly and either stays at a moderately low level of positive energy, in the case of an enduring relationship, or drops to a negative state of depression, remorse, and extreme discomfort, in the case of a failed relationship. Therefore, while intimacy may have a more gradual increase and decline over time, passion is characterized by a rapid initial peak and accelerated decline. The difference, according to Baumeister and Bratslavsky (1999), is that intimacy depends at least in part upon knowledge, which can accumulate through repeated interactions. Passion is based on emotion and does not accumulate in the same sense. Thus, passion is a highly volatile element of love and high levels of passion may be impossible to sustain over extended periods without regular, fundamental, changes in the love relationship to essentially re-start the passion building process (Baumeister & Bratslavsky, 1999).

In regard to a job, passion may also spark high at first, and then diminish over time. In the early days of a job when everything is new, strong feelings, including potentially those of passion, are more likely to occur. In addition, alluring elements such as glamorous travel or high pay may create a heightened sense of attraction and excitement for the job, at least initially. As more about the job is known, the discovery of other, less obvious, aspects of the job may serve to satisfy needs for self-actualization and fulfillment and continue to fuel the fire of passion. But eventually, if the job becomes routine and familiar, or if less desirable elements of the job are exposed, passion is likely to decline. One antidote to the waning of passion, similar to the prescriptions given to keep a marriage "fresh," is to keep embedding surprises and new challenges in the job to spark a sense of wonder and appreciation. Alternatively, or in combination, passion may be enhanced by reducing the elements of the job that cause aggravation, discomfort, or boredom, at work. However, despite these efforts, the romantic love literature (Sternberg, 1986) does indicate that there is likely to be limit to how much passion can be maintained over time, and that limit is unlikely to reach the original highs experienced early in the job tenure.

Sternberg (1986) contends that the course of commitment in a love relationship depends upon the success of the relationship. In his view, there are three types of relationships: successful, flagging, and failed. In the positive case of a successful relationship, commitment builds slowly (even more slowly than intimacy) as more is learned about the object of love, then speeds up once love is confirmed, and finally reaches a steady state of high commitment for the duration of the relationship. Flagging and failed relationships show the same slow build, followed by a sharp up-tick in commitment once love is decided, only to drop off slowly (in a flagging relationship) or rapidly (in a failed relationship) over time.

The experience of commitment in regard to a job may also follow an S-shaped curve. That is, initial levels of commitment may be low while the job is explored, followed by a quick rise in commitment once the job is deemed to be loved. Over time, if the love is sustained, commitment levels will remain high. Otherwise, they will fall until no level of commitment remains and ultimately, the person may leave the job.

It is important, however, to note two things about these predicted life courses of intimacy, passion, and commitment. The first is that the curves described by Sternberg (1986), upon which the current conceptualization is based, are idealized. That is, an actual relationship, whether it is with another person or a job, is likely to be bumpier and less linear than presented. In addition, the elements of intimacy, passion, and commitment are interdependent with one another. The level of commitment, for example, is likely to be highly contingent upon how high the levels of intimacy and passion are at any given moment. Indeed, Baumeister and Bratslavsky (1999) argue that changes in passion are a direct function of changes in intimacy over time.

Overall, then, it remains to be seen how loving a job evolves over the course of time. It may be a highly idiosyncratic phenomenon, dependent upon factors associated with both the individual and the job. If all elements in the equation remain the same, then it could be argued that loving a job is an indefinitely sustainable state of being, even withstanding the likely drops in manifest intimacy and passion. This is the equivalent of a "happily ever after" ending to a love story. But not only do people change over time, jobs and the context in which they are embedded tend to change. Companies get reorganized, supervisors get promoted, economies falter, and tasks get automated. These changes could lead to a resurgence of love, or they could lead to the undermining or even complete loss of love for a job.

2.3. Implications for Future Research

The propositions outlined in the current chapter provide many avenues for empirical investigation into the construct of loving a job. To get started, however, some form of measuring the state of loving a job is required. There are two main approaches that can be used to develop such a measure of job love, referred to here as composite and criterion. The composite approach involves measuring the construct through a set of subscales that capture intimacy, passion, and commitment. To qualify as someone who loves their job, individuals would have to score highly on each of the subscales; otherwise, other types of relationships with a job may be indicated. A composite job love scale could follow the lead of Sternberg's Triangular Love Scale (1997). Sternberg's scale consists of three subscales, each with 15 items, measuring intimacy, passion, and commitment (e.g., respectively, "I have a comfortable relationship with my lover/spouse," "I find my lover/spouse to be very personally attractive," and "Even when my lover/spouse is difficult to deal with, I remain committed to our relationship."). A composite scale would also be similar to measures of job satisfaction that calculate overall satisfaction as the mean of satisfaction with individual aspects of the job, such as pay, supervision, and growth opportunities (Spector, 1997).

On the positive side, a composite job love scale would be relatively straightforward to develop based on the adaptation of Sternberg's (1997) Triangular Love Scale. In addition, the subscales would allow for a more nuanced exploration of the elements of intimacy, passion, and commitment and how they interact in practice. For example, separate predictions about each subscale could be made and tested in regard to particular antecedents, consequences, or patterns over time. Therefore, the creation of a set of subscales capturing the degree to which people experience intimacy, passion, and commitment for their job is a viable and potentially productive means of measuring the construct.

However, there are several disadvantages to measuring the state of loving a job with a composite scale. First, it is an indirect and externally derived means of measuring whether someone loves his job. With such an approach, people are not asked how they feel about their job directly, and are instead categorized by the researcher's algorithm as to whether they love it or not. Therefore, this measure is lacking in face validity relative to other alternatives. In addition, the composite approach relies upon continuous scales and therefore implicitly assumes that loving a job and liking it are quantitatively, but not qualitatively, distinct. Again, without some outside criterion measure of how someone feels about his or her job *overall*, researchers must translate a set of individual item responses into a single gestalt category. A composite job love scale may also be vulnerable to cross-contamination problems between the subscale items and potential correlate measures. For example, the Triangular Love Scale item "I find my lover/spouse to be personally attractive" potentially confounds the experience of passion with a subjective assessment of the love object's attractiveness, which has been identified as an antecedent to love. Similarly, the item "I plan to continue in my relationship with my lover/spouse" may overlap with measures of intention to leave, a predicted consequence of love. Indeed, given the multifaceted nature of job love, developing "pure" measures of its latent constructs which do not overlap with predicted correlates is likely to be quite challenging, although certainly possible.

An alternative approach is to develop a criterion measure of job love. In this case, individuals would be asked directly how they feel about their jobs. Some have argued, for example, that job satisfaction is not the sum of satisfaction with individual aspects of a job and should instead by measured with general job satisfaction measures (Spector, 1997). Therefore, a general measure of job love could be developed, composed of questions such as "All in all, I love my job." However, while this approach would solve the issue of mistaking a sum of parts for the whole, it still assumes that loving a job is a continuous variable moving from hate to love. Therefore, an alternative approach is to ask individuals whether they feel "love," "like," "dislike," or "hate" for their job, and let them categorize themselves into the various buckets. If loving a job is indeed characterized by a short-term decision and acknowledgement that "I love my job," as the current theory describes, then people who do love it should be able to easily answer such a question. People who cannot readily declare their love will likely choose another alternative (c.f., Belkin, 2005). These qualitative responses could later be converted to a continuous scale in which love, like, dislike, and other states, are arrayed, so this approach also has the benefit of affording more flexibility analytically than a composite measure.

One of the downsides to this criterion approach is that there is no external means of validating whether or not someone is accurately representing their feelings for their job. This is a potential shortcoming of many measures in organizational behavior research, especially those in which self-presentation biases are relevant (Spector, 1994). To the extent that people are motivated to present themselves as feeling positively about their job, this type of scale will be subject to self-enhancement bias. This is particularly true for the criterion approach because the nature of the construct being measured is so transparent to respondents. The composite approach would be less vulnerable to this form of bias because individuals would likely have a harder time deciphering and manipulating their image through a long set of discrete subscale questions. In addition, there are a limited number of ways to ask about whether someone loves their job because of the importance theoretically of excluding terms such as "liking" and "being satisfied" with it. In fact, the criterion approach may involve using only a single-item measure of how someone feels about his or her job. For example, the item could be "Please indicate how you feel about your job overall: I love it, I like it, I neither like nor dislike it, I dislike it, or I hate it." Single-item measures are generally avoided in research because they are viewed as inherently less reliable than multi-item measures. However, there is evidence that single-item measures of job satisfaction do nearly as well as their multi-item counterparts empirically (Wanous, Reichers, & Hudy, 1997).

In summary, there are advantages and disadvantages to both approaches to measuring job love. On the one hand, a composite scale measuring intimacy, passion, and commitment follows directly from the Triangular Love Scale (Sternberg, 1997), is more robust statistically, and provides the opportunity to study each subcomponent separately. On the other hand, a criterion scale has greater face validity, is less likely to overlap with related constructs, allows for more flexibility in capturing the construct both qualitatively and quantitatively, and is shorter and easier to administer. Given the relative merits of each approach, the recommendation is for researchers to develop both types of scales and test and compare them empirically.

Once an appropriate means of measuring loving a job is established, there are many pathways to follow with additional research. One is to pursue the propositions made in the current chapter regarding how loving a job is similar to, and different from, liking it and being satisfied with it. For example, a between-subjects design could be used to evaluate the degree to which cognitions, emotions, and behaviors differ between people who love their job and those who like it. In addition, a longitudinal within-subjects design could be used to measure the correlation between satisfaction and love in regard to the same job, and how that relationship evolves dynamically. In addition, the framework shown in Figure 2.1 presents a set of antecedents and consequences that may be studied in regard to job love. It will be particularly important to test these propositions among a broad array of individuals and jobs to get a full sense of how the construct generalizes to different contexts. For this reason, a study involving a national or international sample of adult workers would be very useful. Surveys would naturally lend themselves to this type of investigation. In addition, loving a job is a highly personal and subjective phenomenon and therefore, it should be studied through intimate data collection techniques as well. These methods would include interviews, vignette studies, and perhaps even case studies and ethnographies. Through a broad set of studies using multiple methods, a more complete and accurate understanding of what it means to love a job will be developed.

2.4.   Conclusion

By taking a scientific approach to the question of what it means to love a job, researchers might eradicate any mythology and misinformation regarding this phenomenon that exist in the minds of practitioners today. It is clear even from this initial conceptualization that the construct of job love is a complex one with both positive and negative implications. People who love their job are likely to experience intense fulfillment, excitement, and connection in regard to their jobs, a state that is intrinsically enjoyable and alluring. However, they may pay a price for the devotion and resources they give back to their job in an attempt to perpetuate this love. In particular, loving a job may result in increased vulnerability to rejection and self-esteem loss, disengagement from other areas of life, and work–family conflict. Thus, there is a dark side to loving a job as well as a bright one.

However, the quest for love has never been wholly rational, and knowing the potential pitfalls is unlikely to deter many individuals from pursuing the experience of loving a job. Thus, the ultimate goal of this line of research is not to dissuade people from doing so, but to provide the scientific underpinnings to make their quest and experiences more effective. To adapt the words of Rubin (1988):

> To the extent that the results of love research help people choose partners [jobs] more wisely, cultivate love more resourcefully, and make more realistic demands on their relationships, the research may increase both the quality and the durability of intimate [employment] relationships. (p. xi, words in brackets added)

Hopefully, this chapter will provide both the inspiration and the guidance necessary for researchers and practitioners to systematically investigate this familiar, but not well-understood, form of love.

References

Allen, M. J., & Meyer, J. P. (1990). The measurement and antecedents of affective, continuance and normative commitment to the organization. *Journal of Occupational Psychology, 63*, 1–18.

Aron, A., & Westbay, L. (1996). Dimensions of the prototype of love. *Journal of Personality and Social Psychology, 70*, 535–551.

Ashforth, B. E., & Kreiner, G. E. (1999). "How can you do it?": Dirty work and the challenge of constructing a positive identity. *Academy of Management Review, 24*, 413–434.

Baumeister, R. F., & Bratslavsky, E. (1999). Passion, intimacy, and time: Passionate love as function of change in intimacy. *Personality and Social Psychology Review, 3*, 49–67.

Belkin, L. (2005). Take this job and hug it. *New York Times*, February 13, Section 10, p. 1, Column 1.

Berg, J. H., & McQuinn, R. D. (1986). Attraction and exchange in continuing and noncontinuing relationships. *Journal of Personality and Social Psychology, 50*, 942–952.

Berscheid, E., & Walster, E. H. (1978). *Interpersonal attraction* (2nd ed.). Reading, MA: Addison-Wesley.

Brief, A. P. (1998). *Attitudes in and around organizations*. Thousand Oaks, CA: Sage.

Brief, A. P., & Weiss, H. M. (2002). Affect in the workplace. *Annual Review of Psychology, 53*, 279–307.

Brkich, M., Jeffs, D., & Carless, S. A. (2002). A global self-report measure of person-job fit. *European Journal of Psychological Assessment, 18*, 43–51.

Davis, K. E. (1985, February). Near and dear: Friendship and love compared. *Psychology Today*, 22–30.

Engel, G., Olson, K. R., & Patrick, C. (2002). The personality of love: Fundamental motives and traits related to components of love. *Personality and Individual Differences, 32*, 839–853.

Fehr, B., & Russell, J. A. (1991). The concept of love viewed from a prototype perspective. *Journal of Personality and Social Psychology, 60*, 425–438.

Fisher, C. D. (2000). Mood and emotions while working: Missing pieces of job satisfaction? *Journal of Organizational Behavior, 21*, 185–202.

Fredrickson, B. L. (1998). What good are positive emotions? *Review of General Psychology, 2*, 300–319.

Greenhaus, J. H., & Beutell, N. J. (1985). Sources of conflict between work and family roles. *Academy of Management Review*, *10*, 76–88.

Griffiths, B. (2001). *Do what you love for the rest of your life: A practical guide to career change and personal renewal*. New York: Ballantine Books.

Hackman, J. R., & Oldham, G. R. (1980). *Work redesign*. Reading, MA: Addison-Wesley.

Hazan, C., & Shaver, P. R. (1987). Romantic love conceptualized as an attachment process. *Journal of Personality and Social Psychology*, *52*, 511–524.

Hendrick, S. S., Hendrick, C., & Adler, N. L. (1988). Romantic relationships: Love, satisfaction, and staying together. *Journal of Personality and Social Psychology*, *54*, 980–988.

Herzberg, F. (1966). *Work and the nature of man*. New York: Thomas Y. Crowell Company.

Judge, T. A., Thoresen, C. J., Bono, J. E., & Patton, G. K. (2001). The job satisfaction-job performance relationship: A qualitative and quantitative review. *Psychological Bulletin*, *127*, 376–407.

Lemieux, R., & Hale, J. L. (2002). Cross-sectional analysis of intimacy, passion, and commitment: Testing the assumptions of the triangular theory of love. *Psychological Reports*, *90*, 1009–1014.

Maslach, C., & Leiter, M. P. (1997). *The truth about burnout: How organizations cause personal stress and what to do about it*. San Francisco, CA: Jossey-Bass.

Maslach, C., Schaufeli, W. B., & Leiter, M. P. (2001). Job burnout. *Annual Review of Psychology*, *52*, 397–422.

Mathieu, J. E., & Zajac, D. M. (1990). A review and meta-analysis of the antecedents, correlates, and consequences of organizational commitment. *Psychological Bulletin*, *108*, 171–194.

Murstein, B. (1988). A taxonomy of love. In: R. J. Sternberg & M. L. Barnes (Eds), *The psychology of love* (pp. 13–37). Binghampton, NY: Vail-Ballou Press.

Organ, D. W., & Ryan, K. (1995). A meta-analytic review of attitudinal and dispositional predictors of organizational citizenship behavior. *Personnel Psychology*, *48*, 775–802.

Reis, H. T., & Aron, A. (2008). Love: What is it, why does it matter, and how does it operate? *Perspectives on Psychological Science*, *3*, 80–86.

Rothbard, N. P. (2001). Enriching or depleting? The dynamics of engagement in work and family roles. *Administrative Science Quarterly*, *46*, 655–684.

Rubin, Z. (1970). Measurement of romantic love. *Journal of Personality and Social Psychology*, *16*, 265–273.

Rubin, Z. (1973). *Liking and loving: An invitation to social psychology*. New York: Holt, Rinehart, & Winston.

Rubin, Z. (1974). From liking to loving: Patterns of attraction in dating relationships. In: T. L. Huston (Ed.), *Foundations of interpersonal attraction* (pp. 383–402). New York: Academic Press.

Rubin, Z. (1988). Preface. In: R. J. Sternberg & M. L. Barnes (Eds), *The psychology of love* (pp. vii–xii). Binghampton, NY: Vail-Ballou Press.

Simpson, L. (1999). *Working from the heart: A practical guide to loving what you do for a living*. London: Vermillion.

Sinetar, M. (1987). *Do what you love, the money will follow: Discovering your right livelihood*. New York: Dell Publishing.

Smith, P. C., Kendall, L. M., & Hulin, C. L. (1969). *Measurement of satisfaction in work and retirement*. Chicago: Rand-McNally.

Spector, P. E. (1994). Using self-report questionnaires in OB research: A comment on the use of a controversial method. *Journal of Organizational Behavior*, *15*, 385–392.

Spector, P. E. (1997). *Job satisfaction: Application, assessment, causes, and consequences.* Thousand Oaks, CA: Sage Publications.

Sternberg, R. J. (1986). A triangular theory of love. *Psychological Review, 93,* 119–135.

Sternberg, R. J. (1987). Liking versus loving: A comparative evaluation of theories. *Psychological Bulletin, 102,* 331–345.

Sternberg, R. J. (1988). Triangulating love. In: R. J. Sternberg & M. L. Barnes (Eds), *The psychology of love* (pp. 119–138). Binghampton, NY: Vail-Ballou Press.

Sternberg, R. J. (1997). Construct validation of a triangular love scale. *European Journal of Social Psychology, 27,* 313–335.

Sternberg, R. J., & Grajek, S. (1984). The nature of love. *Journal of Personality and Social Psychology, 47,* 312–329.

Walster, E., Walster, G., Piliavin, J., & Schmidt, L. (1973). "Playing hard-to-get": Understanding an elusive phenomenon. *Journal of Personality and Social Psychology, 26,* 113–121.

Wanous, J. P., Reichers, A. E., & Hudy, M. J. (1997). Overall job satisfaction: How good are single-item measures? *Journal of Applied Psychology, 82,* 247–252.

Weiss, H. M. (2001). Introductory comments. *Organizational Behavior and Human Decision Processes, 86,* 1–2.

Whiteley, R. C. (2001). *Love the work you're with: Find the job you always wanted without leaving the one you have.* New York: H. Holt.

Wrzesniewski, A., Dutton, J. E., & Debebe, G. (2001). Interpersonal sensemaking and the meaning of work. *Research in Organizational Behavior, 25,* 93–135.

Wrzesniewski, A., McCauley, C., Rozin, P., & Schwartz, B. (1997). Jobs, careers, and calling: People's relations to their work. *Journal of Research in Personality, 31,* 21–33.

Chapter 3

Why Do People Overwork? Oversupply of Hours of Labor, Labor Market Forces and Adaptive Preferences

Lonnie Golden and Morris Altman

3.1. Overview

> the innate human desire to improve ones lot is strong enough to make workmen apt to overwork themselves and ruin their health and constitution in a few years.
> — Adam Smith, 1776, *Wealth of Nations*, Book One, Chapter VIII

> Overwork is "working beyond one's endurance and recuperative capacities, ... a hazard in certain personality types engaged in open-ended occupations ... they may at times exceed their bodies' ability to recover ... or make provision for one's physical and emotional needs."
> — J. Rhoads (1977)

> There is a lack of theoretical development on the question of why people work long hours and the nature of "workaholism."
> — E. Douglas and R. Morris (2006)

Two centuries after Smith's astute observation regarding the interaction of the emerging industrial revolution and an aspect of human nature, the concept of overwork has been only a bit more refined. Nor is it less frequent in occurrence. Several key trends across most advanced economic economies have increased both desired hours of work and the salience of working time on well-being. This includes the increasing proportion of the workforce working more than 40 hours per week (Jacobs & Gerson, 2001; Kuhn & Lozano, 2008), multiple-earner households, mothers' employment-to-population ratio, average work hours per household unit (Mishel, Bernstein, & Allegretto, 2005), shift of life cycle leisure time toward

The Long Work Hours Culture
Copyright © 2008 by Emerald Group Publishing Limited
All rights of reproduction in any form reserved
DOI:10.1016/B978-1-84855-038-4.00003-8

retirement years (Hurd, 1996; Charles & Decicca, 2007) and eroding norms of the standard 40-hour-week (Presser, 2003).

Models constructed in the economics discipline offer both labor supply and labor demand reasons to explain why many people are working longer hours level. A chief aim of the theoretical tool of labor supply is to analyze how many hours individuals would want to devote to paid work. The standard microeconomic model of individual labor supply provides a parsimonious foundational starting point to understand the relationship between hours of work, preferences and well-being (utility). However, by focusing on worker responses to changes in the market wage rate, such a minimalist approach is no more than a starting point in understanding work hours trends and worker well-being in the 21st century workforce and workplace.

The main purpose of this chapter is to consider why some people are driven to work beyond their initially preferred extent of commitment toward work ("over-employment") or beyond their own capacity that is self-sustainable in terms of physical or mental well-being ("overwork"). It first establishes the range of factors that determine how many hours a worker wishes to and actually works. It then synthesizes findings from conventional and behavioral economics, and related disciplines, to answer the question, what might cause workers' hours of work to climb? There are both push and pull mechanisms jointly at work. Such mechanisms may exist at the organizational, community, national and perhaps even global levels. It goes on to explore the notion that someone can be working "too much," for their own good, or at least possibly for the family or economy. It explores the potential feedbacks between long hours, overemployment and overwork and raises the possibility for endogeneity of desired labor supply through adaptive preferences for work and income. Finally, it briefly considers implications for individual, organizational and public policy actions that might help promote working hours that would optimize overall well-being by reducing the incidence of overwork and overemployment.

3.1.1.   Conventional Models of Hours of Labor Supply and Labor Demanded: Time for an Update?

Explaining why people work as many hours as they do requires amending the purely economic labor supply function. The conventional labor–leisure choice model portrays optimizing individuals as adjusting their hours of labor supply toward their preferred number per week. The model rests on the three-legged stool of utility maximization behavior, equilibrating markets and stable preferences (Humphries, 1998). The model assumes that workers form their desired number of work hours based on their market wage rate, nonlabor income sources, and innate preferences for work and leisure. Individuals are assumed to possess their own unique, inherent taste or distaste for work. Workers maximize their utility by adjusting their hours until the unique point where the relative preference for an hour of leisure vis-à-vis work exactly equals their market wage rate. The hedonic labor market model assumes that, in the long run, workers and firms sort themselves in ways that match up desired and required hours of work.

In textbook treatments of labor supply, the focus is on wage rate changes and their opposing income and substitution effects. The substitution effect suggests that higher wage rates raise the opportunity cost of hours spent in activities other than working, thus inducing longer desired hours of work. The opposing income effect suggests that as wage rates climb so does the value of nonwork time, inducing shorter desired hours of work. The net effect reveals the slope of their labor supply curve, which may contain a point at which the curve begins to bend backward as wage rates reach relatively higher levels. A key advance was to consider a third option for allocating time, unpaid household production (Becker, 1985). This entails self-produced goods and services, such as cooking and caregiving, which may be substitutes for those paid for market-produced. Because these activities have elements of both work and leisure, they contribute to well-being of the household unit. On the one hand, household production is a type of time allocation that is largely self-directed, like leisure time. On the other, it is considered work because it often involves some combination of routine household tasks, household management and emotional labor (Mederer, 1993). Some analysts actually have considered household labor time in total work hours (e.g., Leete & Schor, 1994).

Insights drawn from behavioral economics would incorporate the various social and psychological reasons that motivate people to work generally (e.g., Wolfe, 1997; Kaufman, 1999; Kelloway, Gallagher, & Barling, 2004; Golden, 2006; Ellingsen & Johannesson, 2007). This would expand the list of determinants beyond the list of the worker's own wage rate, nonwage income and their innate and stable "preferences" assumed by the conventional labor supply model. It requires peering into the black box of "preferences," by recognizing that preferences may become adaptable under social and cultural influences, particularly the inherent inflexibility in many workplaces or jobs that often prevent individuals from getting a desired reduction in their number of work hours. The extent of inflexibilities and degree to which workers eventually internalize them puts at risk labor's long-term sustainability as a productive resource.

3.2. Hours of Labor Demanded: Externally Imposed Work Hours and Overemployment

The wholly separate economic model of firm labor demand creates the groundwork for understanding the role of employers in determining work hours. Most conventional approaches recognize there is a potential divergence of optimally desired hours of labor supply from the hours of labor demand of employers, jobs or relevant labor markets (Hart, 2004). Most workers will at some point face constraints, often binding, imposed on their actual hours of work. Employers often establish fixed shift lengths or minimum hours per employee. These are traced to the fixed costs of adding employees, which increase with the skill requirements in jobs and the cost of contributions to employee benefits, which in the US are commonly structured as fixed per employee rather than per hour worked (Leete & Schor, 1994; Golden, 1996; Cutler & Madrian, 1998; Hart, 2004). Constrained labor supply models incorporate the various cost incentives for employers that preclude downward adjustment of work hours for many workers (e.g., Landers, Rebitzer, & Taylor, 1996; Lang & Kahn, 2001).

Thus, one reason people work as many as hours as they do is at least partly or initially involuntary, outside their direct control. The inability of a sizable segment of the workforce to obtain their optimally desired hours is well recognized in the literature (e.g., Stewart & Swaffield, 1997; Altonji & Oldham, 2003; Böheim & Taylor, 2004). A worker is in a state of overemployment if they would be willing to give up at least some current income, or imminent raises, at prevailing wage rates, to reduce their hours of work burden, but lack that option or realistically exercising that option at their current job. Overemployment represents a case where a worker works too many number of hours to optimize their well-being. Conversely, they are experiencing underemployment if they are unable to get as many hours of work and income as they would prefer at their current job. Understandably, there is more focus on underemployment, given its deleterious effects, especially for those who are part-time and wish full-time work (Feldman, 1996; Dollard & Winefield, 2002; Wilkins, 2007). Estimates of the macroeconomic overemployment rate range widely within for the US, from as little as 6 percent to as much as 50 percent (Schor, 1999; Feather & Shaw, 2000; Jacobs & Gerson, 2001; Lang & Kahn, 2001; Bielinski, Bosch, & Wagner, 2002; Stier & Lewin-Epstein, 2003; Reynolds, 2004; Scacciati, 2004; Messenger, 2004; Schor, 2005). Estimates vary depending on the sample, occupational representation, stage of the business cycle and the way the question is posed about the willingness to trade income for time (Golden & Gebreselassie, 2007).

Generally, at the microlevel, overemployment occurs either when an employer's demand for work hours is escalating beyond the number in the original wage-hour bundle agreed to by the worker, or alternatively, when a worker's preference for shorter working hours, below the expected norm of the workplace or job, is not met or fully accommodated by the employer. It may take the form of unwelcome overtime work, an unfulfilled desire for part-time or part-year work. More formally, workers are overemployed if their actual hours (h) exceed desired hours (h^*) at a current wage and job so long as an employer is not induced to adjust h downward toward h^*. Organizations may overestimate the cost or underestimate the potential payoffs of reducing the costs associated with overemployment (see Golden & Gebreselassie, 2007). In addition, workers may quite rationally remain in the state of overemployment either because switching to a shorter-hours job is too costly, either in terms of a transition to a new career or because the benefit coverage lost with part-time status (at least in the US) is more than proportional to the hours reduction. Indeed, workers are far more likely to attain shorter desired work hours by changing jobs than by finding them within their existing job (Böheim & Taylor, 2004; Senesky, 2005; Reynolds & Aletraris, 2006).

3.3. Overemployment and Overwork: Potential Adverse Effects

The point at which working hours begin to entail escalating risks or harms beyond those associated with normal, standard, agreed-upon hours is considered here to constitute *overwork*. Overwork refers specifically to the cumulative consequences of operating at "overcapacity." Additional hours spent at work eventually creates fatigue or stress so that the worker's physical or mental health, well-being health or quality of life is not sustainable in the longer run. Adverse effects of excess work on various indicators of worker's well-being from individuals and families to employers and the (national or global) economy have been fairly well established empirically. Individuals who work to excess are considered overworkers not because of perceived returns but rather despite a perceived lack of such returns from the organization (Peiperl & Jones, 2001). As Figure 3.1 illustrates, overemployment is fundamentally distinct from the notion of overwork. Many who are working long hours are overworked and/or overemployed, but not all. Many but not all workers with overwork symptoms work long hours. Overwork may occur even if the excess work hours are partly or even wholly voluntary. Many but not all overworked workers prefer reduced hours. Finally, many who prefer reduced work hours work overtime or suffer overwork symptoms, but not all.

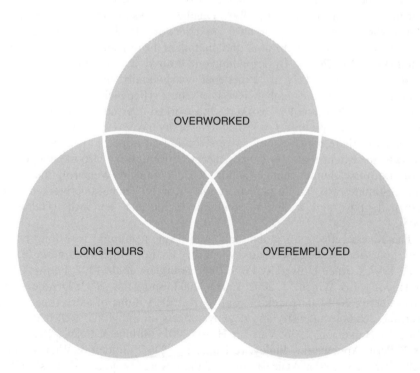

Figure 3.1: Overlap of long work hours, overworking and overemployment.

The point at which work becomes overwork may be fuzzy and less than precise. It varies by the pacing and physical and mental demands of the job, workplace and occupation (Galinsky et al., 2005), not to mention the heterogeneous capabilities of the job incumbent. It also varies by the demands individuals face during nonmarket work time. The potential adverse welfare effects stemming from long hours of work *per se*, such as psychological health and physical health, are becoming ever better documented (e.g., Sparks, Cooper, Fried, & Shirom, 1997; Spurgeon, Harrington, & Cooper, 1997; Burawoy, Fligstein, Hochschild, Schor, & Voss, 2001; Van der Hulst, 2001, 2003; Spurgeon, 2003; Kodz et al., 2003; Dong, 2005; Caruso et al., 2006). Frequent overtime and long work days can be a major cause of stress, chronic fatigue, repetitive motions and exposures to harmful chemicals, leading to chronic or acute health conditions and even occupational burnout (Sparks et al., 1997; Spurgeon et al., 1997; Barnett, Gareis, & Brennan, 1999; Fenwick & Tausig, 2000; Haight, 2001). Evidence abounds that long work hours generally contribute to higher rates of accident rates and thus a greater risk of injury and illness, although this may be attributable at least somewhat to prior health, demographic and compensation characteristics (Allen, Slavin, & Bunn, 2007). For similar reasons of fatigue or work stress, among workers who work overtime hours, depending on factors such as the shift timing, rest breaks and sector of employment, the accident rate typically begins to rise somewhere between the 9th and 12th hour in a day at work (e.g., Rosa, 1995; Hanecke, Silke, Friedhelm, & Grzech-Sukalo, 1998; Dembe, Erickson, Delbos, & Banks, 2005). Those who experience higher levels of overwork levels report a higher scale of stress and depressive symptoms and that their health and self-care are not good (Galinsky et al., 2005). By crowding out desired but unattained nonwork time, families are more likely to experience work–family imbalance or interference (Clarkberg, 2001) and higher levels of stress (Fenwick & Tausig, 2001). For example, over 30 percent of workers who worked over 60 weekly hours experience severe work–family conflict (Cornell University IWS, 1999). More indirectly and longer term, there may be some adverse ecological impacts of more hours spent at work, to the extent that it enhances energy consumption, carbon emissions and the pace of adverse climate change (Schor, 2005; Rosnick & Weisbrot, 2006). The most direct estimates are that 26 percent report recently "feeling overworked" and more than half of workers feeling so sometime in the past 3 months (Galinsky et al., 2005).

The adverse effects on individuals' well-being stemming from long or overtime work hours tend to be exacerbated when they are not entirely voluntary (e.g., Sparks et al., 1997, Cornell University IWS, 1999; Spurgeon et al., 1997; Fenwick & Tausig, 2001; Dollard & Winefield, 2002; Farris, 2002; Spurgeon, 2003; Dembe et al., 2005; Caruso et al., 2006). The lack of control over the volume of work time, particularly overtime, tends to intensify any negative effects on individual well-being indicators (Bliese & Halverson, 1996; Van der Hulst, 2001; Maume & Bellas, 2001; Spurgeon, 2003; Berg, Appelbaum, Bailey, & Kalleberg, 2004; Golden & Wiens-Tuers, 2006; Kelly & Moen, 2007). At least some of the adverse fatigue and stress effects, may traceable to the conditions of work, not only to the individual behavior leading to long number of hours worked (Buelens & Poelmans, 2004). Generally, despite adding to the individual's income and the national output level, overemployment creates four separate types of potential spillover costs: Accident risks that result in injury, illness or adverse public health and safety; time squeeze on family, relationships, children and social capital development; underemployment and negative employment effects and negative effects on average productivity per hour at the organizational and/or national levels.

Feeling driven to work longer is generally more likely to be associated with negative well-being at work outcomes, in contrast to work enjoyment as the prime motivation (Burke, 1999). Workers who work longer hours or more days than they prefer, for reasons such as employer expectations, tend to feel more overworked than others (Galinsky et al., 2005). However, working more hours for personal motivation or financial reasons — such as "to advance at my job" or "to buy things I need" — are not associated with feeling overworked. About 44 percent of those who work more hours than they prefer indicate feeling overworked, markedly more than the 26 percent that express no preference for shorter hours. Similarly, 45 percent of those who are not permitted at their job to change their own work schedules toward their preferred hours experience significantly higher levels of feeling overworked. For those workers facing supervisory pressure to work overtime (Cornell IWS, 1999) and working more than 50 hours a week, the proportion experiencing multiple injuries at work, absenteeism due to illness, somatic stress or "feeling depressed" are all markedly higher. As supervisory pressure intensifies from low, moderate or some levels, workers report almost double greater levels of experiencing multiple injuries at work during the prior year. When overtime is considered involuntary, there are elevated levels of self-reported health problems, and homework interference. For those in low reward work conditions, there are also adverse effects on mental health (Van der Hulst, 2001). Similarly, employees who work overtime on a regular basis are twice as likely to report that they find their job to be highly stressful (Northwestern National Life, 1991). Likewise, lacking flexibility to reduce one's hours leads to higher stress, particularly in the balancing of work and family, or even premature retirement (Barnett et al., 1999; Fenwick & Tausig, 2001; Hill, Hawkins Ferris, & Weitzman, 2001; Charles & Decicca, 2007). The proportion of workers who reported high levels of work–family conflict rose if they faced supervisory pressure to work overtime (Cornell IWS, 1999). The most negative effect of working employer-required overtime is work interference with family.

Overemployment is detrimental not only to the worker but perhaps also to the firm or organization. It is one source of costly worker absenteeism, tardiness or excessive on-the-job leisure (Drago & Wooden, 1992; Yaniv, 1995; Barnett et al., 1999; Kaufman, 1999; Burawoy et al., 2001; Lamberg, 2004). In the extreme case, the worker quits or suffers burnout that results in labor force withdrawal. The mismatch of working more hours than preferred was inversely related to the affective commitment of full-time and male employees (van Emmerik & Sanders, 2005). Conversely, better matching or "congruence" between preferred and actual hours status is associated with employee in-role and extra-role performance

(Holtom, Tidd, & Lee, 2002). Moreover, the rate of overemployment tends to be positively correlated with the rate of underemployment in many industries (Golden & Gebreselassie, 2007). Thus, underemployment of at least some workers seems to be related to the extent that there are overemployed workers in the same industry.

3.4.   The Dynamics of Labor Oversupply and Overemployment

By focusing on work hours preferences primarily as a reflection of changes in wages that generate opposing income and substitution effects, the conventional model of labor supply has paid insufficient attention to the key factors that would shift the entire labor supply curve. These are typically relegated to the status of exogenous changes in innate preferences or constraints. This oversimplification is unfortunate because identifying the source of labor supply shifts is important for understanding recent trends. Survey and experimental evidence suggests that the phenomenon of preference endogeneity, preferences that adapt to market outcomes, rather than being fixed, may be more important than has heretofore been recognized (Schor, 2005). Long hours workers may be "volunteers," who prefer long hours. In contrast, others are "conscripts," who conform themselves to the "ideal worker" norm and carry high levels of consumer debt (Drago, Wooden, & Black, 2006). Thus, we now endeavor to open the "black box" and set out a model of reference-dependent preference formation that underlies desired labor supply.

3.5.   Individual Labor Supply Shifters: What Makes Preferred Work Hours Rise Over Time?

The conventional labor supply model would explain a rise in the desired hours of work straightforwardly, as a reflection of a net substitution effect of rising (after-tax) wage rates that raise the opportunity cost of leisure or household production time. In the event wage rates were constant, then the model would suggest the cause was a decline in nonwage income, or the catch-all, change in "exogenous" preferences toward work or away from nonwork time (see Figure 3.2). However, this is just the beginning, not the end, of the story. A contemporary, comprehensive desired hours of labor supply has five terms: current income compensation, emphasized by the standard model; future targeted income or trajectory, either as human capital investment or signaling behavior; positional goods consumption and relative income concerns, including status conferring, nonmaterial gains; process benefits of work, psychic returns or access to nonwage perks and finally, persistence or addiction, which may actually stem from externally (employer) imposed, unwelcome excess work that becomes internalized. In brief, there are behavioral, social, cultural and institutional forces that might push out an individual's desired work hours, beyond that which would be desired if the individual were living in isolation, *a la* Robinson

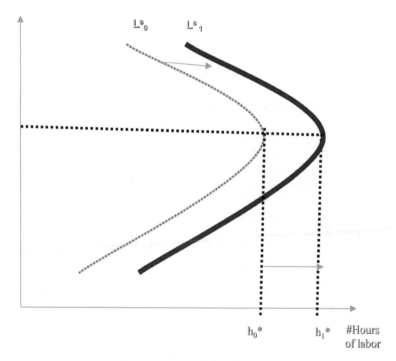

Figure 3.2: An outward shift in individual desired hours of labor supply, wage rate constant, with hours having a signaling, human capital investment or relative positioning function.

Crusoe or *Cast Away*. The same forces create resistance to adjusting hours downward. These forces may be sufficiently strong to offset or even overwhelm the desired leisure enhancing counterforces of rising affluence with higher wage rates or nonwage income.

3.6. Minimum Social Subsistence Level: Backward Bending Labor Supply at Low Wage Rates

The backward bending labor supply curve may exist not only at very high wage rates, but also at very low wages. Thus, if net real wage rates are falling, a worker's desired work hours may rise (Sharif, 2000; Prasch, 2001). Among relatively lower- and middle-income households, the level of consumption considered to be a socially minimum "subsistence" level might be creeping higher over time. Moreover, leisure grants greater well-being in a contemporary economy primarily when there is sufficient income to utilize during the leisure time. At very low levels of income there may be a near-zero marginal value of leisure (Altman, 2001). Accordingly, if social and cultural forces ratchet upward what is considered a minimum, socially acceptable subsistence level of consumption, than either work hours or debt increases will follow.

3.7. Relative Positioning and Signaling at Work and the Workplace

When output quantity cannot be observed directly or productivity monitored at little cost, input time may serve as a proxy for employers. Performing extra work, beyond the norm of a job, workplace or occupation, may be a way for a worker to transmit a signal of promotability or value to employers. This presumes the employer, manager or supervisor interprets face-time as an indication of an employee's level of effort and commitment. An adverse selection model of hiring suggests that employers purposely create longer rather than shorter hours jobs, as a way to screen out potentially less productive workers (Rebitzer & Taylor, 1995). Consequently, workers requesting shorter hours may be passed up in hiring or promotion decisions, at least in professions that reward or valorize long hours, such as law and consulting (Landers et al., 1996; Haight, 1997; Yakura, 2001). Workers may attempt to equal or perhaps exceed the hours worked by their co-workers. The pursuit of long-term relative status through increasing their own work hours promotes a "rat race" with all workers working longer average hours (Landers et al., 1996). Among those who expect to be in managerial positions, there is a clear positive empirical relationship between the number of work hours they prefer and the actual work hours of their co-workers (Eastman, 1998; Brett & Stroh, 2003).

At least as strong may be the incentive to put in extra hours of work is for defensive purposes. If a worker believes their employer uses input time as a screen before an anticipated downsizing or reorganization, they may view longer hours as a protective device or immunization against the risk of future job loss, income loss or demotion (Landers et al., 1996). Rising job and income insecurity also may lead workers to prefer longer hours in order to build up savings to serve as a defensive buffer (Bluestone & Rose, 1998). The notion of presenteeism refers to the tendency to stay at work beyond the time needed for effective performance, as a visible commitment motivated by fear of layoff or hope of promotion (Simpson, 1998).

In the presence of such signaling and incentives, forward-looking labor supply behavior suggests that workers might quite rationally prefer to work longer hours. If the future income trajectory is sufficiently steep (or shorter hours penalty severe) and the time involves at least some element of investment in human capital acquisition, longer work hours may yield greater skills development or credentials that can be applied or pay off in later career stages. By choosing to work longer hours, workers acquire greater skills that do yield better jobs (Michelacci & Pijoan-Mas, 2007). Indeed, all else constant, occupations with longer workweeks are associated with higher current hourly earnings in the US (Hecker, 1998). In "effort-based careers" firms create explicit incentives for employees to work longer hours than the initially bargained ones, creating a robust positive association between workers' hours and their expected probability of promotion in their current job

(Massimiliano & Staffolani, 2007). Supplying (unpaid) overtime work generally improves the probability of positive future earnings outcomes via a signaling process, within given industries that may have different thresholds in what is considered overtime (Anger, 2006). While the response to such incentives may be rational, it is not clear that the outcomes and process are efficient for society. To the extent there is asymmetric information that lead employers to use long working hours as a mechanism to sort or rank the productivity of workers, the high productivity workers will choose to work inefficient long hours and be overemployed (Sousa-Poza & Ziegler, 2003).

3.8. Rising Wage Inequality: Relative Positioning in the Income Spectrum

Generally, the incentives of many workplaces, occupations and labor markets have heightened the economic motivation to strive for promotion. A greater dispersion of earnings within occupations or labor market intensifies the incentives to work relatively longer average hours. The wider is the gap between pay grades or skill grade, the larger the motivation to engage in such positive signaling tactics, while a less tight labor market discourages working time (Bell & Freeman, 2001; Bowles & Park, 2005; Michelacci & Pijoan-Mas, 2007). Consequently, average hours are lengthened while only a few of the workers attain the sought after promotion. However, with the exception of the lower tail of the working hours distribution, the greater inequality of earnings in the US creates no noticeable labor supply incentives among men vis-à-vis Germany (Osberg, 2003). Thus, what may be true within particular labor market may not necessarily be occurring at national levels.

3.9. Amenities in the Workplace and Improved Working Conditions

To the extent a given workplace provides better working conditions, more amenities or fewer disamenities, less hazardous or unpleasant or more satisfying work, the resistance to long work hours is likely to wane. This occurs particularly among those whose alternative is less-alluring household work or family stress (Hochschild, 2005; Cowling, 2007). Thus, if a job is viewed as more intrinsically rewarding, fulfilling, discretionary or autonomous, this brings about a higher level of desired work hours than if it were stressful, anxiety-producing, onerous, routinized and alienating. Some high-paying managerial and professional jobs are also rewarding in terms of the stimulation, social interactions and self-growth, so that their incumbents feel exalted more than exploited and a clear majority love their jobs (Feldman, 2002; Hewlett & Luce, 2006). Workers driven to work additional hours because of nonmonetary features of their job or workplace may be considered a "perkaholic" (Douglas & Morris, 2006).

As the complexity of coordinating job and household production activities grows with more time spent in the paid workforce, it heightens the value of having the working condition of scheduling autonomy or flexibility that enables easier transitions between work, caregiving, commuting and various leisure activities. For a given number of work hours, well-being may be influenced positively by work schedule fit (Barnett et al., 1999). Those lacking flexibility in the timing of work are likely to face more time conflicts or overlapping activities which leads to stress (Floro & Miles, 2003; Hamermesh & Lee, 2007). Indeed, full-time workers having more flexible daily starting and ending times tend to work relatively longer workweeks (Golden, 2008). This association may exist because schedule flexibility moderates some of the potential adverse effects of long hours, such as work–family conflict (Hill et al., 2001; Russo & Waters, 2006). Alternatively, flexibility may be positively related to long hours if supervisors support schedule flexibility for those individuals who are presumed to adhere to the "ideal worker" norm (Drago, Black, & Wooden, 2005). Moreover, if schedule flexibility is viewed as a nonwage perk unavailable to them with other employers, then this intensifies the incentive to work long hours. Finally, workers who appreciate this perk may feel compelled to extend their own work hours on the margin as an act of reciprocity. Extending work hours has been facilitated by the continuing spread of computerization, networking and telecommunications technologies that allow work to be ever more portable (Hübler, 2000; McMillan & O'Driscoll, 2006; Eldridge & Pabilonia, 2007).

3.10. Income-Targeting Behavior

Income-targeting behavior suggests that individuals seek market work sufficient to support their pre-established goals regarding unsatisfied consumption wants and nonmarket time (Altman, 2001). Goals reflect a hierarchical ordering of their physiological and unsatisfied needs, which require income. What restrains desired hours from escalating ever-upward is that there is a hierarchy of needs, which includes the need for nonmarket time. A related case is the finding of a strong negative effect of husbands' health insurance coverage on wives' work hours, particularly in families with children (Buchmueller & Valletta, 1999). Because health insurance benefits are often restricted in the US to full-time workers, wives who have no alternate source of insurance work longer than otherwise preferred hours in order to secure coverage for their families.

3.11. Relative Positioning in Consumption and Consumerism

Some see no harm or negative spillover effects if workers are working long hours as a means to an end of laudable material goals that truly lift their living standard, such as owning a home (Douglas & Morris, 2006). Others, however, see no effective net gain for individuals and many spillovers (Leete & Schor, 1994; Frank, 1999).

The latter stems from a belief that a key motivator for acquisition of material goods and services is less the functionality of them and more the relative positioning it provides. Veblen effects in consumption mean that individuals may compete for higher status by acquiring or accumulating social status conferring goods and services. In particular, income and cars are found to be highly positional; however, more leisure time provides virtually no gain in relative rank (Carlsson, Johansson-Stenman, & Martinsson, 2007). One reference group for workers regarding their income target may be family. More hours may be motivated by keeping pace with siblings (e.g., Neumark & Postlewaite, 1998). Individuals also tend to emulate the consumption patterns of their most affluent reference groups. In the context of recently rising income inequality, with the top income bracket pulling away from the rest, this requires that less well-off individuals or households desire to work more hours in order to gain income to protect their relative position in consumption levels (Altman, 2001; Pingle & Mitchell, 2002). Alternatively, they accumulate more consumer or household debt (Frank, 1999). However, this eventually leads to a desire for more work in order to avoid high-interest balances or risk of personal bankruptcy. Indeed, those who work overtime when it is not mandatory tend to be from relatively higher income households (Golden & Wiens-Tuers, 2006).

Rising consumerism is the primary force behind a rising proportion of full-time workers engaged in very long hours of workweeks (in Australia, see Drago et al., 2005). Arguably behind this is the intensified marketing and advertising that may create tastes for more market goods and services. This creates a perpetual outward movement of the household's income target. The cumulative effects of intensifying promotional efforts for products eventually leads workers to prefer more income to purchase these now familiar products or services (George, 1997; Fraser & Paton, 2003; Cowling & Poolsombat, 2007). As new commodities are introduced, what was once considered a luxury, amenity or novelty item gradually becomes a new want to satisfy. Bandwagon effects suggest that individuals derive satisfaction from consuming goods and services that others are consuming (Altman, 2001).

3.12. Status and Nonmaterial Rewards

Working relatively longer hours than others may confer status in nonmaterial forms, within and outside one's workplace. "Busyness," apparent or real, or even "conspicuous exhaustion" is often conveyed as a prideful mark of high productivity or self-importance (Gershuny, 2005). However, in some occupations, industries or communities, prowess is conferred on those that are productive but work the fewest hours (Haight, 2001). In addition, people work at least in part for what (they believe that) others think about them, i.e., respect (Ellingsen & Johannesson, 2007). Thus, if employers establish long hours as one of the norms of respectability and reward it as a component of good performance, with pay or other forms of recognition, many employees will likely respond accordingly (Peiperl & Jones, 2001).

3.13.   Workaholism and Persistence: Adaptive Preferences and Endogenous Labor Supply

Common to most characterizations of workaholism involves some type of addiction to work, which is manifest at least in part through the quantity of time spent at work (Scott et al., 1997; Snir, Harpaz, & Burke, 2006; Ng et al., 2007). In economics parlance, labor supply becomes persistent and preferences become time-inconsistent — current work time feeds the desire for future work (Hamermesh & Slemrod, 2005). Suggestive evidence of such habituation is that workers express a much stronger preference for reduction in their hours in the more distant future than in the current period (Hart & Associates, 2003). This is not surprising given the greater aversion to income loss than the benefit from an equivalent income gain (Dunn, 1996; Goette, Huffman, & Fehr, 2004). A worker who is overemployed may eventually become more resistant to adjustment downward of their hours of work (Altman & Golden, 2004). That is, a dynamic process may evolve by which workers adapt their preferred number of hours of work, internalizing the external incentives in the labor market, workplace or culture. This exemplifies that the behavioral sources of the drive to work to excess may be motivated more by organizational values than by degree of personal engagement (Burke, 2000; Ciscel & Smith, 2005). This also helps explain the constancy pattern of the overemployment rate over time (see Altman & Golden,

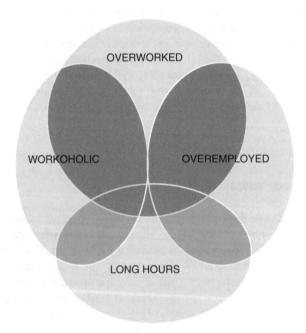

Figure 3.3: Workaholism overlaps with long hours and overworking, but not overemployment.

2004). Thus, what may begin as involuntary overemployment can morph into self-driven overwork and/or compulsive workaholism (Figure 3.3).

Suppose structural incentives lengthen employer work hours demanded above those preferred by an individual. This will tend to create a feeling of time scarcity for the individual or household. This in turn may lead a household to eventually adapt its preferences from self-produced goods and services to those that are more market-produced. It may also shift from time-using goods and services toward the more time-saving type. Furthermore, households are likely to shift preferences from time-intensive to income-intensive leisure activities. All three effects ratchet upward individuals' targeted consumption levels and gradually dissipates the initial desire for shorter work hours (Rothschild, 1982). Working longer than one's initially preferred hours may make individuals acclimated to the higher level of consumption facilitated by the additional income. Since the hierarchy of individuals' needs includes more free time, desired hours would not spiral ever-upward. The action or inaction of the public sector, legislative and regulatory policies, may either reinforce or counteract the pressures that lead to increased hours demanded, hours preferred or both (Rakoff, 2002). There are still spillover costs to the extent individuals become overworked, even if a worker is no longer averse to the excess hours and the risks associated with overwork are discounted or unrecognized.

3.14. Conclusion and Policies to Address Overwork

Why some people work long or longer hours reflects an often complex interaction between workplace constraints, institutions, incentives, working conditions, organizational culture, macroeconomic climate, preference formation, behavioral contagion and innate motivations. From conventional economic models, a climb in hours of work would be a sign of increasing after-tax wage rates that spark a net substitution effect; a wage decrease or nonwage income increase that trigger a net income effect; increasing employer demand for hours to which workers consent; a change in workers' preferences from leisure time toward more income or from time spent in the household toward time spent in the workplace. The standard economic model of labor supply has proven itself quite versatile, in that it has been expanded recently to incorporate behavioral factors such as relative positioning behavior, social norms and reciprocity (Goldsmith, Sedo, Darity, & Hamilton, 2004; Berg, 2006). Nevertheless, the conception of labor supply must be enhanced further to account for the incidence of overemployment, overwork and tendency toward persistence of working longer hours. A comprehensive list of underlying factors opens the "black box" of labor supply preferences. It speaks more to the complexity of the notions of "workaholism" or "overwork." On the one hand, enthusiastic, hard workers should not be denigrated if more work hours reflects a job, workplace or work process that are increasingly satisfying or enriching to the worker (Kelloway et al., 2004; Douglas & Morris, 2006).

Because of the spillover costs of long hours, even when ostensibly voluntary, there remains a "public goods" case for promoting policies and incentives that would help brake the dynamic process that ratchets upward so many workers' desired work hours to the point where they threaten to become counterproductive for individual, family, community health and well-being. Clearly, competitive global market pressures and consumerist forces cannot be reversed for the foreseeable future, but their tendency to spark ever-longer desired hours of work among workers can be tempered. Its habitual character pushes it over the line from work ethic to overwork, for example, continually postponing what had been a planned earlier retirement (Hamermesh & Slemrod, 2005). To the extent this involves mainly highly compensated income individuals, reducing overwork can be net social welfare-enhancing. Because the estimated aversion to loss of income (goods) tends to be greater than the aversion to the loss of time (Dunn, 1996), this asymmetry implies that redistributing work hours from overemployed to underemployed individuals could yield a considerable net gain to social welfare. This would occur so long as hours gains provided to the underemployed outweigh the losses to all those currently employed at longer hours experiencing "forced leisure" (Altman & Golden, 2004; Lin & Yang, 2003). Any restriction of work hours runs real risks of depriving some workers, particularly hourly paid employees, who genuinely need overtime hours (Lautsch & Scully, 2007). Thus, even if some such workers become "overtime junkies," compulsory reductions may be less welcomed than more options. For legal limitations on working time to alleviate the problem of long hours "conscripts," without unduly constraining the long hours of "volunteers" efforts to change institutions must inevitably filter down into corporate cultures and the common workplace, to make them more welcoming of reduced hours options (Drago et al., 2006).

To the extent the sources of longer desired hours reflect underlying, external institutional structures and incentives, they can be more fruitfully addressed with public policy changes. This would entail adopting a tax system with more progressive tax rates, higher taxes on luxury consumption goods and services and lower taxes on household savings, and by transforming payroll taxes from a quasi-fixed to purely variable cost to employers (Frank, 1999; Hamermesh & Slemrod, 2005). Efforts to reverse patterns of persistent long work hours could occur along legal limits and legalized rights. For example, countries with more generous vacation standards do tend to feature shorter annual work hours (Altonji & Oldham, 2003) and those with shorter working time standards and regulations granting requests for reduced workweeks do have a more intensified desire for even shorter work hours (Bielinski et al., 2002; Rakoff, 2002; McCann, 2007). The proposed "working families bill of rights" legislative package would promote minimum standards on various fronts, such as paid personal sick time and parental leave times, as well as establishing a firmer employee right to negotiated flexibility over work hours, such as a right to request reduced work hours with pro-rated benefit coverage and a right to refuse mandatory overtime work. Several US states have been pursuing and already passed many such initiatives, and this activity is likely to continue so long as over-employment and overwork persist.

Acknowledgment

We acknowledge support from the Alfred P. Sloan Foundation, Workplace, Workforce and Working Families Program, Grant #2004-5-32.

References

Allen, H. M., Slavin, T., & Bunn, W. B. (2007). Do long workhours impact health, safety, and productivity at a heavy manufacturer? *Journal of Occupational and Environmental Medicine*, *49*(2), 148–171.

Altman, M. (2001). Preferences and labor supply: Casting some light into the black box of income-leisure choice. *Journal of Socio-Economics*, *30*, 199–219.

Altman, M., & Golden, L. (2004). Alternative approaches of regulating hours. In: M. Oppenheimer & N. Mercuro (Eds), *Alternative approaches in law and economics* (pp. 286–307). Armonk, NJ: M. E. Sharpe.

Altonji, J., & Oldham, J. (2003). Vacation laws and annual work hours. *Economic Perspectives: Federal Reserve Bank of Chicago*, *27*(Fall), 19–29.

Anger, S. (2006). *Overtime work as a signaling device*. Berlin: German Institute for Economic Research (DIW).

Barnett, R., Gareis, K., & Brennan, R. (1999). Fit as a mediator of the relationship between work hours and burnout. *Journal of Occupational Health Psychology*, *4*, 307–317.

Becker, G. (1985). Human capital, effort, and the sexual division of labor. *Journal of Labor Economics*, *3*(1, Part 2), S33–S58.

Bell, L., & Freeman, R. (2001). Working hard. In: G. Wong & G. Picot (Eds), *Working time in comparative perspective* (Vol. 1). Kalamazoo, MI: W.E. Upjohn Institute for Employment Research.

Berg, N. (2006). Behavioral labor economics. In: M. Altman (Ed.), *Handbook of contemporary behavioral economics* (pp. 457–478). New York: M.E. Sharpe.

Berg, P., Appelbaum, E., Bailey, T., & Kalleberg, A. (2004). Contesting time: International comparisons of employee control of working time. *Industrial and Labor Relations Review*, *5*, 331–349.

Bielinski, H., Bosch, G., & Wagner, A. (2002). *Europeans' work time preferences*. Luxembourg: European Foundation for the Improvement of Living and Working Conditions.

Bliese, P. D., & Halverson, R. R. (1996). Individual and nomothetic models of job stress: An examination of work hours, cohesion and well-being. *Journal of Applied Social Psychology*, *26*(13), 1171–1189.

Bluestone, B., & Rose, S. (1998). Macroeconomics of work time. *Review of Social Economy*, *56*, 425–441.

Böheim, R., & Taylor, M. (2004). Actual and preferred working hours. *British Journal of Industrial Relations*, *42*(1), 149–166.

Bowles, S., & Park, Y. (2005). Emulation, inequality, and work hours: Was Thorsten Veblen right? *The Economic Journal*, *115*(507), F397–F412.

Brett, J., & Stroh, L. (2003). Working 61 plus hours a week: Why do managers do it? *Journal of Applied Psychology*, *88*(1), 67–78.

Buchmueller, T., & Valletta, R. (1999). The effect of health insurance on married female labor supply. *Journal of Human Resources*, *34*(1), 42–70.

Buelens, M., & Poelmans, S. (2004). Enriching the Spence and Robbins' typology of workaholism: Demographic, motivational and organizational correlates. *Journal of Organizational Change Management, 17*(5), 440–458.

Burawoy, M., Fligstein, N., Hochschild, A., Schor, J., & Voss, K. (2001). Overwork: Causes and consequences of rising work hours. *Berkeley Journal of Sociology, 45,* 180–196.

Burke, R. (1999). It's not how hard you work but how you work hard: Evaluating workaholism components. *International Journal of Stress Management, 6*(4), 225–239.

Burke, R. (2000). Workaholism in organizations: Concepts, results and future research directions. *International Journal of Management Reviews, 2*(1), 1–16.

Carlsson, F., Johansson-Stenman, O., & Martinsson, P. (2007). Do you enjoy having more than others? Survey evidence of positional goods. *Economica, 74*(296), 586–598.

Caruso, C., Bushnell, T., Eggerth, D., Heitmann, A., Kojola, B., Newman, K., Rosa, R., Sauter, S., & Vila, B. (2006). Long working hours, safety, and health: Toward a national research agenda. *American Journal of Industrial Medicine, 49,* 930–942.

Charles, K. K., & Decicca, P. (2007). Hours flexibility and retirement. *Economic Inquiry, 45*(2), 251–267.

Ciscel, D., & Smith, B. E. (2005). The impact of supply chain management on labor standards: The transition to incessant work. *Journal of Economic Issues, 39*(2), 429–436.

Clarkberg, M. (2001). Understanding the time-squeeze: Married couples' preferred and actual work-hour strategies. *American Behavioral Scientist, 44,* 1115–1136.

Cornell University Institute of Workplace Studies (IWS). (1999). *Overtime and the American worker.* Ithaca, NY: New York State School of Industrial and Labor Relations, Cornell University.

Cowling, K., & Poolsombat, R. (2007). *Advertising and labour supply: Why do Americans work such long hours?* Warwick Economic Research Papers no. 789. Department of Economics, University of Warwick, UK.

Cowling, M. (2007). *Still at work? An empirical test of competing theories of the long hours culture.* MPRA Paper no. 1614, 30 January. Institute for Employment Studies, University of Sussex, Brighton, UK.

Cutler, D. M., & Madrian, B. C. (1998). Labor market responses to rising health insurance costs: Evidence on hours worked. *RAND Journal of Economics, 29,* 509–530.

Dembe, A., Erickson, J. B., Delbos, R. G., & Banks, S. M. (2005). The impact of overtime and long work hours on occupational injuries and illnesses: New evidence from the United States. *Occupational Environment Medicine, 62,* 588–597.

Dollard, M., & Winefield, A. (2002). Mental health: Overemployment, underemployment, unemployment and healthy jobs. *Australian e-Journal for the Advancement of Mental Health, 1*(3).

Dong, X. (2005). Long workhours, work scheduling and work-related injuries among construction workers in the U.S. *Scandinavian Journal of Work, Environment and Health, 3*(5), 329–335.

Douglas, E. J., & Morris, R. J. (2006). Workaholic, or just hard worker? *Career Development International, 11*(5), 394–417.

Drago, R., Black, D., & Wooden, M. (2005). *The existence and persistence of long hours.* IZA discussion Paper no. 1720. Bonn, Germany, August.

Drago, R., & Wooden, M. (1992). The determinants of labor absence: Economic factors and work group norms. *Industrial and Labor Relations Review, 45,* 34–47.

Drago, R., Wooden, M., & Black, D. (2006). *Long work hours: Volunteers or conscripts?* IZA DP no. 2484. Bonn, Germany, December.

Dunn, L. F. (1996). Loss aversion and adaptation in the labor market: Empirical indifference functions and labor supply. *Review of Economics and Statistics, 78,* 441–450.

Eastman, W. (1998). Working for position: Women, men, and managerial work hours. *Industrial Relations, 37,* 51–66.

Eldridge, L., & Pabilonia, S. W. (2007). *Are those who bring work home really working longer hours?* BLS Working Paper no. 406. Washington, DC, May.

Ellingsen, T., & Johannesson, M. (2007). Paying respect. *Journal of Economic Perspectives, 21*(4), 135–149.

Farris, D. (2002). Are transformed workplaces more productively efficient? *Journal of Economic Issues, 36*(3), 659–670.

Feather, P., & Shaw, D. (2000). The demand for leisure time in the presence of constrained work hours. *Economic Inquiry, 38,* 651–662.

Feldman, D. (1996). The nature, antecedents and consequences of underemployment. *Journal of Management, 22*(3), 385–407.

Feldman, D. (2002). Managers' propensity to work longer hours: A multilevel analysis. *Human Resource Management Review, 12,* 339–357.

Fenwick, R., & Tausig, M. (2001). Scheduling stress: Family and health outcomes of shift work and schedule control. *American Behavioral Scientist, 44*(7), 1179–1198.

Floro, M., & Miles, M. (2003). Time use, work and overlapping activities: Evidence from Australia. *Cambridge Journal of Economics, 27,* 881–904.

Frank, R. H. (1999). *Luxury fever.* New York: The Free Press.

Fraser, S., & Paton, D. (2003). Does advertising increase labour supply? Time series evidence from the UK. *Applied Economics, 35*(11), 1357–1368.

Galinsky, E., Bond, J., Kim, S., Backon, L., Brownfield, E., & Sakai, K. (2005). *Overwork in America: When the way we work becomes too much.* New York: Families and Work Institute.

George, D. (1997). Working longer hours: Pressure from the boss or from marketers? *Review of Social Economy, 55*(1), 33–65.

Gershuny, J. (2005). Busyness as the badge of honor for the new superordinate working class. *Social Research, 72*(2), 287–314.

Goette, L., Huffman, D., & Fehr, E. (2004). Loss aversion and labor supply. *Journal of the European Economic Association, 2*(2–3), 216–228.

Golden, L. (1996). The economics of worktime length, adjustment and flexibility: contributions of three competing paradigms. *Review of Social Economy, 54,* 1–44.

Golden, L. (2006). How long? The historical, economic and cultural factors behind overwork. In: R. Burke (Ed.), *Work hours and work addiction: Research companion to workaholism in organizations, new horizons in management* (pp. 36–57). Cheltenham, UK: Edward Elgar.

Golden, L. (2008). Limited access: Disparities in flexible work schedules and work-at-home. *Journal of Family and Economic Issues, 29*(1), 86–109.

Golden, L., & Gebreselassie, T. (2007). Which workers prefer to exchange income for a change in work hours in the US? *Monthly Labor Review, 130*(4), 18–37.

Golden, L., & Wiens-Tuers, B. (2006). To your happiness? Overtime work, worker happiness and satisfaction. *Journal of Socio-Economics, 35*(2), 382–397.

Goldsmith, A., Sedo, S., Darity, W., & Hamilton, D. (2004). The labor supply consequences of perceptions of employer discrimination during search and on-the-job: integrating neoclassical theory and cognitive dissonance. *Journal of Economic Psychology, 25,* 15–39.

Haight, A. D. (1997). Padded prowess: A Veblenian interpretation of the long hours of salaried workers. *Journal of Economic Issues, 31,* 29–38.

Haight, A. D. (2001). Burnout, chronic fatigue, and prozac in the professions: The iron law of salaries. *Review of Radical Political Economics, 33*, 189–202.

Hamermesh, D., & Lee, J. (2007). Stressed out on four continents: Time Crunch or Yuppie Kvetch? *The Review of Economics and Statistics, 89*(2), 374–383.

Hamermesh, D., & Slemrod, J. (2005). *The economics of workaholism: Why we should not have written this paper.* National Bureau of Economic Research Working Paper 11566. Bonn, Germany.

Hanecke, K., Silke, T., Friedhelm, N., & Grzech-Sukalo, H. (1998). Accident risk as a function of hour at work and time of day as determined from accident data and exposure models for the german working population. *Scandinavian Journal of Work Environment Health, 24*(3), 43–48.

Hart, R. (2004). *The economics of overtime working.* Cambridge: Cambridge University Press.

Hart, P., & Associates. (2003). *Imagining the future of work.* New York: Alfred P. Sloan Foundation.

Hecker, D. (1998). How hours of work affect occupational earnings. *Monthly Labor Review, 121*(10), 8–19.

Hewlett, S. A., & Luce, C. B. (2006). Extreme jobs: The dangerous allure of the 70-hour workweek. *Harvard Business Review, 84*(12), 49–55.

Hill, E. J., Hawkins, A., Ferris, M., & Weitzman, M. (2001). Finding an extra day a week: Positive influence of perceived job flexibility on work–family balance. *Family Relations, 50*(1), 49–58.

Hochschild, A. (2005). On the edge of the time bind: Time and market culture. *Social Research, 72*(2), 339–354.

Holtom, B., Tidd, S., & Lee, T. (2002). The relationship between work status congruence and work-related attitudes and behaviors. *Journal of Applied Psychology, 87*, 903–923.

Hübler, O. (2000). All goes faster but lasts longer: Computer use and overtime work. *Ifo Studien, 46*(2), 49–271.

Humphries, J. (1998). Toward a family-friendly economics. *New Political Economy, 3*(2), 223–240.

Hurd, M. D. (1996). The effect of labor market rigidities on the labor force behavior of older workers. In: D. Wise (Ed.), *Advances in the economics of aging, National Bureau of Economic Research Project Report series* (pp. 11–58). Chicago, IL: University of Chicago Press.

Jacobs, J., & Gerson, K. (2001). Who are the overworked Americans? In: L. Golden & D. Figart (Eds), *Working time: International trends, theory, and policy perspectives* (pp. 89–105). New York: Routledge.

Kaufman, B. (1999). Expanding the behavioral foundations of labor economics. *Industrial and Labor Relations Review, 52*, 361–392.

Kelloway, K., Gallagher, D., & Barling, J. (2004). Work, employment and the individual. In: B. Kaufman (Ed.), *Theoretical perspectives on work and the employment relationship.* Urbana, IL: Industrial Relations Research Association Series.

Kelly, E., & Moen, P. (2007). Rethinking the clock-work of work: Why schedule control may pay off at work and at home. *Advances in Developing Human Resources, 9*(4), 487–506.

Kodz, J., Davis, S., Lain, D., Sheppard, E., Rick, J., & Strebler, M. (2003). Working long hours: A review of the evidence. *Employment Relations Research Series, 16*(1).

Kuhn, P., & Lozano, F. (2008). The expanding workweek? Understanding trends in long work hours among U.S. men, 1979–2006. *Journal of Labor Economics, 26*(2), 311–333.

Lamberg, L. (2004). Impact of long working hours explored. *Journal of the American Medical Association, 292*, 25–26.

Landers, R., Rebitzer, J., & Taylor, L. (1996). Rat race redux: Adverse selection in the determination of work hours in law firms. *American Economic Review, 86*, 3229–3248.

Lang, K., & Kahn, S. (2001). Hours constraints: Theory evidence and policy implications. In: G. Wong & G. Picot (Eds), *Working time in a comparative perspective* (Vol. 1). Kalamazoo, MI: Upjohn Institute for Employment Research Institute.

Lautsch, B., & Scully, M. (2007). Restructuring time implications of work-hours reductions for the working class. *Human Relations, 60*(5), 719–743.

Leete, L., & Schor, J. (1994). Assessing the time squeeze hypothesis hours worked in the United States:1969–89. *Industrial Relations, 33*(1), 25–43.

Lin, C.-C., & Yang, C. C. (2003). A labor-adverse selection model of reducing working time. *Journal of Post Keynesian Economics, 25*(3), 515–524.

Massimiliano, B., & Staffolani, S. (2007). Effort-based career opportunities and working time. *International Journal of Manpower, 2*(6), 489–512.

Maume, D. J., & Bellas, M. L., Jr. (2001). The overworked American or the time bind? *American Behavioral Scientist, 44*, 1137–1156.

McCann, D. (2007). Temporal autonomy and the protective individualisation of working-time la: The case of overtime work. *Labour & Industry, 17*(3), 29–43.

McMillan, L. H., & O'Driscoll, M. P. (2006). Understanding workaholism: The case for behavioral tendencies. In: R. Burke (Ed.), *Research companion to working time and work addiction*. Cheltenham, UK: Edward Elgar.

Mederer, H. J. (1993). Division of labor in two-earner homes task accomplishment versus household management as critical variables in perceptions about family work. *Journal of Marriage and the Family, 55*(1), 133–145.

Messenger, J. (2004). *Working time and workers' preferences in industrialized countries finding the balance*. Geneva: International Labor Office Conditions of Work and Employment Programme.

Michelacci, C., & Pijoan-Mas, J. (2007). *The effects of labor market conditions on working time: The US-EU experience*. CEMFI Working Paper 0705 June. Centre for Economic Policy, London, UK.

Mishel, L., Bernstein, J., & Allegretto, A. (2005). *The state of working America, 2004–05*. Washington, DC: Economic Policy Institute.

Neumark, D., & Postlewaite, A. (1998). Relative income concerns and the rise in married women's employment. *Journal of Public Economics, 70*, 157–183.

Ng, T. W. H., Sorensen, K. L., & Feldman, D. (2007). Dimensions antecedents and consequences of workaholism: A conceptual integration and extension. *Journal of Organizational Behavior, 28*(1), 111–136.

Northwestern National Life. (1991). *Employee burnout: America's newest epidemic*. Minneapolis, MN: Northwestern National Life Insurance Co.

Osberg, L. (2003). Understanding growth and inequality trends: The role of labour supply in the US and Germany. *Canadian Public Policy, 29*(Suppl.), S163–S183.

Peiperl, M., & Jones, B. (2001). Workaholics and overworkers: Productivity or pathology? *Group & Organization Management, 26*(3), 369–394.

Pingle, M., & Mitchell, M. (2002). What motivates positional concerns for income? *Journal of Economic Psychology, 23*, 127–148.

Prasch, R. (2001). Revising the Labor supply schedule implications for work time and minimum wage legislation. In: L. Golden & D. Figart (Eds), *Working time: International trends theory and policy perspectives*. New York: Routledge.

Presser, H. (2003). *Working in a 24/7 economy challenges for American families*. New York: Russell Sage Foundation.

Rakoff, T. (2002). *A time for every purpose law and the balance of life.* Cambridge, MA: Harvard University Press.

Rebitzer, J., & Taylor, L. (1995). Do labor markets provide enough short-hour jobs? An analysis of work hours and work incentives. *Economic Inquiry, 33,* 257–273.

Reynolds, J. (2004). When too much is not enough actual and preferred work hours in the united states and abroad. *Sociological Forum, 19*(1), 89–120.

Reynolds, J., & Aletraris, L. (2006). Pursuing preferences: The creation and resolution of work hour mismatches. *American Sociological Review, 71,* 618–638.

Rhoads, J. M. (1977). Workaholism and health. *Journal of the American Medical Association, 237*(24), 2615–2618.

Rosa, R. (1995). Extended workshifts and excessive fatigue. *Journal of Sleep Research, 4*(2), 51–56.

Rosnick, D., & Weisbrot, M. (2006). *Are shorter work hours good for the environment? A comparison of US and European energy consumption.* Washington, DC: Center for Economic Policy Research.

Rothschild, K. (1982). A note on some of economic and welfare aspects of working time regulations. *Australian Economic Papers, 21,* 214–218.

Russo, J., & Waters, L. (2006). Workaholic worker type differences in work-family conflict: The moderating role of supervisor support and flexible work scheduling. *Career Development International, 11*(5), 418–439.

Scacciati, F. (2004). Erosion of purchasing power and labor supply. *Journal of Socio-Economics, 33,* 725–744.

Schor, J. (1999). *The overspent American: Upscaling downshifting and the new consumer.* New York: Basic Books.

Schor, J. (2005). Sustainable consumption and worktime reduction. *Journal of Industrial Ecology, 9,* 37–50.

Scott, K. S., Moore, K. S., & Miceli, M. P. (1997). An exploration of the meaning and consequences of workaholism. Human Relations, *50,* 287–314.

Senesky, S. (2005). Testing the intertemporal labor supply model are jobs important? *Labour Economics, 12*(6), 749–772.

Sharif, M. (2000). Inverted 'S' the complete neoclassical labor supply function. *International Labor Review, 139,* 409–435.

Simpson, R. (1998). Presenteeism power and organizational change long hours as a career barrier and the impact on the working lives of women managers. *British Journal of Management, 9*(s1), 37–50.

Smith, A. (1776). *Inquiry into the nature and causes of the Wealth of Nations.* London: Methuen and Co. Ltd.

Snir, R., Harpaz, I., & Burke, R. (2006). Workaholism in organizations new research directions. *Career Development International, 11*(5), 369–373.

Sousa-Poza, A., & Ziegler, A. (2003). Asymmetric information about workers' productivity as a cause for inefficient long working hours 10 6. *Labour Economics, 10*(6), 727–747.

Sparks, K., Cooper, C., Fried, Y., & Shirom, A. (1997). The effects of hours of work on health a meta-analytic review. *Journal of Occupational and Organizational Psychology, 70,* 391–408.

Spurgeon, A. (2003). *Working time: Its impact on safety and health.* Geneva: Seoul Korea International Labor Organization and Korean Occupational Safety and Health Research Institute.

Spurgeon, A. J., Harrington, M., & Cooper, C. L. (1997). Health and safety problems associated with long working hours: A review of the current position. *Occupational and Environmental Medicine, 54,* 367–375.

Stewart, M., & Swaffield, J. K. (1997). Constraints on the desired hours of work of British men. *Economic Journal, 107,* 520–535.

Stier, H., & Lewin-Epstein, N. (2003). Time to work: A comparative analysis of preferences for working hours. *Work and Occupations, 30*(3), 302.

Van der Hulst, M. a. (2001). Associations between overtime and psychological health in high and low reward jobs. *Work Stress, 15*(3), 227–240.

Van der Hulst, M. a. (2003). Long workhours and health. *Scandinavian Journal of Work, Environment & Health, 29,* 171–188.

van Emmerik, I. J., & Sanders, K. (2005). Mismatch in working hours and affective commitment: Differential relationships for distinct employee groups. *Journal of Managerial Psychology, 20*(8), 712–727.

Wilkins, R. (2007). The consequences of underemployment for the underemployed. *Journal of Industrial Relations, 49*(2), 247–275.

Wolfe, A. (1997). The moral meaning of work. *Journal of Socio-Economics, 26*(6), 559–570.

Yakura, E. (2001). Billables: The valorization of time in consulting. *American Behavioral Scientist, 44*(7), 1076–1096.

Yaniv, G. (1995). Burnout, absenteeism and the overtime decision. *Journal of Economic Psychology, 16*(2), 297–309.

Chapter 4

The Wellsprings of Workaholism: A Comparative Analysis of the Explanatory Theories

Lynley H. W. McMillan and Michael P. O'Driscoll

4.1. Historical Context

Workaholism is an approach to work characterised by intensity, focus, and achievement striving that has its genesis in three inventions; the clock, the light bulb, and consumer finance. Before the 14th century, with the exception of the Roman era, people generally worked until they had enough food and then rested and played in the remainder of their time (Cross, 1990). Time spent working expanded and contracted depending on the family's needs, seasonal availability of food, the weather, and daylight hours. Families worked as intergenerational units that included the very young and very elderly, and labour was distributed according to physical ability to contribute. Work continued until it was finished; if there was no work, there was a lot of play and recuperation. If there was a lot of work, there was no play. Essentially, the boundaries between work and leisure were elasticated (i.e., adjusted according to need).

The invention of the mechanical clock in 1335 introduced a third-party measure of working hours, which shifted people's focus from regulation by the cycles of nature to regulation by minutes on the clock, regardless of daylight, season, or weather. The wide-ranging introduction of machines, factories, and industry enabled more outputs to be produced in one day, and therefore required more consistent input from each individual labour unit. This was the beginning of time crunching — achieving more by working fewer people harder. By 1450, employers began to extend the working day into 12-hour periods, with the less scrupulous hiding clocks (or in some instances, readjusting them) to surreptitiously extract more working time. The Protestants, who disparaged luxury and exalted hard work, supported this new 'meanness' with time (Cross, 1990).

The Long Work Hours Culture
Copyright © 2008 by Emerald Group Publishing Limited
All rights of reproduction in any form reserved
DOI:10.1016/B978-1-84855-038-4.00004-X

In 1866 employees fought for an 8-hour day, but the introduction of the light bulb in 1880 brought a stop to all this. Firstly, it enabled employers to over-ride nature's rhythms of night and day, and secondly, in conjunction with electrically run machines, light bulbs enabled factories to run 24 hours a day. For the next 60 years the general workforce were denied weekends and paid holidays; as the 40-hour week was not introduced until 1938 (Robinson & Godbey, 1992).

Once weekends arrived, however, a new 'time consciousness' evolved, and industry responded to (and some would argue, created) consumer demand for timesaving technological inventions. These inventions included items such as washing machines, electric irons, clothes dryers, dishwashers and automobiles. To meet the demand for these new gadgets, people had to earn more. Ironically, for many families, this meant working longer hours and sending female members into the workplace.

To meet this growing demand for consumption, the final factor that enabled workaholism was shifted into place; consumer credit. This new form of short-term credit allowed people to access more consumer goods than they could immediately pay for. While the need for delayed gratification was decreased, consumer fiancé encouraged people to work beyond strict physiological need. Rather than working to fulfil basic needs, many increased their working day to afford luxuries, such as automobiles, dishwashers, and televisions (Cross, 1990). By the mid-1960s, while many parents marched in unison to the beat of consumerism, their children began to join the hippie movement that rejected parental 'conspicuous consumption' (and its obligatory work ethic) in favour of 'lifestyle' (McMillan, O'Driscoll, & Burke, 2003). It is against this backdrop of societal vacillation between valuing work and alternately leisure that in 1968 the word 'workaholism' was coined as a take on working too hard in an alcoholic-like manner (Oates, 1968).

The next 40 years brought a series of time-savvy devices (mobiles, laptops, Personal Data Assistant (PDAs), e-mails, videoconferencing, broadband) that have mobilised the workforce, blurred the boundary between work and home, and brought workaholism to the fore of public consciousness. By the late 20th century, there were a plethora of media articles on workaholism, Workaholics Anonymous groups, and even some residential treatment centres that purported to offer cures for workaholism.

Today's world is characterised by globalisation of previously small local employers, and 24-hour communication across international time zones. Interestingly, the addition of machines moved *villages into towns*, the application of power evolved *towns into cities*, the innovation of communications consolidated *cities into countries*, and now the incremental improvements of technology are fusing *countries into a global entity*. Together, these factors require many employees to act as global citizens — available to work at the push of a button, at 3am or 3pm. While smart technology and innovative communication devices save time, ironically, global demands to work a 24-hour day rob it back. The mechanisms of change are getting smaller and the mode of application is moving from invention, to innovation, where frequent small improvements produce massive gains. This evolution of technology is shrinking the boundaries between countries, and between work and home; we are living in an increasingly shrinking world.

Combined with the escalating trend towards multinational production lines and portable work devices (such as mobile phones and PDAs), globalisation has accelerated the rise of created elastic-boundaried workplaces (e.g., working from home, the office, off-shore, or in an aeroplane). The tension between work and leisure, including family life, has reached its largest crescendo yet, which has brought workaholism to the fore as a key concern. Employers are curious about the economic value of workaholism, therapists are interested in how to treat it, and workers are keen to maximise benefits and minimise costs. The present chapter briefly summarises contemporary knowledge, and explores the psychological wellsprings (i.e., causes) of workaholism and proposes practical implications and applications for employers.

4.2. Contemporary Knowledge

Today, we define workaholism as a personal reluctance to disengage from work that involves intense enjoyment in work and a strong drive to work, which means that workaholics tend to work or to think about work anytime and anywhere (McMillan & O'Driscoll, 2006). It would not be unusual therefore to find a workaholic quietly thinking about work while appearing to watch television, or to use modern technology such as a laptop computer after formal work hours in diverse environments such as a car, cafe, aeroplane, or at home.

Workaholism is generally understood to involve a distinctive *approach* to work (i.e., *intensity* of working), which has five dimensions: (1) tendency to work or think about work, (2) reluctance to disengage, (3) work at any time in any environment, (4), enjoyment, and (5) drive. These last two factors (drive and enjoyment) are the two critical factors in determining workaholism — they both need to be present for a person to qualify as workaholic. This definition is based on empirical research that cross-validated workaholics', life-partners', colleagues', and academics' definitions of workaholism (McMillan & O'Driscoll, 2006).

Data indicate that workaholism is not the sole preserve of the wealthy and socially mobile — it does not stop once a person achieves a certain net worth or income level. Workaholism has been found to exist it all occupations from factory workers, to nurses, managers, sales people, insurance clerks and company directors, and across all incomes from $20,000 to $100,000 New Zealand dollars per annum (Burke, 1999b; McMillan & O'Driscoll, 2006; Robinson, 2000; Spence & Robbins, 1992). Despite early claims that workaholism was a male-dominated pattern, this was because early research samples did not comprise many females, especially those that sampled management populations (Spence & Robbins, 1992). Furthermore, workaholism is not a wholly Western pattern; research is pouring out of Eastern Bock, Middle Eastern, and Asian countries, in addition to the ongoing programmes in the US, Canada, Britain, Australia, and New Zealand (Burke, 2001; Kanai, Wakabayashi, & Fling, 1996; McMillan & O'Driscoll, 2006; Snir & Harpaz, 2004).

However, while most academics agree that work is healthy and in fact protective from many illnesses, debate has continued over the merits and demerits of workaholism. Early research suggested that it was desirable (Machlowitz, 1978), but later studies disagreed (Robinson, 1996). Essentially, the data depend on which definition of workaholism is defined. If the 'high work-enjoyment, high drive' is used (Spence & Robbins, 1992), then negative health outcomes and relationship distress are negligible (McMillan & O'Driscoll, 2006). This seems to be because high enjoyment is protective of health, even though high drive is harmful. If, however, the '*low* enjoyment, high drive' definition is used, then outcomes include stress (Burke, 1999a; McMillan & O'Driscoll, 2004). However, it is important to note criticism that this high drive/low enjoyment definition of workaholism represents an obsessive compulsive (i.e., psychiatric) diagnosis, and should be researched separately as such (McMillan & O'Driscoll, 2006). To aid readers in interpreting some of these diverse findings about workaholism, the theories that give rise to workaholism will be explicated below.

4.3.   Theories of Workaholism

Theories are used to explain, and to provide a framework for investigating, the causes (wellsprings) of natural phenomena. A sound theoretical base is critical to scientific investigation as it guides enquiry and provides a strategic overview for understanding the data that emerge from research (Schmitt & Klimoski, 1991). Research without strong theoretical underpinnings is merely random experimentation which has little hope of advancing our knowledge. On this basis, a sound theory on workaholism should hold the following properties:

1. explain relationships among a set of variables that influence workaholism,
2. describe and model the precise nature of how the variables interact,
3. state the boundaries and conditions under which the relationships are valid,
4. imply conclusions reasonably expected to follow, based on logical deductions, and
5. able to be subjected to empirical test (Schmitt & Klimoski 1991).

4.4.   Guiding Paradigm: The Biopsychosocial Model

Traditionally, researchers considered human behaviour as strictly biologically driven. In the 1800s, Charles Darwin summarised this in evolutionary theory, proposing that our genes were our destiny. However, in the mid-1900s, Burrhus F Skinner proposed that human behaviour was predominantly learned. Skinner summarised this in Operant Learning Theory, proposing that *all* behaviour was a product of learning. These two eminent scientists' work formed the basis of the nature–nurture debate, which intensified over the ensuing 50 years.

Critically, in the 1990s, as the post-modern philosophy of human behaviour evolved, the additional impact of social systems in the mix was acknowledged. This gave rise to the *biopsychosocial* paradigm of human behaviour, where human behaviour is seen as a *product of the interaction* between biological, psychological, and social factors.

The biopsychosocial paradigm acknowledges the multivariate nature of behaviour and acknowledges that it is an *interaction* between (a) genes, (b) learning, and (c) social systems that produces human behaviour. Today, the biopsychosocial model of human behaviour is widely used in both research and therapy and is widely acknowledged in satisfactorily explaining almost all human behaviour (Copolov, James, & Milgrom, 2001). Because the model is so extensively accepted, it will be used as the guiding paradigm for the present explication on the underlying theories of workaholism.

Explicitly, the biopsychosocial model has five components: (1) inherited biological predispositions, (2) the behaviours people learn to perform, (3) the emotions they experience, (4) the cognitive processes they utilise, and (5) the social systems each person inhabits. This model is presented in Figure 4.1. As illustrated in the model, each of the five categories of variables is believed to interact in a multidirectional manner with each other to produce complex human behaviour such as workaholism. The theories of work-aholism will therefore be presented utilising the biopsychosocial model as the strategic framework, in the following order: biological theory (including personality and addic-tion theories), behavioural theory (including operant conditioning and social learning theory), emotion-focused theory (including psychoanalytic theory), cognitive theory, and social systems theory (including family systems and workplace systems theories).

On this basis, the five groups of theories emanating from the biopsychosocial model that potentially explain the wellsprings of workaholism will be analysed along the following framework:

1. description of the theoretical framework,
2. general principles,

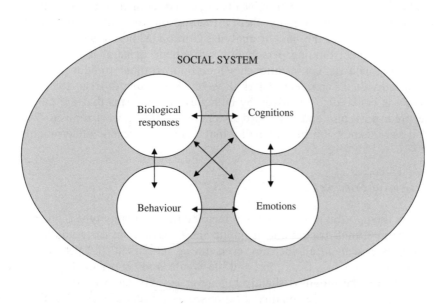

Figure 4.1: Biopsychosocial model of human behaviour.

3. model of how variables interact,
4. predictions implied by the theory,
5. relevance to workaholism,
6. practical applications for the workplace, and
7. Limitations.

At the conclusion of this section a comparative analysis of the theories will be presented, followed by a brief synopsis of the implications for research, therapists, and labour organisations.

4.5. Biological Theory

Biological theory proposes that heredity determines genes, traits, and behaviour. This has led influential psychologists such as John Bowlby to propose that biological processes *create* observable behaviour (Weiten, 1992). There are two relevant biological theories that pertain to workaholism: personality theory and addiction theory; each will be addressed separately below.

4.6. Personality Theory

4.6.1. Description of the Theoretical Framework

Personality is a dynamic and hierarchically organised set of characteristics that typify a particular person. Personality theory focuses on the nature and quality of individual character as the unit of analysis. Gordon Allport (1937) proposed two approaches to understanding personality: nomethetic (general laws that apply to many people such as conscientiousness) and idiographic (unique aspects of a particular individual's character; Clark, Livesley, Schroeder, & Irish, 1996). Because personality is believed to be driven by biological mechanisms that are inherited as genetic predispositions and expressed as character traits, workaholism would be regarded as an expression of personality that has a clear genetic underpinnings.

4.6.2. General Principles

Personality theory is built on five basic principles: (i) personality type is inherited; (ii) environmental stimuli trigger and maintain the behaviour in early adulthood; (iii) personality is evident in all societies, even during retirement; (iv) personality style remains consistent across time, jobs, and life events; and (v) personality is relatively inelastic and can be modified slightly but never entirely removed from a person's repertoire of behaviour. Personality is expressed as clusters of traits. In this context workaholism traits would be regarded as stable characteristics that differ among

Table 4.1: Central traits: Goldberg's 'Big Five'.

Trait	Description
Openness to experience	Degree of willingness to flex and change
Conscientiousness	Degree of orderliness and duty
Extraversion	Degree of sociability
Agreeableness	Degree of conciliatory behaviour
Neuroticism	Degree of emotional reactivity

individuals, influence behaviour, and exist on a continuum (e.g., be exhibited in different intensities that vary markedly between individuals).

4.6.3. Model of How Variables Interact

Personality is widely regarded to comprise three general components. Firstly, cardinal traits are distinguishing characteristics by which an individual is strongly recognised (e.g., an exceedingly passionate leader). Secondly, central traits are the fundamental building blocks of one's individual personality (such as extraversion). Central traits are further subdivided into the 'Big Five' (Weiten, 1992; Table 4.1). Finally, secondary traits are more peripheral characteristics, such as impulsiveness. Specifically, personality theory conceptualises workaholism as a stable behavioural pattern that arises in late adolescence, is stable across multiple workplaces, and is exacerbated by environmental stimuli such as stress (McMillan, O'Driscoll, Marsh, & Brady, 2001).

4.6.4. Predictions Implied by the Theory

Personality theory predicts that the tendency towards workaholism is wired at birth and remains dormant until it is activated by environmental phenomena in late adolescence or early adulthood. On this basis, a workaholic disposition would be evident and relatively habitual by the time a person reached early adulthood and would proceed to increase and consolidate with age (American Psychiatric Association (APA), 1994). In terms of particular traits, workaholism would be likely to arise from an inherited gene that produced the central trait of conscientiousness and secondary traits that produced high obsessiveness and high compulsiveness.

4.6.5. Relevance to Workaholism

Currently, there are two trait-based definitions of workaholism. The first definition is an individual who is highly committed to work and devotes a good deal of time to it, which is evidenced by high involvement in work, compulsion to work, and low work-enjoyment (Spence & Robbins, 1992). The second definition is a personal reluctance to disengage from work evidenced by the tendency to work (or to think about work) anytime and anywhere (McMillan et al., 2001).

The three most probable traits that give rise to workaholism are obsessiveness, compulsiveness, and high energy (Clark et al., 1996). Importantly, each of these characteristics would be evident in the person's life in general rather than specifically limited to the work domain (McMillan et al., 2001). A broad range of data from well-validated measures support this contention, especially with respect to perfectionism (related to obsessiveness), non-delegation (related to compulsiveness), and hypomania (related to high energy; Clark, McEwen, Collard, & Hickok, 1993; McMillan & O'Driscoll, 2006; Spence & Robbins, 1992).

Specifically, Clark et al. (1996) conceptualised workaholism as a pathological aspect of personality and found that workaholism related positively to the dimension of compulsiveness ($r = .41$) and to the higher-order ('Big Five') trait of conscientiousness ($r = .53$). Obsessiveness has correlated with the drive component of workaholism at .35 ($r = .51$ when corrected for measurement error) and compulsiveness at .28 (.37 corrected; McMillan et al., 2001). High energy levels (characteristic of hypomania) have related to workaholism at levels of .19, .25, and .27 (Clark et al., 1993; McMillan et al., 2001). This suggests that a combination of underlying traits may explain workaholism. Thus, it is conceivable that workaholism is a lower-order trait that relates in a hierarchical manner to higher-order 'personality'.

4.6.6.   Practical Applications for the Workplace

Biological theory predicts that workaholism may arise from either simple characteristics such as obsessiveness, or from broader constructs in the 'Big Five' personality factors, such as conscientiousness. Because the theory suggests that some people are 'wired' for workaholism by virtue of their genetic composition, organisations do not have much ability to influence its expression within individual workers. If biological theory holds true, workaholism would demonstrate low responsiveness to organisational change such as promotion, demotion, and remuneration. This would leave organisations with two basic choices, deliberately selected for workaholism — especially if it is found to relate to higher levels of productivity (this contentious prediction has not been tested yet). Alternately, employers could screen for characteristics that act as hallmarks of workaholism (such as obsessiveness and high energy) and deliberately select these people out. Clearly these are both hypothetical propositions that are unlikely to garner popular support.

4.6.7.   Limitations

While trait theory offers multiple explanations of workaholism, it implies a relatively pessimistic view (if workaholism is part of personality it is by implication relatively inflexible). Trait-specific models focus on narrow behavioural patterns, but explain a relatively restricted range of phenomena. For instance, obsessive compulsiveness does not address broader attitudes and values, such as the relative importance of work in a person's belief set. Other limitations include that personality problems require relatively long term and expert therapy to reduce, in extreme examples are intractable across a person's life span, and difficult to diagnose accurately without clinical expertise. Finally, personality theory does not adequately explain the pockets of workaholism that can be found in certain workplaces and professions.

4.7. Addiction Theory

4.7.1. Description of the Theoretical Framework

Addiction involves the uncontrolled or compulsive use of a substance that causes increasing harm to a person, which results in difficulty with social, occupational, or interpersonal functioning and causes marked distress (APA, 1994). Addiction theory focuses on repetitive and harmful cycles of behaviour as the unit of analysis. There are two broad theories of addiction that have relevance to workaholism: the medical model and the psychological model. The medical model predicts that addiction occurs when a person becomes physically addicted to chemicals that are exogenous (e.g., drugs and alcohol), or endogenous (e.g., dopamine; Di Chiara, 1995). The psychological model predicts that addiction continues despite having overt and sometimes distal disadvantages, as it confers some immediate benefits (Eysenck, 1997). Thus, people believe that they cannot function without the repetitive cycle of behaviour, and psychological dependence develops.

4.7.2. General Principles

Addiction involves both physical dependence and psychological dependence. Physical dependence includes symptoms of tolerance (i.e., increased levels of the addictive substance have no linear relationship with the expressed symptoms), craving (an over-riding and irresistible desire to access the addictive substance), and withdrawal (physical symptoms increase upon ceasing the substance, such as headaches, insomnia, illness; APA, 1994). To qualify as an addiction, a behavioural cycle must include increasing tolerance, withdrawal symptoms, and worsening impact over time (i.e., substantial disruption in social, occupational, emotional, or intellectual functioning).

4.7.3. Model of How Variables Interact

Addiction research data demonstrate that addictions produce excessive adrenaline. Adrenaline produces pleasurable somatic sensations which become addictive, and perpetuates an ongoing cycle of addiction. On this basis, addiction theory would suggest that workaholics have low levels of corticosteroids such as dopamine in their neurological systems and inadvertently learn that the stimulation produced by work increases their levels, which yields a pleasurable sensation. Dopamine neurotransmitters are deeply reinforcing, which causes behaviour to be repeated at the expense of other choices, such as spending time with family or friends. Thus a person may 'discover' that working long hours produces desirable physical sensations and continue doing this to achieve more physical highs (Fassel, 1992).

4.7.4. Predictions Implied by the Theory

Addiction theory implies that workaholics perceive some degree of benefit (e.g., a physiological buzz) in perpetually working despite the negative side effects (e.g., tiredness; Rohrlich, 1980). However, the model also implies that if that buzz could be 'earned' by an alternate behaviour (such as competing in sports), then the alternate behaviour (sport) may become the focus of addiction instead. On this basis, workaholism could be potentially be replaced by more adaptive behaviours (such as exercising), but would yield worsening outcomes over time if it was not addressed.

4.7.5. Relevance to Workaholism

The only research reported within the addiction paradigm is that of Bryan Robinson (cf. 1998b, 2001), who defined workaholism as a progressive and potentially fatal disorder that arises from an underlying sense of inferiority and fear of failure that is especially prevalent in dysfunctional families. Robinson (1998b) has reported anecdotal efficacy using counselling based on the alcoholic 10-step programme for addiction. Furthermore, Workaholics Anonymous groups have existed in the United States for over a decade, which suggests some members of the public are finding the framework helpful. On this basis, while there are few empirical data, the model appears to hold intuitive relevance on some level.

4.7.6. Practical Applications for the Workplace

While the model provides an invitingly simple conceptualisation of workaholism, there are few data to support these propositions. For instance, there are no hard data or research designs that have isolated the impact of adrenaline on workaholism. The current dearth of empirical data makes developing a comprehensive addiction theory of workaholism premature, especially as methodological complexities hinder progress and there are no easily accessible measures for the biological substrates of workaholism. Nowadays, few researchers appear to regard workaholism as purely arising from an addiction. In general, scientific evidence indicates that workaholism represents a *value system about the importance of working and achieving*, that does not meet the diagnostic criteria for addiction (APA, 1994), because it is associated with similar quality of health and relationship to the rest of the adult population (McMillan & O'Driscoll, 2004).

4.7.7. Limitations

Addiction theories are constrained by the fact that the hypothesised addictive substance (work-generated adrenaline) is not as easy to isolate and measure as other addictive chemicals (e.g., drugs and alcohol). Given the multifarious variables that produce adrenaline, however (e.g., racing for a deadline), statistically eliminating these mediating variables would be extremely complex and require highly technical biological tests. Unfortunately, while appropriate blood and urine tests are available, they are also open to confounding by the physiological stimulus of taking blood, dietary intake, and circadian rhythms (Di Chiara, 1995). Critically, workaholism does not appear to produce the worsening occupational or social functioning such as unemployment, crime, poor personal hygiene, and illness that is characteristic of all other scientifically recognised addictions. Addiction theory, therefore, generates useful questions and hypotheses about the nature of workaholism, but until more empirical data emerge, is unable to be verified.

4.8. Behavioural Theory

4.8.1. Description of the Theoretical Framework

Behavioural theory considers that all things organisms do (i.e., thinking, feeling, doing) constitutes human behaviour. The core unit of study therefore is behaviour (not the individual, or the system). Behaviour theory comprises operant learning (reinforcement), Pavlovian learning (classical conditioning), and social learning theory. The present section will focus predominantly on operant and social learning as they hold the most relevance for workaholism.

4.8.2. General Principles

Burrhus Skinner proposed that the core principle of operant learning was that consequences change behaviour (Skinner, 1974). In other words, if a behaviour leads to pleasant consequences it would be repeated, as the person attempted to re-experience the pleasing outcome. Thus it was a two-stage process: (i) a discriminative stimuli (trigger) signalled a behaviour, whichs lead to a good consequence, and then (ii) the consequence became a trigger or discriminative stimuli for the next chain of reinforcing behaviour. When testing behavioural theory, Albert Bandura noticed that people tend to observe and then imitate the behaviour of role models. Social learning theory proposes that role modelling evolved as an adaptive response that enables someone to learn faster from successful models rather than experimenting randomly on an individual basis to 'discover' effective solutions to problems. Bandura's research data demonstrated that imitation only occurs when the role model is more potent (i.e., powerful, influential, or with higher social status) than the observer/imitator.

4.8.3. Model of How Variables Interact

Behaviour theories predict that workaholism arises through one of two mechanisms. Firstly, working a few extra hours that yields pleasant peer approval may further increase the likelihood of discretionary working. (While the positive reinforcer in the present example is pleasant, this does not necessarily need to be the case; a negative reinforcer, such as escape from an unpleasant event at home, may also maintain discretionary working). Secondly, a powerful or successful role model who is a workaholic may provide a 'template' for success that is imitated by more junior staff members.

4.8.4. Predictions Implied by the Theory

Operant learning predicts workaholism to be a relatively durable behaviour that is established through operant conditioning when a voluntary response comes under the control of its consequences by earning a desired outcome (Skinner, 1974). Overall, operant conditioning implies that workaholism develops where it leads to desired outcomes, and thus dominates high earning, high-status jobs, especially where home or leisure are unsatisfying. Most controversially, the theory predicts that workaholism could be shaped into anyone given adequately potent and idiopathically suitable reinforcers. Observational learning would predict that if a potent role model (such as a chief executive, senior manager, or mentor) was a strong workaholic, then employees would be likely to model their behaviour on that cultural norm. In other words workaholism would cluster in some families and workplaces. It would also predict that workaholism would be differently distributed in flat structures as opposed to hierarchical systems. Conversely, behavioural theory predicts that workaholism could be faded out of a person's repertoire by altering the relative richness of reinforcement schedules, or by providing a healthy role model of success who was not a workaholic (McMillan et al., 2001).

4.8.5. Relevance to Workaholism

Learning theories are distinguished by their inherent optimism that workaholism can be readily trained out of people. Because the theory avoids invoking reified explanatory fictions (e.g., personality) that are not directly observable, it reduces the number of measurement variables required. Furthermore, the behavioural conceptualisation of workaholism has interesting links with compensation (e.g., non-work activities are on relatively lean reinforcement schedules) and spillover (e.g., busyness generalises from home into the workplace). On this basis, behaviour theory holds broad relevance to workaholism (and associated concepts such as spillover and compensation), especially in terms of interventions and approaches that may help modify or reduce its intensity.

4.8.6. Practical Applications for the Workplace

Behavioural theory is readily applied to the workplace. For instance, promoting the positive benefits of work-life balance in influential role models may reduce level of workaholism in more junior staff members. Alternately, analysing the triggers and maintaining factors in a person's workaholism will by implication supply the treatment and prevention strategies for that particular individual. McMillan and O'Driscoll (2006) present a sequential model that formulates the antecedents, behaviour, and consequence of workaholism which can be used to generate workplace strategies for managing workaholism. In addition, Mudrack (2006) provides a conceptualisation of workaholism as a set of behavioural tendencies. On this basis, learning theory provides generality (explains a large number of individual variances), parsimony (does not invoke extraneous variables), pragmatism (stimulates multiple hypotheses), and presents a feasible basis for explaining workaholism (McMillan et al., 2001).

4.8.7. Limitations

While behavioural theory provides a concise and logically sequential formulation of workaholism, it does not easily account for temporal factors such as childhood experiences that may influence workaholism. It also requires relatively intense analysis of individual's pattern of behaving to yield treatment, which is both time consuming and requires some degree of training. Finally, it does not easily explain the emotional components of workaholism and generally ignores historical variables such as inherited traits and personality styles. Despite these limitations, however, it does provide a logically explicable formulation of workaholism, especially in terms of directly observable behaviour, and therefore provides a sound basis for formulating research designs and workplace interventions.

4.9. Emotion-Based Theory

4.9.1. Description

Emotion-based theories of human behaviour focus on the full spectrum of emotional well-being, in such broad areas as self-actualisation, health, hope, love, and meaning-seeking (Blyth, 1999). This humanistic stance emphasises the *qualitative* and *subjective* aspects of human experience such as joy, sorrow, and personal growth. Humanist therapies include Freud's psychoanalysis, where problems are hypothesised to stem from culturally unacceptable desires that have been suppressed. More latterly, dialectic behaviour theory and acceptance and commitment theory have accentuated the importance of validating human emotions in others and learning effective emotional regulation skills in order to cope successfully.

4.9.2. General Principles

Emotions are powerful internal states that regulate human behaviour. The general principles of the emotion-based theories describe human beings as unique, self-fulfilling individuals that cannot be reduced to components. Humans are regarded as self-actualising individuals (inherently strive to do and be the best they can be), who aim for peak experiences (where they supposedly find unity and meaningfulness in life; Maslow, 1970). The primary goal of most humanist therapies therefore, is to provide emotional maturation for the client. This is usually facilitated by harnessing strengths, catalysing insight, and increasing self-esteem. On this basis, emotion-based theories would conceptualise workaholism as arising from emotional disturbance. This emotional disturbance may be generated by distress, either at home, at work, or internally (e.g., personal issues such as identity crises, mid-life crises, or existential crises).

4.9.3. Model of How Variables Interact

The two key variables in emotional theory are (a) the 'psyche' — an invisible receptacle comprising the 'conscious' and the 'unconscious', and (b) the emotions. Structurally, the psyche contains three components: the 'id' (contains primitive urges, such as sex, hunger, and aggression), the 'superego' (contains internalised norms and), and the 'ego' (mediates between the id and super ego to produce a sense of identity). Specifically, the id is regarded as a (childish) pleasure-oriented part of the personality with no ability to delay gratification, whereas the superego is a 'rules-based' (parental) structure, and the ego is the peace-seeking (adult) that seeks compromise between the id and the rules (Levinson, 1999). Various tensions between urges and rules produce the entire spectrum of human emotions, which are sometimes unpleasant and sometimes socially unacceptable to express. It is this hypothetical 'store' of emotional energy that gives rise to both constructive and destructive human behaviour. On this basis workaholism would arise from emotional distress.

4.9.4. Predictions Implied by the Theory

Humanist theory predicts that when a person is stressed, powerful emotions are distorted into socially acceptable behaviours such as over-working. On this basis workaholism would wax and wane, dependent on a person's internal emotional state. It also predicts that with appropriate insight, a person could 'grow out of' the condition, or at least control the defense mechanisms that trapped them in the pattern. Alternately, it would predict that learning successful stress regulation skills (using such frameworks such as dialectic behaviour therapy) would reduce the intensity of workaholism. Essentially emotion-based theories predict that learning (a) appropriate emotional expression, combined with (b) adequate self-awareness, and (c) effective self-care would decrease the incidence of workaholism.

4.9.5. Relevance to Workaholism

Emotion-based theory regards workaholism as arising from repressed urges or emotional disturbance, where someone uses 'compensation' (adopt one behaviour because they cannot accomplish another, e.g., work excessively because they cannot fall in love) and 'sublimation' (refocus energy away from negative expression into more socially constructive outlets). Killinger (2006) has written extensively about the emotional aspects of workaholism such as fear, boredom, intuition, paranoia, repression, and breakdown and how these may be addressed with emotion-based approaches. It is important to consider however that these suggestions are based in anecdotal clinical experience, not yet in scientifically controlled studies.

4.9.6. Practical Applications for the Workplace

The boundaries of privacy, confidential, and clinical safety around exposing peoples' intimate emotional states in the workplace restricts the practical applicability of these theories to the workplace. For instance, it would be clinically irresponsible to expose a depression or identity crisis in the workplace without having adequately trained professional clinicans on hand to help resolve the risk and distress experienced by the individual. The best course of action when these issues become apparent is to refer the individual to an EAP (Employee Assistance Programme) or qualified professional.

4.9.7. Limitations

Emotion-based theories may explain some of the underlying mechanisms of workaholism, but require qualified professionals to administer the attendant therapy. Furthermore, these theories do not generally isolate one or two causative variables as many problems are regarded to have causes that lie in distant and immeasurable events such as early childhood trauma. This makes concisely conceptualising the causes and consequence of workaholism extremely complex, and makes the incidence of workaholism difficult to predict. This is reflected in part in the literature; psychoanalysis has been critiqued because the early theories arose from clinical case studies as opposed to being grounded in scientific data and empirical rigour.

Some have argued that the theory is not falsifiable, and therefore not scientific. Recent developments in dialectic and acceptance theories however have been empirically measured, particularly in terms of personality disorders and anxiety, but not in terms of workaholism. Thus emotional theories of workaholism add to our general understanding, but are not always practical in terms of suggesting approaches to managing workaholism in the workplace.

4.10. Cognitive Theory

4.10.1.   Description of the Theoretical Framework

An important new development in workaholism research is the analysis of antecedent beliefs. This is based in Donald Broadbent's cognitive theory which has its genesis in the late 1950s (Wells, 1997). Cognitive theory explains how the way people think impacts on their consequent behaviour. In terms of workaholism, cognitive theorists would analyse thought patterns that (a) lead to workaholic behaviour, and (b) perpetuate workaholism. The core unit of analysis is the thought (as opposed to systems theory where groups are the unit of analysis, or personality theory where individual character is the unit of analysis). Cognitive theory rests on Broadbent's paradigm of information processing, where brain function is considered to parallel the manner in which computer software functions (Wells, 1997).

4.10.2.   General Principles

Cognitive theory maps the mental processes by which sensory imputes are stored, computed, and recovered. Cognitive theory proposes that people hold schemata (conceptual frameworks about the world) that are based in core beliefs, assumptions about causality and automatic thoughts, that are maintained and/or changed by these information-processing skills (Beck, 1995). Thoughts are modelled in a logical, sequential manner to essentially mimic in slow motion what happens inside the brain in a millisecond. Cognitive theory asserts that people process data in two broad manners: rational (i.e., linear and logical) or irrational (i.e., impartial and biased). It is this latter irrational data processing that is believed to cause human distress and dysfunctional behaviour. Taken to its logical extreme, this theory implies that addressing irrational thinking can rectify human dysfunction.

4.10.3.   Model of How Variables Interact

The core mechanisms of cognitive theory comprise a four-step information-processing model: (a) attention, selecting which stimuli to attend to; (b) encoding, computing and condensing the information into a manageable format; (c) storage, into either short-term memory, or long-term memory; and (d) retrieval, recovering the data from memory. For example, a person may choose to ignore stimuli such as family demands (selective attention), interpret their request as less important than work (faulty filters and biases), rationalise their behaviour "if I don't put work before family I will fail" (store information as core beliefs), and state that work values them more than their family does (retrieve only relevant perceived data). The tools for changing dysfunctional behaviour into more adaptive behaviour are problem-solving skills and strategising (metacognition). In other words, cognitive theory holds that if cognitions are changed then behaviour will change as a result.

4.10.4. Predictions Implied by the Theory

The cognitive paradigm regards workaholism as arising from (a) a dysfunctional core belief (e.g., I am a failure), which gives rise to (b) faulty assumptions (e.g., if I work hard then I will not fail), and (c) automatic thoughts (e.g., I must work hard). Thus, the beliefs, assumptions and thoughts activate workaholic behaviour, become abbreviated over time to 'work equals worthiness', and therefore maintain high levels of workaholism. However, as outlined above, cognitive theory is a doctrine of optimism; with appropriate problem-solving skills and metastrategies a person can decrease the level of workaholism they experience. Thus workaholism would vary between people and also vary within one person over time, depending on which skills and strategies they are currently using. In sum however it would always logically demonstrable origins and alternatives.

4.10.5. Relevance to Workaholism

Burke (1999a, 1999b) investigated the role of cognitions in workaholism, and found that workaholism was predicted by thoughts about striving against others, moral principles, and proving oneself. This holds important implications for workaholism, because if the data continue to support the theory, there are well-validated therapeutic interventions that modify such core beliefs (such as cognitive therapy and cognitive behavioural therapy; Beck, 1995). For instance, Chen (2006) has prescribed an explicit protocol for delivering rational emotive behaviour therapy. Given the enormous breadth of similar problems that this therapy is statistically validated for, it is highly likely to be clinically efficacious with workaholism.

4.10.6. Practical Applications for the Workplace

Cognitive theory is a promising new development that warrants continued focus. Organisations could potentially impact on peoples' beliefs and cognitions about work through the use of several cognitive mode. These include awareness raising (self-identify workaholism), education programmes (the nature and impact of workaholism), and training programmes (skills to manage workload such as assertiveness and boundary setting). Likewise, provision of internal coaching (from non-workaholic managers) and mentoring programmes with well-respected senior peers, could help people adjust their cognitions and utilise adaptive problem-solving skills to maintain a healthy work-life balance.

4.10.7.   *Limitations*

While cognitive theory holds promising potential in the workaholism field, it has some important limitations. Firstly, purely cognitive frameworks do not generally address emotional states. Secondly, the sequential identification of an individual's thought process to reveal the dysfunctional beliefs and values that create workaholic behaviour, requires substantial training, and expertise. Finally, cognitive theory does not easily encompass historical variables such as inherited traits and personality styles. Despite these limitations, however, it does provide a logically explicable formulation of workaholism, at least in terms of immediately visible behaviour.

4.11.   Social Systems Theory

4.11.1.   *Description of the Theoretical Framework*

Systems theory is based on the work by Gregory Bateson and Margaret Mead who separately observed and then modelled the manner in which systems maintain themselves. In this context, 'system' refers to a group of people such as families, workplaces, and cultures. Essentially the theory treats *groups* as the unit of analysis (rather than individuals). Systems theory recognises the interdependence between groups, individuals, and structures. Systems are believed to be either (a) isolated, which is very rare, (b) closed, as in the case of monasteries, or (c) open, as in the case of workplaces. All systems attempt to maintain homeostasis by adjusting the dynamics between their components (i.e., people). There are two broad systems theories that have relevance to workaholism: workplace systems theory and family systems theory, each will be addressed separately below.

4.12.   Workplace Systems Theory

4.12.1.   *General Principles*

Workplace theory holds that workaholism has its genesis in workplace dynamics. An organisation is conceptualised as a complex web of interconnected relationships that should be treated as such, and not merely as a sum of simple sub-parts. In other words, the focus is on culture, values, remuneration, and structure, rather than specific individual experience. Systems theory proposes that reducing a workplace into component parts (i.e., individual workers) rather than focusing on the whole system (i.e., the entire workplace) would reduce the effectiveness of the entire system.

4.12.2. Model of How Variables Interact

Workplace systems theory considers a workplace a configuration of parts that is connected by a web of relationships, where the emphasis is not on the individual employees, but on the *relationship* between them and the workplace. The focus therefore is on the structure, hierarchy, order, and cultural norms of an organisation. For example, the rewards structure may be seen as a contributing factor in workaholism, if behaviour such as working long hours is remunerated with bonus payments. Alternatively, a culture that esteem workaholism in its senior executives may be seen as responsible for encouraging workaholism in more junior staff members. The assumption is that adequate manipulation of organisational processes, culture, values, and norms will impact on the levels of workaholism expressed by individual employees.

4.12.3. Predictions Implied by the Theory

Systems theory predicts that we must change the structural aspects of the environment in order to change an individual's behaviour. This implies that changing a system, its rules, or its culture, would change workaholism. For example a human resources practitioner may elect to reduce workaholism by altering key performance indicators (KIPs) to ensure that quality (not quantity) of work is rewarded. They may also elect to promote family friendly values and work-life balance programmes in order to normalise healthy work–leisure patterns as a viable alternative. On this basis, human resource managers and senior executives would have considerable influence over workaholism incidence in the workplace, as they are generally resourced to provide organisational level interventions and able to drive organisational culture. However, because systems theory also predicts that the causes of workaholism are located within the system as opposed to the individual, attempting to modify workaholism by providing personal therapy or executive coaching would not be effective *until* the workplace culture was addressed. It also implies that if a family had a culture of workaholism, then the workplace is effectively powerless to intervene until the family addresses its own dynamics and relationships.

4.12.4. Relevance to Workaholism

Workplace systems theory appears to hold intuitive relevance for workaholism. For instance, programmes aiming to address work-life balance have been widely instituted over the last five years. In addition, there has been a recent shift towards developing 'values-based organisations' (i.e., make the leadership and cultural values explicit then embed them into everyday business process, cf. Corporate Leadership Council, 2001a,

2001b). These are both systemic attempts to change culture and modify the workplace behaviour of employees. Furthermore, anecdotal evidence from prominent authors on workaholism also suggest the existence of 'workaholic organisations' and 'addictive organisations' (cf. Fassel, 1992; Burke, 2000; Schaef & Fassel, 1998). Given the relative success of each of these systemic approaches in regulating workplace culture it appears systems theory may have some validity in intervening and modifying workaholism.

4.12.5.   Practical Applications for the Workplace

Systems theory addresses a broad array of contextual variables that may moderate and even exacerbate workaholism. These include generic factors such as organisational values, culture, and norms, in addition to specific factors such as which behaviours are remunerated, pay parity, and leadership style. For instance, encouraging payment for overtime, or providing bonus payments for quantity of work completed may encourage workaholism. In contrast, having leaders who behave congruently with healthy work-life values may discourage workaholism. Human resource practitioners in particular are well placed to measure, monitor, and manage levels of workaholism, and to design interventions that directly alter the systemic structure in the workplace in order to regulate workaholism. A strong working alliance between human resource practitioner, chief executive and senior management would be particularly advantageous in designing effective systemic interventions using such vehicles as culture change, values-based management, and values-based leadership. Workplace systems theory therefore has numerous applications for workaholism.

4.12.6.   Limitations

Workplace systems theory is limited by difficulty in identifying which precise variables cause workaholism and does not easily explain the genesis of a particular individual's workaholism. Because of this, it is arguably difficult to design effective interventions. While the diffuse nature of the theory will limit direct utility, it does have particular use in providing a background explanation of the contextual factors (such as remuneration strategies or company culture) that may encourage or enable workaholism to thrive in the workplace.

4.13.   Family Systems Theory

4.13.1.   General Principles

Family systems theory holds that workaholism has its genesis in peoples' families of origin and is influenced by their current personal relationships. Thus, all behaviour is viewed in the context of interpersonal networks and dynamics, with problems located *within family dynamics*, as opposed to individual pathology (Hayes, 1991). Family theory focuses on relationships *between people* whereas workplace theory tends to focus on the *structural aspects* of the system (such as hierarchy, parity, and remuneration). On this basis, workaholism would be seen to arise directly from difficulties in personal relationships at home.

4.13.2. Model of How the Variable Interact

Family systems theory regards workaholism as a family problem that arises from, and is maintained by, unhealthy dynamics. These dynamics may include blurred parent–child boundaries, over-responsibility, parentified children, circularity (everyone perpetuates the problem), enabling, concealment, and triangulation (parent–child alliances against the working partner; Robinson, 1998a, 2000).

4.13.3. Predictions Implied by the Theory

Hypothetically, family systems theory would suggest that a person with an 'over-responsible' style may express their perceived obligations towards their family by over-working to secure their material needs. The family response may be to enable the over-work by cushioning the worker's stress (e.g., hushing children when the worker arrives home), allowing a mutual dependence to ensue. However, over time the family may come to perceive over-work as a tactic of distancing, and may respond by isolating themselves from the working partner. Thus, workaholism develops in the context of dependence and miscommunication and creates negative outcomes for all parties.

4.13.4. Relevance and Practical Application for the Workplace

Family theory addresses factors that are beyond the scope of the workplace, such as relationship dysfunction, gender roles in the home and structural roles (e.g., division of power and labour) within the home. Furthermore, practical applications of family theory will remain limited until data are published expanding the hypotheses and substantiating the relationship between family dynamics and workplace behaviour. On this basis, having family friendly work practices (e.g., allowing time off for significant family events, such as celebrations, deaths, marriages, births, graduations, sports events, etc.) is probably the most important role a workplace can play in providing a conducive environment for work–family integration.

4.13.5. Limitations

While family dynamics may explain some isolated individual occurrences of workaholism, the theory makes numerous assumptions about life outside the workplace, which have not been subjected to empirical investigation and remain speculative, rather than not scientific. Before these hypotheses can be validated and refined, we require empirical data with which to test the accuracy and appropriateness of family theory for workaholism. In the interim, the relevance of workplace systems theory is limited to identifying if people have personal/family problems, and if so referring them to an EAP or to an alternately qualified counsellor.

4.13.6.   Comparative Analysis

Now that the description of the theoretical framework and the general principles on which each theory rest have been presented, a comparative analysis will be conducted. The analysis is based on four criteria: (a) the explicitness of their modelling of how variables interact, (b) the pragmatism of the predictions implied by each, (c) the generality of the supporting data regarding workaholism, and (d) the breadth of applications for the workplace.

As can been seen in Table 4.2, it is clear that family systems theory, emotion-based theory and addiction theory hold little practical utility in terms of workaholism. While each of these theories clearly outlines hypotheses, cause and effect, and clear hypotheses, the propositions are not measurable. If it cannot be measured, it cannot be disconfirmed, and is therefore not able to scientifically validated. In the case of addiction theory, this is merely because the appropriate research designs have not been innovated yet. As technology progresses, ways to isolate and measure the endogenous addictive substance involved in workaholism may become available. However, in practical terms this is likely to remain relatively cost effective and invasive for research subjects, which may hinder future progress. In terms of family systems and emotion-based theory, the hypotheses are generally too broad and too distal (the causes are proposed to happen years before the effect occurs) which makes accurate measurement and isolation of the independent variables exceedingly complex. As a result there are no empirically generated, scientifically validated data regarding any of these three theories, and the practical applications to the workplace are severely restricted. However, it is important to remember they provide an important context for understanding the remaining theories.

Personality theory and cognitive theory both hold excellent properties in respect to workaholism. The notable disadvantage they present is the level of specialist expertise required to address workaholism in the workplace (i.e., prevent it and reduce it). Cognitive interventions require appropriately trained therapists to produce a valid treatment outcome, although some degree of education can alleviate low-level problems (i.e., those that are below clinical threshold). In contrast, however, personality issues require professionally trained psychological and psychiatric experts to produce even small improvements, and can require many hours and intense resources. While both cognitive and personality theories explain the wellsprings or evolution of workaholism, they are not necessarily helpful on a broad scale in *managing* workaholism.

The two theories that potentially hold the most practical applications to workaholism include workplace systems theory and behavioural theory. However,

Table 4.2: Explanatory theories of workaholism.

		Biological theory personality	Biological theory addiction	Behaviour theory	Emotion-based theory	Cognitive theory	Systems theory workplace	Systems theory family
Explicitness of model	Identifies key variables	Yes	Yes	Yes	Yes	Yes	Yes	Yes
	Details cause and effect	Yes	Yes	Yes	Yes	Yes	Yes	Yes
Pragmatism of predictions	Generates clear hypotheses	Yes	Yes	Yes	Yes	Yes	Yes	Yes
	Propositions are measurable	Yes	No	Yes	No	Yes	Yes	No
Generality of supporting data	Data from multiple countries	Yes	No	No	No	Yes	No	No
	Data from multiple designs	Yes	No	No	No	No	No	No
Breadth of applications to workplace	Outlines preventive strategies	No	No	Yes	No	Yes	Yes	No
	Applicable to multiple disciplines	No	No	Yes	No	No	Yes	No

while the theories both provide measurable hypotheses, neither has been subjected to empirical investigation, to date. Clearly, if the data support the theories, workaholism knowledge could be significantly expanded.

In practical terms however it is most likely that it is an *interaction* of factors that give rise to workaholism. It is entirely viable, for instance, (a) that family systems and emotion-based theories explain the historic factors that set the vulnerability to later workaholic behaviour. It is then feasible that (b) personality theory explains the predisposition to workaholism that is (c) triggered by events inherent within workplace systems theory and then (d) maintained by cognitive patterns and behavioural cycles and (e) eventually becomes entrenched as an addictive pattern. Congruent with the biopsychosocial model of human behaviour, workaholism may have a multifactorial genesis. In fact, given the raft of evidence for this pattern in other behaviour cycles (Copolov et al., 2001), *it is highly unlikely that workaholism arises from one single event, can be explained by one single theory, or treated by only one type of therapy.*

On this basis, it is imperative that we take a multidisciplinary approach to understanding, formulating, treating, and monitoring the rate and nature of workaholism in our workplaces. It is not merely an individual issue; it is a systemic issue, which is the shared responsibility of employers, human resource practitioners, public policy legislators, therapists, executive coaches, families, and individual workers.

4.14. Summary

Workaholism occurs when a person has difficulty disengaging from work (evidenced by the capability to work at any time in any situation), a strong drive to work and intense enjoyment of work (McMillan & O'Driscoll, 2006). Workaholics' most notable characteristics include the tendency to work with a passion that is obvious to the outside observer, think about work four times more frequently after most other people have mentally 'switched off', centre their conversation on work even in social situations, strive for tangible achievements, and work slightly more hours than others. Most researchers concur that workaholism represents a style of working that is neither good nor bad — it is what people do about it and how they manage and respond to it that produces helpful and less helpful outcomes.

The recent surge in research data suggests that the dominant explanatory mechanisms include biological, behavioural, cognitive, emotion-based, and systems theories. While it is tempting to attempt to over-simplify the aetiological mechanisms that act as the wellsprings of workaholism, as this chapter has illustrated, the most accurate explanation is probably provided by the *biopsychosocial model* of human behaviour. In other words, it is a complex interaction of variables that produce workaholism.

Problems that have multiple causes require multiple resources to resolve. Workaholism is *not* an individual issue — it creates implications for families, partners, colleagues, and workplaces. Furthermore, as the world trend towards globalisation, international migration, cross-cultural communication, multinational production lines, mobilised technology, and elastic-boundaried workplaces, shrink the distance between global workplaces, the need for accurate information on workaholism will increase. Further collaborative efforts between researchers, employers, therapists, and governments are imperative in helping to identify therapeutically efficacious and cost-effective interventions for this *multifaceted* condition we are only recently beginning to fully understand.

References

Allport, G. W. (1937). Personality: A psychological interpretation. NY: Holt, Rinehart & Winston. Cited in Weiten, W. (1992). Psychology: Themes and variations (2nd ed.). California: Brooks/Cole.

American Psychiatric Association. (1994). *Diagnostic and statistical manual of mental disorders* (4th ed.). Washington, DC: American Psychiatric Association.

Beck, J. S. (1995). *Cognitive therapy: Basics and beyond.* New York: Guildford Press.

Blyth, F. (1999). Humanistic therapies. In: S. M. Stein, R. Haigh & J. Stein (Eds), *Essentials of psychotherapy.* Oxford, MA: Butterworth Heinman.

Burke, R. J. (1999a). Workaholism in organizations: The role of personal beliefs and fears. *Anxiety, Stress and Coping, 20,* 1–12.

Burke, R. J. (1999b). Workaholism among women managers: Work and life satisfactions and psychological well-being. *Equal Opportunities International, 18*(7), 25–35.

Burke, R. J. (2000). Workaholism in organizations: Concepts, results and future directions. *International Journal of Management Reviews, 2*(1), 1–16.

Burke, R. J. (2001). Editorial: Workaholism in organizations. *International Journal of Stress Management, 8*(2), 65–68.

Chen, C. P. (2006). Improving work-life balance: REBT for workaholic treatment. In: R. J. Burke (Ed.), *Research companion to working time and work addiction.* Cheltenham: Edward Elgar.

Clark, L. A., Livesley, W. J., Schroeder, M. L., & Irish, S. L. (1996). Convergence of two systems for assessing specific traits of personality disorder. *Psychological Assessment, 8,* 294–303.

Clark, L. A., McEwen, J. L., Collard, L. M., & Hickok, L. G. (1993). Symptoms and traits of personality disorder: Two new methods in their assessment. *Psychological Assessment, 5,* 81–91.

Copolov, D., James, J. E., & Milgrom, J. (2001). Biopsychosocial factors in health and illness. In: J. Milgrom & G. D. Burrows (Eds), *Psychology and psychiatry: Integrated medical practice.* Chichester: Wiley.

Corporate Leadership Council. (2001a). *Imbedding values throughout the organisation-literature review.* Washington, DC: CLC.

Corporate Leadership Council. (2001b). *Implementing and evaluating corporate values-fact brief.* Washington, DC: CLC.

Cross, G. (1990). *A social history of leisure since 1600.* Pennsylvania: Venture.

Di Chiara, G. (1995). The role of dopamine in drug abuse viewed from the perspective of its role in motivation. *Drug and Alcohol Dependence, 38,* 95–137.

Eysenck, H. J. (1997). Addiction, personality and motivation. *Human Psychopharmacology*, *12*, S79–S87.

Fassel, D. (1992). *Working ourselves to death*. London: HarperCollins.

Hayes, H. (1991). A re-introduction to family therapy: Clarification of three schools. *Australia and New Zealand Journal of Family Therapy*, *12*(1), 27–45.

Kanai, A., Wakabayashi, M., & Fling, S. (1996). Workaholism among employees in Japanese corporations: An examination based on the Japanese version of the workaholism scales. *Japanese Psychological Research*, *38*(4), 192–203.

Killinger, B. (2006). The workaholic breakdown syndrome. In: R. J. Burke (Ed.), *Research companion to working time and work addiction*. Cheltenham: Edward Elgar.

Levinson, A. (1999). Freudian psychoanalysis. In: S. M. Stein, R. Haigh & J. Stein (Eds), *Essentials of psychotherapy*. Oxford, MA: Butterworth Heinman.

Machlowitz, M. M. (1978). *Determining the effects of workaholism*. Unpublished doctoral dissertation. Yale University.

Maslow, A. H. (1970). *Motivation and personality*. New York: Harper Row.

McMillan, L. H. W., & O'Driscoll, M. P. (2004). Workaholism and health: Implications for organisations. *Journal of Organizational Change Management*, *17*(5), 509–519.

McMillan, L. H. W., & O'Driscoll, M. P. (2006). Exploring new frontiers to generate an integrated definition of workaholism. In: R. J. Burke (Ed.), *Research companion to working time and work addiction*. Cheltenham: Edward Elgar.

McMillan, L. H. W., O'Driscoll, M. P., & Burke, R. (2003). Workaholism: A review of theory, research and future directions. In: C. L. Cooper & I. T. Robertson (Eds), *International review of industrial and organizational psychology* (Vol. 18, pp. 207–230). New York: Wiley.

McMillan, L. H. W., O'Driscoll, M. P., Marsh, N. V., & Brady, E. C. (2001). Understanding workaholism: Data synthesis, theoretical critique and future design strategies. *International Journal of Stress Management*, *8*(2), 69–91.

Mudrack, P. E. (2006). Understanding workaholism: The case doe behavioural tendencies. In: R. J. Burke (Ed.), *Research companion to working time and work addiction*. Cheltenham: Edward Elgar.

Oates, W. E. (1968). On being a "workaholic" (a serious jest). *Pastoral Psychology*, *19*, 16–20.

Robinson, B. E. (1996). The psychosocial and familial aspect of work addiction: Preliminary perspectives and hypotheses. *Journal of Counseling and Development*, *74*, 447–452.

Robinson, B. E. (1998a). The workaholic family: A clinical perspective. *The American Journal of Family Therapy*, *22*, 65–75.

Robinson, B. E. (1998b). *Chained to the desk: A guidebook for workaholics, their partners and children and the clinicians who treat them*. New York: New York University Press.

Robinson, B. E. (2000). Workaholism: Bridging the gap between workplace, sociocultural, and family research. *Journal of Employment Counseling*, *37*, 31–47.

Robinson, B. E. (2001). Workaholism and family functioning: A psychological profile of family members. In: B. E. Robinson & N. D. Chase (Eds), *High performing families: Causes, consequences and clinical solutions* (pp. 3–22). Alexandria: American Counseling Association.

Robinson, J. P., & Godbey, G. G. (1992). *Time for life: The surprising ways Americans use their time*. Pennsylvania: Pennsylvania State University Press.

Rohrlich, J. (1980). *Work and love: The crucial balance*. New York: Harmony.

Schaef, A. W., & Fassel, D. (1998). *The addictive organization*. San Francisco: Harper Row.

Schmitt, N. W., & Klimoski, R. J. (1991). *Research methods in human resources management*. Cincinnati: South-Western Publishing.

Skinner, B. F. (1974). *About behaviorism*. London: Penguin.

Snir, R., & Harpaz, I. (2004). Attitudinal and demographic antecedents of workaholism. *Journal of Organizational Change Management, 17*(5), 520–536.

Spence, J. T., & Robbins, A. S. (1992). Workaholism: Definition, measurement, and preliminary results. *Journal of Personality Assessment, 58*, 160–178.

Weiten, W. (1992). *Psychology: Themes and variations* (2nd ed). California: Brooks/Cole.

Wells, A. (1997). *Cognitive therapy of anxiety disorders*. Chichester: Wiley.

PART II

CONSEQUENCES

Chapter 5

Work Effort and Worker Well-Being in the Age of Affluence

Francis Green

5.1. Introduction

The 1990s was a decade of work intensification in many industrialised countries — most notably in Australia, Belgium, Britain, France, Ireland, Italy, Luxemburg, The Netherlands, Spain and Sweden. Workers in other countries, including the United States and New Zealand, are also likely to have experienced rising work effort in the 1990s, though the evidence is somewhat weaker (Askenazy, Cartron, Coninck, & Gollac, 2007; Green, 2001, 2006; Merllié & Paoli, 2001; Green & McIntosh, 2001; Morehead, Steele, Alexander, Stephen, & Duffin, 1997; Burchell & Fagan, 2002).[1] This widespread intensification has laid a significant foundation for increased stress in the workplace. The same decade also saw, however, a countervailing tendency towards a reduction in average hours of work in most countries.[2]

This chapter aims, first, to provide an update on work intensification and on the trend in working hours up to the middle of the 2000s. Second, I deliver detailed analyses using British data of how levels of required work effort and long hours are distributed across industries and occupations, and asks whether high work loads are being concentrated in specific sectors of the economy. These analyses are then put into perspective through my third objective, the provision of new estimates of the association between work effort, hours of work and employee well-being. The distinctive feature of the analysis here is that it derives from an exceptionally rich nationally representative data set, which provides benchmarks for the distribution of required effort and subjective well-being in the 2000s decade.

---

1. In Finland, the 1980s was the decade of rising work effort (Lehto & Sutela, 2005).
2. European Foundation for the Improvement of Living and Working Conditions (2007, p. 17).

The term "work effort" calls for conceptual clarity, since it is used to mean different things by assorted writers. I use "work effort" to refer to the intensity of mental and/or physical exertion during working time, thus distinguishing the concept from working time itself.[3] In a simple job, involving series of equally demanding tasks, intensity could be encapsulated (negatively) by Marx's metaphor of "porosity", referring to the gaps of idle time during the working day. Most jobs are more complex, however, and involve overlapping tasks that place varying demands on workers.

The measurement of work effort is problematic in most practical work contexts. There being no means of directly measuring mental effort, researchers use the currency of experts' or individuals' reports of effort and of job demands. Both the numbers and the difficulty of job demands have been used as indicators, in specific contexts, of work overload. It is also possible, with safeguards, to use self-reports of the demands of jobs. There are two key aspects to the use of such data in social–scientific analyses. First, it is preferable to focus on required work effort, that is, on the demands of the job itself, rather than asking employees how hard they personally work. Second, it is important to ask job-demand questions across time in identical ways including identical response scales. Providing the time elapsed between surveys is not very large one can defend the assumption that changes in the distribution of responses reflects a genuine change in work effort. Here, I shall utilise an index of required work effort derived from survey responses at successive time points with intervals of less than a decade. While work intensification is implied in several qualitative studies of work organisation (e.g., Erlandsson, 2007), most previous formal studies of work intensification have adopted this procedure.

Europewide evidence so far points to a continued process of work intensification in the 2000s. Thus, according to evidence from The Fourth European Working Conditions Survey, the proportion of employees in all the EU15 countries who were "working at very high speed" more than half the time rose from 43.3% in 1995 to 44.4% in 2000, then 48.5% in 2005; similarly, the proportion who were "working to tight deadlines" rose from 45.9% in 1995 to 48.3% in 2000, then 50.0% in 2005.[4]

However, the picture varies across countries. While the 1990s trend towards intensification in Belgium and Spain continued during 2000–2005, several countries which had not, during the 1990s, shown evidence of work intensification now did so, including Denmark, Germany, Greece and Portugal. Only one European country — The Netherlands — is recorded to have experienced a retreat in work effort over 2000–2005. Effort was stabilised, however, in several other countries, including Austria, France, Ireland, Italy, Luxemburg, Sweden and the UK (European Foundation for the Improvement of Living and Working Conditions, 2007, p. 58). Work effort in Britain had in fact reached a plateau by the late 1990s — there being

---

3. The US-dominated labour economics literature usually treats working time as synonymous with effort.
4. These data are in a forthcoming report on working intensity and working time for the European Foundation for Living and Working Conditions.

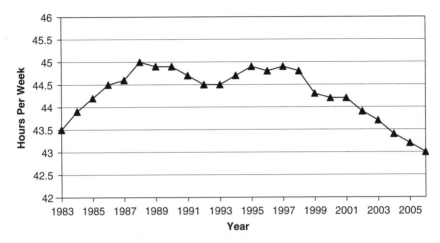

Figure 5.1: Average hours worked per week of full-time employment. UK 1983–2006. *Source*: European Commission, Eurostat Website (http://epp.eurostat.ec.europa.eu/ portal). Data derived from Labour Force Survey.

little evidence of work intensification in the latter few years of the decade according to three separate sources (Burchell & Fagan, 2002; Gallie, 2006; Green, 2006). In addition, recent evidence from the Workplace Employee Relations Surveys implies neither work intensification nor a decline in effort over the period 1998–2004 within establishments having at least 10 workers (Brown, Charlwood, Forde, & Spencer, 2006). Thus, although there remains considerable concern that effort levels were noticeably higher in 2005 than at the beginning of the 1990s, there is at least some relief, from the point of view of employees in Britain, in the finding that matters were not getting still worse.

On top of this partially optimistic finding for Britain comes another welcome development, namely the continued (if slow) decline in weekly work hours (see Figure 5.1). As can be seen, the average hours of full-time workers peaked in 1988, then again in 1997, at 45 h per week, and thereafter steadily declined to 43 h in 2006. A similar decline is found in the proportions working long hours; among males, the proportion working more than 45 h a week peaked at 39.6% in December of 1996, then fell steadily by more than 10 percentage points to 29.3% in March of 2007.[5] The fall in working time may be seen as the resumption of a historical tendency, borne of increasing affluence, that began at the height of the excesses of the industrial revolution in the mid-19th century and has continued ever since, though with several periods of stagnation. An interruption in the decline coincided with the beginning of Margaret Thatcher's new economic regime. The resumption in the mid-1990s

---

5. *Source*: Office of National Statistics, http://www.statistics.gov.uk/statbase. Note that the proportion of long-hours-working females fell only a small amount, from 10.4% to 9.6% over the same period.

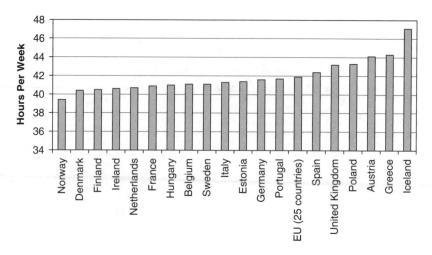

Figure 5.2: Average hours worked per week of full-time employment. Across Europe, 2005. *Source*: European Commission, Eurostat Website (http://epp.eurostat. ec.europa.eu/portal). Data derived from Labour Force Survey, can be downloaded under Population and Social Conditions theme, sub-category: Labour Market/ Employment.

pre-dated the implementation in Britain of the European Directive on Working Time, and is found even in sectors not covered by the Directive (Green, 2003); yet the Directive may have helped to consolidate the progress being made in subsequent years. One consequence of the decline in work hours is that the UK no longer holds top place for working hours in Europe among full-time workers (see Figure 5.2). That dubious honour goes to the workers of Iceland, followed by those of Greece and Austria. Since part-time workers in the UK normally work fewer hours than average, the UK overall weekly hours are not exceptional. Taking all jobs, the average weekly hours worked in the UK stood at 35.4 h in early 2007, compared with an average across the 27 European Union countries of 37.7 h.[6]

Explanations for work intensification in modern economies during the 1990s have centred on the role of technology. In previous work I have proposed the concept of "effort-biased technical change" to describe how prevailing technologies have enabled work to be redesigned in ways that facilitate hard work. In formal analyses work intensification is found to be correlated with organisational and technical innovations, while case studies abound which describe how the process occurs (Green, 2004a, 2006). New technologies can also be designed to heighten surveillance techniques on workers in what has been referred to as a modern "panoptikon". Since

---

6. *Source*: European Labour Force Survey data, reported in Romans and Hardarson (2007).

the new computerised technologies are found across most sectors and occupations, it is not surprising that work intensification is a pervasive phenomenon.

Other factors may also be in play, including the imperative to work hard owing to consumer pressures, and the decline in union power. A lesser role for unions has been matched by successive waves of organisational innovation, ushering in flexible production strategies that have taken advantage of new technologies to redesign jobs in the pursuit, as managers perceive it, of higher productivity. The problem is that managers' perceptions and interests do not necessarily comply with good job design for long-term employee well-being. These factors also apply across all sectors, though there is in principle scope for quite some differentiation. Yet analyses to date have shed no light on whether the intensification of work has been stronger in some sectors of the British economy, or indeed whether there were some sectors that escaped the trend. One aim of this article is to examine the differences across industries and occupations.

Work intensification and trends in work hours matter, because long hours and high work effort are generally thought to be detrimental to the health and well-being of workers. Good reviews about these associations are provided in Warr (2007) and in Wichert (2002). The putative effect of long hours on health has normally had the most purchase on policy. Indeed, the politics that enabled the passing of the European Union Directive on Working Time was that excessive work hours was a health and safety issue, and hence was a requirement that could be voted through without unanimity among countries. Direct legal restraints on work intensification are more difficult to devise.

However, the associations between effort and well-being, and between working time and well-being, are not thought to be linear (Warr, 2007). Employees require some stimulation from external goals, and hence at low levels their well-being can be raised by extra effort and hours. Beyond a certain point the link between effort and well-being becomes first flat then negative. In practice, numerous studies cited by Warr (2007, pp. 165–170) find that high job demands are associated with lower job satisfaction, and lower levels of well-being, while many others find that there is a very low correlation between job satisfaction and effort. The mixed nature of findings is attributed by Warr to different studies operating at different points of the curve: some at the point where extra work effort has a neutral impact on well-being, others at the point where overload has a negative effect. However, another possible cause of the mixed results should not be discounted, namely the varied methodologies and means of measurement used to investigate the effect. Studies are scarce that span the whole range of jobs and therefore capture the putative overall non-linear link between effort and well-being.

An additional factor is that the impact of effort on well-being is found, in line with the "Demand-Control" model, to be moderated by the extent to which workers have autonomy. The impact of high effort on stress and related health disorders is greatest when workers have little control over their work, and are not involved in the organisation (Theorell, 2004). The aim of Section 5.5 later is to investigate the association between effort and mental well-being, allowing both for non-linear effects and for possible interactions with worker autonomy, in the context of a nationally representative sample of jobs.

If a negative association between work effort and well-being prevails, a period of work intensification would lead, others things equal, to a decline in worker well-being. In earlier work I have shown that just such a decline is found, if one looks at the period 1992–2001. During this time there was a rise in Britain in a measure of work strain; at the same time, there was a fall in recorded overall job satisfaction, attributable in part to rising work effort and in part to declining task discretion (Gallie, Felstead, & Green, 2004; Green & Tsitsianis, 2005; Green, 2004b). However, neither overall job satisfaction, nor work strain, can be regarded as comprehensive measures of worker well-being. A more complete picture of subjective well-being at work is provided by the two axes: Enthusiasm-Depression and Contentment-Anxiety developed by Warr (1990). High job demands are typically found to be strongly negatively correlated with the Contentment-Anxiety scale, but the correlation with the Enthusiasm-Depression scale is small, of varying sign, and frequently insignificant. The reason for the latter finding may be that while high effort goes along with "feeling bad" it can also be associated with feelings of arousal. Evidence on the level and change of these measures of well-being is only available on a consistent, representative basis for the 2000s decade, during which time one might expect to find little change, if it is confirmed that effort has continued on a relatively high plateau, and if other determining variables have also remained stable. In Section 5.4 I investigate the changes in the different dimensions of worker well-being during this decade so far.

The earlier discussion has thus raised three main questions in need of further investigation. First, can it be confirmed that effort reached a plateau in Britain in the first half of the 2000s decade; and, even if this is the overall verdict, are there specific sectors or occupations in which work intensification has continued or retreated during this period? Second, what has been happening to the various dimensions of worker well-being in Britain during the period, both overall and within the different sectors? Third, in the context of the full range of jobs across all of Britain, is there an overall negative relation of work effort with well-being, and is that relationship non-linear? In particular, do any detrimental effects of work effort on well-being become greater at higher effort levels? And, is any negative effect on subjective well-being stronger according to the Contentment-Anxiety axis than it is according to the Enthusiasm-Depression axis?

5.2. Data and Description of Work Effort, Well-Being and Job Satisfaction

To address the earlier questions, we make use of data drawn from four British surveys: the Employment in Britain Survey of 1992, and the Skills Surveys of 1997, 2001 and 2006.

The Employment in Britain survey of employed people in 1992 and aged 20–60 comprised an achieved sample of 3869 individuals. Stratified random sampling was used to select households from sectors drawn from the Postal Address File. One person was interviewed face-to-face per household, chosen randomly from those that were found and eligible at each address. Weights were applied to correct for the differential probability of selection depending on the number of eligible persons at each address, and since the achieved sample slightly overrepresented women, compared with Labour Force Survey data, a second small correction was also applied, reducing the weight for women and raising the weight for men so as to match national data. Similar methods were used for the Skills Surveys. While the sampling frame for the 2006 survey extended the age range to those aged up to 65 and to Northern Ireland, for comparison purposes only those data points were used in this chapter which were located in England, Wales or Scotland, and were aged 20–60. For all three years, the analysis was confined to employees only.

Findings based on these data have the attraction of applying to the whole range of jobs to be found in a modern knowledge economy, both the so-called "good jobs" with high rewards and the lower-ranking jobs with poor quality working conditions and less prospects. Details of sampling methods and fieldwork outcomes can be found for each survey in Gallie, White, Cheng, and Tomlinson (1998), Ashton, Davies, Felstead, and Green (1999), Felstead et al. (2002) and Felstead, Gallie, Green, and Zhou (2007).

Required work effort is captured with these data through the use of three items. First, respondents were asked for the strength of their agreement or disagreement with the statement "my job requires that I work very hard"; responses were on a 4-point scale. Second, they were asked the frequency with which their work involved "working at very high speed", and, third, the frequency with which their work involved "working to tight deadlines". A principal components analysis for these three variables, pooled over 2001 and 2006, yielded one component with an eigenvector above one, which explained 56% of the variance. This component was treated as an index, Effort A, for analyses focusing on these two years. A kernel density plot of the distribution of Effort A is given in the left-hand upper quadrant of Figure 5.3. By construction the index has a mean zero but, as can be seen, there is a notable variation around this mean. I defined jobs requiring "high effort" to be jobs where Effort A is more than one standard deviation above the mean — about 18% of jobs. Among high-effort jobs, in eight out of ten cases very-high-speed working is involved "all" or "almost all" of the time; while tight deadlines are involved "all" or "almost all" of the time in nine out of ten cases; and nine out of ten job-holders "strongly agreed" that very hard work was required.

To examine effort over a longer period, bringing in the 1992 data, it was necessary to drop the item on tight deadlines which was not used in the 1992 survey. For this purpose a second index, Effort B, was created by combining the two remaining items, after standardising them, with equal weights, with an equivalent second definition of high-effort jobs.

A common method of measuring mental health in survey work is through instruments to capture affective well-being. A considerable body of research into the structure of emotions and moods has suggested that there are two substantive, though not exhaustive, dimensions, which can be labelled "arousal" and "pleasure". This structure is relevant to describing feelings arising from both work and non-work settings. Within this framework, studies have examined the merits of various

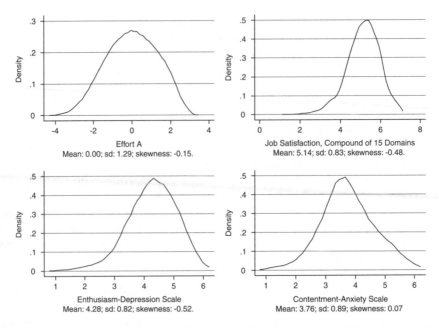

Figure 5.3: The distributions of effort, job satisfaction and well-being at work in Britain. Note: These are plots of Kernel density estimators, with widths clockwise from top left: 0.38, 0.12, 0.20 and 0.20. *Source*: Pooled data from the 2001 Skills Survey and 2006 Skills Survey. Base: employees in Britain aged 20–60.

instruments for tapping combinations of these dimensions. Relatively straightforward scales tend to be needed for occupational research, so as to gain a good balance of practicality and psychometric acceptability.

It seemed likely that the link between effort and well-being at work might be more complex than, simply, positive or negative. Rather, effort could simultaneously be associated with positive emotions such as enthusiasm and negative emotions such as anxiety. Hence there was merit in adopting Warr's two-instrument approach in the Skills Surveys and for this chapter. Warr (1990) examines and validates instruments to tap two correlated axes of affective well-being, namely "Enthusiasm-Depression" and "Contentment-Anxiety". These dimensional axes each comprise combinations of pleasure and arousal. Respondents were asked: "Thinking of the past few weeks, how much of the time has your job made you feel each of the following ...?" There followed a series of adjectives, some positive some negative. To tap Enthusiasm-Depression, the adjectives were "depressed", "gloomy", "miserable", "cheerful", "enthusiastic" and "optimistic". To tap Contentment-Anxiety the adjectives were "tense", "uneasy", "worried", "calm", "contented" and "relaxed". Responses were made against a 6-point frequency scale ranging from "never" to "all of the time". For each axis, an indicator scale was constructed by averaging responses to the six items, with the negative items reversed. The scale reliability coefficient (alpha) for the

Enthusiasm-Depression indicator was 0.803, and for the Contentment-Anxiety indicator was 0.813.[7]

Finally, I derived a compound measure of job satisfaction, averaging responses on a 7-point scale to items covering 15 different domains, including both extrinsic and intrinsic aspects of jobs as follows: promotion prospects, pay, relations with supervisor or manager, job security, the opportunity to use abilities, being able to use own initiative, the ability and efficiency of the management, hours of work, fringe benefits, the work itself, the amount of work, the variety in the work, the training provided, the friendliness of co-workers, and communications between management and employees.

The distributions of the two axes of well-being and of compound job satisfaction are also shown in Figure 5.3. The mean values of Enthusiasm-Depression and of Contentment-Anxiety are 4.28 and 3.76, respectively. As can be seen, there is a considerable variation also in the levels of subjective well-being recorded by workers across jobs in the whole of Britain. There are notable minorities experiencing especially high and others experiencing especially low levels of well-being on both scales. I define jobs with low well-being, on each scale, as being more than one standard deviation below the mean — 13% and 16% of jobs for the Enthusiasm-Contentment and Contentment-Anxiety scales respectively. The Enthusiasm-Depression scale also carries a substantive negative skewness: this means that among the low well-being jobs on this scale there are some with especially low well-being. To give one example: among the people reporting low well-being, 37% reported that their job made them feel depressed much, most or all or the time; this compares with just 1% for the rest of the population. Job satisfaction is a little more tightly concentrated around its mean than the well-being measures, but also carries a negative skewness, signalling the presence of a minority of extremely dissatisfied employees.

5.3. Effort Trends and Variation

To examine work intensification, and the distribution of effort and its trends among sectors of the economy, Tables 5.1 and 5.2 present data effort data in 1992, 2001 and 2006 broken down separately by gender, industry and major occupational group. Given that much of the literature associating work effort with well-being has concentrated on work overload, or on high demands, the data shown are the proportions experiencing high effort required in their jobs, as defined above.[8]

Table 5.1 re-confirms that there was a substantial work intensification between 1992 and 2001, approximately to the same extent for males and females. Moreover,

---

7. Scale reliability indicators of a similar magnitude are given for comparison in respect of a number of other samples in Warr (1990).
8. The pattern of change is largely similar, when results are alternatively presented in the terms of the average levels of the indices.

Table 5.1: High work effort and long hours, 1992, 2001 and 2006, by gender and by industry.

	High effort B (%)			High effort A (%)		Long hours (%)	
	1992	**2001**	**2006**	**2001**	**2006**	**2001**	**2006**
All	10.1	20.4	21.2	17.8	18.7	19.3	14.5
Males	8.6	18.2	18.3	17.0	17.1	30.0	21.6
Females	11.7	23.0	24.1	18.8	20.4	7.2	7.2
Manufacturing	10.0	16.4	19.3	17.8	19.1	22.9	20.9
Construction	12.7	20.5	20.9	18.3	20.6	30.3	21.9
Wholesale & retail	11.6	16.9	18.7	16.9	15.5	17.0	9.1
Hotels & restaurants	11.1	27.0	27.7	25.0	24.6	10.7	14.1
Transport & storage	9.9	20.1	20.6	20.0	20.6	29.4	24.7
Financial	13.4	27.3	19.9	23.7	20.2	16.6	17.4
Real estate & business services	9.0	20.3	20.3	16.5	17.0	22.3	17.4
Public administration	9.3	19.8	18.5	15.4	17.4	13.1	6.9
Education	7.3	28.2	29.4	21.4	22.6	22.9	18.4
Health & social work	11.2	21.4	23.4	15.4	20.3	8.2	6.6
Personal services	9.1	21.0	19.6	15.2	14.1	15.2	7.1

Notes: High work effort is defined as work effort more than one standard deviation above the mean. Long hours working is defined as at least 48 h a week. For definitions of Effort A and Effort B, see text. Industries are classified according to SIC92 codes. Base: Employees in Britain aged 20–60.

Table 5.2: High work effort and long hours, 1992, 2001 and 2006, by occupation.

	High effort B (%)			High effort A (%)		Long hours (%)	
	1992	**2001**	**2006**	**2001**	**2006**	**2001**	**2006**
Managers	9.6	25.9	26.3	23.9	22.9	38.8	30.6
Professionals	6.5	27.8	27	21.6	21.7	32.9	19.7
Associate professionals	12	21.7	25.5	16.7	20.9	15.0	10.1
Administrative & secretarial	12.1	20.8	18.3	16.5	16.3	3.4	3.7
Skilled trades	11.4	13	22	12.7	21	23.7	19.8
Personal service	13.4	20.2	18.1	15.3	13.9	5.2	6.6
Sales	10.6	15.9	15	12.8	11.2	3.3	3.4
Plant & machinery operatives	10.3	15.3	14.2	18.0	15.5	29.3	22.0
Elementary occupations	6.2	17.3	16	19.0	18.4	14.0	9.7

Notes: See Table 5.1. Occupations are classified by SOC2000 Major Groups.

the table indicates that there was no change in the proportions experiencing high work effort in the 2001–2006 period: though the point estimate rose by a little for females, the difference is not statistically significant. It is thus confirmed, and consistent with previous findings on other data sets though covering a somewhat earlier period, that work effort reached a plateau in the first part of the 2000s decade.

The final two columns give the percentages of employees working long hours (defined as at least 48 h per week). As can be seen in Table 5.1, the proportions fell overall in the 2001–2006 period, consistent with the previously cited data which was based on the Labour Force Survey. The Table 5.1 shows, however, that the decline in long hours working was entirely felt by males, who are in any case far more likely to be working long hours than females. For males, the fall in long-hours working was from 30% to 22%, a substantial drop in just five years.

Are these changes present in all sectors? The tables show that the intensification of effort during the 1990s took place within each industry and occupation, with the single exception of Skilled Trades, wherein work effort increased only minimally in the 1990s but substantially in the 2001–2006 period. In the latter period there was also a continued intensification within manufacturing (though the difference was only statistically significant in the case of high Effort B); meanwhile, there was a decrease in work effort in the Financial industry. There was also a marginally significant increase in work effort among Associate Professionals as a whole during 2001–2006. This finding that work intensification took place everywhere is consistent with the explanations cited earlier that the forces underlying intensification are linked to prevailing pervasive technologies or to other generic factors, rather than with the specific characteristics of the evolution of each industry.

Even though work intensification was widespread it was strongest by far in the Education sector, where the share of high-effort jobs soared from just 7.3% to 29%, that is, from the lowest-ranked to the highest-ranked industry. A more-refined analysis is possible within this sector, which shows that the greatest intensification was experienced by school teachers during the 1990s, and that effort for this group has remained exceptionally high. The proportion of teachers in high-effort jobs rose from 10.0% in 1992 to 42.3% in 2001 and to 44.2% in 2006. It seems likely that this intensification reflects the increasing demands upon the education service during the 1990s, combined with the fact of fiscal stringency which limited funds for staff expansion. The Hotels and Restaurants industry experienced the second largest intensification. Among occupations, the largest rises in work effort took place among Managers, Professionals and Associate Professionals.

Cuts in long-hours working during the 2001–2006 period are found for most groups, especially among those most prone to working long hours in the first place, such as Managers and Professionals. But, the cuts in long hours working were not universal: they did not occur either in Manufacturing or in Hotels & Catering.

Comparing effort levels across occupations and industries, it is remarkable that little of the variation in effort shown in Figure 5.1 is associated with the industrial or occupational structure. Within most industries the standard deviation hovers around 1.29, which is the standard deviation for the whole sample. The difference between the largest and smallest means of work effort within industrial groups is just 0.46, a good deal smaller than the standard deviation. As Tables 5.1 and 5.2 show, the proportion of jobs requiring high effort is relatively high in Hotels and Catering, and quite low in Sales occupations, but on the whole there is quite a small range of variation across jobs. What this means is that much of the variation in work effort cannot be accounted for in terms of major occupation groups and single-digit industries. Rather, the findings point to finer disaggregations[9] and to the characteristics of particular jobs, work establishments (and their employers) and individuals as key sources of variation.

5.4. Well-Being and Job Satisfaction

Given that work effort was on a plateau in the 2001–2006 period, one might not expect to find substantial changes in reported well-being in this time. Subjective well-being is also affected by other job design features, and in particular most strongly by discretion and autonomy in jobs. Yet, while evidence points to the fact that the 1990s decline in task discretion was halted in the early part of the 2000s (Felstead et al., 2007; Brown et al., 2006), it remains possible that other factors may have brought about significant changes to workers' emotions and feelings at the workplace.

Tables 5.3 and 5.4 examine whether there have been changes in subjective well-being over the period, either in aggregate or within particular sectors. They show that well-being has been remarkably stable in this period. There have on average been no changes in well-being, either in aggregate or among males and females separately. In both 2001 and 2006, the mean values for both Enthusiasm-Depression and Con-tentment-Anxiety do not significantly differ from their respective pooled averages noted in Figure 5.3. There were also no significant changes within individual sectors or occupations, with one exception being the Transport industry, where the proportions with low well-being fell from 20% to 11%.

Noticeable again is the comparatively small range of mean well-being across occupations or industries. As might be expected, Enthusiasm-Depression is larger in the lower-skilled occupations than among the higher-skilled occupations, a feature it shares with the proportions experiencing low job satisfaction (or high job dissatisfaction). The extent of low well-being according to the Contentment-Anxiety scale, by contrast, varies little across most occupations, though those in Management and Professional occupations are more likely than the rest to experience low well-being.

This observation, along with the similar one made above in respect of effort, implies that most of the differences in well-being are associated with the design of jobs and with personalities, rather than with the particular industry or occupation involved. As can be seen, jobs anywhere can invoke high levels of anxiety; and while low enthusiasm is somewhat more likely in the unskilled occupations, even managerial and professional occupations have their share of low enthusiasm jobs.

---

9. In addition to teachers, another significant group with a large proportion doing high-effort jobs in 2006 were nurses, paramedics and midwives (40.6%).

Table 5.3: Low worker well-being and job dissatisfaction, by gender and by industry.

	Low enthusiasm — high depression (%)		Low contentment — high anxiety (%)		Low satisfaction/high dissatisfaction (%)
	2001	2006	2001	2006	2006
All	13.6	12.8	16.0	15.4	5.1
Males	15.3	13.2	16.1	14.9	5.1
Females	11.7	12.5	16.0	16.0	5.2
Manufacturing	19.0	17.1	14.2	13.4	21.1
Construction	8.4	9.3	12.6	10.8	11.1
Wholesale & retail	14.6	13.3	15.1	11.4	14.9
Hotels & restaurants	13.8	17.2	13.6	14.7	15
Transport & storage	20.4	11.2	20.7	17.2	18.2
Financial	11.8	16.8	14.4	19.4	10
Real estate & business services	9.9	11.7	16.2	17.8	13.2
Public administration	13.8	14	16.5	16.2	9.5
Education	10.9	7.4	20.5	18.4	11.6
Health & social work	9.1	11.3	15.6	17.1	12.3
Personal services	13.1	14.5	15.3	14	12.6

Notes: Low Enthusiasm-Depression, low Contentment-Anxiety and low satisfaction are defined as being more than one standard deviation below their respective means. Base: Employees in Britain aged 20–60.

5.5. The Association between Effort and Well-Being

It follows that policy-makers concerned with improving job quality should focus evidence-based policies on the findings of occupational psychology concerning job design. High work effort is one of several factors associated with the well-being of workers. Given the work intensification that has happened in Britain and elsewhere, one would like to know as precisely as possible the links between effort and well-being on a national scale.

To address this issue, the question of non-linearity, and to identify the components of well-being potentially most affected by work intensification, Table 5.5 presents a selection of multivariate analyses of the determinants of worker well-being and job satisfaction.

Table 5.4: Low worker well-being and job dissatisfaction, by occupation.

	Low enthusiasm — high depression (%)		Low contentment — high anxiety (%)		Low satisfaction/high dissatisfaction (%)
	2001	2006	2001	2006	2006
Managers	8.7	10.9	16.9	20.3	8.8
Professionals	11.9	7.9	25.2	21.2	11.6
Associate professionals	8.4	11.6	16.1	18.6	12.1
Administrative & secretarial	16	14.4	17.6	14.7	12.8
Skilled trades	15	15	9.3	13.1	16.6
Personal service	8	10.8	11.9	10.2	10.3
Sales	15.5	14.9	16.3	9.5	16.6
Plant & machinery operatives	22.6	17.5	14.4	13.5	25.6
Elementary occupations	18.8	15.4	11.9	10.1	19.1

Note: See Table 5.3.

Column (1) confirms that the relationship between Effort A and Enthusiasm-Depression is unambiguously negative, even after controlling for several other facets of the job (including discretion, hours, gender, education, work experience and computing skills).[10] Effort was entered in a quadratic form, as a means of testing whether especially high effort (to proxy work overload) had a larger detrimental association with well-being. As can be seen, this estimate was also negative, confirming that the marginal impact of effort is greater the higher the effort. If well-being were interpreted as "utility" this finding could be seen as consistent with the assumption in economics of an increasing marginal disutility of effort, the assumption that underpins the theory of labour supply. In fact, the marginal effect of effort on well-being is negative throughout the sample range, even at very low levels of effort.

Column (2) includes an interaction term, as suggested by the Demand-Control model, between effort and task discretion. The estimated coefficient is positive and significant as predicted, showing that increases in effort have less of a detrimental

---

10. These variables were included on theoretical grounds and guided by earlier studies of well-being. In fact, the pattern of coefficients (though not their magnitudes) on effort and on effort squared was not sensitive to whether or not all these other variables were included or excluded.

Table 5.5: The relationship of work intensity with worker well-being and with job satisfaction.

	Enthusiasm-depression scale		Contentment-anxiety scale		Job satisfaction, compound of 15 domains	
	(1)	(2)	(3)	(4)	(5)	(6)
Effort A	−0.041	−0.164	−0.147	−0.236	−0.001	−0.089
	(6.19)**	(7.84)**	(21.03)**	(10.62)**	(0.14)	(3.46)**
Effort A^2	−0.009	−0.011	0.000	−0.002	−0.026	−0.028
	(2.11)*	(2.64)**	(0.02)	(0.34)	(4.90)**	(5.22)**
Task discretion times work intensity		0.057		0.041		0.041
		(6.21)**		(4.24)**		(3.60)**
Task discretion	0.278	0.278	0.171	0.171	0.405	0.405
	(21.49)**	(21.56)**	(12.41)**	(12.44)**	(25.21)**	(25.24)**
Hours per week ÷ 10	−0.101	−0.097	−0.129	−0.126	−0.152	−0.148
	(4.38)**	(4.21)**	(5.28)**	(5.16)**	(4.89)**	(4.77)**
$Hours^2 \div 100$	0.013	0.012	0.006	0.005	0.015	0.014
	(4.40)**	(4.15)**	(1.79)	(1.62)	(3.74)**	(3.58)**
Male	−0.033	−0.033	0.147	0.147	−0.044	−0.045
	(1.71)	(1.71)	(7.18)**	(7.19)**	(1.86)	(1.90)
Observations	9672	9672	9677	9677	5957	5957
R^2	0.07	0.07	0.11	0.11	0.13	0.13

Notes: These are weighted least squares estimates, using pooled data from the 2001 Skills Survey and the 2006 Skills Survey. Absolute value of *t* statistics are given in parentheses. Also included as controls in all columns were: 5 education level dummies, a quadratic in work experience, a computing skill index, 1-digit industry dummies, a dummy for 2006, and a constant term. Base: Employees in Britain aged 20–60. *Significant at 5%; **significant at 1%.

effect on well-being when discretion is high. This interaction effect is in addition to the direct positive association between discretion and well-being.

A similar pattern is found for the association between effort and the Contentment-Anxiety scale, except that in this case the estimated coefficient is larger, and there is no significant quadratic relationship. Thus, the negative association prevails across the entire range of high-effort and low-effect jobs. Again, however, the impact is alleviated by higher levels of task discretion.

In the case of job satisfaction, greater effort has an impact only through the quadratic term. This means that at below-average effort levels (that is, below zero for Effort A) higher effort is associated with greater job satisfaction; this contrasts with the previous finding that more effort is unambiguously associated with lower well-being throughout the range. This revelation serves to emphasise that job satisfaction is not a direct measure of well-being; the concept also involves workers' expectations, and it is possible that there are unobserved links between effort and expectations. Finally, as with the well-being measures, task discretion has a substantial and significant association with job satisfaction, both directly and interacting with high effort.

Long hours have also been cited as a scourge on worker well-being. However, the link between hours and the Enthusiasm-Depression scale is estimated to be quadratic: at low hours, an increase in hours is associated with lower well-being on this scale, but above 40 h a week the association becomes positive. Similarly, above 51 h a week the link between hours and job satisfaction turns upwards. A likely explanation for this finding is that long-hours workers may be getting great satisfaction from their work and that may be why they are choosing to work for more hours. In other words, the positive part of the relationship between hours and well-being might be reflecting reverse causation. Other studies reveal similar patterns in the relation between hours and satisfaction (Warr, 2007). Such reverse causation might be thought less plausible in respect of the Contentment-Anxiety scale, and here the estimated association of hours with well-being is unambiguously negative, throughout the observed sample range.

Since these estimates derive from a cross-section analysis, any inference of causation has to be tempered with the qualification that the coefficients could be biased if there is unobserved heterogeneity — that is, there may be other factors, not observed in the data, which affect both well-being and effort. It is therefore safest to record that these are estimates of partial correlations. Nevertheless the Skills Surveys are quite rich in data on job characteristics even if they do not include a comprehensive set of putative determinants of well-being.[11]

With this qualification it is instructive to ask how large are the predicted effects of effort on well-being. It is now conventional to think of "high-strain jobs" being those where the demands are high and control is low. For illustrative purposes, I take these as jobs where Effort A is high (as per the definition in Table 5.1) and where the Task

---

11. In other regressions not shown, carried out to test the robustness of the conclusions, many other job characteristics were included in the regression, but their inclusion did not alter the pattern of coefficient estimates on effort.

Discretion index is at most 2.25, the median value; in the pooled 2001/2006 sample, 9.2% of jobs were "high-strain" according to this measure. By contrast, "low-strain" jobs do not require high effort, and have above-median levels of discretion. Using the estimates in Table 5.5, columns (2) and (4), the differences predict that the two types of jobs will differ on average by 0.46 on the Enthusiasm-Depression scale and by 0.53 on the Contentment-Anxiety scale: that is, by 56% of the standard deviation on each of the two scales.[12] Thus, even though there remain other important factors affecting well-being, taken together the high effort and low discretion involved in high-strain jobs are associated with similarly-large large effects on subjective well-being in both dimensions.

The salience of the combination of high effort and low control outweighs, on these estimates, the potential impact of possible reductions in working time. While job satisfaction and both well-being dimensions are predicted to be higher for part-time workers than for full-time workers, the magnitude of the association, judging by the size of the estimated coefficients, is not all that large. As an illustration, a fall in the working week from 40 to 30 h would be associated with increases in the Enthusiasm-Depression and Contentment-Anxiety scales of 0.01 and 0.09, respectively. Suppose instead that a reduction were to occur among some full-time workers from 50 to 40 h a week. Such a fall would raise their well-being Contentment-Anxiety scale by 0.08, and would have a negligible effect on the Enthusiasm-Depression scale. Were these estimates of associations to be interpreted as estimates of causal effects, it would suggest that the small reductions in working time since the mid-1990s noted in the introduction would not, of themselves, be predicted to have had much of an impact on worker well-being.

To illustrate the practical significance of the stronger association between high-strain jobs and well-being, the growth in the proportion of "high-strain jobs" across the whole economy is shown in Figure 5.4. For the computation of Figure 5.4 the same definition of low discretion (at or below median) is combined with a dummy variable for those who "strongly agree" that their job requires them to work very hard. With this definition, the proportion of high-strain jobs rose in this period from a small beginning, roughly 1 in 11 jobs in 1992, to approximately 1 in 6 jobs (men) and 1 in 5 jobs (women) by 2001. After 2001 the proportion of "high-strain jobs" remained stable for men but for women it rose still further to encompass a quarter of jobs.[13] Thus, especially for this minority of women, the growth of high-strain jobs appears to be an ongoing phenomenon; for this minority the key problem is the combination of high required effort in the job, and a low level of task discretion.

---

12. An alternative comparison would be with "passive" jobs, involving low effort and low control; these yield, relative to high-strain jobs, predicted reductions in the Enthusiasm–Depression and Contentment–Anxiety scales of 0.20 and 0.40, respectively.

13. A remarkably similar growth pattern is found in Sweden, with the rise of high-strain jobs being more persistent for women than for men (Wikman, 2005). It is also interesting to note the findings of Gorman and Kmec (2007), that both in the US and in the UK women's work effort is greater than men's, which, they argue, reflects stricter performance standards for women.

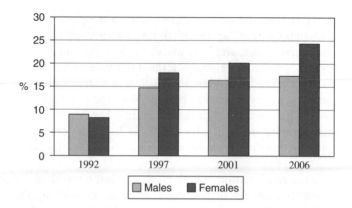

Figure 5.4: Proportion of high-strain jobs, by sex. *Note*: A high-strain job is defined as having high required effort and low task discretion.

5.6.   Conclusion

Among the sicknesses and other horrors of the world that the unfortunate Pandora unleashed from her box, hard work might seem of itself the least unbearable; but it has become a persistent problem in supposedly affluent countries that have conquered many of the other diseases of poverty that escaped her box. Work intensification has been found in very many industrialised countries in the recent era, and became one of the defining features of the 1990s. Yet there are countries where work effort has stabilised during the first half of the 2000s, or even declined. There has also been a renewal of the historical decline in working hours, including a substantive fall in the instance of long-hours working in Britain.

The new analyses presented here have confirmed the intensification of work during the 1990s in Britain, while updating to 2006 the finding that in recent years effort has been travelling on a high plateau, neither rising nor falling significantly. Despite that stability, high effort remains a cause for concern; moreover, the proportion of women in "high-strain" jobs continued to rise in recent years, according at least to the measure utilised in this chapter.

Over the whole 1992–2006 period it has been found that work intensification was pervasive in all sections of industry and in all occupations. Nevertheless, some groups fared differently. School teachers are one large group who experienced an especially strong intensification during the 1990s, a finding which may well be related to the expanded demand for education combined with fiscal stringency during that period. Among occupations generally, it was those at the top — in Managers and Professional occupations — who experienced the largest rises in work effort.

I have also reported benchmark figures for measures of well-being along the Enthusiasm-Depression scale and the Contentment-Anxiety scale for Britain as a whole. There were no significant recorded changes in the averages for either of these well-being measures during the 2001–2006 period.

New estimates of the link between effort and well-being confirm that the association between effort and both measures is negative throughout the range of jobs. In the case of Enthusiasm-Depression, the magnitude of marginal increases in effort on well-being increases as effort becomes higher. The effect of effort on both dimensions of well-being is alleviated in jobs where there is high task discretion. Taking effort and task discretion together, the estimates suggest that the design of a job as a high-strain job, compared with a low-strain job, would make a big difference to the well-being of the job-holder, relative to the existing distribution of well-being. This effect is substantively larger than would be predicted by a large cut in work hours, for example from 40 to 30 h a week.

If the fall in work hours persists for another decade it should have some positive effects on well-being, but the evidence suggests that weekly hours reductions could not be expected in themselves to be greatly beneficial for workers. This finding points in different directions for the development of working-time policies, including the improved matching of working time to employee preferences through, among other routes, the further development of work-life balance strategies.[14] In contrast, any policies that can lead to decent reductions in work overload during existing work hours are likely to have a notable beneficial effect on subjective well-being. Moreover, strategies to improve job design, for example to facilitate greater levels of autonomy and discretion (with associated levels of high trust), would reduce the deleterious impact of high work loads. It is the combination of high work loads and low autonomy workplaces which is most conducive to stress, and unfortunately this combination was growing during the 1990s and, for women, continued to do so in the 2000s. We urgently need to find ways, not just to limit the spread of high-strain jobs but to reverse the trend, if we are to conquer this modern disease.

References

Ashton, D., Davies, B., Felstead, A., & Green, F. (1999). *Work skills in Britain*. Oxford: SKOPE, Oxford and Warwick Universities.

Askenazy, P., Cartron, D., Coninck, F. d., & Gollac, M. (Eds). (2007). *Organisation et intensité du travail*. Toulouse: OCTARÈS Éditions.

Bloom, N., Kretschmer, T., & Reenen, J. V. (2006). *Work life balance, management practices and productivity*. Discussion Paper, Centre for Economic Performance, London School of Economics, London.

Brown, A., Charlwood, A., Forde, C., & Spencer, D. (2006). *Changing job quality in Great Britain 1998–2004*. London: Department of Trade and Industry.

Burchell, B., & Fagan, C. (2002). *Gender and the iIntensification of work: Evidence from the 2000 European Working Conditions Survey*. Conference on Work Intensification, Centre D'Etudes De L'Emploi, 22–23 November, Paris.

---

14. The evidence suggests that work-life balance strategies are not associated with lower productivity (Bloom, Kretschmer, & Reenen, 2006).

Erlandsson, A. (2007). Une rationalistion descendante dans la livraison du courrier et ses effets à court terme. In: P. Askenazy, D. Cartron, F. d. Coninck & M. Gollac (Eds), *Organisation et intensité du travail.* Toulouse: OCTARÈS Éditions.

European Foundation for the Improvement of Living and Working Conditions. (2007). *Fourth European Working Conditions Survey.* Luxembourg: Office for Official Publications of the European Communities.

Felstead, A., Gallie, D., & Green, F. (2002). *Work skills in Britain 1986–2001.* Nottingham: DfES Publications.

Felstead, A., Gallie, D., Green, F., & Zhou, Y. (2007). *Skills at work, 1986 to 2006.* University of Oxford: SKOPE.

Gallie, D. (2006). L'intensification du travail en Europe 1996–2001? In: P. Askenazy, D. Cartron, F. d. Coninck & M. Gollac (Eds), *Organisation et intensité du travail.* Toulouse: OCTARÈS Éditions.

Gallie, D., Felstead, A., & Green, F. (2004). Changing patterns of task discretion in Britain. *Work, Employment and Society, 18*(2), 243–266.

Gallie, D., White, M., Cheng, Y., & Tomlinson, M. (1998). *Restructuring the employment relationship.* Oxford: Clarendon Press.

Gorman, E. H., & Kmec, J. A. (2007). We (have to) try harder. Gender and required work effort in Britain and the United States. *Gender & Society, 21*(6), 828–856.

Green, F. (2001). It's been a hard day's night: The concentration and intensification of work in late twentieth-century Britain. *British Journal of Industrial Relations, 39*(1), 53–80.

Green, F. (2003). The demands of work. In: R. Dickens, P. Gregg & J. Wadsworth (Eds), *The labour market under new labour. The state of working Britain 2003* (pp. 137–149). Basingstoke: Palgrave Macmillan.

Green, F. (2004a). Why has work effort become more intense? *Industrial Relations, 43,* 709–741.

Green, F. (2004b). Work intensification, discretion and the decline in well-being at work. *Eastern Economic Journal, 30*(4), 615–626.

Green, F. (2006). *Demanding work. The paradox of job quality in the affluent economy.* Woodstock: Princeton University Press.

Green, F., & McIntosh, S. (2001). The intensification of work in Europe. *Labour Economics, 8*(2), 291–308.

Green, F., & Tsitsianis, N. (2005). An investigation of national trends in job satisfaction in Britain and Germany. *British Journal of Industrial Relations, 43*(3), 401–430.

Lehto, A.-M., & Sutela, H. (2005). *Threats and opportunities. Findings of Finnish quality of work life surveys 1977–2003.* Helsinki: Statistics Finland.

Merllié, M., & Paoli, P. (2001). *Ten years of working conditions in the European Union.* Dublin: European Foundation for the Improvement of Living and Working Conditions.

Morehead, A., Steele, M., Alexander, M., Stephen, K., & Duffin, L. (1997). *Changes at work: The 1995 Australian Workplace Industrial Relations Survey.* Sydney: Longman.

Romans, F., & Hardarson, O. S. (2007). *Labour market latest trends. 1st quarter 2007 data.* Brussels: Eurostat.

Theorell, T. (2004). Democracy at work and its relationship to health. In: P. L. Perrewé & D. C. Ganster (Eds), *Emotional and physiological processes and positive intervention strategies.* Amsterdam: Elsevier.

Warr, P. (1990). The measurement of well-being and other aspects of mental health. *Journal of Occupational Psychology, 63,* 193–210.

Warr, P. (2007). *Work, happiness, and unhappiness.* London: Lawrence Erlbaum Associates.

Wichert, I. (2002). Job insecurity and work intensification: The effects on health and well-being. In: B. Burchell, D. Lapido & F. Wilkinson (Eds), *Job insecurity and work intensification* (pp. 92–111). London: Routledge.

Wikman, A. (2005). Work Environment Statistics in Sweden. European Foundation for the Improvement of Living and Working Conditions.

Chapter 6

Working Time for Married Couples in 28 Countries

Carla Medalia and Jerry A. Jacobs

Gender roles continue to change throughout the world as reflected in women's labor force participation, educational attainment, age at marriage, divorce rates and fertility levels. Because countries vary in the speed and nature of these transformations, a comparative approach is particularly well suited to studying them. By employing a cross-national analysis, recent research on work and the family has improved our understanding of how the gendered division of paid labor affects the family and society. The time spent on the job by various family members affects the character and extent of work-family conflict as well as gender inequality within the family and economy. While most research in this area focuses on a small sample of mostly industrial countries, this study casts a wider net.

In their analysis of 10 countries, Jacobs and Gornick (2002) and Jacobs and Gerson (2004), examined the length of the workweek for married couples as well as individuals (see also Nock & Kingston, 1988). Furthermore, they reported the fraction of individuals and couples who put in especially long workweeks. Like many studies on working time, the sample of countries they analyzed was limited to all highly developed and industrialized nations in North America and Western Europe. In the current study, we include countries from Eastern Europe, Asia, the Middle East and Latin America along with Western Europe and North America.

Working time is important to study for three reasons. First, the amount of time spent on paid work is one of the key predictors of work-family conflict. This relationship is especially important to examine as women enter the labor force in greater numbers and working time globally is changing for both sexes. Second, unequal amounts of working time for men and women are associated with gender inequality in the labor market and in the home. Therefore, studying working time for individuals and couples is important in order to understand how gender inequality is reduced or reproduced. Finally, many countries have advocated reduced working hours as a tool for lowering unemployment and distributing labor demands more equitably.

The Long Work Hours Culture
Copyright © 2008 by Emerald Group Publishing Limited
All rights of reproduction in any form reserved
DOI:10.1016/B978-1-84855-038-4.00006-3

6.1. Theoretical Considerations

6.1.1. Work-Family Conflict

Work-family conflict refers to situations in which "the role pressures from the work and family domains are mutually incompatible in some respect" (Greenhaus & Beutell, 1985, p. 77). Work-family conflict occurs in two directions: work-to-family conflict occurs when work demands make functioning in the family role difficult, and is characterized by family absences, poor family-role performance, family dissatisfaction and distress. Family-to-work conflict occurs when family demands make it difficult to fulfill employee responsibilities, and is associated with absenteeism from work, tardiness, poor job performance, job dissatisfaction and distress (Voydanoff, 2005, p. 707). In the most extreme manifestation, the spillover from work-to-family can lead to divorce, while the spillover from family-to-work can result in dismissal from one's job.

Three types of work demands are known to influence work-family conflict. Time-based demands are the first type, and occur when work time and schedule conflict with the needs of the family. Non-standard work schedules can also disrupt family life. Thus, working schedules that require evening, night or weekend work can be particularly challenging to working families. Rotating and unpredictable schedules can also be disruptive making childcare arrangements difficult to secure (Presser, 2003). Thus, while we focus on the length of the workweek, it is important to keep in mind that this is just one of several different ways that the time constraints of jobs can affect family life.

The second type, strain-based demands, arises when work stressors produce strain and lead to the inability to fulfill the demands of the family. Finally, the third type is behavior-based demands, noted when patterns of behavior in one role conflict with the need for a different type of behavior in another role. For example, a working mother's adoption of the behavior pattern of a "Type A" executive could come into conflict with the family's need for a warm mother figure.

Of these three types of work demands, much support has been found for the time-based model which explains that working hours are related to work-family conflict. Furthermore, time-based demands are easily measured by working hours. Therefore, in this study, we focus on time-based work demands. If such demands are critical predictors of work-family conflict, then it is important to understand how working time varies across countries.

Specifically, working long hours is related to greater work-family conflict for both men and women (Barnett & Gareis, 2002; Jacobs & Gerson, 2004; van der Lippe, Jager, & Kops, 2006; Wharton & Blair-Loy, 2006). Other research indicates that overtime work, in particular mandatory overtime work, increases work-family conflict (Golden & Wiens-Tuers, 2006). For women who work long hours, experiences of work-family conflict are lessened by the amount of housework husbands do (Barnett & Gareis, 2002). The number of children at home exacerbates work-family conflict (Lundberg, Mardberg, & Frankenhaeuser, 1994; Noor, 2003; Wharton & Blair-Loy, 2006). Age also has a relationship to work-family conflict, with role conflict peaking between the ages of 35 and 39 (Lundberg et al., 1994). Socio-economic status, and education level in particular, has not been found to be related to work-family conflict *per se*, although these factors can affect the nature and extent of job demands (Jacobs & Gerson, 2004; Rice, Frone, & McFarlin, 1992).

While long work hours are associated with a greater likelihood of experiencing work-family conflict, limited working time has been linked to better family outcomes. In a study on couples, Hill et al. (2006) found that the division of work hours between the partners is not as important as the combined number of hours worked by the couple. Couples who work no more than a total of 60 hours per week report significantly greater job flexibility, improved work-family fit, enhanced family satisfaction and less work-to-family conflict.

Many studies have shown how work-family conflict is influenced by gender, though results are mixed. Although women are entering the labor force in increasing numbers, gendered conceptions regarding domestic tasks and childcare remain a part of many cultures cross-nationally. As a result, some studies have shown that women, more than men, are at risk for experiencing work-family conflict (Wharton & Blair-Loy, 2006). However, not all research indicates that women bear the brunt of work-family conflict. Tang and Cousins (2005) found that men experience more work-family conflict regardless of national context. In Western European countries where mothers work part-time hours and are primary caregivers, men report higher levels of work-family conflict. In Eastern European countries where both men and women work full time jobs but where women are still responsible for childcare, men still report experiencing greater work-family conflict.[1]

6.1.2. Gender Inequality

The amount of time spent in the labor market plays a central role in individuals' earnings prospects. Because money is such a central feature of modern societies, working in the labor market increases one's relative power within the family. Thus, working time shapes the extent of gender inequality within the home and in the larger national context. The effect of working time on power is apparent when analyzing the division of housework. A prominent theory on the division of housework, the bargaining model, argues that time spent in the labor market is more valuable than time spent on household chores. Because economic independence is more transferable than skills in the domestic domain, it results in the worker being less dependent on his or her partner (Iversen & Rosenbluth, 2006). Less dependence on one's partner is associated with holding the dominant power in the relationship,

---

1. This paradox may be resolved when the different types of work-family conflict are distinguished. Thus, it may be that men experience job demands that disrupt family life, while women experience more spillover from family to work (Kmec, 1999).

which in turn affects household decision-making, the distribution of housework and other aspects of family life. Because men are more likely to engage in paid work, they typically hold the larger share of power in their familial relationships.

Gender inequality within the home is important because of its connection to the larger national context. Countries with a more equitable division of time spent on housework are also characterized by high proportions of females in the labor force, higher levels of female representation in the government, and more gender egalitarian attitudes.

The relationship between gender inequality in the home and at the national level cuts both ways. First, the division of housework is influenced by several elements of the national context. For example, Hook (2006) and Fuwa (2004) found that countries with more family-friendly social policies, such as the Scandinavian countries and other welfare states, are also characterized by more widespread gender egalitarian ideals and practices. These studies concluded that the degree of gender equality is positively associated with a more egalitarian division of housework, providing support for the gender ideology/socialization perspective regarding the division of housework. Second, gender inequality within the home may "have enduring consequences that contribute to longer-term inequalities in earnings and reinforce patterns of gender segregation in jobs and occupations" (Jacobs & Gerson, 2004, p. 124). Women's earning opportunities in turn can affect their standard of living during retirement (Meyer, 1990) and in cases of divorce (Smock, Manning, & Gupta, 1999). Therefore, studying how working time is divided along gendered lines is important to understanding how greater gender inequalities are reproduced on multiple levels.

6.1.3.   Unemployment

Efforts to reduce unemployment have taken several forms across the world (Went, 2000). For example, in the Netherlands in the 1980s, two new measures were taken to tackle rising unemployment rates. The first effort was a reduction in wages, with the intention of increasing profits which would supposedly result in the addition of new jobs. The second technique was the shortening of the workweek, forcing employers to create new jobs in order to accomplish the workload previously done by fewer employees. These attempts were called the "Third Way," and have had mixed results for the Dutch economy. While employment rates increased by almost 50 percent between 1984 and 2001, unemployment rates have remained relatively static.

To explain this paradox, Spithoven (2002) suggests that the part of the answer may lie in the effect of this legislation on individual workers' productivity. Specifically, he argues that "workers were prodded to complete the former volume of work in less time" (Spithoven, 2002, p. 351). In this way, reduced hours legislation, while it often fails to meet its stated goal of increasing employment, can nonetheless have a positive effect on per-worker economic output. Historian Chris Nyland (1989) finds that this pattern of increased productivity is typical of historical efforts to reduce the length of the workweek.[2]

6.1.4. Cross-National Working Time

Before delving into the analysis at hand, we will outline findings from previous research on working time in various national contexts. The figures we present come from a variety of different sources; while most are from in-depth assessments of individual countries, a few are from large cross-national surveys. Whatever the source, the information is important to place our findings in an established context.

Cross-national data on working time are available from three main sources: Eurostat, the International Labour Organization (ILO) and the Organization for Economic Cooperation and Development (OECD). Below we compare our estimates to those obtained from some of these official reports in order to assess the reliability of the International Social Survey Programme (ISSP) data (Haroarson, 2004).

Some reports (for example, some OECD reports) focus on the total number of hours worked per year in a country. While there is a certain logic to this measure, we feel it is problematic because it combines variation in vacations with the length of the workweek. A single measure for a country also has the disadvantage of combining men and women, and full-time and part-time workers. We prefer more detailed measures that are not fully aggregated to the level of individual countries (see Jacobs & Gerson, 2004, for a more complete discussion of this issue). Other reports (Eurostat and ILO) differentiate between male and female workers. By drawing on micro-data that can be analyzed more fully, we are able to delve further into questions pertaining to working time. In particular, we combine the working time of husbands and wives to give an indication of how busy dual career couples are in different countries. We move the analysis another step forward by examining the prevalence of long workweeks for individuals and couples.

Studies by Jacobs and Gornick (2002) and Jacobs and Gerson (2004) illustrated patterns of working time in 10 Western European and North American countries. Drawing on data from the third or fourth waves of the Luxembourg Income Study (LIS), which were executed between 1991 and 1997, Jacobs and Gornick found that American couples worked more than any other country in their sample, while couples in the Netherlands worked the least. The two Scandinavian countries in their sample, Sweden and Finland had the highest proportion of couples where both partners were employed, while Great Britain had a low proportion of married women in the labor force.

Because American working time falls at the high end of the spectrum, we will review Jacobs and Gornick's other findings about the United States. First,

---

2. Spithoven also notes that other regulations, such as new disability laws which exempted more people from having to work, were introduced at the same time, making it more difficult to assess the unique effects of the shorter hours legislation.

respondents from the United States work long average workweeks; in particular, the working time for women stands out among the other countries in their study. Second, a high proportion of employees work very long hours, with 12 percent of dual earner couples working 100 h or more per week. The United States has the third highest proportion of dual earner couples in the sample, though as discussed, not as high as the Scandinavian countries. Third, wives' working time in the United States is about 20 percent less than their husbands. This figure is greater than the average for the sample; Finnish wives work only 7 percent less than their husbands while Dutch wives work about half as many hours as their husbands. Finally, Jacobs and Gornick discuss the effect of parental status on dual earner couples. While both parents and childless couples work the longest hours in the United States, the impact of parenting differs for mothers and fathers. On average, mothers work about 8.5 fewer hours per weeks than wives without children, while men's working time remains approximately constant. Therefore, the authors conclude that gender equality with respect to working time is greater for women without children in the United States.

Based on the findings of recent research on working time (Bonney, 2005; Jacobs & Gerson, 2004), we predict that working time for British respondents will fall close to the average cross-nationally, despite common perceptions that the British work particularly long hours (Bonney, 2005).

In addition to studying the United States and Western Europe, we will analyze several Eastern European countries, countries in Asia, Latin America and the Middle East. Therefore, it is important to understand general employment patterns in some of those areas before analyzing them cross-nationally.

Eastern Europe's history of communism has led to a different configuration of the labor market than found in Western Europe. Tang and Cousins (2005) reported that both men and women work in high proportions in the Eastern European countries they studied, the Czech Republic, Romania and Hungary. Despite women's long history in the work force, women are still responsible for childcare, placing on them a double burden.

In their study of the Israeli labor force, Cohen and Stier (2006) found an increase in the number of "involuntary part time jobs." When part time jobs are involuntary, it is because the labor market supports part time jobs, forcing workers, regardless of preference for full time jobs, to work part time. Women are more likely than men to be forced into jobs with fewer hours than they prefer. Therefore, we expect to see high proportions of Israeli women working fewer hours per week than in other countries.

In response to the economic crisis and recession in Asia, the labor force participation rate in the Philippines underwent a change. While the unemployment rate for men increased, women entered the labor force in increasing numbers and began to work longer workweeks (Lim, 2000). However, the effect of increased female labor force participation on gender equality is ambiguous, and some argue that the changes did not necessarily lead to greater gender equality for Filipino women, but may actually have decreased their economic status and welfare.

6.2. Data and Methods

This analysis draws on data obtained from the 2002 ISSP: Family and Changing Gender Roles III. The ISSP is a collection of comparable national surveys from countries around the world compiled into one dataset, allowing for cross-national comparisons. The 2002 ISSP asks a broad range of questions about the respondent and the respondent's partner, including questions that consider attitudes toward women in the labor market, the division of housework between partners, weekly hours in the labor market, the degree of control the respondent exercises in making family decisions, income, family composition and other demographic information. The original dataset includes over 45,000 individuals, aged 15–96, from 34 countries.

Because working time is the central focus in this study, we limited the analysis to 28 countries for which there is information regarding the working time for the respondent and his/her partner. Furthermore, the sample was limited to include only the prime working-age population, respondents between the ages of 18 and 64. The countries included in the final analysis are listed in appendix Table 6.A.1, which also provides information on the survey data and the sample size. In most of the countries, the surveys were conducted in 2002 and 2003, with Bulgaria (2001) fielding their survey first and Austria (2003–2004) last in our group.

6.2.1. Measures

The dependent variable in this study is hours of paid work per week. Information on working hours was provided by one respondent per household, who answered questions about both her and her partner's working hours. For the majority of the analysis, we examine only respondents and/or their partners who engaged in at least 1 h of paid labor per week. We examine the workweek from the point of view of individuals as well as the joint hours of paid work of couples. We also report findings on the proportion of individuals in each country who put in especially long workweeks, namely those working 50 or more hours per week.

For the analysis at the level of the couple, we examine respondents who say they are either married (and living as married) or cohabiting (living as married without being officially married). These measures were combined into one variable that indicates whether a respondent has a partner for four reasons. First, a few countries posed the question in such a way that the respondent is asked whether they are "married *or* living as married," as opposed to married *and* living as married, making it difficult to distinguish between marriage and cohabitation. Second, because of the complications surrounding legal marital status in different parts of the world, the meaning of a married individual would vary cross-nationally. Third, we are interested in the joint working time of couples, regardless of the legality of their union. Finally, we calculated average working hours separately for married and cohabiting respondents where possible, and the results were not significantly different.

At the level of couple, we combine both the respondent's and his partner's work hours if at least one of them works a minimum of 1 h per week. We then control for whether both the respondent and partner work, measured by a dummy variable for dual earner status, and whether the couple are parents of children under the age of 17. In addition, we created a categorical variables based on the combined working hours of dual earner couples that indicates whether they work short (less than 80 joint hours per week), moderate (80–99 h) or long (100 h or more) workweeks.

6.3.   Results

6.3.1.   Individual Level Analysis

As the issue of working time is most pressing in the context of dual earner couples, we begin by describing patterns of women's labor force participation. Table 6.1 shows the percentage of women and men who are in the labor force in each of the sample countries. The countries are sorted by the percent of women in the labor force.

Across all of the countries in our sample, the average labor force participation rate for women is 66 percent. However, the proportion of respondents currently in the labor force varies greatly and differs by gender. Women's labor force participation varies from about 50 percent in Brazil, Chile and Hungary to 80 percent in New Zealand and Sweden. To the extent that family life is influenced by women's employment patterns, these data suggest that the pace of family life varies markedly across our sample of countries.

Two quite different groups of countries share the lead in women's labor force participation. The Nordic countries, including Sweden, Denmark and Finland, have long encouraged women's participation in the economy; in each of these countries, women participate in the labor force at relatively high rates. However, the same pattern can be observed in several countries that emphasize an unconstrained labor market. In particular, Great Britain, the United States and New Zealand, have high rates of women's labor force participation based on social arrangements that differ noticeably from the Nordic pattern.

We were somewhat surprised to see low rates of women's labor force participation in some Eastern European countries such as Hungary, given the historically high rates of women's employment in socialist economies. This pattern may reflect the secondary position women have taken in the transition from socialist to market economies (e.g. Plomien, 2006; Pollert, 2003).

The data in Table 6.1 remind us that not all men in their prime working years are employed. Men's labor force participation rate averages 83 percent, and exceeds 70 percent in all of the countries in the sample. Men's labor force participation rate exceeds that for women in all of the countries in our sample. There is a weak positive association between men's and women's labor force participation ($r = .35$). As a result, in some countries, such as the Nordic countries, men's and women's labor force

Table 6.1: Proportion of sample with characteristics by country.

	Labor force participation rate						
	Females	**Males**	**Single females**	**Partnered females**	**Single males**	**Partnered males**	**Percent with partners**
Sweden	80.1	84.9	72.6	83.7	73.5	89.7	74.1
New Zealand	78.5	93.8	87.7	75.5	86.8	95.6	76.5
Denmark	76.5	80.9	63.6	81.3	62.7	87.4	72.8
Great Britain	74.0	83.9	74.3	73.8	80.0	86.1	65.6
USA	72.4	87.4	75.5	70.1	82.6	91.3	56.7
Finland	71.5	81.0	70.6	71.8	68.6	84.9	71.9
Switzerland	71.1	88.9	76.4	68.6	81.0	92.6	69.4
France	70.2	76.4	68.7	71.1	76.6	76.4	77.2
Cyprus	69.9	88.3	64.3	70.6	68.6	98.9	67.5
Latvia	68.7	80.9	63.6	72.4	60.7	90.8	62.2
Norway	67.8	82.7	57.1	71.1	64.5	88.3	76.5
Israel	67.7	80.8	57.1	72.5	67.7	87.9	73.1
Portugal	67.7	85.4	64.8	69.0	82.1	87.5	63.6
Russia	67.6	79.9	60.8	67.2	70.3	84.9	61.0
Bulgaria	67.5	76.7	52.3	73.0	66.7	80.1	74.5
Belgium	67.3	83.3	57.2	70.6	69.3	88.9	72.9
Poland	67.3	77.4	59.9	70.7	68.7	82.8	65.1
The Netherlands	66.3	83.8	72.7	63.4	80.6	85.3	68.8
Taiwan	62.7	89.7	70.1	58.9	79.2	96.1	64.2
Mexico	61.5	88.2	69.3	58.6	84.3	92.1	68.9
Philippines	60.9	85.9	59.8	61.0	69.9	93.0	73.9
Austria	59.7	79.8	60.6	59.1	76.3	81.9	62.7
Spain	59.2	84.3	67.7	54.6	77.9	89.0	61.1
Germany	56.5	79.3	62.1	55.4	69.1	82.9	78.0
Japan	51.9	88.0	60.8	49.2	72.7	94.6	73.5
Hungary	50.4	71.8	74.6	51.8	57.4	78.7	66.8
Chile	48.4	89.8	58.4	42.0	79.8	95.6	62.1
Brazil	45.4	69.9	54.1	39.5	64.4	73.4	63.1
Average	65.3	83.0	65.6	65.2	72.9	87.7	68.7

participation rates are quite similar. In other countries, such as Japan, Chile, Japan, Taiwan and Mexico, women's labor force participation trails far behind that of men.

The last column in Table 6.1 shows the proportion of respondents with a partner by country. The average proportion of respondents with a partner across all countries is 69 percent, with most countries falling into the 60–80 percent range. The United States stands out as having a particularly low percentage of the adult population with partners, owing to a combination of late marriage and a high divorce rate.

We now turn to the length of the workweek. Table 6.2 shows the average hours worked per week by sex and country. Across all countries, the average workweek for men is approximately 45 hours per week. There is nonetheless variation around this average, with country level means ranging from just over 37 hours per week in the Netherlands to over 52 hours per week in Chile. In 19 out of the 28 countries, the average workweek for men is tightly clustered around the average, falling within a 5-hour range between 41 and 46 hours per week.

Table 6.2: Working hours by country and sex.

	Average work hours per week		Percent working 50 hours +	
	Female	Male	Female	Male
Philippines	42.6	44.3	29.7	31.2
Taiwan	46.2	49.7	26.0	37.0
Chile	42.8	51.8	25.8	40.7
Mexico	40.4	47.6	24.0	35.8
Poland	42.7	49.0	21.9	39.7
Hungary	42.4	49.5	21.6	49.8
USA	38.9	45.3	18.7	36.1
Bulgaria	41.8	45.1	16.5	24.2
Brazil	39.2	45.8	16.3	29.6
Latvia	40.4	45.2	14.0	30.3
Japan	34.3	49.8	11.3	51.5
Great Britain	33.7	45.5	10.9	33.2
Russia	38.6	43.9	10.9	23.3
Portugal	38.7	45.1	10.1	24.5
Austria	35.3	43.5	10.0	24.1
Germany	36.3	45.6	9.5	30.6
New Zealand	32.1	44.1	8.6	36.0
Spain	35.5	43.0	7.4	23.5
Belgium	32.5	43.3	7.3	22.6
Switzerland	32.0	44.3	7.3	24.8
Israel	32.0	45.2	7.2	41.2
France	34.6	42.0	5.6	19.2
Norway	33.9	42.8	5.4	24.0
Sweden	36.0	40.2	4.3	12.9
Denmark	35.8	41.6	4.1	18.6
Finland	35.2	39.7	1.7	13.8
Cyprus	38.6	42.2	1.3	11.9
The Netherlands	25.2	37.3	0.8	8.7
Average	37.1	44.7	12.1	28.5

Most of the countries at the high end of the spectrum are relatively poor. For example, men in Chile, Taiwan and Mexico work particularly long workweeks compared to most other countries in the sample. Several Eastern European countries also have relatively long workweeks. Poland and Hungary exemplify this pattern in our sample of countries. Of the richest countries, Japan, Great Britain and the United States are at the high end of the spectrum in terms of the length of men's workweek. For all of the extensive attention paid to the 35-hour workweek in France, it should be noted that men in France typically work just under 42 hours per week, much in line with their counterparts in other countries.

The average workweek for women is shorter than for men in each of the countries in our sample. Women work seven fewer hours for pay on average than do men. In addition, there is more variability across countries in the length of women's workweek. For women, there are eight countries where the average workweek exceeded 40 hours. These included several developing countries: Taiwan, Chile, Mexico and the Philippines. Women also tend to put in long hours in Eastern Europe: Hungary, Poland, Latvia and Bulgaria fit this pattern.

At the other end of the spectrum, there were 7 countries where women work less than 35 hours per week: Japan, Great Britain, Israel, Switzerland, New Zealand, Belgium, Norway, France and the Netherlands. The Netherlands has the shortest workweek for women; it is the only country in our sample where women average less than 30 hours per week on the job.

In general, countries with long workweeks for men also tend to have long workweeks for women. Overall, the correlation between the length of the workweek for men and women is .65. However, there are notable exceptions to this pattern which result in marked cases of gender specialization.

Across the countries in our analysis, the gender gap in the length of the workweek varies markedly. Countries where the gender gap in the length of the workweek is particularly large — 10 hours or more – include Japan, Israel, the Netherlands, New Zealand and Switzerland. Great Britain just misses this cutoff, with British men working almost 10 hours per week more than women. Our findings suggest that a variety of policies and cultures can generate a gendered outcome in the length of the workweek.

Other countries in this sample have a relatively small gender gap in the length of the workweek — less than 5 hours. In a number of instances, these are relatively poor countries where both women and men are expected to contribute to the family income. These countries include Taiwan, the Philippines and Cyprus, as well as several Eastern European countries. Latvia and Bulgaria represent an Eastern European pattern where both employed men and women tend to work in full time jobs. Poland, Hungary and Russia do not quite meet the 5-hour-per-week gap but are not far from it. In the more affluent countries, it is the Nordic model where the gender gap in the length of the workweek is smaller, as exemplified by Sweden and Finland.

The ISSP data on the length of the workweek are reasonably close to the statistics provided by the ILO 2007. We examined the correlation of the average workweeks for the 20 countries included in both data sources (data not shown; results available from the authors). The association was strong for both women ($r = .84$) and men ($r = .78$). For men, the workweek is generally somewhat longer in the ISSP data: the ISSP workweek for men is more than 4 hours longer than that reported in the ILO data for nine countries: Austria, Spain, Belgium, Great Britain, Norway, Portugal, Poland, New Zealand and Chile. For women, only Poland and Portugal have a discrepancy of more than 4 hours per week (again, the ISSP workweek is longer).

Another way to look at working patterns for individuals is to examine the proportion working long hours, measured by the proportion working 50 hours or more per week (also shown in Table 6.2). This indicator begins to zero in on the issue of over-worked individuals. In other words, country averages reflect the typical workweek but also include those who may work part-time. Focusing on those individuals who work 50 hours per week or more gives us a better sense of the prevalence of long workweeks.

While Chile has the longest average workweek for men, Japan and Hungary possess the largest share of men working long hours, approximately 50 percent of employed men. Chilean men still have a large proportion working very long hours, at 41 percent of working men. The Netherlands has the smallest proportion working 50 hours or more per week for both men and women, at just 9 and 1 percent, respectively.

In general, women are less likely to work more than 50 hours for pay than are their male counterparts (of course, adding unpaid labor devoted to housework and child care would change this conclusion). The Philippines stands out as having the highest fraction of women working 50 hours or more per week, followed by Taiwan, Chile, Mexico, Poland and Hungary. In each of these six countries, more than one in five women puts in more than 50 hours per week on the job. Of the most affluent countries, the United States just trails this group at 19 percent. In Great Britain, 11 percent of women work more than 50 hours per week for pay, which is about average for this sample of countries.

6.3.2.   Couple Level Analysis

We have suggested that the issue of busy lives can best be understood in the context of how busy families are. Thus, a 45-hour workweek for a husband of a stay-at-home wife has a very different meaning than if the wife is herself employed full time. Therefore, our analysis now turns to the workweeks of couples.

These results are presented in Table 6.3. The first important point is that the percentage of dual earner couples varies by country, ranging from just one-quarter to almost the entire sample. In the majority of couples, both partners are typically working for pay. The average across the entire sample is 58 percent, and in 21 of the 28 countries, the majority of couples are dual earners.

On average, dual earner couples put in about 82 joint hours per week in paid employment, which is roughly the equivalent of two full time jobs. However, the meaning of being in a dual earner couple varies widely across countries. In other

Table 6.3: Dual earner couples.

	Percent of dual earner couples	Average hours per week		Percent of dual earner couples that work		
		All couples	Dual earner couples	Less than 80 hours	80–99 hours	100 or more hours
Norway	98.9	75.5	75.9	62.5	32.0	5.5
Denmark	98.0	76.5	77.4	68.4	26.0	5.6
Finland	82.3	70.0	76.8	61.6	33.1	5.3
Sweden	80.2	67.9	76.6	47.9	48.1	4.0
New Zealand	70.1	63.6	77.2	52.0	36.5	11.5
Switzerland	68.0	64.0	74.3	57.5	35.1	7.5
Germany	61.7	64.6	81.1	39.6	47.4	13.1
Great Britain	61.7	58.5	77.5	59.0	31.3	9.7
Portugal	61.2	67.2	85.4	28.8	53.7	17.5
Cyprus	60.7	66.8	81.5	42.7	54.3	3.0
Belgium	60.6	56.7	76.3	65.9	24.8	9.2
Latvia	60.0	65.6	86.2	12.5	66.3	21.2
The Netherlands	58.0	48.1	63.4	87.9	10.9	1.2
Poland	56.8	73.2	92.6	17.5	49.3	33.2
Russia	55.8	61.2	83.0	29.8	55.3	14.9
Japan	55.3	66.7	85.1	36.3	42.4	21.3
Austria	54.5	59.5	78.3	57.4	30.3	12.3
Taiwan	53.9	72.6	94.9	15.8	51.3	32.9
France	52.0	56.6	75.9	67.1	27.1	5.7
Israel	51.5	59.4	80.8	42.8	40.0	17.2
USA	50.8	59.6	82.7	36.1	44.6	19.3
Spain	46.0	58.1	79.0	42.0	49.0	9.0
Hungary	44.2	55.6	92.3	11.4	54.2	34.3
Bulgaria	38.4	46.3	84.5	14.6	69.5	16.0
Philippines	36.5	58.3	86.5	36.8	35.8	27.4
Chile	34.5	60.6	91.2	27.1	45.7	27.1
Mexico	34.4	60.4	87.4	34.7	39.6	25.7
Brazil	25.6	48.8	85.7	29.9	50.2	19.9
Average	57.6	62.2	81.8	42.3	42.3	15.4

words, the extent of the joint workweek varies markedly. In Taiwan, Chile, Poland and Hungary, husbands and wives jointly put in more than 90 hours per week on the job. Thus, the busiest couples are not in the richest countries in our sample but rather are in several developing economies in the Eastern European and Asian countries.

The Netherlands stands out as having dual earner couples with the most free time outside of the demands of the workplace. The average dual earner couple in the Netherlands puts in just 63 hours per week on the job, a full 30 hours less per week than in Taiwan. Dual earner couples in the United States work about 83 hours per week and about 77 hours per week in Great Britain.

Another way to understand how busy family life has become is to examine the percentage of couples who work more than 100 hours per week (also in Table 6.3). In Great Britain, about 10 percent of couples put in 100 hours per week or more on the job. The rate in the United States is nearly double that, at 19 percent. Three countries in our sample find one third of couples working 100 or more hours per week (Poland, Hungary and Taiwan). At the other end of the spectrum, 10 countries, all European, have fewer than 10 percent of couples who work 100 hours per week. These countries include Belgium, Spain, Switzerland, France, Denmark, Norway, Finland, Sweden, Cyprus and The Netherlands.

Yet another way to understand the gender gap in working time is to focus on busy parents. It is one thing to have a husband and wife putting in 100 hours per week on the job; it is another matter altogether if they also have children at home. In our sample, parents averaged 7 fewer hours per week on the job than did non-parents. Furthermore, in 22 of the 26 countries we examined, parents worked fewer hours than non-parents.[3] Most of the difference between the working hours of parents and non-parents can be attributed to the reduced working time of mothers (see Table 6.4). In 11 of the 26 countries with available data, mothers put in significantly fewer hours per week than did women without children. In none of the cases where mothers work more than other married women were the differences statistically significant. The difference between the working times of fathers and non-fathers was less clear, and only statistically significant in only three countries, two where fathers worked more and one, Cyprus, where fathers worked less.

We examined whether these "parenting" effects — generally fewer hours on the job for mothers and little difference for fathers — continue to hold true after other relevant factors are taken into account. For example, married mothers may differ from other married women in various ways, including differences in age and education. Can socio-demographic differences between mothers and other married women account for the "parenting effects" we have observed?

To answer this question, we conducted multivariate regression analyses which adjusted the parenting gaps presented in Table 6.4 for differences in education and age. The results indicate that the parenting effects are generally the result of parenting *per se* and are not due to differences in the attributes of mothers compared with other married women. Recall that in 11 of the 26 countries, married mothers put in fewer hours on the job than did other married women. After controlling for age

---

3. The Bulgarian and New Zealand data could not be analyzed in this section due to missing information on children. In four of the countries, parents worked only slightly more than non-parents: Norway (1.53 hours), Portugal (1.20), Switzerland (1.16) and Taiwan (.27).

Table 6.4: Working hours for dual earner couples by parental status.

	Couples			Females			Males		
	No kids	Kids	Difference	No kids	Kids	Difference	No kids	Kids	Difference
Austria	55.82	61.30	5.48	37.2	31.3	5.9	43.9	44.7	−0.8
Belgium	48.30	67.41	19.11	33.9	30.7	3.2	43.5	43.9	−0.4
Brazil	47.62	49.05	1.42	42.1	35.2	7.0	42.5	47.5	−5.0
Chile	56.23	63.18	6.96	42.5	39.2	3.3	52.4	52.2	0.2
Cyprus	56.52	74.05	17.54	38.2	39.0	−0.9	46.4	41.8	4.5
Denmark	76.00	77.03	1.03	37.1	35.4	1.7	41.7	42.0	−0.3
Finland	69.11	71.32	2.21	35.7	36.0	−0.2	39.7	40.9	−1.2
France	46.38	61.03	14.65	35.5	32.7	2.8	41.7	42.7	−1.1
Germany	63.43	64.75	1.32	37.5	33.2	4.3	46.1	46.8	−0.7
Great Britain	57.51	61.16	3.65	35.7	28.5	7.2	46.3	47.7	−1.4
Hungary	50.16	62.96	12.80	41.4	43.1	−1.7	49.1	50.0	−0.9
Israel	53.57	62.04	8.47	35.2	32.9	2.3	45.4	46.6	−1.2
Japan	61.68	70.99	9.31	34.4	30.3	4.2	50.1	50.9	−0.7
Latvia	56.90	71.43	14.53	40.5	39.1	1.4	43.7	48.4	−4.7
Mexico	53.84	62.85	9.01	36.9	38.9	−2.0	45.5	51.1	−5.7
The Netherlands	43.73	53.08	9.35	28.5	21.8	6.7	39.0	40.2	−1.2
Norway	76.36	74.83	−1.53	34.3	33.2	1.1	44.0	43.3	0.7
Philippines	49.50	59.69	10.20	45.8	41.6	4.2	43.7	43.1	0.6
Poland	68.84	75.73	6.89	44.6	42.6	2.1	49.5	51.2	−1.7
Portugal	68.64	67.44	−1.20	38.6	39.3	−0.7	43.8	48.2	−4.4
Russia	49.57	66.70	17.12	40.1	38.7	1.4	44.0	44.8	−0.8
Spain	56.24	60.28	4.04	36.7	33.7	3.0	41.7	44.3	−2.7
Sweden	66.07	70.79	4.72	37.1	34.8	2.4	41.2	40.6	0.6
Switzerland	64.38	63.22	−1.16	32.7	28.6	4.1	45.7	43.3	2.4
Taiwan	72.76	72.49	−0.27	47.5	44.7	2.8	50.9	48.9	2.0
USA	58.80	60.41	1.61	38.6	32.5	6.1	48.9	50.2	−1.3
Average	58.8	65.6	6.8	38.0	35.3	2.8	45.0	46.0	−1.0

and education, this difference remained statistically significant in eight of the countries.

Among men, we found that married fathers generally did not work a longer workweek than did married men without children after age and education were taken into account. While the average workweek for fathers was longer in the majority of cases, the difference was only statistically significant for Cyprus, where fathers actually work less than non-fathers.

These results suggest that the arrival of children reduces the time parents devote to earning money just at the time when families are most in need of additional financial resources. Furthermore, children reinforce gender disparities within the family, with wives' paid working time reduced in the majority of countries while their husbands maintain their time on the job.

Our final analysis examines the difference between the amount of time worked by husbands and wives within each couple in the sample. Table 6.5 shows the weekly hours worked by wives and husbands in dual earner couples and the difference between the amount of time each contributes. In column one, we see a large variation in the length of wives' workweeks, which ranges from 25 to 46 hours per week. Across all countries, wives work an average of 37 hours per week in dual earner couples. Husbands, however, are less varied in the amount of time they work each week, which ranges from 39 to 52 hours per week and averages 45 hours per week across all countries. In the majority of countries, the disparity between the amount of time wives and husbands work is less than 10 hours per week, and on average, wives work 8.5 hours less per week than their husbands. Japan stands out as having the largest gap between husbands' and wives' working time, at 18 hours per week. At the other end of the spectrum, Taiwanese and Filipino wives work almost as much as their husbands, approximately 3 hours less per week.

6.4. Discussion

Our findings modify the conclusions of Jacobs and Gerson (2004) and Jacobs and Gornick (2002). In their analysis of 10 Western European and North American countries, the working time in the United States stood out, both in terms of long average working hours and the proportion of couples working very long hours. However, with the addition of Eastern European, Asian, Middle Eastern and Latin American countries, workers in the United States no longer lead the pack. Non-Western countries have employees who generally work longer hours than employees in Western countries, and are particularly highly concentrated at the high end of the spectrum.

The first pattern worth noting is regarding the proportion of the sample currently employed. Not surprisingly, the rates differ for men and women, but most Western countries have higher rates of employment for both sexes than other geographic areas. This finding contradicts what we expected to find about the formerly communist nations in Eastern Europe. Under communism, it was common for

Table 6.5: Comparison of wives' and husbands' working hours.

	Wife's hours	Husband's hours	Difference
Japan	32.7	51.7	18.4
Switzerland	30.2	44.7	14.6
The Netherlands	24.5	39.0	14.3
New Zealand	31.4	45.1	14.0
Great Britain	31.6	45.8	14.0
Israel	32.8	47.2	13.2
Belgium	32.4	44.3	11.6
Austria	34.0	44.2	10.9
Germany	35.4	45.3	10.9
Chile	40.8	51.7	10.3
USA	37.1	46.2	10.1
Mexico	38.9	49.2	9.8
Norway	33.6	42.4	8.8
Spain	35.8	43.9	7.3
France	34.2	42.1	7.3
Latvia	39.6	46.3	7.1
Hungary	43.0	50.4	7.0
Brazil	39.8	47.6	6.6
Poland	43.6	49.8	6.3
Denmark	35.7	41.7	6.0
Sweden	35.6	40.9	5.4
Russia	39.4	44.2	4.8
Finland	36.0	40.4	4.2
Cyprus	38.8	43.0	3.8
Portugal	40.8	43.9	3.5
Bulgaria	40.9	44.9	3.2
Taiwan	46.2	49.0	2.9
Philippines	41.7	45.5	2.4
Average	36.7	45.4	8.5

women to participate in the labor market (e.g. Tang & Cousins, 2005). However, in comparison to the rest of the sample countries, this region no longer stands out. In all of the five Eastern European countries in the sample, both men and women are employed at lower than average rates.

Jacobs and Gerson (2004) found that dual earner couples in the United States worked the most hours per week than the other countries in their sample. When we broadened the sample to include more countries, we find a somewhat different picture — the workweek in the United States for dual earner couples is just over the average across all of the countries. However, all except for one of the countries that have longer workweeks than the United States were located in Asia, Eastern Europe and Latin America.

We see the same pattern when we observe the proportion of dual earner couples working very long hours. While Jacobs and Gornick (2002) found that America had the highest proportion of dual earner couples working long hours in comparison to Western European and North American countries, this is no longer the case when we include a more diverse sample of countries. Although the United States falls behind nine other countries in terms of proportion of dual earner couples working very long hours, it still leads in comparison to Western European nations. While the United States changes its position relative to the other countries in the sample, the Netherlands, which had the shortest working time in studies by Jacobs and Gornick (2002) and Jacobs and Gerson (2004), also has the shortest workweek with respect to the countries in the 2002 ISSP sample.

Based on our results regarding the working time of dual earner couples, we assert that the meaning of being a partner in a "dual earner couple" varies cross-nationally. First of all, dual earner couples are more commonly found in some countries than others. The majority of the most developed countries have high proportions of dual earner couples while most of the Eastern European, Asian and Latin American countries in the sample have lower proportions of dual earner couples. For example, almost all of the couples from the Scandinavian countries in the sample are dual earner couples, while only one-quarter of Brazilian couples are composed of two workers.

Second, working time for dual earner couples also varies. In some countries, a majority of dual earner couples consist of partners who both work full time. Other countries have different arrangements: one partner may work full time while the other works part time, or both partners may work part time jobs. While dual earners in Taiwan, Poland, Hungary and Chile all work long hours, suggesting that both partners work long hours, the dual earner couples in the Netherlands work much shorter workweeks, indicating a greater proportion of part time jobs.

On the whole, the patterns of labor force participation and working time in Great Britain are about average for men, but the story is a bit more complex for British women. While British women's labor force participation rates are well above average, they tend to work fewer hours per week than other women. Furthermore, the difference between the working time of British mothers and other British women is the greatest in the sample, with British mothers working more than 9 hours less than non-mothers when controlling for age and education. Owing to women's lower than average working time, dual earner couples in Great Britain typically work fewer than 80 joint hours per week, and are less likely to work very long hours than couples in other countries in the sample. Finally, of these dual earner couples, British wives work significantly less than their husbands work each week.

Therefore, while Jacobs and Gerson (2004) found that the American dual earner couples worked the longest combined workweeks of any other country in their sample, the current analysis modifies their findings. We conclude that the United States' combined work hours are long relative to those in Western Europe but are not very long relative to less affluent countries in other parts of the world.

References

Barnett, R. C., & Gareis, K. C. (2002). Full-time and reduced-hours work schedules and marital quality: A study of female physicians with young children. *Work and Occupations, 29*(3), 364–379.

Bonney, N. (2005). Overworked Britons? Part-time work and work-life balance. *Work, Employment and Society, 19*(2), 391–401.

Cohen, Y., & Stier, H. (2006). The rise in involuntary part-time employment in Israel. *Research in Social Stratification and Mobility, 24*(1), 41–54.

Fuwa, M. (2004). Macro-level gender inequality and the division of household labour in 22 countries. *American Sociological Review, 69*(6), 751.

Golden, L., & Wiens-Tuers, B. (2006). To your happiness? Extra hours of labor supply and worker well-being. *The Journal of Socio-Economics, 35*(2), 382–397.

Greenhaus, J. H., & Beutell, N. J. (1985). Sources of conflict between work and family roles. *Academy of Management. The Academy of Management Review, 10*(1), 76.

Haroarson, O. S. (2004). *Statistics in focus: Population and social conditions.* European Communities: Eurostat.

Hill, E. J., Mead, N. T., Dean, L. R., Hafen, D. M., Gadd, R., Palmer, A. A., & Ferris, M. S. (2006). Researching the 60-hour dual-earner workweek: An alternative to the "opt-out revolution". *American Behavioral Scientist, 49*(9), 1184–1203.

Hook, J. L. (2006). Care in context: Men's unpaid work in 120 countries, 1965–2003. *American Sociological Review, 71*(4), 639–660.

International Labour Organization (ILO) (2007). Data from BA Labor Force Survey 2002. Available at http://laborsta.ilo.org/.

Iversen, T., & Rosenbluth, F. (2006). The political economy of gender: Explaining cross-national variation in the gender division of labor and the gender voting gap. *American Journal of Political Science, 50*(1), 1–19.

Jacobs, J. A., & Gerson, K. (2004). *The time divide: Work, family, and gender inequality.* Cambridge, MA: Harvard University Press.

Jacobs, J. A., & Gornick, J. C. (2002). Hours of paid work in dual-earner couples: The United States in cross-national perspective. *Sociological Focus, 35*(2), 169–187.

Kmec, J. (1999). Multiple aspects of work-family conflict. *Sociological Focus, 32*(3), 265–286.

Lim, J. Y. (2000). The effects of the East Asian crisis on the employment of women and men: The Philippine case. *World Development, 28*(7), 1285–1306.

Lundberg, U., Mardberg, B., & Frankenhaeuser, M. (1994). The total workload of male and female white collar workers as related to age, occupational level, and number of children. *Scandinavian Journal of Psychology, 35*(4), 315–327.

Meyer, M. H. (1990). Family status and poverty among older women: The gendered distribution of retirement income in the United States. *Social Problems, 37*(4), 551–563.

Nock, S. L., & Kingston, P. W. (1988). Time with children: The impact of couples' work-time commitments. *Social Forces, 67*(1), 59–85.

Noor, N. M. (2003). Work- and family-related variables, work-family conflict and women's well-being: Some observations. *Community, Work & Family, 6*(3), 297–319.

Plomien, A. (2006). From socialism to capitalism: Women and their changed relationship with the labor market in Poland. In: H.-P. Blossfeld, M. Mills & F. Bernardi (Eds), *Globalization, uncertainty and women's careers: An international comparison.* Northhampton, MA: Edward Elgar.

Pollert, A. (2003). Women, work and equal opportunities in post-communist transition. *Work, Employment and Society, 17*(2), 331–357.

Presser, H. B. (2003). *Working in a 24/7 economy*. New York: Russell Sage Foundation.

Rice, R. W., Frone, M. R., & McFarlin, D. B. (1992). Work-nonwork conflict and the perceived quality of life. *Journal of Organizational Behavior, 13*(2), 155–168.

Smock, P., Manning, W., & Gupta, S. (1999). The effect of marriage and divorce on women's economic well-being. *American Sociological Review, 64*, 794–812.

Spithoven, A. H. G. M. (2002). The third way: The Dutch experience. *Economy and Society, 31*(3), 333–368.

Tang, N., & Cousins, C. (2005). Working time, gender and family: An east-west European comparison. *Gender, Work and Organization, 12*(6), 527–550.

van der Lippe, T., Jager, A., & Kops, Y. (2006). Combination pressure: The paid work-family balance of men and women in European countries. *Acta Sociologica, 49*(3), 303–319.

Voydanoff, P. (2005). Work demands and work-to-family and family-to-work conflict: Direct and indirect relationships. *Journal of Family Issues, 26*(6), 707–726.

Went, R. (2000). Making Europe work — the struggle to cut the workweek. *Capital and Class* (71), 1–10.

Wharton, A. S., & Blair-Loy, M. (2006). Long work hours and family life: A cross-national study of employees' concerns. *Journal of Family Issues, 27*(3), 415–436.

Appendix:

Table 6.A.1:   Survey Information by Country.

	Year(s) of survey	Unweighted sample size	
		Female	**Male**
Austria	2003–2004	1006	651
Belgium	2002	545	521
Brazil	2003	915	889
Bulgaria	2001	435	331
Chile	2002	713	560
Cyprus	2002	465	436
Denmark	2002–2003	622	497
Finland	2002–2003	628	510
France	2002	1136	504
Germany	2002	560	555
Great Britain	2002	872	664
Hungary	2002	438	348
Israel	2002	582	448
Japan	2002	447	395
Latvia	2003	496	372
Mexico	2003	776	516
Netherlands	2002–2003	546	501
New Zealand	2002	480	328
Norway	2002	683	598
Philippines	2002	566	562
Poland	2002	562	439
Portugal	2003	492	353
Russia	2002	859	598
Spain	2003	979	980
Sweden	2002	474	419
Switzerland	2002–2003	392	377
Taiwan	2002	888	837
USA	2002	568	419
Average		647	522

Chapter 7

"I have No Life Other than Work" — Long Working Hours, Blurred Boundaries and Family Life: The Case of Irish Entrepreneurs

Anne Laure Humbert and Suzan Lewis

7.1. Introduction

Far from the rise in leisure once predicted from the technological revolution, many people are now working longer (and more intensively) than ever as attested by other chapters in this volume. With the growth of dual earner and single parent families and the increasing instability of interpersonal relationships, experiences of family as well as working life are being transformed. In this context issues relating to the integration of paid work and the rest of life and particularly the impact of "overwork" in its various forms on family life are often hotly debated. Indeed the very sustainability of families and communities when work takes up so much of people's time and energy, is increasingly questioned (Lewis & Cooper, 1999; Lewis, Gambles, & Rapoport, 2007; Webster, 2004).

In this chapter we first discuss the growing invasiveness of work in people's lives and particularly the blurring of boundaries between work and personal life (especially family). We link the rise and popularity of debates and initiatives on "work–life balance" to these trends and argue that this reflects concerns about the ways in which paid work is dominating people's lives. We then explore some of the reasons why employees are working more and/or are perceiving less "work–life balance". Overworking is often seen as an individual choice and a gender neutral one, but we argue that all choices are socially and structurally constrained and that the trend for work to intrude into family time is both constrained and highly gendered. We explore trends in workplace organisations that encourage and exacerbate long working hours and explore ways in which this can create difficulties in integrating work and family life. In this context, so called flexible working arrangements or work–life policies have limited impact.

The Long Work Hours Culture
Copyright © 2008 by Emerald Group Publishing Limited
All rights of reproduction in any form reserved
DOI:10.1016/B978-1-84855-038-4.00007-5

Many people, especially women, find employment in contemporary organisations incompatible with family commitments and turn instead to self employment to provide more control in their lives (Marlow, 1997; Orhan & Scott, 2001; Belle & La Valle, 2003; Greer & Greene, 2003). We explore this solution in a European context using a study of Irish entrepreneurs as an example. This shows that entrepreneurship only provides a way to reconcile work with family commitments in a minority of cases. We consider a number of questions that these trends raise for future research about the family and wider social impacts of long intense working hours.

7.1.1.   The Blurring of Work–Non-Work Boundaries and Concerns about "Work–Life Balance"

Paid work is increasingly dominating people's lives (Gambles, Lewis, & Rapoport, 2006; Bunting, 2004; Van der Lippe & Peters, 2007 Duxbury, 2008). There is much evidence that workers across the industrialised world are expending more and more time and energy in paid work as working hours are becoming longer and more intensified in many contexts (Lewis & Smithson, 2006; Burchall, Lapido, & Wilkinson, 2002). One consequence is that as time expands in the global 24-hour market place and space and distance are compressed by information and communication technology, temporal and spatial boundaries between paid work and personal life including family life have become increasingly blurred (Sullivan & Lewis, 2001; Brannen, 2005). Work intrudes into family time as many people stay longer at the workplace or work at home during "family time". Work also invades family space as more people bring work into the home, whether as a response to work overload, hot desking, teleworking or expectations of constant availability in the 24/7 market.

Experience of long and/or intensified working hours and blurred work–family boundaries can engender feelings of pressure, lack of time and general "busyness" (Gambles et al., 2006; Bunting, 2004), sometimes signified by metaphors about time such as "the time squeeze" or "time famine" (Hochschild, 1989; Hewitt, 1993) or, in relation to family, the "care deficit" (Warton & Blair-Loy, 2006), that is the question of who will care for the young, old and vulnerable if people are working all the time. These pressures and associated metaphors which have been variously attributed to new forms of work and working patterns, technology and the lure of consumerism and accumulation (Beem, 2005; Bunting, 2004) also engender a feeling of work and non-work "imbalance" (Guest, 2002).

It is in this context that concerns about what is often referred to as "work–family" or more recently "work–life balance", have become hot topics not only in research but also in government, employer and union discussions in the media, and in everyday language. However, the issues are not new. Questions such as whether it is possible to "succeed" in occupational life without sacrificing personal life have grown out of a long tradition of research and discussion on the interface between work, family and the rest of life. Initially this research was a response to demographic trends especially the rise in women's labour force participation in the second half of the twentieth century. The shift in terminology from work–family to work–life was partly a response to the association of family with women and also to emphasise that work has to be integrated with not only family commitments but also other aspects of personal life by both men and women. Work–life balance claims to be gender neutral. However, changing terminology is not sufficient to change practices and can mask ongoing gender inequities at work and at home and the subsequent impact of long working hours on gender dynamics (Lewis, Gambles, & Rapoport, 2007; Warton & Blair-Loy, 2006).

In fact the term work–life balance tends to be used in at least two different ways (Lewis et al., 2007). The *personal control of time* work–life balance discourse focuses on relatively affluent professional and white collar workers — both men and women — especially in the knowledge economy, who have difficulty in finding time for personal life because of the all encompassing nature of many contemporary forms of work. The *workplace flexibility* work–life balance discourse on the other hand focuses on flexibility in working arrangements and tends to be used in discussions of work and family needs, primarily in relation to women. Both discourses incorporate notions of choice and obscure structural and relational constraints. The personal control of time discourse implies human agency and choice to, for example, work harder and longer or to prioritise different aspects of life, and personal responsibility for achieving "balance", overlooking structural, cultural and practical constraints and gender differences in these constraints (Caproni, 2004). Flexibility discourses position work–life balance policies as providing choices for those with non-work (mainly family) commitments, with a focus on workplaces, but again overlooks constraints of gender, workplace culture, norms and assumptions. In both cases it can appear that many people may be "choosing" to spend more time at work than with family. However choice is always socially and structurally embedded, and the trend for work to intrude into family time is no exception.

7.1.2. Are Employees "Choosing" to Spend More Time at Work than with Family when Boundaries are Blurred?

There are many reasons why people work long hours and often experience work–family imbalance, not all of which imply free choice. Technology can facilitate long working hours and blurred work and family boundaries, allowing people to work around the clock. But this is not just a consequence of technology. The nature of work, particularly knowledge work is also changing. For some, work is increasingly interesting, absorbing and challenging, with potential to enhance positive well-being, although it can also encroach into all of workers' time and space, crowding out family life. It seems that work is what some people choose to spend their time on and enjoy doing (Lewis, 2003). Arlie Hochschild (1997) has argued that for many people, at least in the USA, work has become more satisfying than home. Paid work can be absorbing and stimulating and is the source of recognition and status while home becomes just hard work, especially for parents of young children. The more time is spent at the workplace, the more difficult relationships become at home, which reinforces the desire to spend time at work. Work becomes a refuge from home, rather than home a refuge from work as was assumed to be the case in industrial times. It should be noted however, that while for some people work may be more satisfying than family, as Hochschild suggest, the prevalence of this phenomenon is contested (Maume & Bellas, 2001).

The potentially stimulating and absorbing nature of much post industrial work may also explain why, when technology enables the permeation of work and non-work boundaries, it is so often work which become most alluring (Sullivan & Lewis, 2001). Work that has no clear boundaries and can never be clearly "completed" can lure workers away from other activities at any time of the day or night. As communication and information technology enables more people to work at home for part of the working week, in evenings and at weekends, boundaryless work can intrude into the lives of ever growing numbers of workers. However, although both men and women tend to get caught up in these blurred boundaries, women often feel less "free" to choose to work long hours because of gender expectation and the trend for women to retain the greater share of domestic work (Sullivan & Lewis, 2001; Humbert, 2007). Among home-based workers, for example, men tend to be more able to shut themselves away from the family while women are more likely to multitask with both work and family work.

There are also individual difference explanations of the tendency to work long and hard, although these too tend to be underpinned by social values and context. Many people claim to be self-driven, and to achieve intense satisfaction and enjoyment from total involvement in work (Lewis, 2003; Hochschild, 1997). This self attribution of a "driven" personality is reflected in a theory of mastery orientation postulated by Kofodimos (1993), who argues that executives who are high in mastery orientation derive their major source of self-esteem and satisfaction from intense work involvement and career achievement. While this may be viewed as an individual, personality characteristic, it is also strongly related to occupational socialisation and identity in societies which value work-related achievement more than family. In fact, although both Hochschild and Kofodimos appear to be offering individual level explanations of the dominance of work in many people's lives, both relate the tendency to "overwork" to social values which equate self-worth with hard work in paid employment, mastery and career success. They note that status and self-esteem are linked to work rather than other activities or obligations such as family life. Thus while there are clearly some people — men and women — who thrive on long working hours, at least in some stages of the life cycle, and for whom work is as, or more satisfying than family or other activities this must be understood within wider social contexts and the values and status associated with work and with family.

7.1.3. Pressures on Employees

Other explanations of long working hours and the dominance of work in people's lives focus on changes in organisations and the impacts on employees. Trends such as downsizing and reorganisation to deal with global competition, in the private sector and efficiency drives in the public sector mean many employees regardless of occupation have more work to do than before. Often workloads are simply too high for the work to be accomplished in regular working hours (Lewis & Smithson, 2006).

Employers who recognise that employees are feeling pressurised and time squeezed often introduce so called work–life balance policies such as various forms of flexible working arrangements (Lewis, 2003). However, these policies rarely address the deeper issues underpinning employees' experiences of contemporary work pressures and/or absorption in work. Take-up of opportunities to work flexibly or reduced hours tends to be low, particularly among men, but also often among career-oriented women and especially in white collar work where to do so is frequently perceived to be career limiting (Lewis et al., 2002; Perlow, 1998). The low take-up of flexibility by men occurs even in countries with substantial statutory supports to encourage fathers to take family related leaves and be more involved in families (though rates are higher than in other countries) (Haas, Alldred, & Hwang, 2002; Brandth & Kvande, 2001).

Reluctance to make use of flexible working opportunities is related to the traditional, male model of the ideal worker as one who demonstrates job commitment by continuous full-time work and often long hours of "face time" or presenteeism. This ideal is widely embedded in organisational cultures where part time or flexible workers are undervalued and taking up flexible or reduced work hours is perceived as career limiting (Lewis, 1997, 2001; Drew, Emerek, & Mahon, 1998). The overvaluing of traditional full-time work and long hours is deeply gendered, reflecting historically traditional values, based on assumptions that the private sphere of family and the public sphere are separate and unrelated, the one associated with women, the other with men, and the view that ideal workers do not have other time obligations (Acker, 1992; Rapoport, Bailyn, Fletcher, & Pruitt, 2002; Bailyn, 1993). This reinforces traditional gender division in workplaces and in families.

These values may be consistent with traditional male gender identity, but they can create identity issues for women especially mothers of young children (Lewis, 1991) as well as men wishing to be more involved in fathering (Crouter, Bumpus, Head, & McHale, 2001). Ideal worker values are also often internalised and become deeply embedded in notions of occupational or professional identity which may also conflict with gender identity. For example, a study of accountants showed that notions of professional identity are closely tied up with social representation of the client and the client–professional relationship (Lewis, 2003). The need to be constantly available tends to be justified in terms of service to or pleasing clients (Lewis, 2007; Anderson-Gough et al., 2001). Long working hours thus become professional identity affirming. Identity affirming behaviours can and do become absorbing, challenging and exciting (Thompson & Bunderson, 2001; Kofodimos, 1993) and hence the boundaries between work and non-work can become blurred — often resulting in workaholism. Similar processes have been observed in other occupations (Drago, 2001; Perlow, 1998; Yakura, 2001). For example, Drago (2001) argues that among teachers in the US the notion of the ideal worker, incorporating an ideal of teachers as highly trained experts worthy of respect and highly committed to their students, press teachers towards a norm of long hours of work. He argues that teachers have promoted this image against an earlier model, which cast them as mothers of students. Long working hours may be constructed as a choice, and may or may not be enjoyable but they are not necessarily viewed as a choice when considered in relation to professional identity.

The intensification of work is also often cited by employees as a major reason for not taking up flexible working options or even for not taking full holiday entitlements (Lewis & Smithson, 2006). Taking time off for any reason, in the context of high workloads and lean workforces often involves returning to a huge backlog of work. Intense workloads also undermine the capacity of autonomous working teams to enhance flexibility as employees know that if they are not at work they will further overload colleagues who are already working at the height of their capacity (Back Wicklund & Plantin, 2007; Lewis & Smithson, 2006). High commitment management techniques also involve providing employees with more autonomy and the responsibility for getting work done that goes with this. This responsibility tends to be internalised and the consequent intensification or extension of work is then constructed as a choice and a personal responsibility (Perlow, 1998). Perlow (1998, 2001) contends that in knowledge-based workplaces, employees are managed not by the clock, but by organisational culture. She argues that managers use organisational culture to control subordinates' boundaries between work and family lives, by the various ways in which they "cajole, encourage, coerce or otherwise influence the amount of time employees spend visibly at the workplace" (Perlow, 1998, p. 329).

It is possible that some people need stronger work and family boundaries than others, or at different life stages, such as when they have heavy family responsibilities or are particularly involved in certain leisure activities. Arguably the valuing of diversity involves accepting these needs and also those people for whom "work addiction" is a genuine choice. However those who make this "choice" to blur boundaries too often influence workplace cultures and can set impossible standards for others to meet. They are often employees who have a partner at home full time, or working part time and are absolved from family work. This reinforces gendered workplace cultures and the undervaluing of time for family. The subsequent difficulty in sustaining boundaries between work and family is one reason why some employees, including many women move into self employment — to get more control over their lives (Marlow, 1997; Orhan & Scott, 2001; Belle & La Valle, 2003; Greer & Greene, 2003). Does this provide a solution to managing contemporary work demands and family life? We now turn to a study of entrepreneurs to address this question.

7.1.4. The Case of Entrepreneurship

So far, this chapter has shown that despite increases in work–life balance or flexible working arrangements being implemented throughout Europe, there is a danger that quality of life could be undermined by the extension and intensification of work. It could be argued that this is the case in employment due to the lack of workers' control over their environments; for example, control over their imposed and expected workloads and work conditions.

This phenomenon is aggravated by gender and parenthood, itself a gendered factor. The process of work intensification has more serious consequences for women due to their disproportionate responsibilities for household and caring responsibilities. Mothers are least likely to enter and remain in employment, while having children appears to have little impact of father's labour market participation in Europe (Eurostat, 2008; Kalicki, Fthenakis, Peitz, & Engfer, 1998). This has important implications, as women are the ones who will need to find an alternative to employment. If women opt out of employment because of the consequences of work intensification, is entrepreneurship a suitable alternative? Does entrepreneurship allow labour force participants to take back some of the control that may be absent in employment? Is it possible that through entrepreneurship, the process of work intensification is reversed? Do entrepreneurs adopt a model of work and use their time in a way which reverses the work intensification trend? More importantly, does this impact on entrepreneurs' quality of life and that of their family?

This section addresses these questions, drawing on a study of entrepreneurs undertaken in Ireland in 2003–2004. A national survey of entrepreneurship was undertaken with the help and support of the City and County Enterprise Boards, whose aim is to support small businesses creation throughout Ireland. The survey relied on a systematic random sample of male and female owned businesses. A total of 802 respondents (353 male and 449 female) responded to the survey in time to be included, giving a 23 percent response rate, which for a 12-page questionnaire is deemed acceptable. The questionnaire consisted of a mixture of 59 scaled, dichotomous and open-ended questions. Respondents were also encouraged to make qualitative comments at the end of the questionnaire.

The study did not use a matched sample approach. Adopting a matched sample approach would have allowed an examination of the effect of gender alone, while controlling for other factors. Despite the usefulness of this approach in many areas of gender research, the factors that are controlled for are usually strongly associated with gender, as for example sector, size of business or profitability (Ahl, 2004). Indeed, the men and women entrepreneurs in this survey were operating in very different sectors, in line with the prevailing sectoral segregation in the Irish labour market ($p < 0.01$). Men entrepreneurs clearly predominate in sectors such as manufacturing, construction or agriculture, while women entrepreneurs are concentrated in sectors such as professional services or education. We argue as those sectors are themselves highly gendered, any sectoral differences are also contributing to a gendered understanding of differences in entrepreneurship.

7.1.5.   Number of Hours Worked

The hours worked by the entrepreneurs surveyed tend to differ by gender. Men tended to report working longer hours than women ($p < 0.01$). Twelve percent of women entrepreneurs worked fewer than 30 hours per week compared with four percent of men entrepreneurs. The distribution of reported weekly distribution of hours worked is presented in Figure 7.1.

The findings show that overall, men entrepreneurs are much more likely than their female counterparts to work longer than standard hours (in excess of 40 hours of work weekly). A total of 87 percent of men entrepreneurs claimed to work longer than standard hours compared with 69 percent of women entrepreneurs ($p < 0.01$). The vast majority of respondents (89 percent) who worked long hours did not take time off in lieu or pay themselves overtime, while 10 percent took time off in lieu and four percent received overtime payments. In terms of the reported reasons for working longer than standard hours there were no differences between men and women. The most frequently cited reason was a "desire to get the job done", followed by "temporary increase in workload" and "backlog of work". The reasons are detailed in Table 7.1.

Examining working time among entrepreneurs in Ireland provides no indication that entrepreneurship is seen as a mean of working less than in employment. On the contrary, working hours in entrepreneurship are higher than the "standard" 40 hours which is often seen as the norm in white-collar employment, particularly for men entrepreneurs who work a greater number of hours than their female counterparts. Working long hours is seen by some entrepreneurs as part of their identity as an entrepreneur, just as it is for many employees as discussed earlier. For example, two respondents commented:

> Be prepared to work long antisocial hours, a lot of the time without pay. The work becomes a labour of love. (female, working longer than standard hours)

> Advice for new entrepreneurs: no pain-no gain! Unless you are especially gifted and can compress a lot of work and energy into a little amount of time: be prepared to sacrifice a lot of 'politically correct'

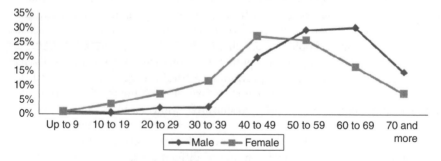

Figure 7.1: Working hours by gender.

Table 7.1: Percentage of respondents reasons working longer than standard hours by reason and gender.

	Male (%)	Female (%)
Own desire to get the job done	74	69
Backlog of work	36	31
Temporary increase in workload	26	40
Part of the organisational culture	21	17
Shortage of staff	17	19
Greater income/incentives	14	16
Covering employees on leave	10	11
Other	10	12
TOTAL	353	449

> qualities and attributes (i.e., family time, personal time, etc.). Be prepared to sacrifice financial security and a nine to five life. (male, working longer than standard hours)

However, one respondent noted that not only was working long hours part of her perceived identity as an entrepreneur but also that it was reinforced by structural factors

> I don't think it is understood the extra hours work that need to be put in to run your own business, that you don't get paid when you don't work and this applies for summer and Christmas holidays, sickness. (female, working longer than standard hours)

These comments suggest that entrepreneurship reinforces blurred boundaries between the public and private spheres. However, many of the entrepreneurs also commented that working long hours is a time investment which was necessary at start-up, but that they did not anticipate it would continue to be the case in the long term, while others commented they had worked long hours initially, but were now working fewer hours:

> [I don't work more than 40 hours weekly] any more, I did in the first two years. (female, not working longer than standard hours)

> I will work any hours over the next 18 months and then start to have more personal time. (female, working longer than standard hours)

> My mission at this stage is to organise my business so that I can work 9 to 5 and get a decent wage. (male, working longer than standard hours)

Some respondents saw this initial time investment in a start-up company as a great sacrifice in terms of other areas of their lives. The common thread arising from those comments was that the time investment made in the company was seen as being quite intense, hence not providing any evidence that entrepreneurship can be less demanding alternative to employment at this stage. For example, two respondents commented:

> The setting-up of the company was a great challenge to my partner and myself, it is only after three and a half years in the business that it is starting to bring financial rewards. The present workload and involvement in the company was really never anticipated by myself and has been a great sacrifice for my family. If I knew then what I know now would I have started? (male, working longer than standard hours)

> Running your own business is very time consuming but obviously very rewarding. During start-up, it is all very consuming and interferes totally with leisure time. In my opinion, it is crucial over the next few years to get a work–life balance. (female, working longer than standard hours)

These comments paint a contradictory picture of entrepreneurship in terms of working hours. It appears that for some, there is a total blurring of boundaries, likely to be reinforced in some cases by working from home. Many of the respondents experience a great deal of personal and family time sacrifice to the benefit of their business. It is also important to note that the single most important reason for working long hours is "to get the job done". This suggests that through ownership of the outcome of their labour, there is a large degree of personal satisfaction. The comments suggest that some entrepreneurs "choose" to work long hours because of an increased sense of achievement and mastery (Kofodimos, 1993).

Nevertheless overworking appears to have consequences that are not all viewed as positive. Indeed, "backlog of work" and "temporary increases in workload" figure in second and third place as reasons for respondents to work longer than the standard 40 hours weekly. It appears that some of the reasons are related to structural factors rather than personal choice. In those conditions, the options for reducing working hours or at least not working longer hours are diminished. This may relate to the structure of respondents' businesses. Below we now examine the relationship between business characteristics and working hours.

7.1.6. Characteristics of Businesses: Number of Hours and Structural Factors

The number of hours worked was closely related to the employment patterns in the respondents' businesses. Size of the business appears to be important. Entrepreneurs without full-time employees worked fewer hours (44) per week than those employing full-time staff (on average between 51 and 53 hours weekly depending on the number of full-time employees) ($p < 0.01$). Table 7.2 shows the average number of hours per

Table 7.2: Average weekly hours worked by number of full-time employees, $N = 606$.

	Total
None	52.69
1–10	56.31
11–20	56.44
21–50	57.22
51 or more	54.45
Total	55.36

week worked by entrepreneurs in relation to their number of full-time employees. While there appeared to be a relationship between the number of full-time employees and working hours, employing part-time workers however did not appear to significantly affect entrepreneurs' working time. The reasons for these differences are difficult to assess. It could be that having more full time employees increases the likelihood of a long hours culture developing — or just be a sign of a greater overall workload.

The reasons why respondents worked long hours in larger businesses (here seen as those with full-time employees) were contradictory. It was claimed that working long hours was linked to not having the necessary resources to diminish respondents' workloads. However, by looking at the figure generated in Table 7.2, it appears that for all but the last category (51 or more employees) the number of hours worked increases with the number of full-time employees. This is very paradoxical as it would seem reasonable to assume that an increasing number of full-time employees would lighten the respondents' burden of work. For example, a temporary increase in workload could be spread out among a greater number of workers, hence reducing the need for the entrepreneur him/herself to work longer hours in order to cope with the increase. To examine this paradox, it might be beneficial to examine the motivations behind respondents' decision to become entrepreneurs as well as their own professional backgrounds in terms of working time.

7.1.7. *Professional Background*

The findings point to a link between motivations for entering entrepreneurship and working long hours. Men and women entrepreneurs who worked longer than standard hours rated motivational factors such as "independence", "excitement and satisfaction" or "looking for a challenge" highest. Those who worked longer than standard hours were more likely to say that they wanted to generate a greater income and dreamt of being an entrepreneur and less likely to be motivated by a desire to balance work and family ($p < 0.05$). Men entrepreneurs who were dissatisfied with employment were less likely to work long hours, possibly because they had become

Table 7.3: Average weekly number of hours worked by reasons for work interruptions.

	No	Yes
Illness[a]	45	51
Child rearing or caring[a]	49	44
Starting a new business	46	47
Furthering education	47	47
Change of residence due to partner	46	48
Unemployment	46	48

[a]Statistically significant.

entrepreneurs to avoid the long hour culture often present in employment. Among women entrepreneurs, those who worked longer than standard hours were more likely to say they were motivated by a dream of being an entrepreneur, perhaps because this is the image that they have of successful entrepreneurs. Career history is also relevant to number of hours worked. Unsurprisingly, for the respondents who had a history of part-time work, the average number of hours worked is lower (46 hours) compared with those who do not (51 hours) ($p < 0.01$). Similarly, the average weekly number of hours worked by entrepreneurs who had a history of work-interruption (for more than six months) was lower (47 hours) than for the average weekly hours reported by those who did not (51 hours) ($p < 0.05$). Respondents who had had a work-interruption lasting more than six months worked a greater amount of hours if this was due to illness, but fewer if their interruption was due to childcare responsibilities (Table 7.3).

Previous working experience relates heavily to the gender of respondents. We have seen that one of the factors related to working hours is caring responsibilities, which remains disproportionately the responsibility of women. It appears that women are at a disadvantage because of this in entrepreneurship as in employment; women's caring responsibilities have a negative impact on the entrepreneurial life (Humbert, 2007). The link between caring, gender and working hours in entrepreneurship are now explored.

7.1.8.   Working Hours, Parenthood and Childcare

The number of hours worked was closely related to the status as a parent. The average number of hours reported among those who had no children was 51 hours weekly compared with 48 hours for parents ($p < 0.05$). Being a parent or not had some implications, particularly because of the problems arising from caring arrangements for children.

The pressure associated with the presence of children and the transition to parenthood was strongly felt in some of the comments made by respondents:

I have two 15 months old twins (babies) so it is difficult to fit in everything. I have a five year old son. (female, not working longer than standard hours)

Did [work longer than standard hours] till I became a mother, not now, before I became a mam over 2 years ago. (female, not working longer than standard hours)

However, the distribution patterns of childcare were widely different for men and women entrepreneurs. The survey examined the responses adopted by parents in caring for their children. The findings show that fathers are able to delegate all childcare responsibilities to their partners, while mothers adopt a jigsaw of responses in trying to cope with their childcare responsibilities. The assumption that it is women, regardless of their professional and/or other commitments, who are expected by Irish society to remain solely or at least principally in charge of childcare responsibilities persists (Table 7.4). This expectation, even though it might have a stronger hold in Irish society, is prevalent throughout Europe (Lewis, 1992; Drew et al., 1998; Humbert, 2007).

Unsurprisingly, the results suggest that there is a link between the number of hours worked per week and the types of caring arrangements used for entrepreneurs who are also parents of dependent children. Table 7.5 shows that there are some differences, particularly for parents who relied on private paid care and themselves or their partners in their set of childcare arrangements. Despite wide gender differences, the results show no real differences by the type of use of childcare in the number of hours worked weekly, except among women entrepreneurs who used a babysitter or domestic help.

Some comments showed the difficulties associated with caring responsibilities. For example, three women entrepreneurs stated:

I am 38 married with five children aged from 13 to two years. Time is a very short with me […] you have to work in the salon all day, get home to let off a baby-sitter, sort out homework and housework. Even though I have someone in the house you still have a lot to do yourself. (female, working longer than standard hours)

Table 7.4: Childcare arrangements by gender.

	Fathers (%)	Mothers (%)
Respondent*	17	41
Private paid care*	23	39
Domestic help*	18	30
Other parent(s)*	66	22
Another family member	13	18

*$p < 0.01$.

Table 7.5: Average weekly working hours by use of childcare arrangements and gender.

	Male		Female		Total	
	No	Yes	No	Yes	No	Yes
Cared for by respondent	55	51	44	44	49*	44*
Cared for by the other parent	55	54	43	46	45*	51*
Cared for by another family member	55	53	44	43	48	46
Cared for by private paid care	55	54	44	43	49*	45*
Cared for by a babysitter or domestic help	54	55	42*	48*	47	50

*$p < 0.01$.

> Our business success is a result of hard work, great effort, great sacrifice, co-operation and understanding on everyone's behalf from the youngest child to my mother (RIP) who contributed greatly by taking care of the children when the business demanded most of my time. (female, working longer than standard hours)

> I work in childcare part-time as at present, it suits me, but I may work elsewhere for more hours when the children are older. (female, not working longer than standard hours)

There was a dramatic parenthood transition for mothers, who felt the impact of being responsible for several areas at the same time due to social expectations that women should remain primarily responsible for caring responsibilities (Humbert, 2007). This was shown in the childcare jigsaw (Baines, Wheelock, & Gelder, 2003) seen in the way fathers and mothers organised childcare. Fathers relied on their partners, while mothers relied on a set of possible responses, including themselves, but also private or family care (Humbert, 2007). This is particularly important in that caring arrangements, which have been shown to be gendered, will also dictate the number of hours worked by respondents. Both private paid care and care for by the respondent him/herself lowered the number of hours worked, while relying on another parent increases the number of hours worked. One childcare arrangement was significant among women entrepreneurs. This consisted of having a higher number of working hours among those that could rely on a babysitter or private paid help. This is not an uncommon childcare arrangement of women entrepreneurs in Ireland and was shown to be very empowering for women entrepreneurs as they were able to delegate responsibilities to another person, usually a woman (Humbert, 2007). This itself has serious implications for gender equality, however, as it pushes the problem further to a poorer and hence probably more vulnerable woman (Ehrenreich & Hochschild, 2003).

One woman entrepreneur pointed out that this problem was affecting women's position in society as business persons:

Lack of childcare (and cost) biggest drawback in women running own business. When my children where small I always went back to work after they were in bed. Never enough hours in a day! (female, working longer than standard hours)

A striking feature of the findings was that all comments made on the relationship between working hours and caring responsibilities were made by women only. This is symptomatic of a wider picture for women's expected position in European society as carers, but it is detrimental to the contribution that women can make to society and to equality in general. If women entrepreneurs continue to have disproportionate responsibilities for caring, then it is likely that their businesses will suffer. As two women entrepreneurs (and carers) put it:

If I am not there my business suffers. I am the primary carer for my father (83) who has Alzheimer's disease. Three years being a full time carer. My caring role has become more demanding. (female, not working longer than standard hours)

My business has gone downhill since becoming a mother, but I regard motherhood as the more important job by far. (female, not working longer than standard hours)

So far, the findings of the survey have shown that entrepreneurs primarily work longer that the standard 40 hours a week, mainly to obtain a feeling of satisfaction and enjoyment, for instance, but not exclusively, through status or (self-)recognition, but also because of a lack of resources which made it difficult to cope with sometimes erratic patterns of work. But the survey also showed a deeply gendered aspect of working hours, in which those with caring responsibilities, often women, are operating on uneven playing fields and have to adopt different patterns of working. The findings hint at a dichotomous relationship between business and family, in which one suffers when the other is looked after.

As it is clear that there is a high prevalence of working long hours in entrepreneurship, we now turn our attention to the impact that this has on the respondents and the functioning of their families by examining the sacrifices they report having made.

7.1.9.   Time Sacrifices

The questionnaire asked respondents about the time sacrifices they felt that they had made. A total of 78 percent of men and women entrepreneurs felt that they had made some or many sacrifices in terms of their free time and 61 percent in terms of social time sacrifices. Among parents, 39 percent felt they had made some or many sacrifices in the time they spent with their children. Similarly, 41 percent of those who were married or cohabiting felt that they made some or many sacrifices with the time spent with their partner. It does not appear that there are gender differences in the time sacrifices perceived by men and women entrepreneurs.

The number of hours worked varied according to whether or not respondents felt they had made sacrifices with their free time ($p < 0.01$), social time ($p < 0.01$), time with their children for those who were parents ($p < 0.01$), and time with their spouse for those who were married or cohabiting ($p < 0.01$). There were no gender differences in this respect.

A total of 35 percent of entrepreneurs prioritised income over personal/family life. There were no gender differences for income prioritisation but some for the expansion of the business ($p < 0.05$). Thirty-eight percent of entrepreneurs prioritised personal and family life over business expansion (43 percent of women entrepreneurs and 31 percent of men entrepreneurs). Being a parent did not affect these figures to any great extent. Nevertheless this raises questions about the impact of these perceived sacrifices on family and social life.

The findings of this study, namely that entrepreneurs, both men and women, tend to work long hours mask the fact that entrepreneurs do not form a homogeneous group. In particular, it would be dangerous to assume that all entrepreneurs work long hours, without realising that many (even though not the majority), use entrepreneurship as a means of obtaining greater flexibility and reduced working hours. For example:

> Being self-employed gives me flexibility, independence, variety and more opportunities for self-improvement. No two days are the same. Working at night is the downside at times but I have learned to accept it. (male, not working longer than standard hours)

> I run my business on a part-time basis to facilitate children, spouse, lifestyle change, but hours very flexible due to changing workload (from 4 to 40 hours per week). (female, not working longer than standard hours)

> I became a Director of this company in 1972 with my first husband. After his death in 1976 I took over the reins and restructured the company. I worked hard to get experience in our particular field of business. Now at 75 years I am working only 3 days per week and continuing to maintain the company's viability. (female, not working longer than standard hours)

Flexibility is of course not synonymous with reduced working hours, and indeed, the entrepreneurs in this study sought greater flexibility, but did not always equate it with a reduction in working hours. Three respondents for example stated:

> We felt we could pay ourselves better and have a better quality of life. We have been successful to date. We have more free time and earn more than friends in the same business. (female, working longer than standard hours)

There's scope for holidays etc. Busy times mean hard work, longer hours, slack times we use as 'fun, leisure' times. (male, working longer than standard hours)

Be also prepared to reap the rewards [of sacrificing family and personal time] with luck more free and flexible time to enjoy your family. (male, working longer than standard hours)

Entrepreneurship brings more control and flexibility than employment, but the results show that flexibility is a double-edged sword. In entrepreneurship, it often entails a greater number of working hours rather than fewer. This poses some important questions, notably on whether flexibility is detrimental or beneficial to family functioning.

In summary, the Irish entrepreneurs study shows that entrepreneurs tend overall to work long hours, sacrificing many aspects of their personal and family life in the process. This process was shown to be highly gendered, with some women respondents, particularly when they become mothers, switching their priorities from business to family life. Men entrepreneurs remained largely unaffected in their response to working time by the transition to fatherhood.

For many respondents, entrepreneurship was dominating their lives, as illustrated by one man who wrote: "Formula: $(Work + Leisure + Childtime + Sleep)/Entrepreneur = Work$ I have no life other than work." (male, working longer than standard hours).

It was clear that there is a perceived conflict between entrepreneurial activities and personal, family or leisure time. The majority of respondents felt that they had made sacrifices in terms of their free time and social time. The numbers for family time sacrifices (sacrificing time with children and/or with partners) were lower across the board. The perception of sacrifices made did not appear to be a gendered one. Overall, the higher the number of hours worked, the higher the perception of sacrifice being made, and this applies across all types of perceived sacrifices.

7.1.10.   Impacts on Families, Family Functioning and Wider Social Impacts

Overall long working hours and work intensification in employment can be problematic if they diminish quality of life. However, in this study of entrepreneurship, the same problems of long hours and intensive workload appear, albeit in the absence of issues of exploitation of labour. This may be problematic, for future generations and for gender or other forms of equality. This raises a number of important issues and questions for future research.

First, what are the likely impacts on children and young people? From the 1960s as more women began to enter into and remain in the labour force there was a spate of research examining the impact of maternal employment on children, reflecting the assumptions that women's place was in the private sphere with men as economic providers. In the 21st century, dual earner families are the norm across the industrialised world, but as we have discussed the nature and pace of work has changed. The more pressing research question now becomes not what happens when both parents work, but what is the impact on children and other family members if two parents (or single parents) are expending so much time and energy at work. Ellen Galinsky (1999) asked children in the United Stares how they felt about their parents' working. This study revealed that it is not parents' working per se, or even the number of hours they work that children are most concerned about, but rather the state and mood of their parents when they return home. Children were upset about parents coming home from work in a "frazzled" state. It appears to be the quality of work and experiences of work that are important. The impacts may also depend on the specific relationships examined. For example Crouter et al. (2001) found that long working hours and role overload were associated with less positive relationships between fathers and adolescents — especially first born adolescents (the negative impact diminished for second born teenagers), but that long hours without role overload were more positive. The nature of physical work–family boundaries may also be important. Some entrepreneurs, and some employed people, perform much of their work at home so there are few if any physical boundaries between work and home. We need to know more about how children are affected when parents feel they have no option but to sacrifice time with families and the nature of work — whether in employment or entrepreneurship — is intense and all consuming and much of it takes place within the family home. There is a substantial literature on the negative aspects of the work–family interface (see e.g., Bellavia & Frone, 2005 for an overview) but of course the relationships between work and home are not necessarily negative, and work and family can, under optimum conditions be mutually enriching (Carlson & Grzywacz, 2008). However, we know much less about the conditions under which work can enrich family and family enrich work. It is important to be able to identify if and under what conditions the intense demands of employment or entrepreneurship could positively impact on children or at least the negative impacts be avoided.

Questions remain also about the impact of long intense work hours on spouses or partners and on other family members. Hochschild (1997) argues that the more time that is spent at the workplace, the more difficult relationships become at home, which reinforces the desire to spend time at work. However Crouter et al. (2001) examining the impact of fathers' long hours and overload on spouse relationships found that although partners working long hours spend less time together this does not necessarily affect the quality of the relationship. Role overload on the other hand did negatively impact on relationships. Again, in the case of entrepreneurs if there are no boundaries between work and home, and sometimes nowhere to go to escape from either work or family, the impact on relationships needs to be considered. Again it is likely that it is the quality of work that is important, but this raises question of whether and in what conditions intensive hours can be enriching or at least, not destructive for family members.

One consequence of current ways of working on the family is a threat to gender equality. Women's greater work time sacrifices may mitigate the impact of all consuming work on children, but at a cost in terms of careers and gender equity. It is difficult for both parents of young children or those with other caring responsibilities to sustain long intensive work hours so this often results in the perpetuation of — or even a shift back to, traditional gendered patterns as women remain more likely than men to reduce work involvement for family reasons. Moreover we have argued in this chapter that this is not confined to those in employment, as women entrepreneurs are more likely than men to cut back on their work. Thus while gendered norms about working parents constrained some women in the mid-twentieth century, despite considerable, if uneven shifts in gender roles and relationships, contemporary trends in working hours contribute to the reproduction of gender in the workplace and the family in the current context. Some working parents manage the intensive demands of full-time work by employing domestic help, often from developing countries. As Ehrenreich and Hochschild (2003) have pointed out, little thought is given to the effects of domestic workers' own families, whose absent mother is enabling more privileged families to manage work and family. This trend also exacerbates global inequalities. We need to understand more about the impact of long working hours on gender relations and how equitable relations can be enhanced and sustained in contemporary contexts.

Long hours can also affect the nature of family relationships. In some contexts it is difficult for those who work long hours to find time to meet potential partners, establish relationships and family formation, although the role of the Internet has proved important in bringing together those for whom there is little time for socialising (Gambles et al., 2007). Declining birth rates in many national contexts have also been attributed the pressures of current forms of work as well as persistent gendered employment experiences (Fagnani, 2007; Hašková, 2007). This raises issues of population sustainability. Current ways of working linked to declining birth rates underestimate the importance of social reproduction for national economies as well as quality of life. In Japan, for example, there is explicit concern about sustaining a future workforce as well as future consumers (Gambles et al., 2006). With ageing populations there is also much concern about the care deficit (Blair Loy & Jacobs, 2003; Hochschild, 1989). Who will care for children, the elderly and sick? In traditional societies extended families can cushion the impact of long working hours of some family members, and yet new ways of working also put strains on extended families and requirements such as relocation are associated with a shift to nuclear families among many knowledge workers, reducing this form of support (Gambles et al., 2006). Long working hours also impact on other relationships. For example many workers now say they have little time to retain friendships (Gambles et al., 2006; Parris, Vickers, & Wilkes, 2008) or for community involvement. This reduces social capital at a time when it can be crucial.

The time squeeze can also impact on family lifestyle. For example, as parents have less time with children they often make up for this by providing more consumer goods, which, in turn, creates further demands, contributing to an intensification of parenting demands as well as work demands (Lewis & Smithson, 2006). As Madeleine Bunting has observed

> The harder you work, the longer and the more intense your hours, the
> more pressure you experience, the more intense is the drive to repair,

console, restore and find periodic escape through consumerism. (Bunting, 2004, p. 157)

7.2.   Socially Sustainable Work — A Long-Term Perspective

This discussion suggests that future debates and research on the nature of work and on workaholic tendencies, whatever their origin, should consider the issues of social as well as economic sustainability of work within contexts where achievement and status associated with work is more valued than family (Lewis & Cooper, 1999; Lewis et al., 2007; Webster, 2004; Brewster, 2004). The sustainability of current forms of paid work is in question in many contexts for a number of reasons; because of rising levels of stress and sickness absence in many contexts (Back Wiklund & Plantin, 2007; Geurts, Kompier, & Grundemann, 2000), declining birth rates and threats to communities and community involvement (Gambles et al., 2006). As Juliet Webster (2004) argues, "we now have to broaden our concerns to consider the impact of the organisation of work on the wider sphere of life beyond paid employment — for the individual, for communities, for society at large. In other words, our concern must now be with enhancing the broader social sustainability of working life" (pp. 62–63). Whether people feel that they "choose" to or are driven by employer demands or entrepreneurial pressures to work all the time and have no other life, the potential impacts extend well beyond individual consequences. Taking a long-term perspective then, it is vital to explore conditions under which long working hours maybe life enhancing or at least not damaging to families and communities. It may also be important to find ways of challenging values that prioritise status and achievement in the world at work to a greater extent than family and community activities.

Acknowledgments

The authors would like to thank the City and County Enterprise Boards for their help in administering the survey. But most importantly, we would like to thank the entrepreneurs who participated in this study, for giving us a little bit of their precious time.

References

Acker, J. (1992). *Gendering organizational analysis.* Newbury Park, California: Sage.
Ahl, H. (2004). *The scientific reproduction of gender inequality: A discourse analysis of research texts on women's entrepreneurship.* Copenhagen: CBS Press.
Anderson-Gough, F., Grey, G., & Robson, K. (2001). In the name of the client. The service ethic in two international accounting firms. *Human Relations, 53,* 1151–1174.

Back Wicklund, M., & Plantin, L. (2007). The workplace as an arena for negotiating the work–family boundary: A case study of two Swedish social services agencies. In: R. Crompton, S. Lewis & C. Lyonette (Eds), *Women, men, work and family in Europe*. London: Palgrave.

Bailyn, L. (1993). *Breaking the mold: Women, men and time in the new corporate world*. New York: Free Press.

Baines, S., Wheelock, J., & Gelder, U. (2003). *Riding the roller coaster: Family life and self-employment*. Bristol: The Policy Press.

Beem, C. (2005). Challenges to change: The invasion of the money world. In: J. Heymann & C. Beem (Eds), *Unfinished work: Building equality and democracy in an Era of working families*. New York: The New Press.

Bellavia, G., & Frone, M. (2005). Work–family conflict. In: J. Barling, E. K. Kelloway & M. Frone (Eds), *Handbook of Work Stress* (pp. 113–147).

Belle, A., & La Valle, I. (2003). *Combining self-employment and family life*. Cambridge: Policy Press and Joseph Rowntree Foundation.

Blair-Loy, M., & Jacobs, J. A. (2003). Globalization, work hours, and the care deficit among stockbrokers. *Gender & Society, 17*, 230–249.

Brandth, B., & Kvande, E. (2001). Flexible work and flexible fathers. *Work, Employment and Society, 15*(2), 251–267.

Brannen, J. (2005). Time and the negotiation of work–family boundaries: Autonomy or illusion? *Time and Society, 14*(1), 113–131.

Brewster, J. (2004). *Working and living in the European knowledge society: The policy implication of developments in working life and their effects on social relations*. Report for the project 'Infowork', Department of Sociology, Trinity College, Dublin.

Bunting, M. (2004). *Willing slaves*. London: Harpers and Collins.

Burchall, B., Lapido, D., & Wilkinson, F. (Eds). (2002). *Job insecurity and work intensification*. London: Routledge.

Caproni, P. J. (2004). Work/life balance. You can't get there from here. *The Journal of Applied Behavioural Science, 40*(2), 208–218.

Carlson, D., & Grzywacz, J. (2008). Reflections and future directions on measurement in work–family research. In: K. Korabik, D. S. Lero & D. L. Whitehead (Eds), *Handbook of Work–Family integration: Theories, Perspectives and Best Practices*. Burlington, MA: Elsevier.

Crouter, A., Bumpus, M., Head, M., & McHale, S. (2001). Implications of overwork and overload for the quality of men's family relationships. *Journal of Marriage and Family, 63*(2), 404–416.

Drago, R. (2001). Time on the job and time with their kids: Cultures of teaching and parenthood in the US. *Feminist Economics, 7*(3), 1–31.

Drew, E., Emerek, R., & Mahon, E. (Eds). (1998). *Women, work and the family in Europe*. London: Routledge.

Duxbury, L. (2008). Too much to do, and not enough time: An examination of role overload. In: K. Korabik, D. Lero & D. Whitehead (Eds), *Work–family culture: Current research and future directions*. Handbook of Work and Family. Burlington, MA: Elsevier.

Ehrenreich, B., & Hochschild, A. (2003). *Global woman: Nannies, maids and sex workers in the new economy*. New York: Metropolitan Books.

Eurostat. (2008). [online] (cited 26 February 2008) Available at < epp.eurostat.ec. europa.eu/portal/page?_pageid = 1090,30070682,1090_30298591&_dad = portal&_schema = PORTAL>.

Fagnani, J. (2007). 'Fertility rates and mothers' employment behavior in comparative perspective: Similarities and differences in six European countries. In: R. Crompton, S. Lewis & C. Lyonette (Eds), *Women, men, work and family in Europe*. London: Palgrave.

Galinsky, E. (1999). *Ask the children. What American children really think about working parents*. New York: Wiliam and Morrow and Co.

Gambles, R., Lewis, S., & Rapoport, R. (2006). *The myth of work–life balance: The challenge of our time for men, women and societies*. Chichester: Wiley.

Geurts, S., Kompier, M., & Grundemann, R. (2000). Curing the Dutch disease. Sickness absence and work disability in the Netherlands. *International Social Security Review, 53*(4), 79–103.

Greer, M. J., & Greene, P. G. (2003). Feminist theory and the study of entrepreneurship. In: J. E. Butler (Ed.), *New perspectives on women entrepreneurs* (pp. 1–24). Greenwich, CT: Information Age Publishing.

Guest, D. (2002). Perspectives on the study of work–life balance. *Social Science Information, 41*(2), 255–279.

Haas, L., Alldred, K., & Hwang, P. (2002). The impact of organizational culture on men's use of parental leave in Sweden. *Community, Work and Family, 5*(3), 319–342.

Hašková, H. (2007). Explanations of fertility decline, postponement of childbearing and increase in childlessness in central and Eastern Europe. In: R. Crompton, S. Lewis & C. Lyonette (Eds), *Women, men, work and family in Europe*. London: Palgrave.

Hochschild, A. R. (1989). *The second shift: Working parents and the revolution at home*. London: Piatkus.

Hochschild, A. R. (1997). *The time bind. When work becomes home and home becomes work*. New York: Henry Holt.

Hewitt, P. (1993). *About time: The revolution in work and family life*. London: IPPR.

Humbert, A. L. (2007). *Female entrepreneurship in Ireland: An exploratory study*. Unpublished thesis. Trinity College, Dublin.

Kalicki, B., Fthenakis, W. E., Peitz, G., & Engfer, A. (1998). Gender-roles at the transition to parenthood. Poster presented at the XVth Biennial ISSBD Meetings, 1–4 July, Berne.

Kofodimos, J. (1993). *Balancing act: How managers can integrate successful careers and fulfilling personal lives*. San Francisco: Jossey Bass.

Lewis, S. (1991). Motherhood and/or employment: The impact of social and organizational values. In: A. Phoenix, A. Woollett & E. Lloyd (Eds), Motherhood: Meanings, practices and ideologies. London: Sage.

Lewis, S. (1997). Family friendly policies: Organizational change or playing about at the margins? *Gender, Work and Organizations* (4), 13–23.

Lewis, S. (2001). Restructuring workplace cultures: The ultimate work–family challenge? *Women in Management Review, 16*(1), 21–29.

Lewis, S. (2007). Working time, client time and family time. Accounting for time in the accountancy profession. In: T. Van der Lippe & P. Peters (Eds), *Competing claims in work and family life*. Cheltenham: Edward Elgar.

Lewis, S. (2003). The integration of paid work and the rest of life: Is post-industrial work the new leisure? *Leisure Studies, 22*(4), 343–355.

Lewis, S., & Cooper, C. (1999). The work–family research agenda in changing contexts. *Journal of Occupational Health Psychology, 4*(4), 382–393.

Lewis, S., Gambles, R., & Rapoport, R. (2007). The constraints of a 'work–life balance' approach: An international perspective. *International Journal of Human Resource Management, 18*(3), 360–373.

Lewis, S., & Smithson, J. (2006). *Final Report of the Transitions Project for the EU Framework 5 funded study "Gender, parenthood and the changing European workplace"*. Manchester: RIHSC, Manchester Metropolitan University. Available at www.workliferesearch.org/transitions.

Marlow, S. (1997). Self-employed women – new opportunities, old challenges? *Entrepreneurship and Regional Development, 9*(3), 199–210.

Maume, D., & Bellas, M. (2001). The overworked American or the time bind? *American Behavioral Scientist, 44*(7), 1137–1156.

Orhan, M., & Scott, D. (2001). Why women enter into entrepreneurship: An explanatory model. *Women in Management Review, 16*(5), 232–243.

Parris, M., Vickers, M., & Wilkes, L. (2008). Fitting friendship into the equation: Middle managers and the work/life balance. *Community, Work and Family* (in press).

Perlow, L. (1998). Boundary control. The social ordering of work and family time in a high tech organization. *Administrative Science Quarterly, 43*(2), 328–357.

Perlow, L. (2001). Time to coordinate: Toward an understanding of work-time standards and norms in a multicounty study of software engineers. *Work and Occupations, 28*(1), 91–111.

Rapoport, R., Bailyn, L., Fletcher, J., & Pruitt, B. (2002). *Beyond work–family balance: Advancing gender equity and work performance*. Chichester: Wiley.

Sullivan, C., & Lewis, S. (2001). Home-based telework, gender and the synchronisation of work and family; perspectives of teleworkers and their co-residents. *Gender, Work and Organisation, 8*(2), 123–145.

Thompson, J., & Bunderson, J. (2001). Work–nonwork conflict and the phenomenology of time. *Work and Occupations, 28*(1), 17–39.

Van der Lippe, T., & Peters, P. (2007). (Eds). *Competing claims in work and family life*. Cheltenham: Edward Elgar.

Warton, A., & Blair-Loy, M. (2006). Long work hours and family life: A cross-national study of employees' concerns. *Journal of Family Issues, 27*(3), 415–436.

Webster, J. (2004). *Working and living in the knowledge society:The policy implications of developments in working life and their effects on social relations*. Report for the project 'Infowork', Department of Sociology, Trinity College, Dublin.

Yakura, E. (2001). Billables. The valorisation of time in consulting. *American Behavioral Scientist, 44*(7), 1076–1095.

Chapter 8

Police Long Work Hours: Causes, Consequences and Alternatives

Bryan Vila and Jason M. Moore

Abstract

In police work, the hazards associated with long work hours are inextricably linked to shift work, schedule disruption and job stress because they all interfere with sleep. In turn, fatigue attributable to lack of sleep appears to be an important causal factor in work-related injuries as well as health and family problems in this critically important occupational group. Shift work, overtime policies and the lack of adequate focus on reducing workplace fatigue increase risks of injury and death for both officers and the communities they serve. Causes of fatigue are discussed as well as some potential methods for addressing fatigue such as education, intervention and assessment. The consequences of failing to address fatigue are dire and increasingly relevant. Suggestions are offered for providing a common ground on which police managers and line officers can collaborate to address fatigue issues effectively.

8.1. Introduction

In police work, the hazards associated with long work hours are inextricably linked to shift work, schedule disruption and job stress because they all interfere with sleep. In turn, fatigue that is attributable to lack of sleep appears to be an important causal factor in work-related injuries as well as health and family problems in this critically important occupational group. Among the 17% of all workers in the United States who work shifts, there are approximately 800,000 full-time, sworn police officers who often work seriously disrupted schedules. Although there is some evidence that problems arising from long, erratic work hours among this group appear to be common to police in other industrialized nations, thus far, the majority of research on this topic has been done in the United States. During the past few years, several

Canadian researchers also have begun focusing on this topic as their policing agencies, officers and labor organizations at every level struggle with long work hours, shift work and resulting fatigue. For the most part, however, this chapter focuses on police in the United States because of the unique obstacles to work-hour reform and research associated with the distribution of this population among roughly 18,000 independent law enforcement agencies serving vastly different communities (Reaves, 2003). This large, essential workforce plays a high-risk/high-demand role in every community because officers must respond to erratic demands for emergency services around the clock regardless of personal needs or preferences.

The health, safety and performance of many police officers is threatened by long and erratic work hours, shift work and occupational stressors — as well as the choices that officers themselves make about work, sleep, family and other personal activities. Officers whose personal choices do not make getting sufficient sleep a priority, or who are required to live chronically disjointed lives by their employers' scheduling and work-hour practices, suffer from disruption of their biological, psychological and social systems. The outcome of this disruption is disproportionately high levels of cardio-vascular, gastrointestinal and metabolic diseases; chronic insomnia, sleep apnea and other sleep disorders; psychological disorders, depression, suicide and family dysfunc-tion (Franke & Anderson, 1994; Franke, Cox, Schultz, & Anderson, 1997; Gershon, Lin, & Li, 2002; Liberman et al., 2002; Luenda, Violanti, Burchfiel, & Vila, 2007a, 2007b; Neylan et al., 2002; Rajaratnam et al., 2007; Toch, 2002; Violanti, Vena, & Petralia, 1998). Research linking long and erratic work hours to these sorts of disorders is substantial and compelling (see Caruso et al., 2006; Durmer & Dinges, 2005).

Nonetheless, police officers in the United States continue to compound the unavoidable physical insults of shift work with large amounts of overtime (Vila, 2006, 2000; Vila, Morrison, & Kenney, 2002; Vila, Kenney, Morrison, & Reuland, 2000). Although there are no comprehensive data about police overtime practices, media reports from around the United States and anecdotal reports from thousands of officers consistently confirm that most officers assigned to patrol and detective assignments work at least occasional double shifts of 16 or more hours and sometimes more than 24 hours straight. When combined with the time it takes to waken, eat, wash, dress and commute to work, these common practices translate into serious levels of impairment. Five separate research studies have found that being awake for 20–24 consecutive hours produces levels of impaired cognition, vigilance, psychomotor skills and simulated driving performance that are equivalent to blood alcohol concentration (BAC) levels of 0.08%–0.10% (Arendt, Wilde, Munt, & Maclean, 2000, 2001; Dawson & Reid, 1997; Lamond & Dawson, 1999; Williamson and Feyer, 2000). Such BAC levels are sufficient to establish drunk driving in most Western nations. For more than a decade, news reports based on timekeeping records have reported extreme cases in which a few officers in an agency worked 2000–3000 or more hours of *overtime* in a single year (e.g., Armstrong, 1996; Cassidy & Armstrong, 1999; Grad & Schoch, 1995; Marisco, 2003). Many officers also moonlight, yet few departments track or restrict the number of hours worked in secondary jobs.

The burden borne by officers and their families as a consequence of work-hour practices is similar to the challenges experienced by other occupational groups (see

Caruso et al., 2006). However, because police officers are required to serve society as law enforcers, first responders to all sorts of emergencies, peace-makers and community problem solvers, these performance-degrading practices also can have severe consequences for the communities they serve. Human performance is impaired by excessive work hours, circadian disruption and inadequate sleep — and this fatigue impairment cannot simply be "toughed out." As the National Aeronautic and Space Administration advised the U.S. Congress in 1999, their research clearly demonstrates that fatigue cannot "be willed away or overcome through motivation or discipline;" rather, it is rooted in physiological mechanisms related to sleep, sleep loss and circadian rhythms. These mechanisms are at work in ... [people] who need to remain vigilant despite long duty days ... and working at night when the body is programmed for sleep." (Mann, 1999; also see Rosekind et al., 1996a, 1996b). However, in contrast to other occupational groups, tired and ill-tempered cops are especially problematic because of the scope of their duties and powers.

Clearly, fatigue-impaired officers can present threats to public safety and expose the communities they serve to substantial liability. As pioneering Stanford University sleep researcher William C. Dement summarized,

> [P]olice work is the one profession in which we would want all practitioners to have adequate and healthful sleep to perform their duties at peak alertness levels. Not only is fatigue associated with individual misery, but it can also lead to counterproductive behavior. It is well known that impulsiveness, aggression, irritability and angry outbursts are associated with sleep deprivation. (as quoted in Vila, 2000, p. xiv)

Perhaps equally troubling are the consequences of drowsy driving as police — like other overworked people — drive home from work while impaired by fatigue.

After reviewing the causes and consequences of police long work hours in the United States, this chapter will discuss the forces and structures that tend to perpetuate current practices. We then will address alternatives for changing police behavior, followed by a discussion of strategies for using police to influence public practices and perceptions regarding long work hours and sleep. In particular, we will argue that drowsy driving prevention and enforcement provides an ideal anchor point for fostering change.

8.2. Causes, Prevalence and Consequences

Long work hours are one of the important factors that cause fatigue (defined here as inappropriate and intrusive sleepiness) among police officers. During the course of an officer's career, long work hours interact with shift work, work scheduling and the demands of work, life and basic human biology to create fatigue that undermines his or her safety, health and performance. Secondary effects of officer fatigue spill over into their families as well as the communities they serve. For decades, researchers, the public and police officers have treated fatigue as a natural and unavoidable part of being a cop (Vila, 1996). Our experience with police fatigue as researchers — and as former police officers — makes it clear that this long-held perception is not correct. A great deal can be done to minimize police fatigue if one understands the organizational and individual processes that promote and perpetuate fatigue and long work hours. Moreover, as we discuss later on, fatigue management and education can provide a fulcrum for efforts to reform work-hour and scheduling practices.

8.2.1. Causes

Police work is a 24/7 activity that requires a large proportion of officers to try to obtain sleep during daylight hours. This deviation from the natural cycle of day work and night sleep disrupts the internal rhythms that synchronize all of the body's major systems. The impact of this disruption is profound because the brain's circadian pacemaker is what one might think of as the conductor for the body's amazingly complex biological symphony. Thus, highest alertness for most people occurs during the morning and in the late afternoon/early evening hours when energy levels are elevated, eyes focus more easily, and physical abilities and coordination peak. When circadian rhythms dip as evening wears on, waves of sleepiness wash over us; appetites diminish, recollection dulls, reaction times slow and we fall asleep (see Dement and Vaughn, 1999; Monk & Folkard, 1992). As a consequence, officers on night shifts struggle to stay awake when their bodies want to sleep and then later try to fall asleep at home when they are naturally primed to be most alert. In fact, the body has defenses against sleeping during the day that make it extremely difficult for people to adapt to shift work under the best of circumstances (Rosekind et al., 1996a). Erratic overtime assignments and shift schedule changes make it impossible for most police officers to adapt at all.

Although the public safety impacts of worker fatigue have become increasingly clear over the past century, there are no laws limiting police officer work hours. The U.S. federal government has controlled the work hours of selected occupational groups such as train engineers, truckers, commercial pilots and, recently, nuclear power plant operators. But neither the national or state governments in the United States control police work hours, even though cops are the most public, sensitive and routinely controversial provider of governmental services. More than 10 years after the first research was published on police fatigue (Vila, 1996), few police agencies have explicit limits on hours worked. Those that have begun to set such limits in response to efforts to raise awareness of this problem tend to set very high limits that approach 100 hours per week.

The lack of legislated work-hour limits does not explain why the police have ignored the impact of fatigue. One likely reason is that policing's "macho" culture makes officers reluctant to complain (or to entertain complaints) about long hours. In addition, hiring, training and paying benefits for new employees is expensive, so many departments use large overtime authorizations to fund extra officers who fill vacancies and staff extra functions. Reliance on overtime can be seductive for chronically understaffed departments. For example, a recent internal audit in

Milwaukee, Wisconsin revealed that the department had paid $17.8 million in overtime in order to make up for 227 vacant police positions in 2006. That amount would have been sufficient to fund 380 more officers (Barton & Poston, 2007; Morics, 2007; also see O'Shaughnessy, 2006; Marisco, 2003; Miller & Delfiner, 2003). On a personal level, shift-differential pay and overtime work, as well as secondary employment, can provide strong motivation for officers to work considerably more than the traditional 40-hour week (e.g., see Vila, 2000).

8.2.2. *Prevalence*

Nationally representative data to provide individual-level information about police work hours and overtime do not exist in the United States — in part because police responsibilities are fragmented among so many agencies at different levels of government. However, the Center for Design of Industrial Schedules (CDIS) found that work schedule arrangements and requirements for off-duty court appearances in the Philadelphia Police Department resulted in "a state of cumulative sleep deprivation for most ... officers" that reduced performance and safety, and that "the officers had one of the worst profiles of alertness/sleepiness among shift workers evaluated by CDIS nationwide" (Czeisler, 1988, p. 4). Recent data also suggest that non-supervisory patrol officers in large urban departments tend to average between 15 and 40 hours of overtime work per month (Vila, 2000, 2006; Vila & Taiji, 1999). However, as is common in many occupational groups, overtime tends to be unevenly distributed (Coleman, 1995). It appears quite common for officers to average 80 or more hours of overtime per month and 1000 or more hours per year. This is an *enormous* amount given that the typical 40-hour, 50-week schedule results in 2000 hours per year. More extreme examples collected from jurisdictions scattered across the United States identify officers who have worked more than 3000 hours of overtime a year (Armstrong, 1996; Cassidy & Armstrong, 1999; Grad and Schoch, 1995; Marisco, 2003; Miller & Delfiner, 2003). Another telling piece of information emerged in August 2005, when the Boston Police Department began enforcing a long-standing rule that limited total work time to 96 hours per week. Within six months, 85 officers had been disciplined for exceeding even that extreme limit (Estes & Slack, 2006; Slack & Cramer, 2006). It is important to note that these figures fit well with the observations of the authors during their careers as police.[1] They also are consistent with the responses of more than 1000 police officers and executives who have attended talks and workshops on police fatigue issues during the past 10 years (Vila, 2006, p. 976).

---

1. Vila for 17 years and Moore for 10 years.

8.2.3. Consequences

Both the immediate and long-term consequences of fatigue and long work hours can increase health risks. Over the short-term, the probability of accidents, injuries and illness is increased by fatigue (Durmer & Dinges, 2005) and long work hours (Spurgeon, 2003). In policing, reduced performance in cognition, situational awareness, psychomotor skills and decision-making may be expected to translate into more traffic crashes, vulnerability to assault and sub-optimal interactions with the public. In a review of occupational injury surveillance data, Houser and his colleagues at the RAND Corporation found that nearly 90% of police fatalities on the job in the United States result from either assaults or vehicle crashes and most of the rest are heart attacks provoked by overexertion. Nearly half of all lost-time injuries are caused by assaults (27%) and vehicle accidents (16%). Other common causes of lost-time injuries are physical stress or overexertion (25%) and falls (19%) (Houser, Jackson, Bartis, & Peterson, 2004, pp. 46–49).

The long-term impact of being chronically sleep deprived because of shift work, schedule disruption and long work hours can be severe because day-to-day fatigue interacts with life stressors and human physiology to perpetuate a vicious cycle in which fatigue reduces ability to cope with stress constructively and undermines health and fitness, then stress, illness and poor physical fitness interfere with sleep. Over the course of a career in policing, the consequences of chronic fatigue include increased stress levels and diminished ability to cope with the sorts of complex, threatening and corrosive situations that police officers often are called on to handle.

Thus far, only a few studies have been completed that assessed the impact of fatigue and long work hours on police officers' health. But all of their results point to substantial health problems. For example, the "Tired Cops" study, which tested officers in four medium-sized police departments in different regions of the United States (379 officers, 60,000 potential work days) found that 14% of officers reported that they were always or usually tired at the *beginning* of their work shifts. During the previous month, 16% reported having trouble staying awake while driving, eating meals or engaging in a social activity more than once a week. Officers also reported averaging far less sleep than the general public — 53% of police, as compared with 38% of the general public, averaged 6.5 or fewer hours of sleep daily. Sleep quality scores on a standardized instrument were twice as high (indicating poorer sleep) as those for the general public. Forty-one percent of the officers' scores indicated that they should seek medical attention for possible sleep disorders (Vila et al., 2000, pp. 48–52). Newly announced results of a self-report study of 4471 U.S. and Canadian police officers demonstrated similar levels of sleep disorders: 38.4% of officers screened positive for sleep disorders and, among those, more than a third suffered from obstructive sleep apnea and nearly 7% had insomnia (Rajaratnam et al., 2007).

Another study of 747 police officers in the San Francisco Bay area and New York City found similar levels of low sleep quality and that stress from officers' general work environment was strongly associated with poor sleep quality. Sleep disturbances in this study were strongly associated with post-traumatic stress symptoms and general psychopathology as measured using well-validated psychometric instruments. Moreover, health problems associated with post-traumatic stress symptoms were mediated by sleep disturbances. Traumatic stress symptoms were significantly related to both somatic symptoms (r-squared $= 0.18$, $p < 0.001$) and health functioning (r-squared $= 0.02$, $p < 0.01$). Further, sleep partially mediated the relationship between somatic symptoms and traumatic stress symptoms ($p < 0.001$), and fully mediated the relationship between traumatic stress symptoms and health functioning (Neylan et al., 2002).

A retrospective mortality study by Violanti and Vena in Buffalo, New York provides a chilling picture of the potential impact of a career in policing. Using official records, they assembled data on 2693 white males who had been employed as police officers for at least 5 years by the city of Buffalo between 1950 and 1990, then compared it with corresponding age- and time-specific U.S. mortality rates for white males to calculate expected numbers of deaths (Violanti et al., 1998). The cohort included officers who were: retired (53%), actively employed (27%), died in service (13%) and resigned or left service (7%). In all, 58,474 person years were included in the study's modified life-table analysis. When compared with persons of similar age, race and sex in the general population, officers and former officers from Buffalo had significantly higher rates for all causes of mortality. These rates were highest among those who had been on the job from 10 to 19 years, those aged 50–69, and those who began their careers prior to age 24. Malignant neoplasms, cirrhosis of the liver and suicide were particularly elevated — the latter even though police suicides often tend to be underreported (Violanti, Vena, Marshall, & Petralia, 1996).

These findings also are consistent with a previous study by the same research team that compared the 1950–1979 Buffalo police officer cohort with municipal workers from the same region of New York (Vena, Violanti, Marshall, & Fiedler, 1986). Police officer mortality rates in that study for heart disease, cancer and suicide were elevated relative to the municipal workers to much the same degree as in the 1998 study. Although the Buffalo study did not specifically include work-hour data, it is relevant to the current discussion because it provides striking evidence of the health burden associated with police work. As was noted previously, all of the mortality factors that were elevated for these officers have firmly-established links with shift work and sleep disruption.

Many of the persistent work-hour and scheduling practices that cause or enable officers to work while impaired by fatigue also are likely to contribute to the major causes of officer deaths: assaults, accidents and suicide. Figure 8.1, which was constructed using data from the U.S. Federal Bureau of Investigation and from the Centers for Disease Control, compares the proportion of police law enforcement officers who were killed each year by criminal acts, in accidents and by suicide. As this figure shows, there has been a gradual shift in the proportion of on-duty law enforcement officers who were killed accidentally, as opposed to feloniously.[2]

---

2. Felonious killings include those associated with assaults, vehicle pursuits or other serious criminal acts. Accidental deaths involve vehicle accidents and other causes ranging from falls and aircraft accidents to accidental firearms discharges.

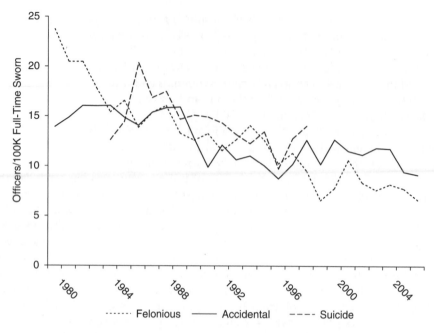

Figure 8.1: Police officers killed in the United States from 1980 to 2006 by on-duty felonious and accidental causes (U.S. Department of Justice, FBI annual) and by suicide (CDC 1984–98) from 1980 to 2006.

Although total death rates have declined significantly since 1980, almost all of that change has been driven by reductions in felonious killings. Accidental deaths have declined almost not at all and neither have deaths by suicide. The most likely explanations for the decline in felonious killings are the introduction of soft body armor in the early 1970s, steady refinements in officer survival training and tactics, and declines in violent crime since the mid-1980s. Accidental deaths are dominated by vehicle-related accidents such as crashes and being struck accidentally by a vehicle. The lack of improvement in accidental death rates, despite dramatic changes in vehicle safety technologies, may well be related to the fact that shift work and long work-hour practices have changed little during the past three decades. Similarly, the impact of proximate and chronic fatigue on a person's ability to keep stressors in perspective, maintain positive affect and overall psychological well-being is likely to increase the risks of suicide.

8.2.4.   *Family and Social Living*

Just as fatigue degrades police officers' performance, health and safety, it also can interfere with the kinds of familial and social relations that connect them to society and help protect them from the corrosive environment in which they work. Shift work, like working during weekends, tends to separate officers from society at large because it imposes a contrarian rhythm to their lives. It also reinforces the insular tendency of cops that arises because police have unique legal powers and perform an often unpleasant job which tends to bring them in contact with people who are dysfunctional, angry, agitated, inebriated, in crisis and sometimes armed. Social life, particularly family life, gives officers the kinds of contact with normal people in normal settings that help put their abnormal experiences on the job in perspective. Unfortunately, fatigue also is likely to increase the probability that officers will bring the anger, violence and general dysfunction of the streets home with them. Sometimes these problems erode relationships with family and friends. All too often, the result is domestic violence.

Shift work and erratic work hours are considered risk factors for domestic partner violence, so are exposure to danger on the job and the presence of weapons in the home — all inevitable aspects of having a cop in the family (Finn & Tomz, 1997; Wetendorf, 2000). The job itself tends to increase the risk of domestic violence because officers are routinely exposed to critical incidents and trained to use psychological and physical force (Kirschman, 1997). Not surprisingly, the result often appears to be marital discord, dissatisfaction and divorce (Finn & Tomz, 1997; Gershon, 1999). Gershon and her colleagues' survey of work stress among 1100 police officers found that intimate partner violence was significantly correlated with perceived job-related stress (Gershon, Patten, & Johnson, 1999).

The prevalence of intimate partner violence among police families is difficult to establish because of underreporting due to pressures within families and police agencies — in the United States, police officers who have been convicted of domestic violence lose their jobs because they are no longer able to use or possess firearms (42 USC 136, 1994). Compared to the estimated 10% prevalence of intimate partner violence among the general public, estimates for police families range from 25% in a small study (Neidig, Russell, & Seng, 1992) to approximately 7% in Gershon et al.'s (1999) large, anonymous self-report study (Gershon et al., 1999). The fact that 8% of a small sample of police spouses ($n = 48$) who also were queried in that study reported being physically assaulted lends credence to the lower estimate (Gershon, 1999). A later study by Gershon compared officers in a large, urban police force who had been charged with committing intimate partner violence with officers who were not charged. The accused officers were significantly more likely to be assigned to a high-crime district and to be members of a racial or ethnic minority (Gershon, Tiburzi, Lin, & Erwin, 2005). These findings are consistent with the correlation of police stress with physical violence against intimates in their 1999 study. They also are consistent with the long work-hours/stress/ dysfunction hypothesis advanced in this chapter because officers assigned to high crime areas are more likely to work overtime and be involved in critical incidents.

8.2.5. Community Issues

The impact of police fatigue on a community obviously includes such things as elevated risks of vehicle crashes and suboptimal decision making. But fatigue also can harm a community by degrading the millions of mundane contacts between police and the public — such as calls for information and advice, resolving simple disagreements, responding to passing comments during a meal break or routine traffic stops — that are the basis of much public opinion about the police. Fatigue's impact here may be akin to repeated microtraumas that gradually erode police–community relations. A short-tempered, rude or dismissive police officer provides a handy excuse for stereotyping the officer, his or her department, and the profession in a way that degrades the effectiveness of the police. Lowering the effectiveness of a police department increases the net cost of policing. It also undermines justice.

Police officers in the United States have broad discretionary powers and often function with substantial autonomy. Many of their most difficult and complex decisions are made in fluid, ambiguous and emotionally charged situations where lives, property and liberty can be lost in a split second. Even the more routine decisions made by officers can have serious consequences for individuals, families and communities. Officers decide when and how to drive emergency vehicles, confront disturbed and violent individuals, make arrests and use deadly force — usually with minimal supervision. In order to grasp how enormous the impact of officers' decisions can be, consider the impact of even a minor arrest on a young person's job prospects, what is at stake when an officer drives a little bit too fast responding to a call for service and causes a serious accident, or the long-term impact on a city when an ill-tempered officer's actions spark a riot.

Police officers in the United States are held accountable for their actions by a large, complex web of laws, regulations and policies. Sanctions including reprimands, suspension, termination from employment, or even criminal prosecution are imposed against officers who use their substantial discretionary powers improperly. The assumption behind these sanctions is that negative consequences will deter officers from behaving inappropriately. However, deterrence requires that the officers *think about* the potential consequences of their actions prior to engaging in illegal or prohibited behavior. Unfortunately, a substantial body of scientific evidence demonstrates that usual and accepted police work-hour and scheduling practices in the United States are likely to neutralize the ability of officers to make truly rational decisions. This is because they produce levels of sleep deprivation that can significantly impair the parts of the brain required for planning, weighing consequences and applying moral principles. If officers are unable to fully consider the potential consequences of their actions prior to acting, then the effectiveness of deterrence-based controls is diminished. Failure to control the police undermines justice itself.

To add insult to injury, police misconduct or impaired performance also exposes communities to unnecessary legal liability — and that liability is growing in the United States. Increasing public and professional awareness about fatigue exposes police officers and the jurisdictions for which they work to new and potentially serious legal liabilities. Although law in this area is still not fully formed, fatigue is being raised more and more frequently in civil suits regarding industrial and traffic accidents. In general, employers are being held responsible for the actions of overly fatigued employees under the theory that an employer has an affirmative duty to intervene if an employee has worked so many hours without rest that their impairment constitutes an unreasonable and foreseeable risk to others (Coburn, 1996; Moore-Ede, 1995; 892 P. 2^d 703; 462 F. Supp. 2^d 663; 2006 WL 2238913). Now that research has established that many officers work long hours, a substantial proportion of them are seriously impaired by fatigue, and roughly half of them are likely to have sleep disorders, police executives and the political leaders to whom they answer are obligated to address fatigue issues to the best of their ability. Officers and police administrators must cooperate to take meaningful and proactive steps toward addressing the issue of fatigue. It seems obvious that effective fatigue management is in the best interest of all police officers, regardless of rank, as well as the jurisdictions and communities they serve.

8.3. Changing Police Behavior

Police in the United States tend to be rather cynical and suspicious of change, and labor relations in many police agencies are strained. Understandably, work-hour issues tend to be one of the most difficult labor/management negotiations these organizations face. The number of hours an officer works affects how much she or he earns, and the scheduling of those hours affects almost every other aspect of family and social life. Despite this difficulty, both labor and management must cooperate fully in order to manage police fatigue. The reason is simple: no matter how well fatigue management policies are designed, if officers fail to get sufficient sleep during their off hours, they will be impaired on the job. Conversely, no matter how conscientiously an officer tries to obtain sufficient sleep, she or he will fail if work-hour policies and practices result in overly long work days and erratic scheduling practices — or if these practices work against, rather than with, the body's natural rhythms.

8.3.1. *Common Ground for Labor and Management*

Fortunately, experience with this problem during the past decade provides some guidance about how to go about developing and implementing policies and programs that help improve officer health, safety, performance and interactions with their communities. The first step is to clear a common ground on which both sides can work. The second step is to bring each side evidence that is so compelling that they cannot ignore it. Once that is done — once they realize that they *must* work together to address the tangle of performance, safety and health issues that surround work-hour issues — it is possible to bring science to bear so that they can schedule and allocate personnel in a way that balances the needs of the community for police services with the needs of officers for, rest, recuperation, social interaction and adequate earnings.

The common ground on which police management and labor can come together is bounded by four issues: risk management, human capital management, officer safety and officer health. Once managers become aware of the risks and legal liabilities associated with police fatigue and the ways in which fatigue wastes human capital, they must deal with the problem. Personnel costs account for more than 90% of most police budgets, and police services tend to be one of the largest expenses for most local governments. Police executives who fail to manage risks and conserve human capital jeopardize their careers and violate their public trust. Similarly, police unions and other collective bargaining units' primary responsibilities center on officer safety and health, all else is secondary. Individual officers also must respect safety and health issues associated with fatigue, if not for their own sake, because of their obligation to protect and support their fellow officers effectively in the field and because of their duty to the public. Once they become aware of the evidence about police fatigue, neither managers, labor leaders or individual officers can fail to try to develop solutions.

If this sounds overly optimistic, consider that since *Tired Cops: The Importance of Managing Police Fatigue* (Vila, 2000) was published, pleas for help in managing police fatigue have come from large — and roughly equal — numbers of police executives, union leaders and individual cops. In many instances, calls and e-mails have come from people who were frustrated because they could not get either labor or management to listen to reason. For every department whose police chief or sheriff cannot get a collective bargaining unit to discuss changing work shifts to manage fatigue or putting reasonable limits to hours worked per day, week or month, there seems to be a police bargaining unit leader, sergeant or line officer who cannot get his or her chief or sheriff to discuss the same things. Moreover, not one of the thousands of police officers of all ranks who have attended dozens of talks, workshops and consulting sessions put on by one of us (Vila) has failed to agree that fatigue is a serious problem and that it must be addressed. This level of agreement from police audiences about any issue, especially a conditions-of-work issue, is most unusual.

Police work-hour policies and practices must be tailored to meet the unique needs of each agency because local differences in critical variables such as demand for service peaks, crime rates, customs, laws, climate and geography create a work environment that requires different numbers of officers with different skill sets at different times of the day, week and year. Individual differences such as age, family obligations, educational aspirations, location of residence and commute times also need to be taken into account. A full description of the policy development process is beyond the scope of this chapter, but suggestions are provided in Vila (2000) and Vila et al. (2002). However, the keys to beginning this process are education and training.

8.3.2.   Education and Training

Meaningful change requires that executives, managers, supervisors and officers learn about the importance of managing fatigue and work hours. Starting in police academies and continuing throughout their entire careers officers are trained extensively and intensively to do their jobs well. Although there are signs of change, they receive almost no training about how to recognize or deal with the debilitating effects of fatigue related to shift work, long work hours or sleep deprivation.

Early in their careers — preferably during their academy training — officers should be taught about the impact of fatigue on decision making, performance, safety and health. As with other critical knowledge and skills, they also should receive periodic refresher training. After all, the most important piece of safety equipment an officer has is her or his brain. When officers are promoted to supervisory, management or executive ranks this training should be expanded. Supervisors need to monitor the alertness of officers and assure that they are sufficiently rested to perform their duties properly, just as they monitor the functionality of subordinates' safety equipment. They also need to learn to train officers to manage fatigue and employ fatigue countermeasures (see Caldwell, Caldwell, & Schmidt, 2008; Caldwell & Caldwell, 2003). Managers and executives need an even deeper understanding of the causes and consequences of fatigue and strategies for balancing the needs of officers with those of the community in a way that minimizes risks associated with long work hours, shift work and the challenges of police work.

One method for instilling an appreciation of the effects of fatigue on performance might be to assess the quality of officers' sleep, educate them about fatigue-related issues and policies, then sleep deprive them in a controlled setting where they can be tested using training simulators so they can see how fatigue affects critical job skills such as ability to communicate effectively, drive and handle deadly force situations. Most police academies already use simulators to train officers, so this added use would be easy to implement. The "show me" aspect of this type of training could increase awareness and acceptance of work-hour limitations since officers could experience firsthand how their abilities are impacted by working long hours.

Another important component of any fatigue-training program would be to periodically screen officers for potential sleep pathologies such as apnea, insomnia and stress-induced sleep issues. This would identify officers who had developed sleep disorders and reinforce the importance of sleep and fatigue management. Officers found to potentially have sleep disorders would then be referred to a licensed sleep professional for diagnosis and treatment.

Members of officers' families also should be encouraged to learn about fatigue. Experience in industry has demonstrated that educating and training employees works much better if their families also are given opportunities to learn about fatigue, why it is important, and how to help their shift worker make sleep a priority in a household that likely is on a different schedule (see Coleman, 1995; Monk & Folkard, 1992; Moore-Ede, 1993). Family support is a vital part of managing officer fatigue.

8.3.3. *Police Changing Public Behavior*

Yet another way to change current police practices and culture is to increase officer involvement in drowsy driving prevention, enforcement and accident investigation. Drowsy driving is a serious and frequently overlooked problem in the United Sates.

Even though it is seriously undercounted, the U.S. National Highway Traffic Safety Administration estimates that drowsy driving causes at least 100,000 police-reported crashes — 71,000 of which produce injuries — and kills more than 1550 Americans each year (NHTSA 2005; National Sleep Foundation, 2007). Just like the general public, few police officers appreciate the risks associated with driving while drowsy or even understand serious hazards such as the synergy between fatigue and alcohol (Arendt et al., 2000, 2001; Horne, Reyner, & Barrett, 2003; Krull, Smith, Sinha, & Parsons, 1993; Powell et al., 1999; Roehrs & Roth, 2008). As a consequence, people who would never consider driving drunk often think nothing of driving while drowsy. According to the 2005 Sleep in America poll, 60% of adult American drivers report driving while drowsy in the past year and 37% report actually falling asleep at the wheel. Most political jurisdictions in the highly decentralized United States do not currently consider drowsy driving education a priority. Although most states include information about fatigue or drowsy driving in their driver licensing manuals, in many cases this information was misleading or minimal (National Sleep Foundation, 2007).

Increasing police involvement in counter drowsy-driving activities could help improve public safety by reducing drowsy driving, and it also is likely to help anchor the importance of fatigue management in the officers involved in counter drowsy-driving activities. Standing in front of audiences to teach people about the dangers of drowsy driving, arresting drowsy drivers and investigating drowsy-driving crashes will tend to make officers avoid driving drowsy themselves. The more officers understand fatigue issues, the less they will be able to avoid feeling hypocritical if they drive drowsy or report to work overly fatigued. And the more a high-profile, macho occupational group like the police treats fatigue management as a way to improve performance, health and safety — to get the alertness edge — the more other people are likely to follow suit. Police often are viewed as role models and public icons. Focusing more of their efforts on drowsy driving provides a solid fulcrum for leveraging changes in both their behavior and that of the general public.

8.4. Summary

Long work hours and insufficient good-quality sleep often are likely to impair the performance of police officers in the United States even though public safety and justice itself depend on the soundness of their decisions and the skill with which they operate the tools of their job. In order to deal with this problem, managers need to understand how to balance the costs and benefits of compressed work shifts, flexible schedules, overtime and officer performance against demands for service, officer safety, legal liability and the hazards of burn-out or early retirement. Officers and their families need to know how to manage shift work, long work hours and job-related stress as well as how to maximize alertness. They also need to understand the likely consequences of overwork, second jobs and inadequate sleep. All of this knowledge must be predicated on clear evidence about the relationships between causal variables and their impact on officers day-to-day throughout their careers and into retirement.

Finally, both management and labor must be held accountable for managing fatigue because each has control over different parts of the problem. Their roles are inextricably intertwined; managers schedule and staff, officers make choices about what portion of their time off to devote to sleep, and the amount of time that they have available for sleep and recuperation is reduced by work time. There are no excuses for not dealing rationally with police fatigue other than, perhaps, sudden catastrophic events. Even then, there are ways to manage fatigue during unexpectedly long shifts using caffeine management, short naps and environmental change (Caldwell et al., 2008; Caldwell & Caldwell, 2003; Committee on Military Nutrition Research, 2001; Mitler, Dinges, & Dement, 1994; Moore-Ede, 1993; Naitoh, Kelly, & Babkoff, 1990). Although fatigue sometimes is caused by things beyond an officer's control such as a sick child or competing family responsibilities, once an officer has been properly trained about fatigue management he or she must stand up like a professional and say "I've been awake for 20 hours straight and I'm not ready to work the streets." This is the essence of personal accountability for fatigue. Similarly, even when understaffing and demand for services make overtime the only option, managers must endeavor to distribute that overtime reasonably evenly. In extreme circumstances, they also must decline to send sleep-impaired officers on non-emergency calls despite pressure from political leaders or the public.

References

Arendt, J. T., Wilde, J. S., Munt, P. W., & Maclean, A. W. (2000). Simulated driving performance following prolonged wakefulness and alcohol consumption: Separate and combined contributions to impairment. *Journal of Sleep Research*, 9, 233–241.

Arendt, J. T., Wilde, J. S., Munt, P. W., & Maclean, A. W. (2001). How do prolonged wakefulness and alcohol compare in the decrements they produce on a simulated driving task? *Accident Analysis and Prevention*, 33, 337–344.

Armstrong, D. (1996). Troopers' extra hours spur worry overtime, details on pike pile up despite regulations. *Boston Globe*, p. A1, September 12.

Barton, G., & Poston, B. (2007). In 2006, Milwaukee police worked enough overtime to hire 380 more officers. *Milwaukee Journal Sentinel*. Downloaded on 30 September from www.jsonline.com/story/index.aspx?id = 669050.

Caldwell, J. A., & Caldwell, J. L. (2003). *Fatigue in aviation, a guide to staying awake at the stick*. Burlington, VT: Ashgate.

Caldwell, J.A., Caldwell, J.L., & Schmidt, R.M. (2008). Alertness management strategies for operational contexts. *Sleep Medicine Review*, doi:10.1016/j.smrv.2008.01.002.

Caruso, C. C., Bushnell, T., Eggerth, D., Heitmann, A., Kojola, B., Newman, K., Rosa, R., Sauter, S., & Vila, B. (2006). Long work hours, health, and safety: Toward a national occupational research agenda. *American Journal of Industrial Medicine*, 49(11), 930–942.

Cassidy, T., & Armstrong, D. (1999). State police overtime soaring. *Boston Globe* (September), B1.

Coburn, E. (1996). Managing the costs of worker fatigue. *Risk Management News*, July, 3–4.

Coleman, R. M. (1995). The Twenty-Four Hour Business: Maximizing Productivity Through Round-The-Clock Operations. New York: American Management Association.

Committee on Military Nutrition Research, Food and Nutrition Board. (2001). *Caffeine for the sustainment of mental task performance: Formulations for military operations.* Washington, DC: National Academy Press.

Czeisler, C. A. (1988). *Final report on the Philadelphia police department shift rescheduling program.* Boston: Center for Design of Industrial Schedules.

Dawson, D., & Reid, K. (1997). Fatigue, alcohol and performance impairment. *Nature, 388*, 235.

Dement, W. C., & Vaughn, C. (1999). *The promise of sleep: A pioneer in sleep medicine explores the vital connection between health, happiness, and a good night's sleep.* New York: Delcorte.

Durmer, J., & Dinges, D. (2005). Neurocognitive consequences of sleep deprivation. *Seminars in Neurology, 25*, 117–129.

Estes, A., & Slack, D. (2006). Boston reports a wage drop: Payroll decreases by $13m since '04. *Boston Globe* (March), A1.

Finn, P., & Tomz, J. E. (1997). *Developing a law enforcement program for officers and their families* (pp. 1–219). Washington, DC: U.S. Department of Justice, National Institute of Justice.

Franke, W. D., & Anderson, D. F. (1994). Relationship between physical activity and risk factors for cardiovascular disease among law enforcement officers. *Journal of Occupational Medicine, 36*, 1127–1132.

Franke, W. D., Cox, D. F., Schultz, D. P., & Anderson, D. F. (1997). Coronary heart disease risk factors in employees of Iowa's department of public safety compared to a cohort of the general population. *American Journal of Industrial Medicine, 31*, 733–777.

Gershon, R. R. M. (1999). *Domestic violence in police families.* Baltimore, MD: Mid-Atlantic Regional Community Policing Institute.

Gershon, R. R. M., Lin, S., & Li, X. (2002). Work stress in aging police officers. *Journal of Occupational and Environmental Medicine, 44*, 160–167.

Gershon, R. R. M., Patten, M., & Johnson, O. (1999). Project shields. *Proceedings of the National Symposium on Law Enforcement Families*, San Antonio, TX.

Gershon, R., Tiburzi, M., Lin, S., & Erwin, M. (2005). Reports of intimate partner violence made against police officers. *Journal of Family Violence, 20*(1).

Grad, S., & Schoch, D. (1995). Cities' top 25 lists show employees generously paid. *Los Angeles Times*, September, B1.

Horne, J., Reyner, L., & Barrett, P. (2003). Driving impairment due to sleepiness is exacerbated by low alcohol intake. *Occupational and Environmental Medicine, 60*, 689–692.

Houser, A., Jackson, B., Bartis, J., & Peterson, D. (2004). *Emergency responder injuries and fatalities: An analysis of surveillance data (TR-100-NIOSH).* Santa Monica, CA: RAND.

Kirschman, E. (1997). *I love a cop.* New York: Guilford.

Krull, K., Smith, L., Sinha, R., & Parsons, O. (1993). Simple reaction time event-related potentials: Effects of alcohol and sleep deprivation. *Alcohol Clinical Experimental Research, 17*(4), 771–777.

Lamond, N., & Dawson, D. (1999). Quantifying the performance impairment associated with fatigue. *Journal of Sleep Research, 8*, 255–262.

Liberman, A., Best, S., Metzler, T., Fagan, J., Weiss, D., & Marmar, C. (2002). Routine occupational stress and psychological distress in police. *Policing: International Journal of Management, 25*, 421–439.

Luenda, C., Burchfiel, C., Violanti, J., Vila, B., Hartley, T. A., & Slaven, J. (2007a). Shift work and sleep: The Buffalo police health study. *Policing: An International Journal of Police Strategies & Management, 30*, 215–227.

Luenda, C., Violanti, J., Burchfiel, C., & Vila, B. (2007b). Obesity and sleep: The Buffalo police health study. *Policing: An International Journal of Police Strategies & Management, 30*, 203–214.

Mann, M. (1999). Testimony on pilot fatigue before the Aviation Subcommittee of the Committee on Transportation and Infrastructure, U.S. House of Representatives. Congressional Record, August 3. (Downloaded August 18, 2004 via Verity Information Server.)

Marisco, R. (2003). 200 P.A. officers at least doubled pay with overtime: Money for extra shifts sets agency record. *Star Ledger* (May), 1–22.

Miller, A., & Delfiner, R. (2003). Overtime king: Nonstop bridge cop adds 210G to salary. *New York Post*, May, 17.

Mitler, M., Dinges, D., & Dement, W. (1994). Sleep medicine, public policy, and public health. In: M. Kryger, T. Roth & W. Dement (Eds), *Principles and practice of sleep medicine* (2nd ed.). Philadelphia, PA: W.B. Saunders.

Monk, T., & Folkard, S. (1992). *Making shift work tolerable*. London: Taylor & Francis.

Moore-Ede, M. (1993). *The 24-hour society: Understanding human limits in a world that never stops*. Reading, MA: Addison-Wesley.

Moore-Ede, M. (1995). When things go bump in the night. *ABA Journal* (January), 56–60.

Morics, W.M. (2007). Audit of Milwaukee Police Department Overtime. City of Milwaukee, Wis., common council file, June.

Naitoh, P., Kelly, T. L., & Babkoff, H. (1990). Napping, stimulant, and four-choice performance. In: R. J. Broughton & R. D. Ogilvie (Eds), *Sleep, arousal, and performance*. Boston: Birkhaüser.

National Aeronautic and Space Administration. (1999). Hearing on pilot fatigue before the aviation subcommittee of the Committee on Transportation and Infrastructure, U.S. House of Representatives Transcript, August 3.

National Highway Transportation Safety Administration. (2005). Drowsy Driving and Automobile Crashes: NCSDR/NHTSA Expert Panel on Driver Fatigue and Sleepiness. Downloaded 09 April 2008 from www.nhtsa.dot.gov/people/injury/drowsy_driving1/drowsy.html#NCSDR/NHTSA

National Sleep Foundation. (2007). *State of the states report on drowsy driving*. Washington, DC: National Sleep Foundation.

Neidig, P., Russell, H., & Seng, A. (1992). Interspousal aggression in law enforcement families: A Preliminary Investigation. Police Studies.

Neylan, T. C., Metzler, M. A., Best, S. R., Weiss, D. S., Fagan, J. A., Liberman, A., Rogers, C., Vedantham, K., Brunet, A., Lipsey, T. L., & Marmar, C. R. (2002). Critical incident exposure and sleep quality in police officers. *Psychosomatic Medicine, 64*, 345–352.

O'Shaughnessy, B. (2006). Overtime costs local taxpayers millions. *Indianapolis Star*, August 6. Download from www.indystar.com.

Powell, N., Riley, R., Schechtman, K., Blumen, M., Dinges, D., & Guilleminault, C. (1999). A comparative model: Reaction time performance in sleep-disordered breathing versus alcohol-impaired controls. *Laryngoscope, 109*(10), 1648–1654.

Rajaratnam, S., Barger, L., Lockley, S., Cade, B., O'Brien, C., White, D., & Czeisler, C. (2007). Screening for Sleep Disorders in North American Police Officers. *Sleep, 30*: Abstract Supplement, A209.

Reaves, B. A. (2003). *Census of state and local law enforcement agencies, 2000. Bureau of justice statistics bulletin.* Washington, DC: U.S. Department of Justice.

Roehrs, T., & Roth, T. (2008). Sleep, sleepiness, and alcohol use. National Institute on Alcohol Abuse and Alcoholism, National Institutes of Health. Downloaded from pubs.niaaa.nih.gov/publications/arh25-2/101-109.htm on March 27.

Rosekind, M., Gander, P., Gregory, K., Smith, R., Miller, D., & Oyung, R. (1996a). Managing fatigue in operational settings1: Physiological considerations and counter-measures. *Behavioral Medicine, 21*, 157–164.

Rosekind, M., Gander, P., Gregory, K., Smith, R., Miller, D., & Oyung, R. (1996b). Managing fatigue in operational settings 2: An integrated approach. *Behavioral Medicine, 21*, 157–164.

Slack, D., & Cramer, M. (2006). 82 Officers punished for excess workload. *Boston Globe*, Al, February 17.

Spurgeon, A. (2003). Working time: Its impact on safety and health. International Labour Office report. Geneva: International Labour Organization.

Toch, H. (2002). *Stress in policing.* Washington, DC: American Psychological Association.

U.S. Department of Justice, Federal Bureau of Investigation. Annual. Law Enforcement Officers Killed and Assaulted. Washington, DC: http://www.fbi.gov/ucr/killed/2006/index.html

Vena, J. E., Violanti, J. M., Marshall, J. R., & Fiedler, R. (1986). Mortality of a municipal worker cohort III: Police officers. *American Journal of Industrial Medicine, 10*, 383–397.

Vila, B. (1996). Tired cops: Probable connections between fatigue and the performance, health, and safety of patrol officers. *American Journal of Police, 15*(2), 51–92.

Vila, B. (2000). *Tired cops: The importance of managing police fatigue.* Washington, DC: Police Executive Research Forum.

Vila, B. (2006). Impact of long work hours on police officers and the communities they serve. *American Journal of Industrial Medicine, 49*(11), 972–980.

Vila, B., Kenney, D., Morrison, G., & Reuland, M. (2000). *Evaluating the effects of fatigue on police patrol officers.* Washington, DC: U.S. Department of Justice.

Vila, B., Morrison, G., & Kenney, D. (2002). Improving shift schedule and work-hour policies and practices to increase police officer health, safety and performance. *Police Quarterly, 5*(1), 4–24.

Vila, B., & Taiji, E. (1999). Police work hours, fatigue and officer performance. In: D. Kenney & R. McNamara (Eds), *Police and policing* (2nd ed.). Westport, CT: Praeger.

Violanti, J., Vena, J., & Petralia, S. (1998). Mortality of a police cohort: 1950–1990. *American Journal of Industrial Medicine, 33*, 366–373.

Violanti, J. M., Vena, J. E., Marshall, J. R., & Petralia, S. (1996). A comparative evaluation of police suicide rate validity. *Suicide & Life-Threatening Behavior, 26*, 79–85.

Wetendorf, D. (2000). *Police domestic violence: A handbook for victims* (pp. 1–34). Des Plaines, IL: Life Span.

Williamson, A. M., & Feyer, A.-M. (2000). Moderate sleep deprivation produces impairments in cognitive and motor performance equivalent to legally prescribed levels of alcohol intoxication. *Occupational and Environmental Medicine, 57*, 649–655.

COURT CASES

Court of Appeals of Oregon v. McDonald's Restaurants of Oregon, Inc. 892 P. 2^d 703 (133 Or.App. 514892 P. 2^d 703)

U.S. v. Sandhu. 462 F. Supp. 2^d 663 (E.D. PA, 2006)

Darling v. J.B. Expedited Services. 2006 WL 2238913 (U.S.D.C. M.D. Tenn)

Violence Against Women Act of 1994, 42 USC 136, Sub. III

Chapter 9

It Takes Two to Tango: Workaholism is Working Excessively and Working Compulsively

Wilmar B. Schaufeli, Toon W. Taris and Arnold B. Bakker

Since the term "workaholism" was coined by the American minister and psychologist Wayne E. Oates in 1968 to denote his own work addiction, it has rapidly become a colloquial notion. From the onset, workaholism was a well-liked topic in the popular, business, and self-help press (Robinson, 1998). In sharp contrast to its colloquial use, relatively few scholarly publications on workaholism have appeared. Recently, 131 articles on workaholism were identified, of which only 28 were empirical in nature (Ng, Sorensen, & Feldman, 2007). One of the main reasons for this large discrepancy between public and scientific interest in workaholism is the lacking agreement on its definition. Although for the lay public workaholism is synonymous with working excessively hard, scholars have proposed several more elaborate definitions (for a recent overview see McMillan & O'Driscoll, 2006). Nevertheless, to date, a generally accepted definition of workaholism is still lacking.

In this chapter, we propose a straightforward two-dimensional notion of workaholism. Based on a review of the literature, we conceive workaholism as an irresistible inner drive to work excessively hard (Section 9.1). Following this definition, a self-report questionnaire is introduced — the Dutch Workaholism Scale (DUWAS) — that includes subscales tapping working excessively and working compulsively. A national Dutch database is used to examine relationships of workaholism with age, gender, working hours, and occupational group (Section 9.2). Next, the validity of our two-dimensional approach to workaholism is studied in greater detail in a sample of medical residents, a prototypical risk-group for workaholism (Section 9.3). More particularly, both subscales of the DUWAS are related to various job demands, job resources, and outcomes in order to identify their key correlates. In short, this chapter introduces a two-dimensional notion of workaholism and seeks to demonstrate its validity.

The Long Work Hours Culture
Copyright © 2008 by Emerald Group Publishing Limited
All rights of reproduction in any form reserved
DOI:10.1016/B978-1-84855-038-4.00009-9

9.1. Two Core Components: Working Excessively and Working Compulsively

The most obvious characteristic of workaholics is that they work beyond what is required. Consequently, they devote much more time to their work than to others (e.g., Buelens & Poelmans, 2004; Mudrack & Naughton, 2001). For instance, North American workaholics work on average 50–60 h per week (Brett & Stroh, 2003; Burke, 1999). However, conceiving workaholism exclusively in terms of the number of working hours would be misleading because it neglects its addictive nature. People may work long hours for many reasons such as financial problems, poor marriage, social pressure, or a strong desire for career advancement, without being *addicted* to it.

Rather than being motivated by such external or contextual factors, a typical work addict is motivated by an obsessive internal drive that cannot be resisted. This follows from the overview of earlier theory and research as performed by Scott, Moore, and Miceli (1997), who found three common characteristics of workaholism that feature across most definitions. First, workaholics spend a great deal of time on work activities when given the discretion to do so — they are excessively hard workers. Second, workaholics are reluctant to disengage from work and they persistently and frequently think about work when they are not at work. This suggests that workaholics are obsessed with their work and therefore driven to work excessively — they are compulsive workers. The third element in Scott et al.'s (1997) overview is that workaholics work beyond what is reasonably expected from them to meet organizational or economic requirements. This is a specification of the first and the second feature, because it deals with the motivation for spending an excessive amount of time to work. That is, workaholics work harder than is required out of an obsessive inner drive, and *not* because of external factors such as financial rewards, social pressure, poor marriage, or career perspectives. In a similar vein, in seven of the nine workaholism definitions that were listed by McMillan and O'Driscoll (2006), working excessively hard and being propelled by an obsessive inner drive are mentioned as core characteristics. Also, another analysis of scholarly definitions concludes that hard work at the expense of other important life roles and an obsessive internal drive to work are the two core aspects of workaholism (Ng et al., 2007).

Hence, we define workaholism as the tendency to work excessively hard in a compulsive way. The former — working excessively hard — points to the fact that workaholics tend to allocate exceptionally much time to work and that they work beyond what is reasonably expected to meet organizational or economic requirements. The latter — working compulsively — recognizes that workaholics are obsessed with their work and persistently and frequently think about work, even when not working.

Our conceptualization of workaholism corresponds with the meaning of the term as it was originally used by Oates (1971), who described workaholism as "… the compulsion or the uncontrollable need to work incessantly" (p. 11). For workaholics, their need to work is so exaggerated that it endangers their health, reduces their happiness, and deteriorates their interpersonal relations and social functioning, he argued. Many other scholars agree with the original view that workaholism is an addiction akin to alcoholism (e.g., Killinger, 1991; Robinson, 1989). As Porter (1996) has put it: "Whereas an alcoholic neglects other aspects of life for the indulgence in alcohol, the workaholic behaves the same for excessive indulgence in work" (pp. 70–71). We agree with Porter and Kakabadse (2006), who called on students of workaholism to stick to the origin of the term, meaning that workaholism should be interpreted as a behavioral addiction that "... involves engaging in a specific behavior for relief, comfort, or stimulation and which results in discomfort or unease of some type when discontinued" (p. 536).

In addition, our conceptualization of workaholism agrees with lay perception. This is illustrated by McMillan and O'Driscoll (2006), who asked workers, colleagues, and partners the question "How would you describe someone who is workaholic?" After content analysis, it appeared that the two most often mentioned answering categories were "time spent working or thinking about work" (39%) and "obsessive personal style" (22%), together representing 61% of the responses.

9.1.1. Is Workaholism Positive?

Some scholars have argued that workaholism may also be seen in positive terms. For instance, Machlowitz (1980) distinguish between "fulfilled" and "unfulfilled" workaholics, Scott et al. (1997) consider achievement-oriented workaholics as "hyper performers", and Buelens and Poelmans (2004) write about some workaholics as "happy hard workers". In a similar vein, Ng et al. (2007) propose — in addition to the behavioral dimension (excessive working) and the cognitive dimension (obsessive or compulsive working) — a third affective dimension; joy in working. And last but not least, the most popular model of workaholism assumes three underlying dimensions — the so-called workaholic-triad — consisting of work involvement, drive, and work enjoyment (Spence & Robbins, 1992). Different combinations of these three dimensions are assumed to produce different workaholic types. For instance, "real workaholics" are high in involvement, high in drive, and low in enjoyment, whereas "work enthusiasts" are high in involvement and enjoyment, and low in drive. Elsewhere, we argued that "work enthusiasts" closely resemble what we defined as engaged workers, who have a sense of energetic and effective connection with their work activities, and see themselves as able to deal well with the demands of their job (Schaufeli, Taris, & Van Rhenen, 2008). Moreover, the discriminant validity of workaholism (as tapped by the DUWAS; see later) vis-à-vis work engagement was successfully demonstrated in a sample of managers. This means that Spence and Robbins (1992) subsume conceptually and empirically distinct types of employee well-being under the same heading of "workaholism". We strongly believe that by introducing "good" forms of workaholism that include work enjoyment as a constituting element, the meaning of the term is blurred. This is also noted by Mudrack (2006, p. 109), who concluded after reviewing various definitions of workaholism: "... work enjoyment, whether it is high or low, is simply not a defining characteristic of workaholism". So for the sake of conceptual clarity, instead of discriminating between "good" and "bad" forms of workaholism, we proposed to discriminate between workaholism — being "bad" — and work engagement — being "good" (Schaufeli et al., 2008; Schaufeli, Taris, & Bakker, 2006).

9.2.   The Measurement of Workaholism: The Dutch Workaholism Scale (DUWAS)

In line with our conceptualization, we have operationalized workaholism in terms of two scales, namely *Working Excessively* (WE) and *Working Compulsively* (WC). Originally, these scales were taken from two frequently used workaholism inventories: the *Work Addiction Risk Test* (WART; Robinson, 1999) and the *Workaholism Battery* (WorkBat; Spence & Robbins, 1992), respectively. The original label of the WART-scale that we used to assess excess work (Control Tendencies) was somewhat misleading, because most of its items refer to working hard without any reference to the underlying motivation, whereas the remaining items refer to the inability to relax and to feeling guilty when not working. For that reason, we re-labeled the Control Tendencies-scale as WE. Using three independent Dutch samples, it was shown that the 9-item work excess-scale could be used as short version of the full 25-item WART (Taris, Schaufeli, & Verhoeven, 2005). In other words, working excessively hard seems to be equivalent to the way workaholism was operationalized by Robinson (1999) using the WART.

Studies on the factorial validity of the WorkBat failed to confirm Spence and Robbin's (1992) three-factor model of workaholism that includes work involvement, work enjoyment, and drive (Kanai, Wakabayashi, & Fling, 1996; McMillan, Brady, O'Driscoll, & Marsh, 2002). Instead, the data suggest the elimination of the work involvement factor, leaving a two-factor model with enjoyment and drive as the core components of workaholism. We employ only the drive component because — as was argued earlier — we excluded "good" workaholism that is characterized by enjoyment. The 8-item Drive-scale of the WorkBat that explicitly refers to the compulsiveness of excessive work behavior, was re-labeled as WC so that it matches our definition of workaholism.

A Dutch study using an Internet-based survey revealed that two WE-items load on the WC-scale: "I feel guilty when I am not working on something" and "It is hard for me to relax when I am not working" (Schaufeli et al., 2006). It is clear from the content of these items that they reflect the negative consequences of a compulsive tendency to work rather than excess work. After changing the composition of both scales accordingly, the internal consistencies of the WE- and WC-scales were satisfactory (Cronbach's α values of .80 and .86, respectively), whereas the correlation between both latent workaholism factors was .75.

Because of the "wrongly" loading WE-items and because of the length of questionnaire, an improved and shortened version of the DUWAS was developed using samples from The Netherlands and Japan (Schaufeli, Shimazu, & Taris, 2008).

A 10-item version of the DUWAS emerged, with five items in each scale (see Appendix 9.A.1). Correlations between the original and the shortened scales ranged between .90 and .95 in the Dutch and Japanese samples, and values of Cronbach's α of both short scales ranged between .68 and .78. Correlations between both latent workaholism factors were .50 and .59 in the Dutch and Japanese samples, respectively.

Hence, it seems that the 10-item DUWAS is an appropriate research tool to study workaholism. Therefore, it will be used in the remainder of this chapter. Below, the same Dutch sample is employed as in the study of Schaufeli et al. (2008) but new additional results will be presented on the relationships of workaholism with various background variables, including age, gender, work hours, and occupational group. In Section 9.3, the correlates of workaholism as measured with the DUWAS are examined in a national Dutch sample of medical residents.

9.2.1. The Relationship of Workaholism with Demographic and Work-Related Factors

The Dutch database ($N = 7,594$) is a composite sample consisting of 52% women and 48% men with a mean age of 36.4 years (SD = 9.5). The majority (71%) was approached by their organization or occupational health service to participate in an employee satisfaction survey or in a health check-up, and filled out either a computerized or a paper-and-pencil questionnaire. The remaining responders (29%) were recruited through the Internet.

Men score significantly higher than women on both workaholism scales. Mean WE-scores for men are $M = 2.61$ (SD = .60) and for women $M = 2.46$ (SD = .59) ($t_{(7446)} = 10.82; p < .001$); mean WC-scores for men are $M = 2.04$ (SD = .64) and for women $M = 1.98$ (SD = .62) ($t_{(7446)} = 3.67; p < .001$). Moreover, although the correlation of WC with age is statistically significant ($r = -.05; p < .05$), it lacks practical relevance. No significant correlation with age was observed for WE.

As expected, the actual number of work hours per week correlates positively and significantly with both workaholism scales; correlations are stronger for WE ($r = .43; p < .001$) than for WC ($r = .15; p < .001$). Correlations with contractual work hours are also positive and significant but weaker: WE ($r = .24; p < .001$) and WC ($r = .06; p < .01$). The fact that relationships of long working hours with WE are stronger than with WC underscores the content validity of the former scale that assesses working excessively hard. These results, particularly regarding WE, agree with studies that showed positive correlations between workaholism and the time committed to the job, e.g., working during weekends and taking work home (Burke, 1999; Kanai et al., 1996; Kanai & Wakabayashi, 2001; Spence & Robbins, 1992; Taris et al., 2005).

Figure 9.1 shows that levels of WE ($F_{(9,6243)} = 54.96; p < .001$) and levels of WC ($F_{(9,6243)} = 8.39; p < .001$) differ systematically between various occupational groups. Post-hoc analyses of variance revealed that compared to other occupational groups, managers, entrepreneurs, executives, and medical residents have the highest WE

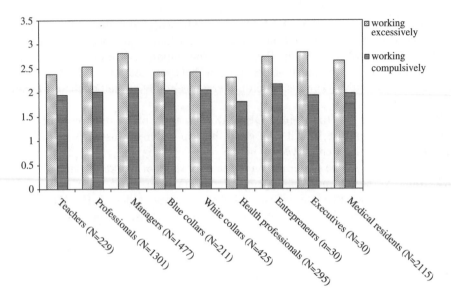

Figure 9.1: Levels of workaholism in various occupational groups.

scores, whereas health professionals, and blue and white-collar workers have the lowest WE scores. A slightly different picture emerges regarding WC with differences being somewhat smaller. Again, the highest WC scores are observed for entrepreneurs and managers, but blue and white-collar workers also score high. The lowest scores on WC are for health professionals and for executives. Since WE and WC have the same number of items and are scored on similar answering scales, their levels can be compared. It appears that, overall, levels of WC are significantly lower than levels of WE ($t_{(7479)} = 70.19$; $p < .001$). Taken together, workaholism seems most prevalent in entrepreneurs and managers, whereas executives seem to work hard, but do less compulsively so.

In sum, based on our analysis of a large Dutch database we conclude that: (1) men score slightly higher on workaholism than women; (2) workaholism is not meaningfully related to age; (3) workaholism is positively related to the total working hours as well as to the contractual working hours, although the former relationship is stronger than the latter; (4) systematic differences exist among occupational groups with managers, entrepreneurs, executives, and medical residents showing the highest workaholism scores; and (5) the previous results are more salient for the excess work component than for the compulsive work component.

9.3. A Study of Workaholism among Medical Residents

Medical residents work excessively hard. Compared to all other occupational groups included in the Dutch database, they spend most time at their jobs, both formally

($M = 43.86$, SD $= 4.99$ vs. $M = 28.23$, SD $= 7.89$; $t_{(5860)} = 284.19$; $p < .001$), as well as actually ($M = 50.75$, SD $= 7.25$ vs. $M = 44.80$, SD $= 4.94$; $t_{(5860)} = 242.08$; $p < .001$). In a national US-survey on working conditions of medical residents it was found that, on average, residents were 56.9 h per week on call in the hospital (Daugherty, DeWitt, & Rowley, 1998), a figure that is comparable to our Dutch sample. So an important precondition for workaholism seems to be met by many medical residents; they work excess hours.

To our knowledge, no quantitative study exists on workaholism among medical residents, despite the fact that they are seen as a prototypical risk-group (e.g., Harpaz & Snir, 2003; Scott et al., 1997). The stressful nature of medical residency is well-documented. For instance, a recent systematic overview found 15 articles on resident burnout that suggests that burnout levels are high among residents and may be associated with depression and problematic patient care (Niku, 2004). Since it has been argued that workaholism might act as a root-cause of burnout (Maslach, 1986), it can be speculated that the combination of excess working hours and high burnout levels makes it likely that workaholism is quite prevalent among medical residents. And indeed, as shown in the previous section medical residents are among the occupational groups with the highest levels of workaholism, as measured with the DUWAS.

9.3.1. Correlates of Workaholism

Below we will examine in greater detail the correlates of workaholism among a nationally representative sample of Dutch medical residents ($N = 2,115$). More specifically, relationships will be studied with job demands, job resources, and outcomes.

9.3.1.1. Job demands   It is expected that both workaholism scales show positive relationships with various job demands because in their attempts to continue working, workaholics may go as far as to actively create more work for themselves; for instance, by making their work more complicated than necessary or by refusing to delegate work (Machlowitz, 1980). Accordingly, positive relationships were found between workaholism and job demands such as work overload and role problems (Burke, 2000; Burke & Koksal, 2002; Kanai et al., 1996; Kanai & Wakabayashi, 2001). Taris et al. (2005) showed that the relationship between workaholism and exhaustion was partly mediated by perceived job demands: workaholics experience high job demands, which in turn are related to exhaustion. Also, positive relations were found between workaholism and number of work hours (Aziz & Zickar, 2006; Schaufeli et al., 2008) and work–home conflict (Aziz & Zickar, 2006; Bonebright, Clay, & Ankenmann, 2000; Schaufeli et al., 2008; Taris et al., 2005); workaholics work long hours and therefore feel that their jobs interfere with their personal lives.

In the present study we included in addition to more general job demands (i.e., work overload, working hours, role problems, and work–home conflict), mental and organizational, and emotional demands. We feel that these demands are particularly important for medical residents because they have to process large quantities of information and make complicated decisions (mental demands), they work in a complex organizational environment (organizational demands), and they must deal with suffering patients and their families (emotional demands).

9.3.1.2. Job resources Compared to job demands, relationships of workaholism with job resources have not been studied often, perhaps with the exception of career prospects (Burke, 2001) and social relationships at work (Buelens & Poelmans, 2004; Schaufeli et al., 2008) which both appeared to be negatively related to workaholism. This agrees with the idea that even in unresourceful jobs workaholics work very hard because they are propelled by an obsessive inner drive rather than by extrinsic factors (Brett & Stroh, 2003). In the present study, we included in addition to more general job resources (i.e., social support from colleagues, job control, and participation in decision-making), also more specific resources that are particularly important for the resident's traineeship such as opportunities for learning and development, supervisory coaching, and performance feedback.

9.3.1.3. Outcomes Workaholics report relatively high levels of job strain and (mental) health complaints, particularly burnout (Andreassen, Ursin, & Eriksen, 2007; Burke, Richardsen, & Mortinussen, 2004; Schaufeli et al., 2008; Taris et al., 2005). This is compatible with the notion that by working excessively hard workaholics drain their energy backup which leaves them mentally exhausted (Maslach, 1986). Previous research has shown that working long hours is associated with elevated levels of strain and ill-health (Van der Hulst, 2003, for a review), presumably because workers who work hard have insufficient opportunity to recover from their excessive efforts (Sonnentag & Zijlstra, 2006). For that reason, in the present study not only burnout but also recovery was assessed.

In addition to poor mental health (i.e., burnout), workaholism is also consistently found to be related to poor subjective well-being (Aziz & Zickar, 2006; Bonebright et al., 2000; Buelens & Poelmans, 2004; Schaufeli et al., 2006). Since workaholism is conceived as an addiction this would imply that workaholics are unhappy with their lives.

So far, behavioral indicators of health have rarely been studied in relation to workaholism. An exception is the study of Burke and Matthiesen (2004) among Norwegian journalists, which showed no relationship between workaholism and number of sickness absence days during the previous year. This null-finding might be caused by the fact that instead of absence frequency absence duration was used as an outcome. The latter is namely considered to be an indicator of "involuntary" absenteeism that results from the inability rather than the unwillingness to come to work (Hensing, Alexanderson, Alleback, & Bjurulf, 1998). In contrast, absence frequency is considered to be an indicator of "voluntary" absenteeism and hence a function of employees' motivation. Therefore, we also included absence frequency in our study among medical residents. It is expected that workaholics are less frequently absent because they are — almost literally — driven to work. Even more so, when feeling ill they might nevertheless decide to come to work (presenteeism; Aronsson, Gustafsson, & Dallner, 2000). Because of their strong inner drive to work we expect a positive relationship between workaholism and presenteeism: workaholics — although feeling ill — come to work.

Whereas some authors maintain that workaholics are extremely productive (e.g., Machlowitz, 1980; Peiperl & Jones, 2001), others have claimed the opposite (Oates, 1971; Porter, 2001). The latter argue that workaholics work hard rather than smart. Moreover, workaholics create difficulties for their co-workers, they suffer from perfectionism, they are rigid and inflexible, and they do not delegate (Killinger, 2006; Porter, 2001). Unfortunately, virtually no empirical research has been carried out on the relationship between workaholism and job performance (see Schaufeli et al., 2006, for an exception). We expect that, given the long list of negative attitudes and behaviors that might interfere with job performance (Scott et al., 1997, p. 291), workaholics are not necessarily good and perhaps even poor performers.

In sum: we expect workaholism to be: (1) positively related to job demands; (2) negatively related to job resources; and (3) positively related to burnout and presenteeism, and negatively related to happiness, sickness absence (duration and frequency), and performance.

9.3.2. Methods

9.3.2.1. Procedure and sample All 5245 Dutch medical residents who were at October 1, 2005 included in the national register of the Royal Dutch Medical Association received a questionnaire by mail. A small group ($N = 119$) indicated that they were no longer residents, which makes the total population $N = 5126$. A cover letter was included that explained the purpose of the study — a working conditions survey — and emphasized anonymity. In total 2115 medical residents responded (41.3%). The top three reasons for not responding were: "I am too busy" (22%), "The questionnaire is too long" (22%), and "I lack energy" (11%). The majority of the participants is female (60.7%) and the mean age of the sample is 31.5 years (SD = 3.5). Almost 77% is married or lives together with a partner, and 32% of the respondents have one or more children.

9.3.2.2. Measures Workaholism was measured with the 10-item DUWAS (see earlier) that includes two scales: *WE* (5 items, $\alpha = .67$) and *WC* (5, items $\alpha = .77$). Both scales were scored on a 5-point rating scale, ranging from 1 ("never") to 5 ("always") and correlate positively ($r = .46$, $p < .001$). A confirmatory factor-analyses revealed that the hypothesized two-factor structure of the DUWAS fitted well to the data ($\chi^2(34df) = 360.46$; GFI = .97; AGFI = .95; RMSEA = .07, NFI = 92; NNFI = .91, CFI = .93). The correlation between both latent factors was estimated .55 ($p < .001$).

Job demands   *Work overload* (4 items; α = .87), *mental demands* (4 items; α = .77), *organizational demands* (5 items; α = .64), *emotional demands* (4 items; α = .71), were assessed with shortened scales (e.g., Bakker, Demerouti, De Boer, & Schaufeli, 2003; Bakker, Demerouti, Taris, Schaufeli, & Schreurs, 2003) of the Questionnaire on the Experience and Evaluation of Work (QEEW), which is widely used by applied researchers in The Netherlands (Van Veldhoven, De Jonge, Broersen, Kompier, & Meijman, 2002). Example items are: "Do you have to work very fast?" (work overload); "Do you have a lot of meetings?" (organizational demands); "Does your work demand a lot of concentration?" (mental demands); "Does your work put you in emotionally upsetting situations?" (emotional demands). *Work–home conflict*, was measured with three items from the Survey Work-home Interference Nijmegen (SWING; Geurts et al., 2005; see Demerouti, Bakker, & Bulters, 2004). Participants were asked to indicate the extent to which their work negatively influences the home situation, e.g. "How often does it happen that you find it difficult to fulfill your domestic obligations because you are constantly thinking about your work?" (1 = "never", 5 = "always"). *Role conflict* was assessed with a self-constructed, 4-item scale that focuses on role conflicts between the resident's role as a doctor and as a trainee (α = .64). An example item is: "How often does it happen that because of your training, it is difficult to fulfill the requirements as a doctor?". Finally, an index was calculated of the percentage of *overtime* using the formula $[(a-c)/c] \times 100$, whereby a equals the number of actual work hours per week and c equals the number of contractual working hours per week. The mean percentage of overtime is 16.5% (SD = 14.7), meaning that, on an average, employees worked 16.5% longer than they should according to their official labor contract (M = 43.8; SD = 5.0).

Job resources   Using shortened scales of the QEEW, six job resources were assessed: *social support from colleagues* (3 items; α = .87), *job control* (3 items; α = .73), *opportunity to learn and to develop* (3 items; α = .80), *performance feedback* (5 items; α = .83), *supervisory coaching* (6 items; α = .86), and *participation in decision making* (4 items; α = .77). Example items are: "If necessary, can you ask your colleagues for help?" (social support); "Do you have freedom in carrying out your work activities?" (job control); "Do you learn new things in your work?" (opportunities to learn and to develop); "Does your work provide you with direct feedback on how well you are doing your work?" (feedback); "My supervisor stimulates me to develop my talents" (coaching); (participation in decision making). All demands and resources items were scored on a 5-point rating scale ranging from 1 ("never") to 5 ("always").

Outcomes   Six different outcomes were measured, using nine indicators. First, burnout was assessed with three scales of the Dutch version (Schaufeli & Van Dierendonck, 2000) of the Maslach Burnout Inventory-Human Services Survey (MBI-HSS; Maslach, Leiter, & Jackson, 1996): *Emotional exhaustion* (8 items; α = .89), *depersonalization* (5 items; α = .73), and *personal accomplishment* (7 items; α = .78). Example items are: "I feel emotionally drained from my work" (exhaustion), "I don't really care what happens to some recipients" (depersonalization), and "I have accomplished many worthwhile things in this job" (personal accomplishment). All items were scored on a 7-point scale ranging from 0 ("never") to 6 ("always"). High scores on exhaustion and cynicism and low scores on personal accomplishment are indicative of burnout. Second, *recovery* after work was assessed with a self-constructed scale (4 items; $\alpha = .71$). An example item is "When I come home from work I have time to recover". The answering scale ranges from 1 ("never") to 5 ("always"). Third, subjective well-being was assessed in terms of *happiness* (Diener, Suh, Lucas, & Smith, 1999) by a single item ("Taken everything together, how happy are you with your life?") that was scored on a 10-point scale ranging from 0 ("totally unhappy") to 10 ("extremely happy") ($M = 7.7$, SD = 1.1). Fourth, sickness absence was measured by asking the residents "How many days in the previous 12 months did you not work because of illness?" (*absence duration*), and "How many times have you stayed home because of illness" (*absence frequency*). The answering format was the number of days ($M = 4.1$; SD = 13.1) and a scale running from "0 times" (35.1%), via "1–3 times" (58.3%), "4–7 times" (4.8%) to "over 8 times" (1.1%), respectively. Fifth, *presenteeism* was measured with a single item "How often did you go to work in the previous year despite feeling sick?". Answering categories were "0 times" (21.2%), via "1–3 times" (66.3%), "4–7 times" (10.1%) to "over 8 times" (2.2%). Finally, *medical performance* was assessed with a self-constructed scale (6 items; $\alpha = .69$). An example item is: "I make mistakes that have negative consequences for my patients" (1 = "has never occurred", 4 = "has often occurred").

9.3.3. Results

First, we analyzed both dimensions of workaholism separately. That is, we identified the most important job demands, job resources, and outcomes that are associated with WE and WC separately. Next, we *combined* scores on both dimensions in order to compare the job demands, job resources, and outcomes of "workaholics" (who score high on both dimensions), with that of "hard workers" (high on WE and low on WC), "compulsive workers" (high on WC and low on WE), and "relaxed workers" (low on both dimensions). Following the logic of the introduction of this chapter we expect that, compared to the three other groups, "workaholics" work in the most stressful and least resourceful jobs, and have the most unfavorable outcomes.

9.3.3.1. Predicting working excessively and working compulsively Using hierarchical multiple regression, both workaholism scales were independently regressed on job demands, job resources, and outcomes, respectively. So in total six regression analyses were performed. Age and gender were included in the first step because previous analyses (see earlier) revealed that these biographical variables were related to workaholism. In the next step, job demands, job resources, and outcomes were entered stepwise in order to identify the most important predictors within each of

Table 9.1: Predicting working excessively (WE): Standardized regression coefficients (β).

	Separate clusters	Simultaneous analysis
Job demands		
Step 1: Gender (1 = female, 2 = male)	.05**	.03*
Step 2: Work overload	.42***	.39***
Work–home conflict	.24***	.21***
Overwork %	.07***	.08***
Role conflict	.08***	
Mental demands	.07***	.07***
Organizational demands	.06**	.05**
Percentage explained variance	44.8	
Job resources		
Step 1: Gender (1 = female, 2 = male)	.04*	
Step 2: Support colleagues	−.15***	−.07***
Participation decision-making	−.13***	
Feedback	−.10**	
Coaching	−.08**	−.08***
Percentage explained variance	6.0	
Outcomes		
Step 1: Gender (1 = female, 2 = male)	.06***	
Step 2: Exhaustion	.44***	.14***
Poor medical performance	.10***	.08***
Presenteeism	.08***	.03*
Depersonalization	.07**	.08***
Recovery	−.06**	
Happiness	−.05*	
Absence frequency	−.04*	
Percentage explained variance	33.3	47.0

Note: *$p<.05$, **$p<.01$, ***$p<.001$.

these three clusters.[1] Tables 9.1 and 9.2 (first column) provide an overview of the results for WE and WC, respectively.

As expected from the analyses in the previous section, male residents score higher on WE than female residents. With the exception of emotional demands, *all* job demands that are included in the regression equation show positive relations with WE. The strongest relationships are observed for work overload and work–home

---

1. Please note that the term "predictors" is used as a technical statistical term. Since a cross-sectional design is used no causal inferences can be made.

Table 9.2: Predicting working compulsively (WC): Standardized regression coefficients (β).

	Separate clusters	Simultaneous analysis
Job demands		
Step 1: Gender (1 = female, 2 = male)	.05*	.04*
Step 2: Work–home conflict	.34***	.24***
Role conflict	.12***	.07**
Mental demands	.10***	.08***
Emotional demands	.08***	.07**
Work overload	.06**	
Organizational demands	.06**	
Percentage explained variance	28.6	
Job resources		
Step 1: Gender (1 = female, 2 = male)	.06**	
Step 2: Opportunity to learn	−.16***	
Support colleagues	−.14***	−.07***
Feedback	−.11***	
Participation decision making	−.09***	
Coaching	−.08**	
Percentage explained variance	10.0	
Outcomes		
Step 1: Gender (1 = female, 2 = male)	.05*	
Step 2: Exhaustion	.38***	.24***
Depersonalization	.10***	.08***
Happiness	−.08***	
Recovery	−.08***	
Presenteeism	.07**	.05**
Absence frequency	−.06**	−.05**
Percentage explained variance	27.7	35.0

Note: *$p<.05$, **$p<.01$, ***$p<.001$.

conflict. Residents who work excessively hard experience work overload, work–home conflict, mental and organizational demands, and role conflict, and they perform more overwork than is specified in their labor contract.

As far job resources are concerned, relationships with WE are less strong – 6% explained variance vs. 44.8% for job demands. Moreover, two resources (i.e., job control and opportunities for learning) were *not* included in the regression equation of WE. The remaining four job resources indicate that, compared to residents who work less hard, those who work excessively hard experience less social support from their colleagues, participate less often in decision-making, and receive less performance feedback and supervisory coaching.

Clearly, emotional exhaustion is the outcome that is most strongly related to WE. Except personal accomplishment and absence duration, all other outcomes are significantly related to WE in the expected direction. That is, compared to residents who work less hard, those who work excessively hard perform more poorly, depersonalize their patients more often, recover less well after a day on the job, and are less happy with their lives. On the other hand, they work more often while being ill (presenteeism) and are less frequently absent. In total 33.3% of the variance in WE is explained by these six outcomes.

Taken together, the results of regression analyses sketch a gloomy picture of excessively hard working, dutiful yet overburdened, exhausted, and unhappy medical residents, who neglect their patients and perform poorly.

Next, in order to reduce the overlap and identify the key variables that are associated with WE *across* the three clusters (job demands, job resources, and outcomes), the significant predictors that emerged from the previous three separate analyses were now included simultaneously into one hierarchical regression analyses. Again, we controlled for age and gender.

Work overload emerges as the most powerful predictor of WE, followed by work–home conflict, and emotional exhaustion, respectively: those who work excessively hard feel that they are overloaded and exhausted, and that their excessive work behavior triggers work–home conflicts. In addition to quantitative job demands like work overload and overwork, residents high on WE also suffer from high quantitative demands (i.e., mental and organizational demands). Only two job resources are maintained in the final analyses; poor support from colleagues and poor supervisory coaching. Quite alarmingly, depersonalization of patients and poor medical performance remain significant predictors of the resident's WE-score, meaning that working excessively hard is bad from the perspective of patient care. Finally, presenteeism is associated with working excessively hard.

Taken as a whole, our expectations that working excessively hard is related to job demands, lacking resources, and poor outcomes is corroborated, whereby job demands contribute most and job resources contribute least in explaining WE.

Similar analyses were carried out for WC. As can be seen from Table 9.2, men are also more compulsive workers than women.

As far as the job demands are concerned, the picture of WC differs from that of WE in the sense that qualitative demands (i.e., work–home conflict, and mental, emotional, and organizational demands) are more important than quantitative demands. To illustrate this point, the relationship with work overload is relatively weak and overwork percentage is not included in the regression equation at all. Regarding job resources; opportunity for learning is now included in the regression equation of WC together with the other resources that also predicted WE. As far as the outcomes are concerned, a similar pattern for WE emerges with emotional exhaustion as the most important predictor of WC. However, in contrast with WE, poor medical performance is not included in the regression equation of WC.

Taken together, compared to WE, percentages of explained variance of WC are somewhat higher for job resources but lower for outcomes and particularly for job demands. The patterns of associations also differ slightly; in case of WC quantitative demands seem to be more important than qualitative demands, and poor learning opportunities are associated with WC (and not with WE), whereas poor medical performance is not associated with WC (but with WE).

Again, a hierarchical regression analyses was performed including all significant predictors that emerged from the three previous analyses. Emotional exhaustion and work–home conflict emerge as the most powerful predictors of WC, meaning that residents who work compulsively feel exhausted and experience conflicting demands between work and home. Furthermore, residents who work compulsively experience qualitative rather than quantitative demands; instead of being bothered by large quantities of work and long working hours, their obsession with work seems to be associated with qualitative demands (i.e., mental and emotional demands). Except for poor support from colleagues, job resources do not seem to play a role for residents who work compulsively. As far as outcomes are concerned, compulsively working residents seem to be dutiful because, rather than reporting sick when they feel ill, they continue working. Finally, like hard working residents, compulsive residents also tend to depersonalize their patients.

In sum, our expectations that working compulsively is related to job demands, lacking job resources, and poor outcomes is corroborated. Moreover, despite some differences, WE and WC are largely associated with similar demands (work–home conflict and mental demands), lack of resources (poor social support from colleagues), and outcomes (exhaustion, depersonalization, and presenteeism). This suggests that WE and WC assess a similar underlying construct: workaholism.

9.3.3.2. Combining working excessively and working compulsively Based on a median split, residents who scored high or low on WE and WC, respectively, were identified. Next, by combining high and low scores on WE and WC, four types of residents were distinguished: (1) "workaholics" ($N = 827$) — who score high on WE and WC; (2) "hard working residents" ($N = 286$) — who score high on WE and low on WC; (3) "compulsively working residents" ($N = 238$) — who score low on WE and high on WC; and (4) "relaxed residents" ($N = 633$) — who score low on WE and WC. In order to compare mean values on the three clusters of variables (i.e., 7 job demands, 6 job resources, and 9 outcomes) across these four groups, multivariate analyses of variance were carried out with gender as covariate.

We expected that, compared to the other three groups, workaholic residents would have unfavorable scores on job demands, job resources, and outcomes. A significant, overall multivariate effect was observed ($F_{(66,5703)} = 18.42$; $p < .001$), indicating that scores on all 22 dependent variables differed systematically across the four groups. As can be seen from Table 9.3, subsequent univariate analyses revealed that — except for sickness absence duration — differences between groups were significant and in the predicted direction for *all* dependent variables.

Testing of post-hoc contrasts across all four groups resulted in a consistent picture. As expected, compared to the other three groups, workaholics exhibited the most unfavorable scores on most variables: 16 out of 21 (i.e., 76%). Moreover, on the remaining five variables workaholics scored less favorably than the relaxed group,

Table 9.3: Differences in job demands, job resources, and outcomes between "workaholics" ($N = 827$), "hard working residents" ($N = 286$), "compulsively working residents" ($N = 238$), and "relaxed residents" ($N = 633$).

	Workaholic	Hard working	Compulsively working	Relaxed	$F_{(3, 1920)}$
Demands					
Work overload	3.72^{ab}	3.63^{cd}	3.01^{ad}	2.96^{bc}	163.58^{***}
Overwork %	19.27^{ab}	18.74^{cd}	13.43^{bc}	13.41^{ad}	25.29^{***}
Work–home conflict	2.75^{abc}	2.39^{adf}	2.15^{bef}	1.91^{sde}	229.30^{***}
Role conflict	2.36^{abc}	2.11^{adf}	2.00^{bef}	1.81^{cde}	132.12^{***}
Mental demands	4.19^{abc}	4.01^{ad}	4.01^{be}	3.83^{cde}	47.64^{***}
Emotional demands	2.77^{abc}	2.60^{ad}	2.60^{be}	2.46^{cde}	38.01^{***}
Organizational demands	3.01^{abc}	2.96^{adf}	2.78^{bef}	2.62^{cde}	67.81^{***}
Resources					
Support colleagues	3.55^{abc}	3.59^{ad}	3.60^{be}	3.81^{cde}	36.10^{***}
Coaching	2.77^{ab}	2.89^{a}	2.84^{c}	2.97^{bc}	9.38^{***}
Job control	2.91^{abc}	3.09^{a}	3.05^{b}	3.12^{c}	11.10^{***}
Feedback	2.94^{ab}	3.12^{ac}	3.03^{d}	3.42^{bcd}	19.87^{***}
Opportunity to learn	3.56^{abc}	3.82^{ad}	3.69^{bde}	3.90^{ce}	35.87^{***}
Part in decision making	2.80^{abc}	3.09^{a}	3.04^{bd}	3.17^{cd}	30.13^{***}
Outcomes					
Exhaustion	2.68^{abc}	2.07^{adf}	1.88^{bef}	1.43^{cde}	221.87^{***}
Depersonalization	1.78^{abc}	1.41^{ad}	1.48^{be}	1.14^{cde}	69.47^{***}
Accomplishment	2.32^{abc}	2.23^{adf}	2.13^{bef}	2.02^{cde}	36.59^{***}
Recovery	2.83^{abc}	2.96^{ad}	3.08^{b}	3.16^{cd}	19.32^{***}
Happiness	7.27^{abc}	7.72^{ad}	7.77^{be}	8.02^{cde}	63.87^{***}
Presenteeism	2.07^{abc}	1.97^{ad}	1.91^{b}	1.82^{cd}	18.81^{***}
Absence frequency	1.77^{ab}	1.73	1.67^{a}	1.68^{b}	2.89^{*}
Absence duration	4.49	4.98	3.95	3.94	.51

Note: Similar superscripts indicate significant differences between the corresponding means.
$^{*}p<.05$, $^{**}p<.01$, $^{***}p<.001$.

meaning that on *all* variables (except absence duration) workaholic residents scored more unfavorably than their relaxed fellow residents. No significant difference was observed between workaholic residents and hard working residents concerning work overload, overwork percentage, and absence frequency. This means that 85% of the variables showed significant differences in the expected direction between workaholics and hard workers. No significant difference was observed between the workaholic residents and the compulsively working residents as far as work overload, coaching, and feedback is concerned. This means that, again, 85% of the variables showed significant differences in the expected direction between workaholics and compulsive workers. Although few non-significant contrasts between groups were observed (15%), no significant unexpected differences were found. Hence, it can be concluded not only that workaholic residents score more unfavorably on *all* variables compared to the opposite group of relaxed residents, but also that the *combination* of working excessively hard and working compulsively is associated with more unfavorable job characteristics and outcomes than either working excessively hard or working compulsively separately.

9.4. Conclusion and Discussion

In this chapter a two-dimensional notion of workaholism is proposed. The first dimension — working excessively hard — agrees with the layman's perception that workaholics "always" work (McMillan & O'Driscoll, 2006). They work far beyond what is required by their jobs or their organization, or by what is necessary from an economic perspective. However, defining workaholism exclusively in terms of the number of working hours would be a mistake because it denies the underlying motivation that sets workaholics apart from mere hard workers. There are numerous reasons to work hard without being addicted to it. Therefore, we added a second constituting dimension, namely the obsession with work that manifests itself in working compulsively. Workaholics are propelled by an obsessive inner drive that urges them to work hard, even when they feel like not doing so. In other words it is the compulsive nature of the hard work that makes the difference.

Thus, we conceive workaholism as an obsessive, irresistible inner drive to work excessively hard. Not only is this definition in line with the ideas of the founding father of the concept of workaholism (Oates, 1968, 1971), but both constituting elements are also found in the majority of definitions that have been proposed during the past four decades or so (for reviews see Scott et al., 1997; McMillan & O'Driscoll, 2006; Ng et al., 2007). Seen from this perspective, our synthetic definition is the least common multiple of existing descriptions of workaholism.

9.4.1. Measuring Workaholism

Based on our definition of workaholism, a self-report instrument — dubbed Dutch Workaholism Scale (DUWAS) — is proposed that includes two subscales of five items each: WE and WC. Both scales are moderately correlated, sharing between about 20% and 30% of their observed and latent variances, respectively. The psychometric features of the DUWAS in terms of internal consistency and factorial validity are satisfactory. Moreover, its conceptual validity was demonstrated because WC and particularly WE were positively related to the number of working hours, which is a necessary (albeit not sufficient) hallmark of workaholism.

For the first time, workaholism has been studied using a large national database that includes a wide range of occupational groups. It appeared that the DUWAS is sensitive to differences in levels of workaholism across these groups. Workaholism seems to be particularly high among managers, entrepreneurs, executives, and medical residents. This is not very surprising because work in these jobs is never done and such "open ended" work environments constitute a fertile ground for workaholism to develop, particularly among those with an obsessive inner drive to work. Conversely, such individuals might also land in managerial, entrepreneurial, executive, or medical specialist jobs, of course.

It is concluded that the DUWAS is a reliable and valid self-report tool to assess workaholism that can be used — for instance — in future cross-national studies on the prevalence of workaholism. So far, such studies have relied on rather unsatisfactory proximal measures for workaholism such as the number of weekly working hours (e.g., Snir & Harpaz, 2006).

9.4.2.   Workaholism among Medical Residents

The validity of our workaholism measure has been studied in more detail in a national representative sample of Dutch medical residents, an occupational group that is considered prototypical for exhibiting workaholism (Harpaz & Snir, 2003; Scott et al., 1997). We defined workaholism as a "syndrome" — that is, as a set of two characteristics that occur together. This means that both scales that tap these characteristics should not only be interrelated, but should also be associated with similar features such as job demands, job resources, and outcomes. This was indeed the case. Separate regression analyses for job demands, job resources, and outcomes revealed that virtually all variables that were included in the analyses predicted WE and WC, with job demands explaining most variance (ranging between 29% and 45%), followed by outcomes (ranging between 28% and 33%), and job resources (ranging between 6% and 10%), respectively.

A more comprehensive analysis that included all predictors *simultaneously* — and thus accounting for overlap between the three clusters — revealed that work–home conflict and emotional exhaustion are the most powerful common predictors of WE and WC. This agrees with the notion that workaholics neglect their lives outside work and are literally "tired from working" (Killinger, 2006). In addition, other common yet less pronounced predictors of WE and WC were high mental demands, poor support from colleagues, depersonalization, and presenteeism. Thus residents who score high on either WE or WC experience high mental work demands, poor support from their fellow residents, they treat their patients in a callous way, and they come to work even when they feel sick. The major difference between predictors of WE and WC is that the former is more strongly related to quantitative job demands, notably work overload and overwork. This is not surprising given the nature of the WE-scale. Furthermore, it appeared that 7 out of 12 significant predictors of WE (58%) are similar to those of WC, whereas on the other hand, 7 out of 10 predictors of WC (70%) are similar of those of WE. Thus, a substantial overlap exists between predictors of WE and WC — in qualitative as well as quantitative terms — so that we may conclude that the DUWAS assesses the workaholic *syndrome*.

This conclusion is corroborated when the scores on the WE and WC-scales are combined into four groups: "workaholics", "hard workers", "compulsive workers", and "relaxed workers". Of all four groups, the workaholic group scores most unfavorable on *all* 22 variables that were included in the analyses, except sickness absence duration. Previous studies also failed to show a relationship between workaholism and absence duration (e.g., Burke & Matthiesen, 2004), presumably because this is a measure of involuntary absenteeism (Hensing et al., 1998).

More detailed comparisons revealed that, compared to the relaxed residents, the workaholic group scored significantly more unfavorably on *all* variables, whereas compared with the hard working and the compulsively working group this was the case for 85% of the variables. Notable exceptions were that workaholics did not differ from hard workers in terms of work overload, overwork, and absence frequency, and from compulsive workers in terms of coaching, feedback, and absence frequency. The former results make sense because almost by definition hard workers feel overloaded and work long hours. The latter results agree with Porter (2001), who showed that perfectionists, who believe that no one else works to the same high standards, have poor social relationships at work that are characterized by anger and frustration. Porter's definition of workaholics as perfectionists comes close to our compulsive workers.

In sum, our analyses showed that the *combination* of working excessively hard and working compulsively is particularly powerful in producing significant results that are not obtained when both dimensions are treated separately. In other words, it takes two to dance the workaholism tango.

9.4.2.1. Outlook Virtually all people, laymen and scholars alike, would agree that that working excessively hard constitutes the hallmark of workaholism. This overt, behavioral manifestation of workaholism is undisputed. The problem is with the covert mental processes that drive this excessive work behavior. Or framed differently, the basic issue in understanding workaholism is to identify the motivational process that is responsible for working so excessively hard. In doing so, we feel that it is crucial to make a sharp distinction between "good" and "bad" workaholism, whereby the former is defined as work engagement (Schaufeli & Salanova, 2007). This is not merely a semantic issue. First, there is accumulating evidence that workaholism — as defined as an irresistible inner drive to work excessively hard — can be distinguished empirically from work engagement — as defined in terms of vigor, dedication, and being pleasurably absorbed in one's work (Schaufeli et al., 2008; Schaufeli et al., 2006). Secondly, and most important from a theoretical perspective, it can be speculated that the underlying psychological mechanisms — i.e., motivational systems — differ fundamentally.

More particularly, workaholics are likely to be motivated by so-called performance goals, whereas engaged workers are motivated by mastery goals (Elliot,

2005). The former are competitive, other-referenced, and extrinsic, whereas the latter are directed at self-enhancement, self-referenced, and intrinsic. This agrees with observations of workaholics as perfectionists and narcissists: "Caught up in a compulsive drive to gain personal approval and public recognition of their success, these driven men and women live in a gerbil-wheel, adrenalin-pumping existence rushing from point A to point B, narrowly fixated on the next desired goal or accomplishment" (Killinger, 2006, p. 61). On the other hand, engaged employees work so hard because for them work is fun and they keep looking for new challenges in their jobs because they are motivated to learn and to develop themselves; essentially, they try to realize their full personal potential through their jobs (Bakker & Schaufeli, 2008; Schaufeli & Salanova, 2007).

In a somewhat similar vein, it can be argued that the work behavior of workaholics is primarily regulated by a prevention focus, whereas that of engaged employees is regulated by a promotion focus. Based on regulatory focus theory (Higgins, 2005), it can be speculated that workaholics are being pushed towards work because they want to prevent feeling bad (i.e., guilty or worthless) when they do not work — so basically they are propelled by an *avoidance* motivation. Engaged workers, on the other hand, are being pulled towards work because it promotes possibilities for learning and development — so basically they are propelled by an *approach* motivation.

To date, we can only speculate about possible different motivational systems, but by making a conceptual distinction between workaholism and work engagement, a new and exciting avenue for future research is opened. It seems that again, it takes two to tango.

References

Andreassen, C. S., Ursin, H., & Eriksen, H. R. (2007). The relationship between strong motivation to work, "workaholism", and health. *Psychology & Health, 22*, 625–629.

Aronsson, G., Gustafsson, K., & Dallner, M. (2000). Sick but yet at work. An empirical study of sickness presenteeism. *Journal of Epidemiological Community Health, 54*, 502–509.

Aziz, S., & Zickar, M. J. (2006). A cluster analysis investigation of workaholism as a syndrome. *Journal of Occupational Health Psychology, 11*, 52–62.

Bakker, A. B., Demerouti, E., De Boer, E., & Schaufeli, W. B. (2003). Job demands and job resources as predictors of absence duration and frequency. *Journal of Vocational Behavior, 62*, 341–356.

Bakker, A. B., Demerouti, E., Taris, T. W., Schaufeli, W. B., & Schreurs, P. J. G. (2003). A multi-group analysis of the job demands-resources model in four home care organizations. *International Journal of Stress Management, 10*, 16–38.

Bakker, A. B, & Schaufeli, W. B. (2008). Positive organizational behavior: Engaged employees in thriving organizations. *Journal of Organizational Behavior, 29*, 147–154.

Bonebright, C. A., Clay, D. L., & Ankenmann, R. D. (2000). The relationship of workaholism with work–life conflict, life satisfaction, and purpose in life. *Journal of Counseling Psychology, 47*, 469–477.

Brett, J. M., & Stroh, L. K. (2003). Working 61 plus hours per week: Why do managers do it? *Journal of Applied Psychology, 88*, 67–78.

Buelens, M., & Poelmans, S. A. Y. (2004). Enriching the Spence and Robbins' typology of workaholism: Demographic, motivational and organizational correlates. *Organizational Change Management, 17*, 459–470.

Burke, R. J. (1999). It's not how hard you work but how you work hard: Evaluating workaholism components. *International Journal of Stress Management, 6*, 225–240.

Burke, R. J. (2000). Workaholism in organizations: Psychological and physical well-being consequences. *Stress Medicine, 16*, 11–16.

Burke, R. J. (2001). Workaholism components, job satisfaction, and career progress. *Journal of Applied Social Psychology, 31*, 2339–2356.

Burke, R. J., & Koksal, H. (2002). Workaholism among a sample of Turkish managers and professionals: An exploratory study. *Psychological Reports, 91*, 60–68.

Burke, R. J., & Matthiesen, S. (2004). Workaholism among Norwegian journalists: Antecedents and consequences. *Stress & Health, 20*, 301–308.

Burke, R. J., Richardsen, A. M., & Mortinussen, M. (2004). Workaholism among Norwegian managers: Work and well-being outcomes. *Journal of Organizational Change Management, 7*, 459–470.

Daugherty, S. R., DeWitt, C. B., & Rowley, B. D. (1998). Learning, satisfaction, and mistreatment during medical internship: A national survey of working conditions. *Journal of the American Medical Association, 279*, 1194–1199.

Demerouti, E., Bakker, A. B., & Bulters, A. (2004). The loss spiral of work pressure, work–home interference and exhaustion: Reciprocal relationships in a three-wave study. *Journal of Vocational Behavior, 64*, 131–149.

Diener, E., Suh, E. M., Lucas, R. E., & Smith, H. L. (1999). Subjective well-being: Three decades of progress. *Psychological Bulletin, 125*, 267–302.

Elliot, A. J. (2005). A conceptual history of the achievement goal construct. In: A. J. Elliot & C. S. Dweck (Eds), *Handbook of competence and motivation* (pp. 52–72). New York: Guilford.

Geurts, S. A. E., Taris, T. W., Kompier, M. A. J., Dikkers, S. J. E., Van Hooff, M., & Kinnunen, U. (2005). Work–home interaction from a work-psychological perspective: Development and validation of a new questionnaire, the SWING. *Work & Stress, 19*, 319–339.

Harpaz, I., & Snir, R. (2003). Workaholism: Its definition and nature. *Human Relations, 56*, 291–319.

Hensing, G., Alexanderson, K., Allebeck, P., & Bjurulf, P. (1998). How to measure sickness absence? Literature review and suggestion for five basic measures. *Scandinavian Journal of Social Medicine, 26*, 133–144.

Higgins, T. (2005). Value from regulatory fit. *Current Directions in Psychological Science, 14*, 209–213.

Kanai, A., & Wakabayashi, M. (2001). Workaholism among Japanese blue-collar employees. *International Journal of Stress management, 8*, 129–203.

Kanai, A., Wakabayashi, M., & Fling, S. (1996). Workaholism among employees in Japanese corporations: An examination based on the Japanese version of the Workaholism scales. *Japanese Psychological Research, 38*, 192–203.

Killinger, B. (1991). *Workaholics: The respectable addicts*. New York: Somin & Schuster.

Killinger, B. (2006). The workaholic breakdown syndrome. In: R. J. Burke (Ed.), *Research companion to working time and work addiction* (pp. 61–88). Northampton, MA: Edward Elgar.

Machlowitz, M. (1980). *Workaholics: Living with them, working with them.* New York: Simon & Schuster.

Maslach, C. (1986). Stress, burnout and workaholism. In: R. R. Killberg, P. E. Nathan & R. W. Thoreson (Eds), *Professionals in distress: Issues, syndromes and solutions in psychology* (pp. 53–73). Washington, DC: American Psychological Association.

Maslach, C., Leiter, M. P., & Jackson, S. E. (1996). *Maslach burnout inventory — manual* (3rd ed.). Palo Alto, CA: Consulting Psychologists Press.

McMillan, L. H. W., Brady, E. C., O'Driscoll, M. P., & Marsh, N. V. (2002). A multifaceted validation study of Spence and Robbin's (1992) wokaholism battery. *Journal of Occupational and Organizational Psychology, 75,* 357–368.

McMillan, L. H. W., & O'Driscoll, M. P. (2006). Exploring new frontiers to generate an integrated definition of workaholism. In: R. J. Burke (Ed.), *Research companion to working time and work addiction* (pp. 89–107). Northampton, MA: Edward Elgar.

Mudrack, P. E. (2006). Understanding workaholism: The case for behavioral tendencies. In: R. J. Burke (Ed.), *Research companion to working time and work addiction* (pp. 108–128). Northampton, MA: Edward Elgar.

Mudrack, P. E., & Naughton, T. J. (2001). The assessment of workaholism as behavioral tendencies: Scale development and preliminary testing. *International Journal of Stress Management, 8,* 93–112.

Ng, T. W. H., Sorensen, K. L., & Feldman, D. C. (2007). Dimensions, antecedents, and consequences of workaholism: A conceptual integration and extension. *Journal of Organizational Behavior, 28,* 111–136.

Niku, K. T. (2004). Resident burnout. *Journal of the American Medical Association, 292,* 2880–2889.

Oates, W. (1968). On being a 'workaholic' (A serious jest). *Pastoral Psychology, 19,* 16–20.

Oates, W. (1971). *Confessions of a workaholic: The facts about work addiction.* New York: World Publishing Co.

Peiperl, M., & Jones, B. (2001). Workaholics and overworkers: Productivity or pathology? *Group and Organization Management, 26,* 369–393.

Porter, G. (1996). Organizational impact of workaholism: Suggestions for researching the negative outcomes of excessive work. *Journal of Occupational Health Psychology, 1,* 70–84.

Porter, G. (2001). Workaholic tendencies and the high potential for stress among co-workers. *International Journal of Stress Management, 8,* 147–164.

Porter, G., & Kakabadse, N. K. (2006). HRM perspectives on addiction to technology and work. *Journal of Management Development, 25,* 535–596.

Robinson, B. E. (1989). *Work addiction.* Dearfield Beach, FL: Health Communications.

Robinson, B. E. (1998). *Chained to the desk: A guidebook for workaholics, their partners and children and the clinicians who treat them.* New York: New York University Press.

Robinson, B. E. (1999). The work addiction risk test: Development of a tentative measure of workaholism. *Perceptual and Motor Skills, 88,* 199–210.

Schaufeli, W. B., & Salanova, M. (2007). Work engagement: An emerging psychological concept and its implications for organizations. In: S. W. Gilliland, D. D. Steiner & D. P. Skarlicki (Eds), *Research in social issues in management (Volume 5): Managing social and ethical issues in organizations* (pp. 135–177). Greenwich, CT: Information Age Publishers.

Schaufeli, W. B., Shimazu, A., & Taris, T. W. (in press). Being driven to work exceptionally hard. The evaluation of a two-factor measure of workaholism in The Netherland and Japan. *Cross-Cultural Research.*

Schaufeli, W. B., Taris, T. W., & Bakker, A. B. (2006). Dr. Jekyll and Mr. Hide: On the differences between work engagement and workaholism. In: R. Burke (Ed.), *Work hours and work addiction* (pp. 193–252). Northampton, MA: Edward Elgar.

Schaufeli, W. B., Taris, T. W., & Van Rhenen, W. (2008). Workaholism, burnout and engagement: Three of a kind or three different kinds of employee well-being? *Applied Psychology: An International Review, 57,* 173–203.

Schaufeli, W. B., & Van Dierendonck, D. (2000). *Handleiding van de Utrechtse Burnout Schaal (UBOS) [Manual Utrecht Burnout Scale].* Lisse, The Netherlands: Swets Test Services.

Scott, K. S., Moore, K. S., & Miceli, M. P. (1997). An exploration of the meaning and consequences of workaholism. *Human Relations, 50,* 287–314.

Snir, R., & Harpaz, I. (2006). The workaholism phenomenon: A cross-national perspective. *Career Development International, 11,* 374–393.

Sonnentag, S., & Zijlstra, F. R. (2006). Job characteristics and off-job activities as predictors of need for recovery, well-being, and fatigue. *Journal of Applied Psychology, 91,* 330–530.

Spence, J. T., & Robbins, A. S. (1992). Workaholism: Definition, measurement, and preliminary results. *Journal of Personality Assessment, 58,* 160–178.

Taris, T. W., Schaufeli, W. B., & Verhoeven, L. C. (2005). Internal and external validation of the Dutch work addiction risk test: Implications for jobs and non-work conflict. *Applied Psychology: An international Review, 54,* 37–60.

Van der Hulst, M. (2003). Long work hours and health. *Scandinavian Journal of Work, Environment and Health, 29,* 171–188.

Van Veldhoven, M., De Jonge, J., Broersen, S., Kompier, M., & Meijman, T. F. (2002). Specific relations between psychosocial job conditions and job-related stress: A three-level analytic approach. *Work & Stress, 16,* 207–228.

Appendix 9.A.1

Working excessively (WE)

1. I seem to be in a hurry and racing against the clock.
2. I find myself continuing to work after my co-workers have called it quits.
3. I stay busy and keep many irons in the fire.
4. I spend more time working than on socializing with friends, on hobbies, or on leisure activities.
5. I find myself doing two or three things at one time, such as eating lunch and writing a memo while talking on the telephone.

Working compulsively (WC)

1. It's important to me to work hard even when I don't enjoy what I'm doing.
2. I feel that there's something inside me that drives me to work hard.
3. I feel obliged to work hard, even when it's not enjoyable.
4. I feel guilty when I take time off work.
5. It is hard for me to relax when I'm not working.

Chapter 10

Work Motivations, Satisfactions, and Health: Passion versus Addiction

Ronald J. Burke

Over the past decade, work hours have increased among managers and professionals in several countries (e.g., the US and the UK), and across the board in these and other countries, while decreasing among blue collar workers in these same countries (Golden, 2007). Working long hours and working long hours of overtime have been found to be generally associated with lower levels of job and family satisfaction, psychological well-being and physical health (Burke, 2007; Dembe, Erickson, Delbos, & Banks, 2005; DeRaeve, Jansen, & Kant, 2007; Sparks, Cooper, Fried, & Shirom, 1997; van der Hulst, 2003). The Japanese have even coined a word "Karoshi" to refer to death from overwork (Kawahito, 1991; Uehata, 1990).

Why do people work hard and does their motivation for working long hours matter in terms of their satisfaction and well-being? Several streams of research bear on these questions. First, a growing body of research on workaholism has shown that different types of workaholics exist (Scott, Moore, & Miceli, 1997; Spence & Robbins, 1992) and that some types seem to be work satisfied and psychologically healthy while other types are dissatisfied with their jobs and careers, with their family relationships, and in psychological distress (Buelens & Poelmans, 2004; Burke, 2007; Machlowitz, 1980; Kanai, Wakabayashi, & Fling, 1996; Robinson, 1998; Spence & Robbins, 1992).

Second, extensive research on sources of motivation (e.g., the effects of intrinsic versus extrinsic goals) and different processes or motivations for realizing these goals (e.g., internal versus external motivations) – the "what" and "why" of goal pursuits – has shown that individuals motivated by extrinsic goals and external sources of motivation report lower levels of satisfaction and psychological health (Deci & Ryan, 1985, 2000; Deci, Koestner, & Ryan, 1999; Ryan & Deci, 2000; Srivastava, Locke, & Bartol, 2001). Burke (2007) has shown that different types of workaholics are motivated by different beliefs and fears about people and their larger social and work environment.

The Long Work Hours Culture
Copyright © 2008 by Emerald Group Publishing Limited
All rights of reproduction in any form reserved
DOI:10.1016/B978-1-84855-038-4.00010-5

Third, although working long hours has generally been associated with more negative work and health outcomes, dramatic exceptions to this trend have also been observed. Hewlett and Luce (2006) reported some work and family experiences of men and women working in "extreme jobs", jobs in which they worked 70 or more hours per week and under high work intensity (e.g., an unpredictable flow of work, responsibility for clients 24/7, and a fast paced flow of work). Respondents were senior-level managers and executives in large US and international-based corporations earning huge salaries and working in prestigious jobs having lots of perks. Their respondents indicated great work satisfaction resulting in part from the challenge, meaning and rewards from their jobs. They were passionate about their work and their jobs. Respondents did indicate, however, that they hoped to work a few hours less in future and some were concerned about potential negative effects of their work hours on personal and family lives. Brett and Stroh (2003), in a sample of alumni of a prestigious US business school, also reported positive reasons among both men and women for working over 61 hours per week.

Fourth, it is only recently that passion in the workplace has begun to be explored. Vallerand and his colleagues (Vallerand et al., 2007; Vallerand et al., 2003a) have proposed a dualistic approach to passion. Passion is defined as a strong inclination towards an activity (e.g., work in our case) that is important, liked and involves investing considerable time in its pursuit. They distinguish between a Harmonious Passion (HP) that is well integrated into one's identity and undertaken freely and willingly and an Obsessive Passion or addiction (OP) that is not well integrated into one's identity and is the result of internal pressure (e.g., to increase one's self-esteem in the eyes of others). The activity controls the person under OP; the person controls the activity under HP. They hypothesized and found that HP leads to more positive affect, less negative affect and higher levels of flow while OP produced the opposite effects. Because the activity is freely chose under HP, the individual is engaged in the activity more fully and flexibly leading to greater concentration, absorption, flow and positive affect. They developed measures of both types of passion and found they were significantly and positively correlated with each other, and similarly and positively correlated with evaluations and liking for a self-chosen activity. They also found that levels of HP were higher than levels of OP for the chosen activity. They further suggest that HP would likely be correlated with psychological health and OP with psychological distress. Thus passion can create motivation, increase well-being and provide meaning in one's life but it can also lead to negative emotions, rigid persistence and unbalanced life.

Fifth, two of the three workaholism components in the most widely used measure of workaholism developed by Spence and Robbins (1992) – Feeling driven to work because of inner pressure (D) and Work enjoyment (WE) have been found to relate in different directions and to different outcome (see Burke, 2007, for a review). WE, not surprisingly has been shown to be positively related to various work outcomes whereas D was shown to be negative related to many of these work outcomes. However, D was found to be negatively related to measures of psychological health while WE was unrelated to these health indicators. In addition, WE and D related differently to potential antecedents of workaholism such as perceptions of organizational climate supporting work-personal life balance and perceptions of people and, their motives and how to succeed in the world. Other researchers have also reported different relations between WE and D and a number of different work and well-being outcomes (e.g., Graves, Ruderman, & Ohlott, 2006; Johnstone & Johnston, 2005; Schaufeli, Taris, & Bakker, 2007; Virick & Baruch, 2007). For the purposes of the present exploratory study, WE is considered to be similar to Passion while D is considered to be similar to Addiction.

Graves et al. (2006), using both WE and D, examined their relationship to job performance ratings based on 360-degree feedback perceptions. Self-reports of WE were positively related to performance ratings self = reports of D moderated the effects of WE on performance ratings; when D was low, WE was positively related to performance ratings, and when D was high, WE was not related to performance ratings. They concluded that high levels of D seemed to interfere with the performance-enhancing aspects of WE.

Virick and Baruch (2007), in a sample of 575 employees of a high tech firm, found that organizational identification, self-reliance and outcome orientation were positively related to both D and WE. Work-family culture had a significant negative relationship with D but not WE. D lowered work-life balance and life satisfaction but enhanced employee performance. WE was positively associated with work-life balance and both job and life satisfaction.

Johnstone and Johnston (2005), in a study of two occupational groups, (Business Services, Social Services), found that only Work Pressure was significantly related to D. Work pressure, involvement, co-worker cohesion and supervisor support were all related to WE. In addition, employees in Business Services reported higher levels of D and lower levels of WE than did employees working in Social Services suggesting effects of occupational type as well as organizational climate on WE and D.

Schaufeli et al. (2007) make a distinction between "good" and "bad" workaholics, reporting that the former score higher on measures of work engagement while the latter score higher on measures of burnout. They suggest that some people work because they are engaged, satisfied and challenged while other people work hard because they are addicted to work seeing job contribution as a way of finding identity and value.

These studies indicate different patterns of correlations, both antecedents and consequences, of WE and D. WE and D represent different underlying motivations or orientations to work and therefore have different effects of both work and well-being outcomes. D is likely to hamper performance. WE likely to facilitate performance (Vallerand, Salvy, Mageau, Elliot, & Denis, 2003a; Vallerand, Blanchard, Mageau, Koestner, & Ratelle, 2007). D is likely to be associated with persistence, rigidity, perfectionism and heightened levels of job stress. D is likely associated with working harder not smarter. D may also be associated with the setting of unrealistic performance expectations and deadlines. The positive emotions of WE are likely to spur higher levels of performance through increasing social resources and creativity, building trust with colleagues and reducing levels of debilitating stress.

Vallerand et al. (2003a, 2000b, 2007) suggest four hypotheses relating to their two types of motivation, Passion and Addiction. First, Passion and Addiction are likely to be positively correlated. Second, respondents will generally score higher on Passion than on Addiction. Third, Passion is likely to be related to positive work outcomes and psychological health. And fourth, Addiction is likely to be associated with negative work outcomes and psychological distress.

This chapter presents the results of three studies involving different occupational groups and conducted in different countries that examine the four hypotheses suggested by Vallerand et al. (2003a, 2007).

10.1.   Study 1: Managers and Professionals in Canada

10.1.1.   Procedure

Mail questionnaires were sent to about 1000 male and 1000 female MBA graduates of a single university in Canada. Responses were received from 591 individuals, a response rate of about 35%, with elimination of questionnaires returned because the person had moved. The sample decreased to 530 when individuals who indicated they were no longer working full-time were excluded.

10.1.2.   Respondents

Table 10.1 presents personal demographic characteristics of the sample ($N = 530$). A fairly wide range of response was present on most items. Ages ranged from under 35 to over 50, with about half falling between 36 and 45. Almost 80% were married and 70% had children. MBA degrees were obtained over a range of years, most (almost 60%) before 1985. Almost 40% had also achieved one or more professional designations (CA, CFA, etc.). Almost one-third worked 46–50 hours per week. About half had incomes between $50,000 and $100,000. Almost three quarters had been with their present employers 10 years or less and in their present jobs 5 years or less. Employing organizations ranged in size from under 10 to over 85,000 with about one-third less than 100 employees.

10.1.3.   Measures

10.1.3.1.   Personal characteristics   Individual demographic characteristics were measures by single items: for example, age sex, marital status and parental status.

10.1.3.2.   Work situation characteristics   Work situation characteristics were also measures by single items: e.g., organizational level, job and organizational tenure and organizational size.

Table 10.1: Demographic characteristics of sample.

	N	%		N	%
Age			**Professional designation**		
35 and under	91	17.2	Yes	206	39.0
36–40	139	26.2	No	322	61.0
41–45	138	26.2			
46–50	102	19.3	**Level of management**		
Over 50	58	11.1	Non-management	62	11.9
			Lower management	37	7.1
Children			Middle management	197	37.9
Yes	370	70.3	Senior management	234	43.1
No	156	29.7			
Number of children			**Hours worked**		
1	81	21.8	35 or less	18	3.4
2	184	49.6	36–40	58	11.3
3	80	21.6	41–45	85	16.2
4	18	4.9	46–50	198	30.1
5	7	1.9	51–55	76	14.4
6	1	.3	56–60	90	17.4
			61 or more	38	7.2
Marital status			**Sex**		
Single	71	13.4	Males	251	52.5
Divorced/widowed	44	8.3	Females	227	47.5
Married	415	78.3			
Length of marriage			**Year of MBA**		
1–5 years	47	11.3	1980 or before	142	27.2
6–10 years	103	24.7	1981–1985	158	30.0
11–15 years	84	20.4	1986–1990	188	35.8
16–20 years	92	22.0	1991 and later	36	7.0
21 years of more	89	21.6			
Years present position			**Years present employer**		
5 years or less	350	76.3	5 years of less	179	36.4
6–10 years	79	17.2	6–10 years	158	31.9
11 years or more	30	6.5	11–15 years	62	12.5
			16 years or more	95	19.2
Organizational size			**1996 Income**		
100 or less	152	30.0	$50,000 or less	50	10.3
101–1000	138	27.4	$50,001–100,000	263	53.6
1001–10,000	126	25.0	$100,001–150,000	104	21.1
Over 10,000	89	17.6	$150,001–200,000	29	5.9
			Over $200,000	45	8.1

Table 10.1: (*Continued*)

	N	%		N	%
1999 Income			2000 Income		
$40,000 or less	73	24.7	$40,000 or less	58	19.3
$41,000–50,000	99	33.6	$41,000–50,000	86	28.5
$51,000–60,000	63	21.4	$51,000–60,000	78	26.0
$61,000–70,000	24	8.1	$61,000–70,000	28	9.3
$71,000–80,000	10	3.4	$71,000–80,000	21	6.9
$81,000–90,000	7	2.4	$81,000-90,000	7	2.4
$91,000–100,000	8	2.7	$91,000–100,000	7	2.3
Over $100,000	11	3.7	Over $100,000	16	5.3

Passion and Addiction: Passion was measured by the 10 item scale (alpha = .88) developed by Spence and Robbins (1992). One item was "My job is more life fun than work" Addiction was measured by the seven-item scale (alpha = .80) developed by Spence and Robbins (1992). An item was "I often feel that there's something inside me that drives me to work hard." Respondents indicated their agreement with each item on a 5-point scale (1 = strongly agree and 5 = strongly disagree).

10.1.3.3. Antecedents of passion and addiction   Two antecedents were included, one individual and one organizational.

Beliefs and fears   Three measures of beliefs and fears developed by Lee, Jamieson, and Earley (1996) were used. One, Striving against others (alpha = .77) had six items (e.g., "There can only be one winner in any situation."). A second, No moral principles (alpha = .79) had 6 items (e.g., "I think that nice guys finish last."). The third, Need to prove yourself (alpha = .87) had nine items (e.g., "I worry a great deal about what others think of me."). Responses were made on a 5-point Likert scale (1 = strongly disagree; 5 = strongly agree). As these three scales were strongly and positively intercorrelated, a total score was obtained by combining them.

Organizational culture values   Organizational values encouraging work-personal life balance and imbalance were measured by scales created by Kofodimos (1993). Organizational values encouraging balance was measured by nine items (alpha = .86) (e.g., "Setting limits on hours spent at work."). Organizational values supporting imbalance (alpha = .83) was measure by eight items (e.g., "Traveling to and from work destinations on weekends."). Responses were made on a 5-point Likert scale (1 = very negatively values, 5 = very positively valued). A total balance score was obtained by combining both scales, reversing the imbalance scores.

10.1.3.4. Work investment Four indicators of work investment were included

Hours worked was measured by a single item; respondents indicated how many hours they worked in a typical week.

Extra-hours worked was measured by six items (alpha = .68). Respondents indicated how frequently they did each item (e.g., "Go to work early.").

Job involvement was measured by an eight item scale (alpha = .81) developed by Spence and Robbins (1992) One item was "I am deeply committed to my job."

Time to job a measure of the psychological conception of time invested, was measured by seven items (alpha = .82) developed by Spence and Robbins (1992). An item was "I devote more time to my work than most people."

10.1.3.5. Job behaviors Two job behaviors were considered.

Perfectionism was measured by eight items (alpha = .90) developed by Spence and Robbins (1992). One item was "I can't let go of projects until I'm sure they are exactly right."

Non-delegation was assessed by seven items (alpha = .87) also developed by Spence and Robbins (1992). An item was "I feel that if you want something done correctly you should do it yourself."

10.1.3.6. Work outcomes *Job satisfaction* was measured by a seven item scale (alpha = .79) developed by Kofodimos (1993). One item was "I feel challenged by my work."

Career satisfaction was assessed by a 5-item scale (alpha = .91) developed by Greenhaus, Parasuraman and Wormley (1990). One item was "I am satisfied wit the success I have achieved in my career."

Career prospects was measured by a three item scale (alpha = .66) also developed by Greenhaus et al. (1990). An item was "I expect to advance in my career to senior levels of management."

Job stress was measured by nine items (alpha = .89) developed by Spence and Robbins (1992). One item was "Sometimes I feel like my work is going to overwhelm me."

10.1.3.7. Extra-work satisfactions Three extra-work satisfactions were included.

Family satisfaction was measured by a seven item scale (alpha = .89) developed by Kofodimos (1993). One item was "I have a good relationship with my family members."

Friends satisfaction was measured by three items (alpha = .85) also developed by Kofodimos (1993). An item was "My friends and I do enjoyable things together."

Community satisfaction was measured by four items (alpha = .80) developed by Kofodimos (1993). One item was "I contribute and give back to my community."

10.1.3.8. Psychological well-being Three indicators of psychological well-being were included.

Psychosomatic symptoms was measured by nineteen items (alpha = .84) developed by Quinn and Shepard (1974). Respondents indicated how often they experienced each physical condition (e.g., headaches) in the past year.

Emotional health was measured by six items (alpha = .77) developed by Kofodimos (1993). An item was "I actively seek to understand and improve my emotional well-being."

Physical health was assessed by five items (alpha = .72) also developed by Kofodimos (1993). One item was "I participate in a regular exercise program."

10.1.4. *Results*

Correlation of Passion and Addiction
   Passion and Addiction were significantly and positively correlated: $r = .25$, $p < .001$, $N = 524$).
   Levels of Passion and Addiction.
   Respondents indicated similar levels of Passion and Addiction, the mean scale values being 2.5 and 2.7, respectively, contrary to predictions.

10.1.4.1. Work Investments The correlations between the measures of both Passion and Addiction with four indicators of work investment are shown in the top fifth of Table 10.2. All were positive and significantly different from zero ($p < .001$). As hypothesized managers and professionals scoring higher on Passion, and on Addiction, were more involved with their jobs and work (e.g., worked more hours, more extra-hours, more job involved).

10.1.4.2. Antecedents of Passion and Addiction The next fifth of Table 10.2 shows the correlations of Passion, and of Addiction, with two potential antecedents. All correlations here were significantly different from zero ($p < .001$) Managers scoring higher on Passion scored lower on the measure of beliefs and fears and higher on the measure of organizational support for work-personal life balance; managers scoring higher on Addiction also scored higher on the measure of beliefs and fears and lower on the measure of organizational support for work-personal life balance. As hypothesized, the pattern of correlations were the direct opposite.

10.1.4.3. Job Behaviors The next fifth of Table 10.2 presents the correlations of Passion and Addiction with two job behaviours: perfectionism and non-delegation. All correlations were significantly different from zero ($p < .001$). Managers scoring higher on Passion, and managers scoring higher on Addiction, also scored higher on perfectionism; however managers scoring higher on Passion scored lower on non-delegation whereas managers scoring higher on Addiction scored higher on non-delegation. These findings provide partial support for our hypotheses.

10.1.4.4. Work Outcomes The middle fifth of Table 10.2 shows the correlations of both Passion and Addiction with four work outcomes. Most correlations were

Table 10.2: ^aCorrelates of passion and addiction.

Work investment	Passion	Addiction
Hours worked	.18***	.26***
Extra hours	.17***	.33***
Job involvement	.51***	.31***
Time to job	.21***	.46***
Antecedents		
Beliefs and fears	−.25***	.39***
Organizational culture	.28***	−.29***
Job behaviors		
Perfectionism	.13***	.40***
Non-delegation	−.18***	.19***
Work outcomes		
Job satisfaction	.53***	−.19***
Career satisfaction	.30***	−.10*
Career prospects	.33***	.02
Job stress	−.27***	.54***
Extra-work satisfactions		
Family	.18***	−.11*
Friends	.10*	−.14**
Community	.11*	−.24***
Psychological well-being		
Psychosomatic symptoms	−.27***	.31***
Emotional health	.24***	−.28***
Physical health	.16***	−.22***

***$p < .001$, **$p < .01$, *$p < .05$; $p < .10$.
^aNs range from 486 to 511.

significantly different fro zero. Managers scoring higher on Passion also indicated more favourable work outcomes across the board (more satisfaction). Lower levels of stress: managers scoring higher on Addiction also indicated less job and career satisfaction and higher levels of stress. Scores on addiction were not correlated with perceptions of future career prospects. Once again, as hypothesized, the pattern of correlations were in the opposite direction.

10.1.4.5. Extra-Work Satisfactions The next fifth of Table 10.2 shows the correlations of scores on Passion, and of Addiction, with three indicators of extra-work satisfaction. All correlations were significantly different from zero ($p < .05$). Managers scoring higher on Passion were also more satisfied in all three extra-work areas; managers scoring higher on Addiction were less satisfied in all three areas of extra-work satisfaction. As hypothesized, the pattern of correlations were in opposite directions, but weak.

10.1.4.6. Psychological Well-Being   The bottom fifth of Table 10.2 presents the correlations between Passion and Addiction and three indicators of psychological health. All correlations were significantly different from zero ($p < .001$). Managers scoring higher on Passion reported higher levels of psychological well-being whereas managers scoring higher on Addiction reported lower levels of psychological well-being.

In summary, the pattern of findings shown in Table 10.2 provides strong support for the hypotheses proposed in the introduction. In almost all instances, Passion and Addiction showed opposite relationships with the antecedent and outcome variables under investigation.

10.1.5. Discussion

Consistent with our hypotheses, our findings indicated marked differences in the correlates of two sources of work motivation, Passion and Addiction, potential antecedents and both work and psychological well-being outcomes. Before examining these differences, it should be noted that, as predicted, both Passion and Addiction were significantly correlated with job and work investment (e.g., hours worked, job involvement) consistent with earlier reported results (Vallerand et al., 2003a, 2007). In addition, again consistent with the conclusions of Vallerand et al. (2003a, 2007) scores on Passion and Addiction were moderately and positively correlated, and respondents indicated higher levels of Passion than Addiction as sources of work motivation. There was one other noteworthy area of similarity; scores on both Passion and Addiction were significantly and positively correlated with a general measures of perfectionism (see Table 10.2) suggesting that Perfectionism as operationally defined here may have some desirable features in the workplace. Future research might employ more differentiated measures of perfectionism (Flett & Hewitt, 2002; Hewitt et al., 2003).

There were also widespread differences in the direction of correlation of Passion and Addiction with antecedents, job behaviours, work and extra-work satisfactions and indicators of psychological well-being. Passion was always correlated with favourable work, extra-work and psychological well-being outcomes and less obsessive job behaviours. These findings were consistent with an emerging view that positive emotions are likely to be associated with favourable outcomes (Fredrickson, 2001; 1998; Lyubormirsky, King, & Diener, 2005; Pressman & Cohen, 2005). Addiction was almost always correlated with less favourable work, extra-work and psychological well-being indicators, and less constructive job behaviours (e.g., more difficulty delegating). In summary, our results suggest significant differences in the effects of a healthy commitment to one's work versus a harmful, psychologically and physically damaging compulsion to work.

Why should Passion and Addiction, as sources of work motivation, produce such different patterns of findings? These findings, along with previous conceptualization and empirical work (Deci & Ryan, 1985; Burke, 2007; Srivastava et al., 2001; Villerand et al., 2003a) suggest interesting potential explanations. First, managers scoring higher on Addiction also scored higher on the Beliefs and fears measure, seeing their world as more "dog eat dog": and have a greater need to prove themselves (lower self-esteem). The workaholism literature, particularly Killinger (1991) and Robinson (1998) see low self-esteem coupled with strong needs to prove one-self, associated with extrinsic goals and psychological distress. In addition, managers scoring higher on Addiction are also more perfectionistic and have greater difficulty in delegating to others likely leading to heavier workloads (see Burke, 2007, for supporting evidence). Both perfectionism and the inability to delegate because of alack of trust in subordinates is likely to influence both the nature of one's work experience and workload, resulting in greater work stress. Mangers scoring higher on Addiction indicated less satisfying work and extra-work outcomes associated with higher levels of job stress, more work-personal life conflict and less satisfying relationships outside of work likely reflecting less reflecting less social support as well. It was not surprising then, that Addiction as a source of work motivation was associated with diminished psychological functioning.

10.2. Study 2: Female Psychologists in Australia

10.2.1. Procedure

Mail questionnaires were sent to 3561 members of the Australian Psychological Society in the state of Victoria. A total of 658 completed surveys were returned, a 19% response rate. Respondents were similar to the total membership of the Australian Psychological Society on some dimensions (age, sex) for which data were available. Only female respondents were chosen for this study.

10.2.2. Respondents

Table 10.3 presents personal demographic characteristics of the sample ($N = 324$). A fairly wide range of response was present on most items. Most of the respondents were married (66%), had children (49%), were between 41 and 50 years of age (28%), worked 36–40 hours per week (39%), had been in their present jobs 5 years of less (76%), with their present organizations 5 years or less (58%), worked in organizations having 100 or fewer employees (53%) and earned between 41,000 and 60,000 Australian dollars (59% in 1999 and 54% in 2000).

Table 10.3: Demographic characteristics of sample.

	N	%		N	%
Age			Marital status		
30 or less	67	20.7	Single, divorced, widowed	111	34.3
31–40	82	25.4			
41–50	89	27.5	Married	213	65.7
51–60	80	24.6			
61 or more	6	1.9	Length of marriage		
			5 years or less	54	25.5
Parental status			6–10	47	22.2
			11–15	18	8.5
Children	137	48.9	16–20	24	11.3
Childless	164	51.1	21 or more	76	33.5
Number of children					
0	170	52.5	Worked continuously		
1	30	9.3	Yes	170	52.5
2	63	19.4	No	153	47.4
3	26	8.0			
4	19	5.9	Years present job		
5 or more	16	4.9	5 or less	242	75.6
			6–10	45	14.1
Hours worked per week			11–15	19	5.9
			16–20	8	2.5
35 or less	16	5.0	21 or more	6	1.9
36–40	125	38.8			
41–45	66	20.5	Years present employer		
46–50	67	20.8			
51–55	9	2.8	5 or less	183	58.3
56–60	26	8.1	6–10	64	20.4
61 or more	13	4.0	11–15	35	11.1
			16–20	19	6.1
			21–25	5	1.6
Organizational level			26 or more	8	2.5
Non-management	110	35.6			
Supervisor	29	9.4	Organization size		
Lower management	41	13.3	25 or less	90	28.8
Middle management	57	18.4	26–50	37	11.8
Senior management	30	9.7	51–100	42	13.4
Executive	22	7.1	101–200	34	10.9
Divisional head	8	2.6	201–500	16	5.1
CEO	12	3.9	501–1000	19	6.1
			1001–2000	16	5.1
			2001–4000	20	6.4
			4001–8000	16	5.1
			Over 8000	23	7.3

10.2.3.   Measures

10.2.3.1.   Personal characteristics   Individual demographic characteristics were measures by single items: for example, age sex, marital status, and parental status.

10.2.3.2.   Work situation characteristics   Work situation characteristics were also measures by single items: e.g., organizational level, job and organizational tenure, and organizational size.

Passion and Addiction: Passion was measured by the 10 item scale (alpha = .88) developed by Spence and Robbins (1992). One item was "My job is more life fun than work" Addiction was measured by the seven item scale (alpha = .80) developed by Spence and Robbins (1992). An item was "I often feel that there's something inside me that drives me to work hard." Respondents indicated their agreement with each item on a 5-point scale (1 = strongly agree; 5 = strongly disagree).

10.2.3.3.   Antecedents of passion and addiction   Two antecedents were included, one individual and one organizational.

Beliefs and fears   Three measures of beliefs and fears developed by Lee et al. (1996) were used. One, Striving against others (alpha = .77) had six items (e.g., There can only be one winner in any situation."). A second, No moral principles (alpha = .79) had six items (e.g., "I think that nice guys finish last."). The third, Need to prove yourself (alpha = .87) had nine items (e.g., "I worry a great deal about what others think of me."). Responses were made on a 5-point Likert scale (1 = strongly disagree, 5 = strongly agree). As these three scales were strongly and positively intercorrelated, a total score was obtained by combining them.

Organizational culture values   Organizational values encouraging work-personal life balance and imbalance were measured by scales created by Kofodimos (1993). Organizational values encouraging balance was measured by nine items (alpha = .86) (e.g., "Setting limits on hours spent at work."). Organizational values supporting imbalance (alpha = .83) was measure by eight items (e.g., "Traveling to and from work destinations on weekends."). Responses were made on a 5-point Likert scale (1 = very negatively valued, 5 = very positively valued). A total balance score was obtained by combining both scales, reversing the imbalance scores.

10.2.3.4.   Work investment   Four indicators of work investment were included
Hours worked was measured by a single item; respondents indicated how many hours they worked in a typical week.
Extra-hours worked was measured by six items (alpha = .68) Respondents indicated how frequently they did each item (e.g., "Go to work early.").
Job involvement was measured by an eight item scale (alpha = .81) developed by Spence and Robbins (1992). One item was "I am deeply committed to my job."

Time to job a measure of the psychological conception of time invested, was measured by seven items (alpha = .82) developed by Spence and Robbins (1992). An item was "I devote more time to my work than most people."

10.2.3.5.   Job behaviors   Two job behaviors were considered.

Perfectionism was measured by eight items (alpha = .90) developed by Spence and Robbins (1992). One item was "I can't let go of projects until I'm sure they are exactly right."

Non-delegation was assessed by seven items (alpha = .87) also developed by Spence and Robbins (1992). An item was "I feel that if you want something done correctly you should do it yourself."

10.2.3.6.   Work outcomes   *Job satisfaction* was measured by a seven item scale (alpha = .79) developed by Kofodimos (1993). One item was "I feel challenged by my work."

Career satisfaction was assessed by a 5-item scale (alpha = .91) developed by Greenhaus et al. (1990). One item was "I am satisfied wit the success I have achieved in my career."

Career prospects was measured by a three item scale (alpha = .66) also developed by Greenhaus et al. (1990). An item was "I expect to advance in my career to senior levels of management."

Job stress was measured by nine items (alpha = .89) developed by Spence and Robbins (1992). One item was "Sometimes I feel like my work is going to overwhelm me."

10.2.3.7.   Extra-work satisfactions   Three extra-work satisfactions were included.

Family satisfaction was measured by a seven item scale (alpha = .89) developed by Kofodimos (1993). One item was "I have a good relationship with my family members."

Friends satisfaction was measured by three items (alpha = .85) also developed by Kofodimos (1993). An item was "My friends and I do enjoyable things together."

Community satisfaction was measured by four items (alpha = .80) developed by Kofodimos (1993). One item was "I contribute and give back to my community."

10.2.3.8.   Psychological well-being   Three indicators of psychological well-being were included.

Psychosomatic symptoms was measured by nineteen items (alpha = .84) developed by Quinn and Shepard (1974). Respondents indicated how often they experienced each physical condition (e.g., headaches) in the past year.

Emotional health was measured by six items (alpha = .77) developed by Kofodimos (1993). An item was "I actively seek to understand and improve my emotional well-being."

Physical health was assessed by five items (alpha = .72) also developed by Kofodimos (1993). One item was "I participate in a regular exercise program."

10.2.4. Results

10.2.4.1. Work Investments The correlations between the measures of both Passion and Addiction with four indicators of work investment are shown in the top fifth of Table 10.4. All were positive and significantly different from zero ($p < .001$). As hypothesized female psychologists scoring higher on Passion, and on Addiction, were more involved with their jobs and work (e.g., worked more hours, more extra-hours, more job involved).

10.2.4.2. Antecedents of Passion and Addiction The next fifth of Table 10.4 shows the correlations of Passion, and of Addiction, with two potential antecedents. Three of the correlations here were significantly different from zero ($p < .05$). Female

Table 10.4: [a]Correlates of passion and addiction.

Work investment	Passion	Addiction
Hours worked	.21***	.23***
Extra hours	.22***	.17***
Job involvement	.54***	.21***
Time to job	.26***	.33***
Antecedents		
Beliefs and fears	−.20***	.34***
Organizational culture	.14*	.03
Job behaviors		
Perfectionism	.04	.47***
Non-delegation	−.12*	.18**
Work outcomes		
Job satisfaction	.54***	−.19***
Career satisfaction	.36***	−.17
Career prospects	.27***	.20***
Job stress	−.20***	.50***
Extra-work satisfactions		
Family	.08	−.15**
Friends	.20***	−.12*
Community	.12*	−.12*
Psychological well-being		
Psychosomatic symptoms	−.15*	.27***
Emotional health	.16**	−.22***
Physical health	.09	−.21***

***$p < .001$; **$p < .01$; *$p < .05$
[a]Ns range from 289 to 320.

psychologists scoring higher on Passion scored lower on the measure of beliefs and fears and higher on the measure of organizational support for work-personal life balance; female psychologists scoring higher on Addiction also scored higher on the measure of beliefs and fears. As hypothesized, the pattern of correlations were the direct opposite.

10.2.4.3.   Work Outcomes   The middle fifth of Table 10.4 shows the correlations of both Passion and Addiction with four work outcomes. Almost all correlations were significantly different from zero. Female psychologists scoring higher on Passion also indicated more favourable work outcomes across the board (more satisfaction, lower levels of stress): female psychologists scoring higher on Addiction indicated less job satisfaction and higher levels of stress. Scores on both Passion and Addiction were positively correlated with perceptions of future career prospects. Once again, as hypothesized, the pattern of correlations were in the opposite direction.

10.2.4.4.   Extra-Work Satisfactions   The next fifth of Table 10.4 shows the correlations of scores on Passion, and of Addiction, with three indicators of extra-work satisfaction. Most correlations were significantly different from zero ($p < .05$). Female psychologists scoring higher on Passion were also more satisfied in two extra-work areas; female psychologists scoring higher on Addiction were less satisfied in all three areas of extra-work satisfaction. As hypothesized, the pattern of correlations were in opposite directions, but weak.

10.2.4.5.   Psychological Well-Being   The bottom fifth of Table 10.4 presents the correlations between Passion and Addiction and three indicators of psychological health. Almost all correlations were significantly different from zero ($p < .001$). Female psychologists scoring higher on Passion reported higher levels of psychological well-being whereas female psychologists scoring higher on Addiction reported lower levels of psychological well-being.

In summary, the pattern of findings shown in Table 10.4 provides strong support for the hypotheses proposed in the introduction. In almost all instances, Passion and Addiction showed opposite relationships with the antecedent and outcome variables under investigation.

10.2.5.   Discussion

Consistent with our hypotheses, our findings indicated marked differences in the correlates of two sources of work motivation, Passion and Addiction, potential antecedents and both work and psychological well-being outcomes. Before examining these differences, it should be noted that, as predicted, both Passion and Addiction were significantly correlated with job and work investment (e.g., hours worked, job involvement) consistent with earlier reported results

(Vallerand et al., 2003a, 2007). In addition, again consistent with the conclusions of Vallerand et al. (2003a, 2007) scores on Passion and Addiction were moderately and positively correlated, and respondents indicated higher levels of Passion than Addiction as sources of work motivation. There was one other noteworthy area of similarity; scores on both Passion and Addiction were significantly and positively correlated with a general measures of perfectionism (see Table 10.2) suggesting that Perfectionism as operationally defined here may have some desirable features in the workplace.

There were also widespread differences in the direction of correlation of Passion and Addiction with antecedents, job behaviours, work and extra-work satisfactions and indicators of psychological well-being. Passion was always correlated with favourable work, extra-work and psychological well-being outcomes and less obsessive job behaviours. Addiction was almost always correlated with less favourable work, extra-work and psychological well-being indicators, and less constructive job behaviours (e.g., more difficulty delegating).

10.3. Study 3: Journalists in Norway

10.3.1. Procedure

Data were collected from 211 journalists working in the city of Bergen Norway using anonymously completed questionnaires representing a response rate of 43%. Five hundred questionnaires were sent out by the journalists' union and completed questionnaires were returned to a university address. Measures originally appearing in English were translated into Norwegian by members of the research team using the back-translation method; other measures (e.g., Maslach Burnout Inventory) had already been translated into Norwegian from English and used by others in their research projects.

10.3.2. Respondents

Table 10.5 presents personal demographic characteristics of the sample ($N = 211$). Two thirds of the sample were male (676%), most were married (70%), worked in permanent jobs (89%), were under 40 years of age, (65%), worked between 31 and 40 hours per week (55%), had relatively low levels of job and organizational tenure (42% had 4 years of less of organizational tenure and 46% had 2 years of less of job tenure), and most had no supervisory responsibilities (74%).

Table 10.5: Demographic characteristics of sample.

	N	%		N	%
Age			**Organizational tenure**		
29 or less	42	20.1	1–2 years	47	22.5
30–39	94	45.0	3–4 years	41	19.6
40–49	38	18.2	5–10 years	65	31.1
50–59	31	14.8	Over 10 years	56	26.8
60 or over	4	1.9	**Journalism Tenure**		
Gender			1–3 years	28	13.5
Males	138	67.0	4–10 years	95	45.7
Females	68	33.0	10–20 years	53	25.5
			Over 20 years	32	15.4
Marital status			**Organization size**		
Single	47	22.8			
Married	145	70.4	15 or less	22	10.8
Separated/divorced	13	6.3	16–100	31	15.2
Widowed	1	.5	101–150	44	21.6
			151 and over	107	52.4
Children at home			**Unit Size**		
Yes	95	45.7			
No	113	54.3	1–15	81	39.3
			16–100	62	30.1
Education beyond primary			101–150	57	27.7
0–3	27	13.0	151 or more	6	2.9
4–6	83	39.9			
7 or more	98	47.1	**Job tenure**		
			Less than 1 year	30	14.6
Title			1–2 years	65	31.6
Journalist	178	85.2	3–4 years	48	23.3
Layout designer	14	6.7	5–8 years	36	17.5
Photographer	15	7.2	9 years or more	27	13.1
Work status			**Income**		
Permanent	185	89.4	275,000 or less	42	20.4
Temporary	16	7.7	275,000–350,000	65	31.6
Freelance	6	2.9	351,000–450,000	64	31.1
			451,000 or more	35	17.0
Hours worked			**Leadership responsibility**		
30 or less	14	6.8			
31–40	114	55.0	Yes	54	26.0
41–50	75	36.3	No	134	74.0
51 and above	4	1.9			

10.3.3. Measures

10.3.3.1. Personal characteristics   Individual demographic characteristics were measured by single items: for example, age, sex, marital status, and parental status, level of education, and income.

10.3.3.2. Work situation characteristics   Work situation characteristics were also measured by single items: e.g., hours worked, unit and organizational size, job, organization and journalism tenure, and leadership responsibility.

10.3.3.3. Passion and addiction   Passion was measured by the 10 item scale (alpha = .80) developed by Spence and Robbins (1992). One item was "My job is more life fun than work" Addiction was measured by the seven item scale (alpha = .88) developed by Spence and Robbins (1992). An item was "I often feel that there's something inside me that drives me to work hard." Respondents indicated their agreement with each item on a 5-point scale (1 = strongly agree; 5 = strongly disagree).

10.3.3.4. Work investment   Two indicators of work investment were included
  Hours worked was measured by a single item; respondents indicated how many hours they worked in a typical week.
  Work-family conflict
  Work-Family Conflict was measured by two items (alpha = .63) taken from the General Questionnaire for Psychological and Social Factors at Work (QPS Nordic) developed by Lindstrom et al. (1997). Responded indicated the extent to which work demands interfered with family and family demands interfered with work.

10.3.3.5. Work outcomes   Four work outcomes were included.
  Intrinsic Motivation was assessed by a three item scale (alpha = .68) taken from the QPS (Lindstrom et al., 1997). Respondents indicated how important each item would be in their ideal job. One item was "imagination and creativity."
  Extrinsic motivation was measured by a three item scale (alpha = .71) also from the QPS (Lindstrom et al., 1997). An item was "money."

10.3.3.6. Organizational Commitment   Organizational commitment was measured by three items (alpha = .78) taken from the QPS (Lindstrom et al., 1997).

Flow   Flow is a positive experiential state when an individual is totally connected to the task in a situation where personal skills are equal to the required challenges; flow is the subjective experience of full involvement with one's job and work (Csikszentmihalyi, 1990). In this research, flow was measures to a 36-item instrument developed by Jackson and Marsh (1996). This scale measures nine dimensions: challenge-skill balance, action-awareness merging, clear goals, unambiguous feedback, concentration on task at hand, sense of control, loss of self-consciousness, transformation and autotelic experience. Reliabilities of these nine four-tem scales

(Cronbach's alpha) ranged from .75 to .82. Respondents were asked to identify a challenging professional work experience they had encountered in the past few weeks and indicate how descriptive each statement was of this concrete event (e.g., "I felt like time stopped while I was working" on a 5-point scale ($1 =$ strongly disagree, $3 =$ neither agree nor disagree, $5 =$ strongly agree). A total flow score was created (alpha $= .89$) since the nine dimensions were all positively and mostly significantly correlated ($p < .05$).

10.3.3.7. Psychological Well-Being Psychological well-being indicators included three scales from the Maslach Burnout Inventory and measures of positive and negative affect.

Burnout Three burnout components were measured by the Maslach Burnout Inventory–General Survey (MBI-GS) developed by Schaufeli, Maslach, Leiter, and Jackson (1996). Exhaustion had five items (alpha $= .90$) and assess fatigue, Cynicism had five items (alpha $= .81$) reflects indifference or a distant attitude towards one's work. Professional Efficacy (6 items, alpha $= .83$) includes both social and non-social aspects of occupational accomplishments. Respondents indicated how frequently they experiences each item on a seven point frequency scale ($0 =$ never, $6 =$ always).

Affect Positive and negative affect were measured using the PANAS scales (Watson, Clark, & Tellegen, 1988). Positive and negative affect (alphas $= .89$ and .83, respectively) were each measured by 10 terms or words that describe different feelings and emotions. Respondents indicated the extent to which each work described their feelings on a 5-point scale ($1 =$ very slightly or not at all, $3 =$ moderately, $5 =$ extremely).

10.3.3.8. Work Investments Passion tended to work more hours ($p < .10$) and reported more work-family the top quarter of Table 10.6 shows the correlations of the measures of Passion and Addiction with two indicators of work investment. Journalists scoring higher on conflict; journalists scoring higher on Addiction worked more hours and reported more work-family conflict.

10.3.3.9. Work Outcomes The next quarter of Table 10.6 presents the correlations of Passion and Addiction with four work outcomes: Intrinsic motivation, Extrinsic motivation, Organizational commitment and Flow. Six of the eight resulting correlations were significantly different from zero ($p < .05$) and the direction of these correlations was opposite in the two work motivation sources (Passion versus Addiction). Journalists scoring higher on Passion also scored higher on Flow, Organizational commitment and Intrinsic motivation; Passion was uncorrelated with levels of Extrinsic motivation (but negative in sign). Addiction was negatively correlated with Flow and Organizational commitment and positively correlated with level of Intrinsic motivation and tended to be positively correlated with level of Extrinsic motivation ($p < .10$). Thus Passion and Addiction were differentially correlated with Flow, Organizational commitment and Extrinsic motivation (but in

Table 10.6: [a]Correlates of passion and addiction.

Work investment	Passion	Addiction
Hours worked	.13[b]	.21**
Work-family conflict	.15*	.31***
Work experiences and Outcomes		
Flow	.35***	−.20**
Organizational commitment	.32***	−.19**
Intrinsic motivation	.34***	.17*
Extrinsic motivation	−.10	.14a
Psychological well-being		
Burnout		
Exhaustion	−.35***	.51***
Cynicism	−.36***	.41***
Efficacy	.09	−.01
Affect		
Positive	.22**	−.46***
Negative	−.41***	04

***$p < .001$; **$p < .01$; *$p < .05$,
[a]Ns range from 195 to 209.
[b]$p < .10$.

the latter case not significantly so), and similarly correlated with levels of Intrinsic motivation.

10.3.3.10. Psychological Well-Being   The bottom half of Table 10.6 shows the correlations of Passion and Addiction with three burnout components and two measures of affect; seven of the ten resulting correlations were significantly different from zero ($p < .01$). Journalists scoring higher on Passion also scored lower on Exhaustion, Cynicism and Negative affect and scored higher on Positive affect. Journalists scoring higher on Addiction also scored higher on Exhaustion and Cynicism and lower on Positive affect. Neither Passion not Addiction was correlated with levels of Efficacy; Addiction was also uncorrelated with levels of self-reported Negative affect.

In summary, the pattern of findings shown in Table 10.6 provides strong support for the hypotheses proposed in the introduction. In almost all instances, Passion and Addiction showed opposite relationships with the outcome variables under investigation.

10.3.4. Discussion

The pattern of results shown in Table 10.6 was generally consistent with our hypotheses. First, journalists scoring higher on Passion, and on Addiction, were more involved in their jobs and work (worked more hours a week, had more work-family conflict). Second journalists scoring higher on Passion also reported more favourable work experiences and outcomes (more flow at work, more organizational commitment, higher levels of Intrinsic motivation) whereas journalists scoring higher on Addiction also reported less flow and organizational commitment, and higher levels of Intrinsic motivation. The latter also tended to report higher levels of extrinsic motivation as well ($p < .10$). Third, journalists scoring higher on Passion reported higher levels of psychological well-being (less exhaustion, cynicism, and negative affect and higher levels of positive affect) whereas journalists scoring higher on Addiction reported lower levels of psychological well-being (more exhaustion and cynicism, less positive affect). Interestingly neither Passion nor Addiction were correlated with self-reports of efficacy on the job.

10.4. Overall Implications

The findings obtained in the three studies discussed above showed convincingly that different sources of work motivation – Passion and Addiction – had dramatically different relationships with a range of job satisfactions, work outcomes and indicators of psychological health. Though moderately and positively correlated, Passion and Addiction had the opposite relationships with these dependent variables.

It has previously been shown that "why one works hard" – the motives make a difference (see Burke, 2007; Hewlett & Luce, 2006; Schaufeli et al., 2007). The intriguing question then becomes though Passion was associated with positive outcomes and Addiction was associated with negative outcomes, are individuals who score high on either sources of motivation still "slaves"?

10.5. Future research Directions

The most important future research need is to strengthen the measures of both Passion and Addiction. As noted above, the two measures used here were initially developed to address related -but different- concepts. The work of Villerand and his colleagues (Vallerand et al., 2003a, 2007) provides a useful starting point. Some of their items could be reworded and added to those contained in the Spence and Robbins (1992) measures. It is important to get at deeper levels of both Passion and Addiction (e.g., "I cannot live without my work," "My work is in harmony with other activities in my life."). It is also vital to better understand the drivers of both Passion and Addiction. Where do Passion and Addiction come from? It is also critical to better understand how both Passion and Addiction get translated into different job behaviours and work and extra-work experiences and health outcomes. Is the process one involving attitudes and/or behaviours on and off the job? Work investments are likely to be the same so is it a matter of expectations and appraisal? Is the cup half-full or is it half-empty? In addition, it would be important to identify potential boundary conditions for the observed findings. These might involve number of work hours and national values. It is possible that these findings would be mitigated among employees working in occupations that limit the hours employees work because of contractual relationships (thus working fewer hours) or in countries that place a higher value on family and leisure.

Acknowledgement

Preparation of this manuscript was supported by York University. Graeme MacDermind, Stig Mattheisen, Zena Burgess and Fay Oberklaid assisted with the collection of the data in the three studies; Lisa Fiksenbaum participated in data analysis; and Susan Lorr contributed to manuscript preparation.

References

Brett, J. M., & Stroh, L. K. (2003). Working 61 plus hours a week: Why do managers do it? *Journal of Applied Psychology, 88*, 67–78.

Buelens, M., & Poelmans, S. A. Y. (2004). Enriching the Spence and Robbins typology of workaholism: Demographic, motivational and organizational correlates. *Journal of Organizational Change Management, 17*, 446–458.

Burke, R. J. (2007). *Research companion to working time and work addiction*. Cheltenham,UK: Edward Elgar.

Csikszentmihalyi, M. (1990). *Flow: The psychology of optimal experience*. New York: Harper Collins.

Deci, E. L., Koestner, R., & Ryan, R. M. (1999). A meta-analysis review of experiments examining the effects of extrinsic rewards on intrinsic motivation. *Psychological Bulletin, 125*, 627–668.

Deci, E. L., & Ryan, R. M. (1985). *Intrinsic motivation and self-determination in human behavior*. New York: Plenum.

Deci, E. L., & Ryan, R. M. (2000). The "what" and "why" of goal pursuits: Human needs and the self-determination of behavior. *Psychological Inquiry, 11*, 227–268.

Dembe, A. E., Erickson, J. B., Delbos, R. G., & Banks, S. M. (2005). The impact of overtime and long work hours on occupational injuries and illnesses: New evidence from the United States. *Occupational and Environmental Medicine, 62*, 588–597.

DeRaeve, L., Jansen, N. W. H., & Kant, I. J. (2007). Health effects of transitions in work schedule, work hours and overtime in a prospective cohort study. *Scandanavian Journal of Work, Environment and Health, 33*, 105–113.

Flett, G. L., & Hewitt, P. L. (2002). *Perfectionism: Theory and research*. Washington, DC: American Psychological Association.

Fredrickson, B. L. (1998). What good are positive emotions? *Review of General Psychology, 2*, 300–319.

Fredrickson, B. L. (2001). The role of positive emotions in positive psychology: The broaden-and-build theory of positive emotions. *American Psychologist, 56*, 218–226.

Golden, L. (2007). How long? The historical, economic and cultural factors behind working hours and overwork. In: R. J. Burke (Ed.), *Research companion to working time and work addiction* (pp. 36–60). Cheltenham, UK: Edward Elgar.

Graves, L. M., Ruderman, M., & Ohlott, P. J. (2006). Effect of workaholism on managerial performance: Help or hindrance. Paper presented at the Academy of Management, Atlanta, August.

Greenhaus, J. H., Parasuraman, S., & Wormley, W. (1990). Organizational experiences and career success of black and white managers. *Academy of Management Journal, 33*, 64–86.

Hewlett, S. A., & Luce, C. B. (2006). Extreme jobs: The dangerous allure of the 70-hour work week. *Harvard Business Review, 84*(December), 49–59.

Jackson, S. A., & Marsh, H. W. (1996). Development and validation of a scale to measure optimal experience: The flow state scale. *Journal of Sport and Exercise Psychology, 18*, 17–35.

Johnstone, A., & Johnston, L. (2005). The relationship between organizational climate, occupational type and workaholism. *New Zealand Journal of Psychology, 34*, 181–188.

Kanai, A., Wakabayashi, M., & Fling, S. (1996). Workaholism among employees in Japanese corporations: An examination based on the Japanese version of the workaholism scales. *Japanese Psychological Research, 38*, 192–203.

Kawahito, H. (1991). Death and the corporate warrior. *Japan Quarterly, 38*(April–June), 149–156.

Killinger, B. (1991). *Workaholics: The respectable addicts.* New York: Simon & Schuster.

Kofodimos, J. (1993). *Balancing act.* San Francisco: Jossey-Bass.

Lee, C., Jamieson, L. F., & Earley, P. C. (1996). Beliefs and fears and Type A behavior: Implications for academic performance and psychiatric health disorder symptoms. *Journal of Organizational Behavior, 17*, 151–178.

Lindstrom, K., Dallner, M., Elo, A. L., Gamberale, F., Knardahl, S., Skogstad, A., & Orhade, E. (1997). *Review of psychological and social factors at work and suggestions for the General Nordic Questionnaire (QPS).* Copenhagen: Nordic Council of Ministers.

Lyubormirsky, S. L., King, L., & Diener, E. (2005). The benefits of frequent positive affect: Does happiness lead to success. *Psychological Bulletin, 131*, 803–855.

Machlowitz, M. (1980). *Workaholics: Living with them, working with them.* Reading, MA: Addison-Wesley.

Pressman, S. D., & Cohen, S. (2005). Does positive affect influence health? *Psychological Bulletin, 131*, 925–971.

Quinn, R. P., & Shepard, L. J. (1974). *The 1972–73 quality of employment survey.* Ann Arbor, MI: Institute for Social Research, University of Michigan.

Robinson, B. E. (1998). *Chained to the desk: A guidebook for workaholics, their partners and children and the clinicians who treat them.* New York: New York University Press.

Ryan, R. M., & Deci, E. L. (2000). Self-determination theory and the facilitation of intrinsic motivation, social development, and well-being. *American Psychologist, 55*, 68–78.

Schaufeli, W. B., Maslach, C., Leiter, M. P., & Jackson, S. E. (1996). *Maslach burnout inventory – general survey.* Palo Alto, CA: Consulting Psychologists Press.

Schaufeli, W. B., Taris, T. W., & Bakker, A. B. (2007). Dr. Jekyll or Mr. Hyde: On the difference between work engagement and workaholism. In: R. J. Burke (Ed.), *Research companion to working time and work addiction* (pp. 193–220). Cheltenham, UK: Edward Elgar.

Scott, K. S., Moore, K. S., & Miceli, M. P. (1997). An exploration of the meaning and consequences of workaholism. *Human Relatins, 50*, 287–314.

Sparks, K., Cooper, C. L., Fried, Y., & Shirom, A. (1997). The effects of hours or work on health: A meta-analytic review. *Journal of Occupational and Organizational Psychology, 70*, 391–400.

Spence, J. T., & Robbins, A. S. (1992). Workaholism: Definition, measurement, and preliminary results. *Journal of Personality Assessment, 58*, 160–178.

Srivastava, A., Locke, E. A., & Bartol, K. M. (2001). Money and subjective well-being: It's not the money, it's the motives. *Journal of Personality and Social Psychology, 80,* 959–971.

Uehata, T. (1990). *Karoshi: When the corporate warrior dies.* Tokyo: Mado-sha.

Vallerand, R. J., Blanchard, C. M., Mageau, G. A., Koestner, R., Ratelle, C., Leonard, M., & Gagne, M. (2003a). Les passions de l'ame: On obsessive and harmonious passion. *Journal of Personality and Social Psychology, 85,* 756–767.

Vallerand, R. J., & Houlfort, N. (2003b). Passion at work: Toward a new conceptualization. In: D. Skarlicki, S. Gilland & D. Steiner (Eds), *Social issues in management* (Vol. 3, pp. 175–204). Greenwich, CT: Information Age Publishing.

Vallerand, R. J., Salvy, S. J., Mageau, G. A., Elliot, A. J., Denis, P. L., Grouzet, F. M. E., & Bouchard, C. (2007). On the role of passion in performance. *Journal of Personality, 75,* 505–533.

van der Hulst, M. (2003). Long work hours and health. *Scandinavian Journal of Work, Environment and Health, 29,* 171–188.

Virick, M., & Baruch, Y. (2007). Factors determining workaholism, its positive and negative consequences. Paper presented at the Academy of Management, Philadelphia, August.

Watson, D., Clark, L. A., & Tellegen, A. (1988). Development and validation of brief measures of positive and negative affect: The PANAS scales. *Journal of Personality and Social Psychology, 54,* 1063–1070.

PART III

CHOICES

Chapter 11

Animal Farm, Baby Boom and Crackberry Addicts

Gayle Porter and Jamie L. Perry

As French critic and novelist Alphonse Karr said "Plus ça change, plus c'est la même chose" — "The more things change, the more they are the same." To examine the topic of work addiction, it is important to look at current trends that contribute to excess work. However, it can be equally valuable to recognize the tendencies that have been constant over time. Further, the problem of balancing work and personal life has become a topic of personal discussion among workers in many industries and job types and has been a popular topic of mainstream media. In recent years, there also has been an increase in scholarly attention to work hours and the potential for work addiction. All of these perspectives, considered together, are important for imagining the future of work and working hours.

Among the trends over the past decade is the shift from an industrial-based national economy to an information-based global economy, which has caused a transformation in the division of work and personal life (Hill, Ferris, & Märtinson, 2003). As a result, the job market has shifted to require more flexibility in work hours of the employee, in order to compete in the global marketplace. Some feel this global competition has changed the workforce and created a need for committed employees, who are willing to work longer hours (Friedman, Christensen, & DeGroot, 1998). But, an unquestioned shift to longer hours, especially when part of a pattern of work addiction, can create negative effects on an employee's personal life, such as physical and mental well-being and relationship issues (cf. Robinson, 2007). It can also result in less than optimal working relationships on the job (Porter, 1996) and lessen the link between work enjoyment and job performance (Graves, Ruderman, Ohlott, & Weber, 2008).

External forces can encourage people to work longer hours. For example, company pressures to cut costs and/or monitor activity around the globe are two factors that may press workers to expand their time devoted to work. With limited resources and greater demands, working more hours may seem necessary to keep their current jobs or to be seen as deserving of future promotion or pay increase. However, some individuals are internally driven to work long hours beyond what can be accounted for by financial need (Harpaz & Snir, 2003) and the external pressure provided by the company serves as a convenient excuse when a partner/ spouse or children complain about excess work at the expense of family life (Porter & Kakabadse, 2006). Because companies tend to reward workaholic behavior, people with this internal compulsion to work are not often recognized as having any type of "work disturbance," even though "it is probably more characteristic or contemporary culture" than other difficulties of personal development (Axelrod, 1999, p. 47).

In this chapter, we draw from both popular media and research support, along with anecdotal examples drawn from conversations accumulated as part of our own prior studies. Our goal is to present reminders that working hours are a personal life choice, even with external demands, but a choice that is influenced by elements of the individual's working situation. The implications of a choice for long working hours are shown through use of two past "hard working" icons from popular media, one from the 1940s and one from the 1980s. Discussion continues into current time with an overview highlighting advances in technology that provide expanded work opportunities but, also, exacerbate tendencies toward work addiction.

11.1. *Animal Farm*

The book *Animal Farm*, written by George Orwell in 1946, is considered classic literature and a well-known commentary on social change, particularly working-class rebellion. This book is about workers (in this case farm animals) who realize their own strength and rise against the elite (the humans) who have been exploiting them. In addition, it highlights the risk that rebellion leaders may eventually transition into a new elite adopting the undesirable traits of their predecessors. It is a message about social institutions and the use and abuse of power.

The animals Orwell features in this book are dissatisfied because they are doing all the work and receiving little benefit. They long for happiness and freedom and a chance to fulfill their own dreams. When hunger pushes them into open rebellion, they drive out the humans, declare themselves a democratic society, and create a doctrine of "Animalism" represented in seven principles they write on the barn wall — similar to the way company's display their vision statements on walls or banners. As difficulties arise, the quick-witted pigs find they can take advantage of the others and, consequently, they become corrupted by power. The seven principles are compromised one by one and conditions return to their earlier state, the pig leaders having replaced the humans to exploit the other animals.

Woven throughout this tale of power and corruption is the story of Boxer, the loyal, honest and kind workhorse of the farm. Much of the progress the animals make toward their new society is due to Boxer's devotion to working hard. Boxer has two personal slogans by which he faces every challenge. The first is "I will work harder." The second is "[the leader] is always right." The first governed his personal behavior, and the second kept him from questioning priorities.

Though Boxer's work was critical to the animals' achievements, they warned him that he might be overdoing it. He continues, following the goals set out by the leader and, at every obstacle, remarking, "I will work harder."

One day, Boxer decides he can complete more work by waking up a half hour earlier in the morning. This helps for awhile but, eventually, he arranges to be awakened 45 min earlier instead of a half hour. In his spare time, which becomes increasingly rare due to the extension of the regular work day, he would go back to the work site alone to complete tasks that did not require assistance. At times, "Boxer would even come out at nights and work for an hour or two on his own by the light of the harvest moon" (Orwell, 1946, p 59).

As the animals' situation deteriorates to starvation conditions, cruelty and bloodshed resurface, but now it is animal against animal. Boxer — who rarely voices a personal opinion — makes this speech:

> I do not understand it. I would not have believed that such things could happen on our farm. It must be due to some fault in ourselves. The solution, as I see it, is to work harder. From now onwards I shall get up a full hour earlier in the mornings. (Orwell, 1946, p. 72)

And Boxer Returns to Work.

Over time, injuries and age cause Boxer to think he may not be able to continue work at the level he has in the past. Yet he perseveres for two reasons: it is the only life he knows and he will be rewarded at a future time. The rules of their new society include a pension policy, by which horses can retire at age 12, and Boxer is now 11. The corner of a pasture had been fenced off for retiree grazing; each retiree is guaranteed a generous allotment of basic food with a carrot or possibly an apple on public holidays. Again, others warn Boxer that he should slow down, but he wants to see a particular project well underway before he accepts his honorable shift to the promised retirement. Boxer works harder than ever. His appearance suggests health deterioration, but he will admit to no difficulty. Others observe that as he works his mouth often forms the words, "I will work harder" although he has no voice left to speak them aloud.

Finally, one day Boxer drops to the ground. Lying on his side, eyes glazed, he cannot even raise his head. His lungs have given out. He is now within a month of retirement and believes he has at least left the work in a condition that others can carry on without him. Soon, Boxer is being taken away in a large van. The other animals are saying goodbye, thinking it is transportation for medical treatment promised by the leader. But, Benjamin the Donkey, one of the few animals other than the pigs to have learned to read, shouts that the words on the van are ALFRED SIMMONDS, HORSE SLAUGHTERER AND GLUE BOILER. They yell to Boxer that he is being taken to his death and must escape. They can hear him kicking at the van doors, but Boxer no longer has the strength to break free.

Boxer's story is a good example of workaholism or work addiction (the terms used synonymously here). His story applies to a number of people. As challenges increase, these people seem to have the same guiding philosophy as Boxer — I will work harder. Most organizations contain individuals who others refer to as a "workhorse"; some may admit to that profile or even take pride in identifying themselves by that label. It is important to differentiate the loyal, honest and kind worker who is willing to do extra on occasion from the work addicted individual who ignores clear evidence of a need to cut back and continues to sacrifice all else in life for the job.

Correctly identifying that difference is complicated by that fact that many successful people attribute their own advancement to workaholic behavior, and they expect the same from the people who work for them. Many who achieve higher ranking positions make the common observation that: "This job would be a piece of cake, if I had myself working for me" — if the next in line were a person willing to give the hours and devotion this individual did. Looking around, they wonder what is wrong with those other people who do not have the same willingness to give up everything for the job. Too often the newly promoted fill in the gaps by, once again, working harder. Given the chance to identify, hire and keep people of a like mindset, workaholics will influence norms until expectations for excess time on the job gradually dominate the organizational culture (Schaef & Fassel, 1988).

Also like Boxer, an increasing number of people have adopted the solution of getting up earlier each morning to create or accommodate more work time. More and more people are scheduling in less and less sleep as a way to pack more working hours into each day. This trend seems to be particularly common among working mothers, some surviving on as little as 3.5 h of sleep per night (Frith, 2005). Some mothers rise at 4 a.m. in order to have a few hours to work while the house is quiet, but this solution is not without cost. Numerous comparisons have reported that people are working more hours than in the past (e.g., Schor, 1993). Yet, according to the US National Institute for Occupational Safety and Health, people have five more hours of leisure time per week than they did in times past (Sauter et al., 2002). All those extra hours are coming from somewhere and, increasingly, it seems to be through people deciding they can make do with less sleep.

The term sleep deprivation applies to a person that lacks adequate sleep for the span of a few days. The two most common causes for lack of alertness while driving are alcohol and sleep deprivation, and researchers have estimated that between 16% and 60% of road accidents involve sleep deprivation. Studies reveal that people who have been awake for 17–19 h perform worse on driving tests than those with a blood alcohol level of .05%, which is legally drunk in many Western European countries (CNN, 2000).

In the attempt to compress sleeping into fewer hours, people often take mild sedatives to ensure being able to get to sleep quickly and stay asleep. Even after having awakened and resumed activity, residue of these drugs in the system has the potential to impair memory of events (National Sleep Foundation, 2006). Overall, it seems an unproductive cycle — sleeping less (often enable by use of drugs) leading to inattention, poor memory, and acceptance of risky behavior. While it is a routine that provides more hours for work, it does not represent the quality of work we could otherwise expect from these same individuals. More is not always better and, in this case where residue effects are common, more does not seem to be even as good.

Another clear example from Boxer's story is that working too hard is likely to directly and negatively affect one's health and well-being. When a person is addicted to work, it goes beyond loyalty to the cause or demands of the job. A person who is addicted to work will continue to choose work even when negative impact becomes apparent. For example, when presented with a choice between giving up work or experiencing significant personal loss — most commonly loss of health or destruction of close personal relationships — those who continue to choose work are exhibiting an unhealthy relationship to their work (Porter, 1996; Robinson, 2007). When Boxer realized he had given too much, he no longer had the strength to escape his ill fate. Similarly, people may finally realize they have given too much to the job but find they have already initiated long-term health problems or have irreversibly alienated family and friends.

Even when an individual recognizes the dilemma, the choice is not easy if excess work has become the prominent life-style. For example, a director of a large technology company has stated, "After my heart attack at age thirty-seven, my doctor told me, 'Get a new job or you won't make forty.' I knew the important things in my life were health and family, but I loved my work and I couldn't face the prospect of giving it up. Isn't there any way to have a life and still do what I love to do?" (Bailyn, Fletcher, & Kolb, 1997, p. 11). Again, the person of concern here is the one who would face this dilemma and choose work rather than health and family. The implications of choosing work over health were recognized in the 1940s when Orwell wrote *Animal Farm*, and they are still relevant today.

It is like that old joke about going to the doctor saying, "It hurts when I do this" and the doctor replies, "don't do that." When someone is on their second heart attack and the doctor says slow down on your working hours or it is going to kill you ... When someone has children who no longer even expect appearance at birthdays or other events because the parent's work demands have consistently taken priority over the years ... When there is clear indication that the choice to continue the current level of work will have dire consequences and work is still the choice — this is a person we refer to as a workaholic or one addicted to work. Someone who is, in fact, a workaholic has given priority status entirely to work. This is an act of accepting that work is always the correct response and whether there is any life left for other things is a function of waiting for work demands to ease up telling us it is OK to have other interests. This is reminiscent of Boxer's second slogan, "the leader is always right." Accepting that work is always the highest priority without questioning the required sacrifices would mean that work has become the unquestioned leader in all life choices.

It is not easy to step back away from a job in progress. Many tend to think, as Boxer did, that it is only for now, it is only to meet a certain need, its behavior I will engage in only until ...

– things are in good enough shape for another to take over,
– I reach the next promotion level,

– my company wins a particular large contract I have been working on,
– my retirement account reaches a certain level.

Perhaps the image of Boxer on his way to the glue factory might help people invest a little more thought into their choices about integrating work with other life values.

11.2. *Baby Boom*

In the 1980s, actress Diane Keaton starred in a movie called *Baby Boom*, about a hard-driving businesswoman forced to reconsider her total devotion to career. The beginning of this movie is filled with powerful examples of workaholic behavior. The film opens with Diane's character, J.C. Wyatt, walking to her office at a major advertising agency. The consummate multi-tasker, she is reading the *Wall Street Journal* as she walks, still managing to notice and greet an individual who is apparently an important business contact. J.C.'s entrance to the office is a flurry of demands to the staff that jump at her every command. At one point, a woman hesitates when told they have to work this weekend. When questioned, she admits having tickets to the ballet, tickets she waited six months to obtain. With a single look from J.C., she immediately reassures that there is no problem and she will be there to work.

A second scene shows J.C. at dinner with her boss who announces he wants to suggest she be made a partner in the firm, but he wants reassurance that she is not going to suddenly decide on marriage and children which would, of course, negate her ability to perform as expected in that role. She assures him that she does not want to "have it all," she only wants the career. During this conversation, her excitement over the possible promotion is visible to viewers who are shown her leg bouncing under the table — that knee jiggle that so many people do when they must sit still but have nervous energy to release. Although her boss cannot see this, he does hear the resulting tap as her other foot (she is sitting with legs crossed at the knee) taps against the table support. When he asks about the tapping sound, she tries to stop, but her excitement is so strong that she can not subdue it completely.

Now some contrast. The next scene involves J.C. and her equally career-driven partner Stephen in their bedroom. She is propped up in bed with work and newspapers spread around her, carrying on a conversation with Stephen as he gets ready for bed. Soon he comes in and asks if she wants to make love. She keeps the other conversation going until, a few minutes later, realizing that he is serious and waiting for a response. She says "Oh, OK," moves some paperwork, takes off her glasses and the scene fades out showing the bedside clock at 11:46. The scene fades back in on the clock at 11:50 as she sits up, puts her glasses back on, and returns attention to the paperwork.

It is good to love your work. It is good to be excited when your talents are recognized through promotion or other rewards. And, it is good to have a spouse or partner who respects your choice to give significant time and energy to a career that offers personal fulfillment. The demonstration in this film that is important, however, is J.C.'s unemotional acquiescence to four minutes of intimacy with her partner in comparison to her absolutely uncontrollable physically reaction to a potential promotion, even while guaranteeing she is willing to increase her already 60–80 h per week given to the job.

In the movie, J.C. inherits a baby when a cousin and his wife die in an auto accident. At first she tries everything to unload this burden, but softens to the little girl eventually. Even with all her management skills, she cannot maintain her previous level of job involvement and has to make drastic changes in when, where, and how she works. Stephen departs at this point without a second thought. J.C. leaves her high-powered job, moves to the country and faces enormous new challenges. Over a period of time, she develops and successfully markets her own brand of baby food. As the new business grows, her old firm wants to bring her back in, at an even higher level position, as part of a deal to acquire her company.

During deal negotiations, she steps out to the ladies room in an attempt to regain control of her emotional reaction. The old excitement is taking over. She is BACK!!! She has won by doing things her way and now they are asking her to return. Then the reality sets in of what she would be coming back to and the life she would be giving up — a life in which she can experience somewhat more low-key success but control her time, be with her daughter and enjoy other relationships and activities. This is a life she has learned to value, but there is no question in the viewers mind that the prospect of returning to her previous high-pressure situation sparks a "high" that is very different from the gentler contentment of her more recent situation. If she succumbs to the cycle of pursuing that high — a cycle in which every success only shifts the bar higher for what it will take for the next adrenalin surge — that choice and the accompanying sacrifices would suggest work addiction. She does not return to her former life.

One difficulty in studying the topic of workaholism is separately identifying those who are addicted to work in contrast to those who are only reacting to external pressure and would ease back if given the chance. In today's working environment, there are many demands — growing global competition, changing preferences among customers, changing priorities of society and potential or real changes in laws and regulations to meet those priorities. Identifying true work addiction requires looking deeper than the surface behaviors, because so many people are working well beyond a 40-hour week.

Here is an accumulation of information across multiple sources, with emphasis on work habits in the US:

- Fifty-one percent of American men and 30% of the women say they work more than 40 h per week. Further, 35% of employed adults in the US do not take all of their awarded vacation days for the year, typically relinquishing 3 days each year of an average 14 days entitlement. Only a small proportion of people (14% of the men and 9% of the women) are paid for unused vacation, so most of the estimated 574 million unused vacation days represent time donated to the company (Expedia.com, 2007).

- Compared to workers in the US, Australians, Canadians, Japanese and Mexican workers are on the job 100 h less per year (2.5 weeks), Brazilians and British employees 250 h less (> 5 weeks) and Germans 500 h less (12.5 weeks). However, Czechs put in 100 h more than the Americans and South Koreans almost 500 h more (Anderson, 2001).
- Thirty-seven percent of Americans with household income over $100,000 say they typically work 41–50 h per week, with another 17% report that their usual is more than 50 h (Lorenz, 2007).
- Nineteen percent of men and 14% of women say they work overtime everyday; 8% of workers exceed their schedule work hours once per week and 15% either take work home or work overtime 2–3 times per week (Work/personal boundaries, 2001).

However, workaholism is not a problem unique to the United States. A 2005 study of Canadian social trends showed that one in three workers between the ages of 19 and 64 describe themselves as workaholics. Sixty-five percent of these self-declared workaholics admitted a sacrifice of time with family and friends. Overall the workaholics were more likely to feel trapped, rushed and unable to meet goals for each day; over half of them said they had no time for fun (Study: Workaholics, 2005). In Japan, widows can receive compensation for loss of a spouse to Karoshi, or death by overwork. Germans have a term, arbeitssucht, which means work craze, a disease in which people are driven to work (e.g., Heide, 1999). Books in the Czech Republic warn about the dangers of developing an unhealthy relationship with one's work so that it becomes excess (e.g., Nespor, 1999). Business press in Brazil has highlighted workaholism (Correa, 2002). Researchers have also been testing for and finding workaholic tendencies among professionals in Turkey, Norway and Australia, just to name a few additional countries (Ersoy-Kart, 2005; Burke, Richardsen, & Martinussen, 2004; Burke, Burgess, & Oberklaid, 2003, respectively).

As work increasingly spills over into personal time, there is some evidence of backlash from those who do not enjoy workaholic behaviors. By the end of the 1990s, white-collar workers including managers and professionals in banking, sales, engineering, programming, journalism, insurance and law, had begun to file lawsuits to claim overtime pay, and many of them won generous settlements. Although pay for overtime was traditionally seen as applicable to blue-collar workers, the flattening of organizational hierarchies has resulted in a wide scope of jobs that did not clearly fall within the definition of overtime exemption specified in U.S. federal laws (Conlin, 2001).

More commonly, workers are simply deciding that the spillover of work into personal time entitles them to consider the boundary permeable in both directions. This can certainly seem justified, but who will determine the appropriate amount of trade-off? One survey indicates that 75% of today's workers attend to personal tasks while on the job. Among this 75%, people report an *average* of 1.35 h per day spent on personal tasks (Work/personal boundaries, 2001).

Now that the door is open to integrated lives where work and non-work activities overlap, rather than segmented lives where there are clear maintained boundaries, it is a definite struggle to manage the understanding between company and employee about appropriateness. This would include the explicitly stated expectations (which are difficult to define and, therefore, avoided by most companies) and implicit agreements or evolving norms of behavior which have as much or more impact on organizational results as stated agreements. One manager explained that he felt it was his job to push people toward realizing all their potential, and the employee was responsible for letting him know when the pressure became too much. With the lack of job stability over the past decade, it has become more difficult for employees to feel they can give that type of response to their manager. The organizational culture, therefore, may evolve into one that requires workaholic behaviors to survive, one in which some workers will struggle to survive while those with work addiction tendencies will adapt, appear to thrive, and make similar demands and those around them (Porter, 2001).

Steve Prentice is an author who writes about the benefits of slowing things down, not just because it is good for us but also because we are more efficient and effective in our work when we have breaks. In his latest book, *Cool Down*, he reminds the reader that breaks are critical by calling to mind the cheetah, the fastest animal on earth (Prentice, 2007). A cheetah can run 90 miles per hour, but a cheetah is also smart enough to not try to run 90 miles an hour every hour of every day. The Cheetah might be considered the Corporate Athlete (a term from Groppel & Loehr, 2000) of the animal kingdom — intense when the job must get done but smart enough and able to rest for times in between. Both companies and individual employees should be looking for ways to ensure those rest times are available in some form.

A 2002 survey supported by the temporary staffing agency OfficeTeam asked 567 full-time workers to identify their number one career concern. Thirty-two percent responded by stating, "Being able to balance work and family demands" (OfficeTeam, 2002). As referenced earlier, many people are truly seeking to have a meaningful work life without allowing work to become the single focus. A small group, estimated to be between 5% and 23% of the workforce (Burke, 2000) will instead show patterns of work addiction. Rather than incorporating rest like the cheetah, these people will work like Boxer in *Animal Farm*. They will face a similar fate as that workhorse, unless they recognize the imbalance of their sacrifices in time to stop while they have energy enough to make change.

As seen in the example of J.C., the main character of *Baby Boom*, people can make a change when the right motivation presents itself. The attraction to work does not go away. Just as J.C. started to feel the old excitement when offered a chance to return to her workaholic life, any work addict will likely have similar times of remembering that adrenalin high and need to renew their commitment to alternate work patterns. As shown by the examples of Boxer and J.C., there is nothing new about the problem of people working to the exclusion of other life interests or even self-preservation. But, there are new tools — enablers — that add to the temptation and facilitate indulgence in work addiction.

11.3. Crackberry Addicts

Since the advent of Internet technology, people have gained the ability to communicate and conduct business transactions from any place in the world within seconds. This has resulted in access to an endless supply of information readily available 24 h a day. Although, this technology helps business keep up with expanding markets, it may also contribute to an unhealthy working environment for employees. Again, some employees struggle with meeting these new demands, while others find the increased access through technology as an avenue to support their addiction to their work (Porter & Kakabadse, 2006).

Korn/Ferry International (2006) studied 2300 executives across 75 countries. They found that 80% of executives are connected to work through mobile devices. The majority of them (77%) felt the mobility enhanced work-life balance, but approximately one-third found the devices to be addictive. That may sound somewhat contradictory, but a mixed reaction is very common. As one manager in another interview stated, the devices are invaluable for handling business across time zones but are "like owning a cat. You don't know who's in charge" (Crandell, 2007, p. 41). Work addiction research estimates that 5–25% of the working population is workaholic (Burke, 2000) is compatible with the results from the Korn/Ferry study on use of technology. Addictive behavior related to work and addictive behavior related to technology are mutually reinforcing forces. A workaholic who wants to take work home, continue working on vacation, or sneak in a fix anytime anywhere, can do so more easily now than in the past, because these devices are easily transported. A person who becomes addicted to technology, seeking excuses to justify the activity to a complaining spouse or friends, can use demands of the job to explain the necessity of excess.

Users often will admit to the addictive potential of technology, but it is always the "other guy" who is having the problem. This rationalizing is similar to what alcoholics or drug addicts might say prior to seeking help. Other typical responses noted by Crandell (2007) include:

• "My friends think I have a problem, but I don't."
• "It affects every aspect of my life, but I don't think that's a bad thing."
• "It affects relationships negatively, but it helps in so many other ways."

One suggestion for identifying whether work addiction is a problem is for the subject to draw a family organization chart based on allocation attention, not on what they think it should be but what it really is. If the technology device is above your spouse, that is likely a problem. If your children do not appear on the chart, that is another sign of trouble (Crandell, 2007).

Other researchers compare workaholism to obsessive-compulsive disorder, or OCD, (e.g., Mudrack, 2004) as an alternate interpretation to addiction. As described by Crandell (2007), evaluating email is one example resembling OCD behavior. This behavior occurs when you "overvalue" incoming messages, assigning each one with a sense of urgency and feel that if you do not answer, something catastrophic will result. Similar to the fears an addict experiences, there is often an underlying (perhaps unidentified) feeling that, if I am not available every minute, people might realize they do not need me (Crandell, 2007).

One benefit of technology is that far more women with children under the age of 18 think that part-time work is their best option, compared to 10 years ago. In 2007, 60% of women in this category said part-time work was preferable compared to 48% in 1997 (Crary, 2007). The choices they were given included full-time, part-time or not working. This shift to part-time preference comes entirely through lowering of preference for full-time; the proportion saying they prefer "not-working" has held constant. One reason is that technology today enables people to work part-time in terms of hours on the job while at the same time maintaining a strong professional presence in the workforce. In other words, 10 years ago, it was necessary to work full-time to be involved in certain types of work and at certain professional levels, whereas now there is more flexibility on what can be done from the vantage point of part-time hours.

However, technology can encourage taking dangerous risks. The *Wall Street Journal* (Cooper, 2007) reported last March on a 5-vehicle pileup attributed to text-messaging while driving — what has now been referenced as DWT, or driving while texting. Nationwide Insurance company (2007) conducted a survey of 1200 Americans to find that 73% of drivers talk on cell phones while behind the wheel but that, among drivers identified as the Gen Y age group (those born in 1981 or later and also called "millenniums"), 37% text while driving their vehicles. Several states are considering laws to address this specifically. Not all drivers that text or talk on their cell phones while driving are addicted, but those who are addicted will be far more inclined to discount the risk to maintain that technology interaction or their contact with the job.

Where is the tipping point where technology shifts from a benefit to a problem? And, is it a serious problem? Consider these situations:

- Women in a line of chairs receiving pedicures — promoted as a relaxing break — have been seen to all be actively using handheld devices. They may be denying themselves some of the benefits of that relaxing break — personally harmful in that respect.
- Instead of meeting new people in an unfamiliar social setting, some people will maintain focus on a handheld device, which eliminates social interaction beyond, perhaps, a quick nod. This social crutch provides some relief from stress of the situation, but it is not likely the best long-term solution, particularly if the social event has career implications or high personal importance.
- At any kind of meeting — business, children's schools, or volunteer activities — people feel compelled to multi-task by checking messages or organizing their schedule on a device while the meeting is in session. Granted, there are often gaps or discussion sidesteps that seem unproductive but, frequently, information must be repeated and misunderstandings corrected — adding meeting time due to split attention.

In addition to technology helping us with work we have always had to do, it is important to also recognize that demands have increased and consider whether we would stand any chance at all of meeting those demands if not for improvements in technology. What has changed; what is the same? In the US, some expectations are deeply engrained in the collective psyche. When the country was in early stages of development "popular stories by Horatio Alger and other authors emphasized the theme of individuals rising from rags to riches. The main character would always begin from a disadvantaged position but, through hard work and perseverance, would reach success. This fostered the belief in America being the 'land of opportunity' in which anyone willing to put in the effort deserved to achieve a higher social position and material wealth. An unfortunate side-effect was the implication that people who do not improve their standing must be deficient in either ability or ambition to not have capitalized on that opportunity" (Porter, 2008).

Other countries have their own stories initiating pressure to succeed. In this example, the premise starts people off with a felt obligation to improve from wherever they start, and the pressure builds from there. The increasing amount of available information is one factor that adds demand on time and energy, and rate of increasing information is accelerating. The term "cumulative codified information base" means the sum of all human intelligence that has ever been written down. In the 1930s scientists estimated the base to double every 30 years; by the 1970s they estimated it was doubling every 7 years; by 2010 it is expected to double every 11 h (Bontis, nd). That is a tremendous amount of available information, and we are already inundated with more than we can process for most decision-making.

From a study of international business managers, researchers estimated that as many at 60% were suffering from "cognitive overload" — high stress, loss of job satisfaction, physical symptoms like headaches and dizziness, and felt exhausted but had difficulty sleeping (Maslach, Schaufeli, & Leiter, 2001). Any time people are asked to mentally process more than they can handle, the tendency is to become more impulsive, to make decisions without getting complete information, to opt for short-term closure, to be tactical rather than strategic (Nichols, 2007). We also will begin to avoid tasks that require focused mental effort. When there is too much data, it can cause people to indefinitely put off reaching a decision; some may reach a stage of burnout. People suffering from "serious burnout," estimated at 3–5% of the working population (Maslach et al., 2001), have lost the capacity to make sound judgments, their mental and physical health is compromised, they feel chronically exhausted and have difficulty maintaining relationships. Feeling exhausted at the end of a tough workday is normal, but the difficulty arises when there is no structure in which to recover. Something like those vacations we discussed earlier that people in the US are not taking.

Not only are people at risk for Burnout from trying to do too much, but many have developed a belief that hard workers can and should do multiple things at once. *Harvard Business Review*, in its recent listing of "Breakthrough ideas for 2007" describes what they call "Continuous Partial Attention," an adaptive behavior that has emerged over the past two decades (Stone, 2007). Continuous partial attention is different from what is referred to as multi-tasking, or simply doing more than one thing at a time. In a business setting, we typically restrict simultaneous activities to the overlapping of fairly automatic tasks that do not require much mental processing — Internet scanning while talking on the phone or eating lunch and things like that. Continuous partial attention is a higher cognitive activity in which we are constantly shifting among things that are all demanding and all relative high priority, so it is more taxing and focus deteriorates unless there are recovery opportunities. NASA has studied human ability to truly do two tasks at once and found that it typically does not work well, even when the person is highly skilled at the required work (as described by Beaton, 2007).

People often do not always realize the loss experienced through constant interruption. Several years ago, Hewlett-Packard commissioned a study at King's College in London, in which they tested whether distractions of phones ringing and email pinging would impact scores on an IQ test. The results show that the interrupted group scored an average of 10 points lower than those who were not interrupted. Additionally, the interrupted group had average scores 6 points lower than the group that took the same test while high on marijuana (Pimentel, 2005). It is the misuse of technology — not use but MISUSE of technology — that has contributed to the rising incidence of burnout and gives a false sense of having the ability to constantly split attention in multiple directions. Those addicted to technology or using technology to enable their work addiction will likely be attracted to situations of misuse, because maintains the appearance of working hard and, ultimately, may even increase the time needed to complete the work, thereby maintaining the need to keep working.

Mr. Dennis Kneale, a Managing Editor with *Forbes Magazine*, participated in an experiment as part of a series in which the NBC television network challenged people to "Do Without" something that had become an important fixture in their life (Could you do without?, 2007). This is a man who started each day with a cup of coffee, two laptops, a cell phone and his BlackBerry, and they challenged him to go one week without those pieces of technology. He lasted only 40 h before he tearfully gave up and asked that all his devices be returned. In that short time:

- He had anxiety attacks.
- He had experienced phantom rings (he would hear his cell phone ringing but did not even have it with him).
- He bounced two checks because he could not rely on his usual online funds management.
- He broke the rules by borrowing a cell phone from a cab driver to make a call.

One could assume this man was a competent businessperson before all the electronics were available to him but, he did not revert to what he had done as past practices. Rather, he attempted to operate as usual but without the tools that supported it. He could not do it and that result is not so surprising, given the pace he was trying to maintain.

His anxiety and rule breaking are suggestive of an addictive pattern, but there is another side-effect worth mentioning. Mr. Kneale's friends, family and business contacts had learned to expect a quick reply and got angry when they did not hear back on their messages in a short period of time. Our expectations of each other have changed dramatically. Today's average knowledge worker receives 75 emails per day, but some people receive as many as 400 per day (Beaton, 2007). Although email allows for asynchronous communication, users will develop a particular "responsiveness image" and calibrate their behaviors to match their primary correspondents. The communication becomes "peri-synchronous" with very clear norms as to when to reach each other by email and how long a wait to expect before response (Tyler & Tang, 2003).

When everyone is expecting quick response, how does one handle that demand? One suggestion is that we all become more adept at speed reading. Yet, the issue is not just reading fast enough to get through the messages but the extent to which we are willing to interrupt other activities to simply monitor the arrival of new messages. A McKinsey survey of 7800 managers in multiple countries reports that 25% consider the burden of voicemail, email and meetings to be either nearly or completely unmanageable. Within the total time they spend with these communications, nearly 40% reported spending a half to a full day on messages that are not valuable to them (as reported in Mandel, Hamm, Matlack, Farrell, & Palmer, 2005).

One difficult aspect of email to manage is the proportion of messages which are directed to another person and then copied, or CC'ed, to a full distribution list. Some describe CC'ing as an act of aggression, because so often the message is of no interest to all the parties on the CC list, but the sender felt a need to cover bases by distributing broadly. One manager reports sorting his mail so that everything on which he is CC'd drops into a separate mail folder — something he views as slightly, but not much, above a spam or junk mail folder which he can separately review at a later time, rather than have to wade through those to find the real messages every day. A close cousin to the CC aggravation is the proliferation of return notes that only say thanks or I agree and are done through a "reply all" command.

Email has become a tool of survival for many businesspeople and a prime activity for those who are addicted to technology, work, or any combination of the two. According to a survey of more than 4000 individuals around the world, 15% of the Americans believe they are addicted to email. Here are some usage numbers to consider. Of users with portable devices, 59% say they check each time a new message arrives and 43% "keep the devices nearby when they are sleeping to listen for incoming mail." In addition, not only do 40% say they have checked in the middle of the night, but also 26% report doing email in bed in their pajamas (AOL, 2007). This is not really new but, rather, the same work behavior as J.C. in the *Baby Boom*. The only difference is that in the 1980s she was shown with paperwork spread all over the bed and now we have done away with the paper.

Those who manage other people might want to stop for a moment and think about what is being communicated to the employees that translates into thinking they need to be working on email in bed or while driving. Some managers have explained that they put thoughts into email over the weekend simply as a way to deal with something on their minds. Once the thought is recorded in the email, they can move on to other activities without worry of forgetting to ask the question or offer the instruction Monday morning. It is not their intention that the employee receiving that message read it and responds over the weekend. It is sent out for personal convenience. Unfortunately, in today's volatile work environment, employees do not feel they can take the chance of not responding. As the habit spreads, a norm develops and carries the suggestion that those who want to succeed in the company will be available at any time and quickly responsive. It would communicate a very different message if the managers saved those messages in draft mode and sent them all out first thing Monday morning.

The same is true with people away on vacation. In a 2006 survey, even though a very small percentage of employees (4%) report that they have been directly asked to stay connected while away, a much higher number say there is an unspoken expectation in their company to stay connected. Sixty-one percent of executives reported feeling obligated to stay connected, 36% of middle managers and 27% of those in non-management positions. Further, 81% of Human Resource professionals said that their companies provided the means to stay connected — cell phones, laptops and or handheld devices (Victor, 2007). There may or may not be a difference in perception (company versus employee) about whether company-supplied devices are intended to communicated an expectation of 24/7 availability, but there would seem to be potential for differing interpretations of both intent and outcome. Of 155 Executives asked about work–life balance, 56% felt their electronic devices had helped improved balance; 44% said the devices did not improve their ability to balance. In the same survey, only 10% said it is *not expected* that they can be reached outside of traditional working hours (Can't disconnect? You are not alone, 2007).

Again, not everyone who is a heavy user of technology is addicted to technology or to their work. Much of what we see on a daily basis that causes concern can also be rudeness. We are still sorting through how to meet changing expectations and how to communicate to others what those expectations can be before crossing the boundary into unreasonable. In a study commissioned by T-Mobile, 90% of BlackBerry users said they consider their handset vital to business, but two-third of them also said it improves their status and makes them look more professional (Crandell, 2007). It may be this latter statistic that begins to cause problems. An accessory that adds to status will be used frequently and once the habit develops it will spread to more times and places unless social norms develop that communicate what is generally considered appropriate.

In a recent radio broadcast, they had polled a listener group to find the answer to this question: What is the one thing a man can do on a first date that will immediately end any further interest by the woman? Having determined the number one answer, they now were offering a prize to the caller who could correctly match that top answer. The very first caller to guess said, "He takes calls on his cell phone." That was not the number one answer, so she did not get the prize, but it initiated a sharing of horror stories about having dates who have done that. It is far too easy to learn more than one wants to know about strangers' personal lives while riding in airport shuttles or sitting in coffee shops. These unwanted exposures through overhearing cell phone conversations are the flip side of the frustrations of wanting to have a face-to-face conversation with a person whose attention is cast downward onto their electronic device. Social norms have not yet evolved to cover the rudeness potential of using new technology. As norms develop, it will become easier to identify those who routinely violate them as potentially having an addiction problem.

11.4.   A Look to the Future

Just like J.C. in *Baby Boom*, people can make a decision to curb their immersion in work, whether focused on technology or more traditional workaholism. While one heavy technology user eliminated arguments with his wife by getting her a device of her own (to which she became somewhat addicted), others have achieved better harmony on the home front by disciplining themselves to leave the device by the front door or agreeing to blackout times of non-use. Steve Prentice (2007) recommends that each family designate two nights a week that everyone will put away their personal devices, PDAs as well as music and phones, to have dinner together. Sadly, two nights of dinner together might be a difficult transition for many households, with or without the electronic device ban. It is not just the working adults that are overly busy and distracted from home life but the young people, as well.

Many of the articles about technology reference the comparative ease with which the younger generation accepts both the technology and the pace and scope of interaction that it brings. Does this mean they will be better at handling the work-related technology demands than their predecessors? There is evidence that some might while others might not. College counselors are increasingly advised to watch for signs of Internet addiction among the student population. Students can become so engrossed in their net world that they ignore coursework and fail classes before realizing they have sabotaged their own long-term goals. They go off to school where they have unlimited Internet access, large blocks of time that are unstructured and free of parental control, and faculty encouraging them to use Internet resources. Many are highly stressed when first at college, feeling pressure about grades, parents' expectations for success and constant reminders about competition for jobs when they finish. The signs of a problem are fatigue from lack of sleep, dropping grades and progressive withdrawal from other social activities. They deny there is any serious problem, rationalize that the Internet offers better information than their college courses, lie about the amount of time they spend online and claim "I can cut back or quit any time I want" (Young, 2007).

A contrasting example is someone like Victor De Leon who has been competing on the professional video game circuit for five years and, at his current age of nine, may be the world's youngest professional gambler. His story was featured on the television show *60 Minutes* in a segment naming the seven most amazing youngsters. In answer to people critical of his parents' allowing this focus on video gaming, his father responds that those people do not live in his house and should not criticize. As the father explains, when Victor is not in preparation for a specific competition, he spends about two hours per day with the games, but he also enjoys riding his bike every day. His other interests are playing the violin and playing with Star War toys; he has a hamster and a dog (Lambert, 2007). From this account, it appears Victor is able to "work" at his competitions, which happen to be based on technology, but still maintain other sources of satisfaction in life. He does not yet show signs of work addiction.

Although the upcoming generation seems more comfortable working with technology, the potential of addiction to working with technology will likely continue to be a problem for some while others are able to maintain balance. The messages given to employees about acceptability of long working hours could make a difference. The workplace and society in general need not glorify workaholic behavior. Companies can have policies that encourage better balance and, even more importantly, enforce those policies as the preferred standard rather than simply an available option that might limit one's career if utilized. Although colleagues cautioned Boxer that he should slow down, their organization did not require that he take a day off each week for recovery time. If it had not only allowed for but insisted he take time for rejuvenation, he might have accomplished as much and lasted much longer. If J.C.'s company had offered better consideration for family responsibilities, she would not have been faced with an "all or nothing" career decision. The element of personal choice is paramount, but that choice happens in a larger context. Only when social norms and company cultures discourage excess, will those individuals unable to give up their excess stand out as addicted people creating a problem for themselves and the organization.

In 2002, the Department of Health and Human Services published a report on "The Changing Organization of Work and the Safety and Health of Working People." Within their recommendations, they emphasized the need for more research attention on the changes in how work is organized and how that might impact the safety and health of employees (US National Institute for Occupational Safety & Health, 2002). This chapter has referenced some of the ways in which the organization of work has changed, considering the increasing demands of globalization, the impact of restructuring and flattening of organizational hierarchies, and the adjustment to technology that makes available more information while it demands more availability of the workers who use that information. Much of the research referenced here fits as response to the call for investigation of the employees' safety and health, because the impact of behavioral addictions is directly tied to employee well-being.

In addition to scholarly research, many references have been incorporated here from popular media in the belief that what people are talking about, reading in magazines, hearing about on television or finding on websites is a strong indicator of where the general public will set priorities. These priorities hold valuable information for defining content of future research on work behaviors.

The icons used to structure this discussion — Boxer from the 1940s, J.C. from the 1980s and crackberry addicts in the new millennium — offer a progression into current time that considers many changes impacting today's world of work, without losing track of the potential for individual choice that remains constant. A person's work can be a source of fulfillment and personal growth. Individuals can pursue work that enriches their lives, rather than consuming their lifetime. Organizations and societies can decide to create and maintain workplaces that nurture this enrichment, rather than enforcing demands. Although no clear answers are offered here, perhaps some images are relayed that will help both workers and organizational decision-makers stay mindful of the positive and negative potentials of choices.

References

Anderson, P. (2001). Study: U.S. employees put in most hours. CNN.com. Available at archives.cnn.com/2001/CAREER/trends/0830/ilo.study. Retrieved on January 5, 2008.

AOL. (2007). Think you might be addicted to email? You're not alone. Available at press.aol.com/article_display.cfm?article_id = 1271. Retrieved on December 26, 2007.

Axelrod, S. D. (1999). *Work and the evolving self: Theoretical and clinical considerations.* Hillsdale, NJ: The Analytic Press.

Bailyn, L., Fletcher, J. K., & Kolb, D. (1997). Unexpected connections: Considering employees' personal lives can revitalize your business. *Sloan Management Review, 38*(4), 11–19.

Beaton, E. (2007). Work is driving me crazy. *Atlantic Business, 18*(4), 36–45.

Bontis, N. (nd). Speech promotion. Available at http://www.bontis.com/BontisOnePage.pdf. Retrieved on January 6, 2008.

Burke, R. J. (2000). Workaholism in organizations: Concepts, results and future research directions. *International Journal of Management Reviews, 2*(1), 1–16.

Burke, R. J., Burgess, Z., & Oberklaid, F. (2003). Workaholism and divorce among Australian psychologists. *Psychological Reports, 93*(1), 91–92.

Burke, R. J., Richardsen, A. M., & Martinussen, M. (2004). Workaholism among Norwegian senior managers: New research directions. *International Journal of Management, 21*(4), 415–426.

Can't disconnect? You are not alone. (2007). *HR Magazine*, February, *52*(2), 2.

CNN. (2000). Sleep deprivation as bad as alcohol impairment, study suggests, September 20. Available at archives.cnn.com/2000/HEALTH/09/20/sleep.deprivation. Retrieved on September 28, 2007.

Conlin, M. (2001). Revenge of the "Managers." *Business Week Online*. Available at www.businessweek.com/print/magazine/content/01_11/b3723067.htm. Retrieved on January 6, 2008.

Cooper, C. (2007). 'Driving While Texting' linked to accidents. *Wall Street Journal*, March 29. Available at http://global.factiva.com/ha/default.aspx. Retrieved on January 6, 2008.

Correa, C. (2002). Procura-se atleta corporative. *Exame, 36*(3), 32–41.

Could you do without? (2007). NBC Series segment, February 19. Available at www.youtube.com/watch?v = 7zroOj3RvNM. Retrieved on September 23, 2007.

Crandell, S. (2007). Why am I leading the crackberrry life? *Delta Sky, 40–43*(June), 104.

Crary, D. (2007). Part-time jobs ideal, working moms say. Available at seattletimes.nwsource.com/html/nationworld/2003785581_momwork12.html. Retrieved on July 12, 2007.

Ersoy-Kart, M. (2005). Reliability and validity of the workaholism battery (Work-BAT): Turkish form. *Social Behavior and Personality, 33*(6), 609–617.

Expedia.com. (2007). Expedia.com survey reveals vacation deprivation among American workers is at an all time high. Press release. Available at press.expedia.com/index.php?s = press_releases&item = 311. Retrieved on January 5, 2008.

Friedman, S. D., Christensen, P., & DeGroot, J. (1998). Work and life: The end of the zero-sum game. *Harvard Business Review*, 76(6), 119–129.

Frith, M. (2005). Working mothers suffer record levels of sleep deprivation. *The London Independent*. Available at findarticles.com/p/articles/mi_qn4158/is_20050602/ai_n14651251. Retrieved on January 5, 2008.

Graves, L. M., Ruderman, M. N., Ohlott, P. J., & Weber, T. J. (2008). Effect of workaholism on managerial career satisfaction and performance: Help or hindrance? Manuscript submitted for publication.

Groppel, J. L., & Loehr, J. (2000). *The corporate athlete*. Indianapolis: Wiley.

Harpaz, I., & Snir, R. (2003). Workaholism: Its definition and nature. *Human Relations*, 56(3), 291–319.

Heide, H. (1999). Work craze: Sketch of the theoretical bases. Available at www.labournet.de/diskussion/arbeit/asucht.html. Retrieved on August 13, 2004.

Hill, J. E., Ferris, M., & Märtinson, V. (2003). Does it matter where you work? A comparison of how three work venues (traditional office, virtual office, and home office) influence aspects of work and personal/family life. *Journal of Vocational Behavior*, 63, 220–241.

Korn/Ferry International. (2006). Press release. Available at http://www.kornferry.com. Retrieved on December 26, 2007.

Lambert, B. (2007). He's 9 years old and 56 pounds, and a video-game circuit star. *New York Times*, June 7, A1, B6.

Lorenz, M. (2007). More money means longer hours. *CNN.com*. Available at cnn.com/2007/LIVING/worklife/10/24/cb.money.hours/index.html. Retrieved on January 5, 2008.

Mandel, M., Hamm, S., Matlack, C., Farrell, C., & Palmer, A. T. (2005). The real reasons you're working so hard. *BusinessWeek*, October 3. Available at www.businessweek.com/magazine/content/05_40/b3953601.htm. Retrieved on January 5, 2008.

Maslach, C., Schaufeli, W. B., & Leiter, M. P. (2001). Job burnout. *Annual Review of Psychology*, 52, 397–422.

Mudrack, P. E. (2004). Job involvement, obsessive-compulsive personality traits, and workaholic behavioral tendencies. *Journal of Organizational Change Management*, 17(5), 490–508.

National Sleep Foundation. (2006). Press release. Available at www.sleepfoundation.org/site/apps/nl/content2.asp?c = hulXKjMOIxF&b = 2424611&ct = 3453975. Retrieved on September 28, 2007.

Nationwide Insurance Company. (2007). Press release. Available at vocuspr.vocus.com/vocuspr30/Temp/Sites/2625/1ad0f5725cdb4adbbadfd89a6562c902/Nationwide%20Survey%20On%20the%20Go%20w.tips.pdf. Retrieved on December 26, 2007.

Nespor, K. (1999). *Zavislost* (Work addiction). Prague: Grada Publishing.

Nichols, E. (2007). Hyper-speed managers. *HR Magazine*, April, pp. 107–109.

OfficeTeam. (2002). The power of balance. Press release. Available at www.officeteam.com/portal/site/ot-us/template.PAGE/menuitem.f641a8b96a6cc83772201cb2   02f3dfa0/?javax.portlet.tpst = 2bc7e8a27266257872201cb202f3dfa0&javax.portlet.prp_2bc7e8a27266257872201cb202f3dfa0_releaseId = 251&javax.portlet.prp_2bc7e8a27266257872201cb202f3dfa0_request_type = RenderPressRelease&javax.portlet.begCacheTok = com.vignette.cachetoken&javax.portlet.endCacheTok = com.vignette.cachetoken. Retrieved on January 6, 2008.

Orwell, G. (1946). *Animal farm*. New York: Harcourt, Brace and Company.

Pimentel, B. (2005). E-mail addles the mind. *The San Francisco Chronicle*, May 4, p. C-1.

Porter, G. (1996). The organizational impact of workaholism: Suggestions for researching the negative outcomes of excessive work. *Journal of Occupational Health Psychology, 1*(1), 70–84.

Porter, G. (2001). Workaholic tendencies and the high potential for stress among Co-workers. *International Journal of Stress Management, 8*(2), 147–164.

Porter, G. (2008). Excessive work and its consequences. In: C. Wankel (Ed.), *Handbook of 21st century management* (pp. 148–156). Thousand Oaks, CA: Sage.

Porter, G., & Kakabadse, N. K. (2006). HRM perspectives on addiction to technology and work. *Journal of Management Development, 25*, 535–560.

Prentice, S. (2007). *Cool down: Getting further by going slower.* Toronto: Wiley.

Robinson, B. E. (2007). *Chained to the desk: A guidebook for workaholics, their partners and children and the clinicians who treat them.* New York: New York University Press.

Sauter, S. L., Brightwell, W. S, Colligan, S. L., Hurrell, J. J., Katz, T. M., LeGrande, D. E., & Lessin, N. (2002). The changing organization of work and the safety and health of working people: Knowledge gaps and research directions. Available at www.cdc.gov/niosh/pdfs/02-116.pdf. Retrieved on December 13, 2007.

Schaef, A. W., & Fassel, D. (1988). *The addictive organization.* San Francisco: Harper & Row.

Schor, J. (1993). *The overworked American: The unexpected decline of leisure.* New York: Basic.

Stone, L. (2007). Living with continuous partial attention. *Harvard Business Review, 85*(2), 28–29.

Study: Workaholics and time perception. (2005). *The Daily.* Available at www.statcan.ca/Daily/English/070515/d07515c.htm. Retrieved on January 6, 2008.

Tyler, J. R., & Tang, J. C. (2003). When can I expect an email response? A study of rhythms in email usage. *Proceedings of the eighth European conference on computer-supported cooperative work,* Helsinki, Finland (pp. 239–258).

US National Institute for Occupational Safety & Health. (2002). The changing organization of work and the safety and health of working people. Available at 222.cdc.gov/niosh/pdfs/02-116.pdf. Retrieved on January 6, 2008.

Victor, J. (2007). 2006 workplace vacation: Poll findings. Society for Human Resource Management. Available at www.shrm.org/. Retrieved on December 26, 2007.

Work/personal boundaries shifting. (2001). Office Solutions. Available at www.allbusiness.com/human-resources/employee-development-employee-ethics/961307-1.html. Retrieved on January 6, 2008.

Young, K. (2007). Surfing not studying: Dealing with internet addiction on campus. Available at www.netaddiction.com/articles/surfing-not-studying.htm. Retrieved on September 15, 2007.

Chapter 12

Recovery After Work: Unwinding from Daily Job Stress

Carmen Binnewies and Sabine Sonnentag

Experiencing stress at work and at home are concomitants of the changing nature of work employees are increasingly struggling with (Burke & Ng, 2006; Schabracq & Cooper, 2000). Work-related stressors, including long working hours are detrimental for employees' health and well-being in the short and in the long run (De Lange, Taris, Kompier, Houtman, & Bongers, 2003; Sluiter, De Croon, Meijman, & Frings-Dresen, 2003; Sonnentag & Frese, 2003). Organizations can counteract the negative consequences of work-related stressors by redesigning the workplace in order to minimize stressors, by implementing stress management interventions or work–life policies that allow employees to successfully cope with job demands and to recover from work-related stress (Gerkovich, 2006; Semmer, 2003). In addition, employees themselves have the opportunity to prevent and reverse negative effects of work-related stress by actively seeking recuperation from job demands in their leisure time.

Experiencing relief from job-related stress by taking vacations is one recovery possibility for employees (Etzion, 2003; Westman & Etzion, 2001). The positive effects of vacations, however, fade out quickly (Fritz & Sonnentag, 2006; Westman & Eden, 1997). Therefore, recovery during vacations is not sufficient to prevent negative consequences of work-related stress that may occur every day. Conse-quently, it is important to know how employees can successfully recover from a stressful working day after work, that means during daily leisure time or during the weekend. This chapter gives an overview over research on recovery from work-related stress with a focus on daily recovery after work. We first describe the recovery process and indicators of recovery. Afterwards, we turn to the concept of need for recovery and summarize research examining antecedents of need for recovery. We then outline theoretical frameworks in the context of recovery, methodological approaches to examine recovery after work, and the importance of recovery for individuals and organizations. In the following, we sum up theoretical assumptions and empirical research investigating which activities or experiences during leisure

The Long Work Hours Culture
Copyright © 2008 by Emerald Group Publishing Limited
All rights of reproduction in any form reserved
DOI:10.1016/B978-1-84855-038-4.00012-9

time contribute to the recovery process. We further discuss the role of sleep in the recovery process and factors that facilitate or impede recovery. Finally, we point out implications for individuals and organizations that result from our knowledge about recovery after work.

12.1.   Recovery After Work: A Process Opposite to the Strain Process

During the working day employees' physical and mental resources are depleted because employees have to spend energy and effort to fulfill their tasks and to cope with job-related stressors (Meijman & Mulder, 1998). Thus, most people experience fatigue at the end of the working day and feel a need for recovery (Sluiter, van der Beek, & Frings-Dresen, 1999). After work, that is usually in the evening, employees have time to rest and to unwind from job demands encountered during the day. An employee's drained resources are no longer taxed and can be replenished. This process of restoration is called *recovery*. Alternative terms for the recovery process are unwinding process (Frankenhaeuser & Johansson, 1986), recuperation (Strauss-Blasche, Ekmekcioglu, & Marktl, 2002), or restoration (Hartig, Böök, Garvill, Olsson, & Gärling, 1996). Recovery is the process that reverses the negative consequences of job demands and allows an individual's functional system to return to a baseline level (Craig & Cooper, 1992).

Successful recovery is indicated by a reduction of the negative effects of work-related stressors, for example by a reduction in experienced fatigue, or by a decreasing heart rate, or adrenaline excretion (Linden, Earle, Gerin, & Christenfeld, 1997). Furthermore, recovery is indicated by increased positive outcomes, such as an improved well-being or a higher subjective feeling of being recovered. As dealing with daily work demands involves an increase in fatigue and negative mood (Fuller et al., 2003; Jones & Fletcher, 1996; Zohar, 1999; Zohar, Tzischinski, & Epstein, 2003) and a decrease in positive mood (Fuller et al., 2003), recovery after work also comprises mood restoration, specifically a decrease in negative mood and an increase in positive mood. Taken together, during the recovery process an individual's mood, well-being, ability, and willingness to face new tasks and demands are (re)established. In the following we summarize research on need for recovery that is the state that characterizes how much people wish and require recovering from work-related demands.

12.1.1.   Need for Recovery

While working individuals have to invest effort to accomplish their tasks and to cope with job-related stressors (Meijman & Mulder, 1998), spending effort in any work setting and kind of working activity pursued over a longer period of time requires some degree of recovery (Meijman & Mulder, 1998). However, individuals differ in their need to recover after work. Generally, one can assume that the more stressful the work and the longer hours a person is working the higher is this person's need for recovery (deCroon, Sluiter, & Blonk, 2004; Jansen, Kant, Van Amelsvoort, Nijhuis, & Van Den Brandt, 2003).

Need for recovery can be described as transient state in which "feelings of 'wanting to be left alone for a while', or 'wanting to lay down for a while'" (Sluiter, Frings-Dresen, van der Beek, & Meijman, 2001) are predominant. In everyday language need for recovery is experienced as a wish for *recharging one's batteries*. A person who feels a high need for recovery is reluctant to accept new demands. Need for recovery has been described as an early sign of prolonged fatigue and psychological distress (Jansen, Kant, & van den Brandt, 2002). Persons who experience a high need for recovery have more difficulties in performing well on the job. For example, a recent study reported that need for recovery was related to a decrease in concentration at work (Demerouti, Taris, & Bakker, 2007).

Empirical research supports the assumption that certain aspects of the work situation are related with a person's need for recovery. For example, job demands such as a high pace and amount of work were found to be associated with a high subjective need for recovery (Sluiter et al., 2001). In addition to these psychological job demands, also other demands (e.g., physical job demands), and low job control were related to a high need for recovery in a sample of truck drivers (deCroon et al., 2004). Sonnentag and Zijlstra (2006) reported similar findings with various job stressors being positively related to need for recovery and job control showing a negative relation.

In a large-scale study with more than 12,000 participants, Jansen et al. (2003) found that long working hours (per week and per day) were positively related to need for recovery, particularly in men. For women, short working hours (less than 25 h per week) were associated with a low need for recovery. Moreover, in men and women, frequent overtime work was related to a high degree of need for recovery, particularly when overtime work was experienced as troublesome. Similar findings on overtime and need for recovery were also reported in other studies (e.g., Sonnentag & Zijlstra, 2006).

Taken together, these studies suggest that persons facing a high degree of job stressors and long work hours have a higher need for recovery. The finding that job control is negatively related to need for recovery warrants additional attention. The pattern of relations suggests that not only job stressors increase a person's need for recovery by exhausting resources, but also that job control protects a person from feeling quickly in need for recovery. It might be that jobs with a high level of control provide employees with the opportunity to adjust their specific work activities and work pace to their momentary state (Taris et al., 2006). This would imply that when experiencing fatigue employees enjoying a high level of job control can decide to do different things or to slow down a little bit in order not to exhaust their resources too much. Employees however, who do not have job control cannot influence what to do and how to do it and as a consequence the fatigue process will progress and need for recovery will further increase. After summarizing research on need for recovery, we now turn to theoretical frameworks in the context of recovery.

12.1.2. Theoretical Frameworks in the Context of Recovery

Three theoretical frameworks, the *Allostatic Load model* (McEwen, 1998, 2004), the *Effort-Recovery model* (Meijman & Mulder, 1998), and the *Conservation of Resources theory* (Hobfoll, 1989) can explain certain aspects and mechanisms of the recovery process.

In the *Allostatic Load model*, McEwen (1998, 2004) describes the process of adaptation to stress and how this process proceeds in a normal or a maladaptive way. When facing a demand or stressor an individual's physiological system responses with an adaptation process in order to achieve stability or *homeostasis*. This adaptation process is called *allostasis* (McEwen, 1998). *Allostasis* is characterized by changes in various physiological indicators, such as increased heart rate, blood pressure, or adrenaline excretion (McEwen, 1998). This process is normal and essential for physiological functioning under changing conditions as long as the physiological system shuts down its adaptation response when the demand or stressor is no longer present (McEwen, 1998, 2004). However, the process of allostasis can turn into a maladaptive process called *allostatic load* (McEwen, 1998, 2004). *Allostatic load* occurs when the individual is exposed to frequent stress, thus preventing the physiological system to recover, or when the physiological system fails to shut down after the stressor is no longer present, or when the physiological system shows an inadequate response, indicated for example by a decreased response to adapt to stressors (McEwen, 1998). According to the *Allostatic Load model*, recovery from work-related stress can be seen as the process of shutting down the adaptation response after work when demands are no longer imposed on the individual. Therefore, recovery can be measured by changes in the cardiovascular or endocrinological system after a period of rest (Rau, 2006; Steptoe, Lundwall, & Cropley, 2000).

According to the *Effort-Recovery model* (Meijman & Mulder, 1998; cf. also Geurts & Sonnentag, 2006), recovery occurs through the absence of work demands. Work demands usually require employees to spend effort in order to fulfill the assigned work tasks and goals, and thus, drain on employee's resources causing "load reactions" such as work-related fatigue (Meijman & Mulder, 1998, p. 9). Usually such load reactions are reversible. If an individual stops working and no longer depletes the resources that are needed at work, recovery occurs automatically and an individual's functional systems return back to the baseline level (Meijman & Mulder, 1998). Therefore, recovery is mainly a function of time not spent on the job and on job-related or similar activities that are further burdening the resources used at work. If time for recovery is not sufficient, an individual's functional systems do not return to their baseline level and the individual experiences a state that is suboptimal for performing his or her tasks when back at work. Consequently, the individual has to spend compensatory effort in order to maintain the fulfillment of tasks and goals (Meijman & Mulder, 1998). When recovery lacks over longer periods of time insufficient recovery and increased fatigue can accumulate and result in irreversible consequences, such as severe health complaints that cannot be easily reversed during the usual rest periods.

Consistent with the Effort-Recovery model, the *Conservation of Resources (COR) theory* (Hobfoll, 1989, 1998) assumes that work demands deplete an individual's resources. Hobfoll (1989) supposes that people generally strive to increase their resources, gain new resources, and regain their lost resources in order to prepare themselves for future encounters with stressors and the associated possibility of resource loss. Resources are defined as "those objects, personal characteristics, conditions, or energies that are valued by the individual or that serve as a means for attainment of these objects, personal characteristics, conditions, or energies" (Hobfoll, 1989, p. 516). If resources are threatened to be lost, if an actual loss of resources has happened, or if a resource gain after an investment of resources is not possible, individuals are assumed to experience stress (Hobfoll, 1989). However, a gain of resources will not occur automatically, but has to be initiated by the individual, and often requires the investment of some other resources. For example, engaging in sport activities involves investing a certain amount of energy and self-regulatory resources, but is beneficial for people's recovery (Hansen, Stevens, & Coast, 2001; Rook & Zijlstra, 2006; Sonnentag, 2001). Applying COR theory to recover from work-related stress, it is assumed that people strive at arranging their leisure time in a way that helps them to conserve, regain, or build up resources in order to be prepared for upcoming work demands (Zijlstra & Cropley, 2006).

12.2.   Methodological Approaches to Examine Recovery After Work

When examining recovery after work several researches conducted diary studies to investigate the processes that lead to recovery and well-being of individuals (Klumb & Perrez, 2004). Assessing data by diaries has the advantage that activities and experiences during the working day and during leisure time can be captured more in real time (Bolger, Davis, & Rafaeli, 2003; Klumb & Perrez, 2004). Thus, influences of memory deficits or changed interpretations of retrospective answers are minimized (Bolger et al., 2003). As an example, we describe the design of a diary study of Sonnentag and Zijlstra (2006) to illustrate how recovery after work can be examined. Sonnentag and Zijlstra (2006) investigated in one of their study if chronic job demands and job control as well as different activities during off-job time were related to need for recovery and well-being at bedtime. Data was assessed by a questionnaire and a diary survey. Participants first responded to the questionnaire, indicating their chronic level of job demands and job control, filled in items assessing negative affectivity, and provided demographic data. Afterwards, participants had to fill in diary surveys for five consecutive workdays twice a day, namely when returning home from work and before going to bed. In the diary survey after work, participants indicated their well-being when returning home, and in the diary survey at bedtime participants reported how much time they spent on different categories of activities during leisure time (we refer to these categories and their relationships with recovery later in this chapter) and indicated their need for recovery and well-being at bedtime. Thus, need for recovery and well-being at bedtime were taken as measures of successful recovery. The authors examined if the chronic level of job demands and job control and certain recovery activities were related to need of recovery and well-being at bedtime over and above well-being when returning home. Thus, a change in well-being occurring during daily leisure time (after returning home until going to bed) was taken as an outcome of the recovery process after work. Other studies on recovery after work used a similar approach to examine predictors and processes of recovery during daily leisure time (for examples, see Cropley & Purvis, 2003; Rook & Zijlstra, 2006; Sonnentag & Bayer, 2005; Steptoe et al., 2000).

12.2.1. *Importance of Recovery for the Individual and for Organizations*

Recovery is assumed to contribute to an individual's health. A recent study demonstrated the importance of incomplete recovery for the risk of cardiovascular death (Kivimäki et al., 2006). In a 28-year follow-up study with a sample of industrial workers, Kivimäki and his coworkers showed that incomplete recovery from work during the weekends predicted a higher risk for cardiovascular death over and above other well-known risk factors, such as increased blood pressure or smoking. A 9-year follow-up study with a sample of men with a high risk for coronary heart disease provided evidence that the more vacations one had within the last months (frequency of vacations) the lower was the risk of death, and especially of cardiovascular death (Gump & Matthews, 2000).

Moreover, studies that examined the relationship between recovery and job performance further stress the importance of successful recovery. A study of Sonnentag (2003) focusing on daily recovery showed that when individuals felt more recovered in the morning they experienced higher work engagement during the day and showed more proactive behaviors at work, specifically personal initiative and pursuit of learning. Furthermore, Binnewies, Sonnentag, and Mojza (in press) reported that when individuals felt more recovered in the morning, they showed a higher level of task performance, personal initiative, and helping behavior at work and spent less compensatory effort at work. Fritz and Sonnentag (2005) examined recovery during the weekend and found evidence that specific recovery processes, namely social activities (meeting friends, performing activities with others) and positive work reflection (thinking about the positive aspects of one's job) were related to improved job performance after the weekend. Specifically, social activities predicted improved task performance and positive work reflection predicted improved pursuit of learning. In addition, a study of Trougakos, Beal, Green, and Weiss (2008) examining recovery during breaks in a sample of cheerleader instructors found that pursuing respite activities, such as taking a nap, relaxing, or socializing was positively related to subsequent performance. Moreover, the authors showed that the relationships were partially mediated by positive emotions. Taken together, empirical research provides evidence that recovery is important for an individual's health and job performance. In the following we will summarize research on recovery activities and experiences and their benefits for individuals' recovery.

12.3. Recovery Activities and Recovery Experiences: What is Beneficial for Successful Recovery?

Recovery processes can occur during different periods of rest, including micro breaks at work, daily time for recovery after a working day, during the weekend, or during vacations, or other respites. One of the most important questions in the study of recovery is, what should people do or avoid to do during their leisure time in order to successfully recover from work-related stress? How should leisure time be arranged and what processes and experiences are important for successful recovery? In the following section, we summarize research that addressed these questions. As the focus of this chapter is recovery after work we concentrate on studies examining recovery during the working week or during the weekend. First, we resume studies that investigated what activities are beneficial or detrimental for employees' recovery. Second, we outline research that examined underlying psychological experiences of recovery activities and the benefits for employees' recovery.

12.3.1. Recovery Activities

People engage in various activities during their leisure time in order to be relieved from job demands and to satisfy their need for recovery. From a theoretical point of view activities that do not place demands upon individuals and do not further deplete the resources that were previously drained should be most beneficial for recovery (Zijlstra & Cropley, 2006). However, not all activities pursued during the non-work time are completely free of demands. Accordingly, Sonnentag (2001) differentiated between leisure activities with a high duty-profile that have to be accomplished and pose further demands on the individual, and leisure activities with a potential for recovery that are voluntarily pursued by the individual and are less demanding. Activities with a high duty-profile are generally assumed to be detrimental for employees' recovery and to raise employees' fatigue, because they put further demands on an individual, further deplete an individual's resources and prevent the individual from gaining resources (Rook & Zijlstra, 2006; Sonnentag, 2001; Zijlstra & Cropley, 2006). In contrast, low-effort activities, social activities, and physical activities are assumed to be beneficial for recovery (Rook & Zijlstra, 2006; Sonnentag, 2001; Zijlstra & Cropley, 2006). Activities with a high duty-profile include *domestic activities* (e.g., doing housework, taking care of children) as well as *work-related* (e.g., finishing a task, preparing oneself for the next working day) and other *task-related activities* (e.g., paying bills, working on one's private finances). Sonnentag (2001) further divided activities with a potential for recovery into three major categories: *low-effort activities* (e.g., watching television, taking a bath), *social activities* (e.g., meeting friends, going out), and *physical activities* (e.g., sports, exercise).

Some studies using a diary survey design examined which kind of activities are beneficial or detrimental for employees' recovery. Empirical research shows that time spent on physical activities is beneficial for employees' recovery because it is positively related to situational well-being (Sonnentag, 2001), positive mood (Sonnentag & Bayer, 2005), and vigor (Sonnentag & Natter, 2004), and negatively related to need for recovery (Sonnentag & Zijlstra, 2006), fatigue (Rook & Zijlstra, 2006; Sonnentag & Zijlstra, 2006), and depressed mood (Sonnentag & Natter, 2004).

Time spent on social activities is also beneficial for recovery because it is positively associated with situational well-being (Sonnentag, 2001) and negatively related to need for recovery (Sonnentag & Zijlstra, 2006). However, there was one notable exception: In a sample of flight attendants time spent on social activities was related to increased depression indicating a detrimental effect (Sonnentag & Natter, 2004). This finding supports the assumption that demands of recovery activities have to be opposite to job demands in order to benefit employees' recovery (Zijlstra & Cropley, 2006). Flight attendants' job demands require *emotional labor* (Heuven & Bakker, 2003; Hochschild, 1983). Employees who perform *emotional labor* have to regulate their emotions in order to fulfill interaction expectations (Grandey, 2000). Engagement in social activities might further draw on the resources needed to regulate one's emotions and to deal with other people. Thus, for employees performing emotional labor at work engaging in social activities during leisure time might be detrimental for recovery from job-related demands (Sonnentag & Natter, 2004).

A study examining recovery during the weekend with a sample of emergency service workers confirmed that employees who engaged more in social activities during the weekend showed improved well-being and an increase in task performance in the following working week (Fritz & Sonnentag, 2005). With regard to low-effort activities only one study with a sample of school teachers demonstrated a beneficial effect, specifically on improved situational well-being (Sonnentag, 2001). Taken together, empirical research on the benefits of leisure time activities demonstrated positive effects of physical activities, mainly positive effects of social activities and sometimes positive effects of low-effort activities. Consistent with these findings, Iso-Ahola and Mannell (2004) and Haworth and Lewis (2005) argue that pursuing active leisure activities has a greater restorative effect than pursuing passive leisure activities, because the former are intrinsically motivating and build up resources, such as positive mood and increased self-esteem (Haworth & Lewis, 2005).

In accordance with theoretical assumptions, time spent on work-related activities is detrimental for employees' recovery because it is negatively related to situational well-being (Sonnentag, 2001; Sonnentag & Zijlstra, 2006) and vigor (Sonnentag & Natter, 2004) and positively related to need for recovery (Sonnentag & Zijlstra, 2006) and fatigue (Sonnentag & Natter, 2004; Sonnentag & Zijlstra, 2006). Considering time spent on domestic activities, none of the studies confirmed the assumed detrimental effect on employees' recovery. An explanation might be that pursuing domestic activities are both demanding and restorative. Steptoe et al. (2000) examined differences in recovery after work between individuals living with a family including children, with a partner or living alone. Recovery after work was operationalized by changes in cardiovascular functions measured during the working day and in the evening. A decrease in heart rate and blood pressure indicates that the physiological systems returned to their baseline level, suggesting that successful recovery has occurred. Steptoe et al. (2000) showed that a decrease in blood pressure during the evening was largest for individuals living with a family including children, intermediate for individuals living with a partner, and smallest for individuals living alone. Consequently, individuals with a family recovered most successfully from work stress during the evening. Results are in line with an enhancement model of multiple roles (Ruderman, Ohlott, Panzer, & King, 2002; Tiedje et al., 1990) that suggests that multiple social roles, such as marriage, parenthood, or paid employment are beneficial for individuals' health (Steptoe et al., 2000).

12.3.2. Recovery Experiences

Research summarized so far has shown that specific off-job activities seem to be beneficial for recovery whereas others are not. In addition, there is empirical evidence that not only the type of activities persons pursue during their non-work time is related to their well-being and subsequent job performance. Also the way how individuals *experience* these activities may matter (Sonnentag & Natter, 2004). For example, one person may perceive cooking a nice meal for friends as a relaxing off-job activity that provides joy and fulfillment, whereas the same activity might be dull and a pure burden for a second person. This second person might find joy and fulfillment by reading a novel or by playing a music instrument. Sonnentag and Fritz (2007) suggested four specific psychological experiences associated with recovery activities that may account for variance in individual well-being: psychological detachment, relaxation, mastery, and control during off-job time.

Psychological detachment from work during off-job time implies to refrain from job-related activities as well as from job-related thoughts. When psychologically detaching from work, the person "switches off" mentally and gains some kind of distance to his or her job. When not psychologically detaching from work, the person continues to think about work-related issues and may even ruminate about his or her job (Cropley & Purvis, 2003). In a cross-sectional study, Sonnentag and Fritz (2007) found negative relationships between psychological detachment from work during off-job time and health complaints, emotional exhaustion, depressive symptoms, sleep problems, and poor life satisfaction. Similarly, Sonnentag and Kruel (2006) reported that teachers who psychologically detached from work during their off-job time, felt more recovered than teachers who did not fully detach. Similarly, also Aronsson, Svensson, and Gustafsson (2003) argued that worrying about work during non-work time is a core indicator of poor recovery.

A daily survey study showed that professionals who succeeded in psychologically detaching themselves from their jobs during after-work hours experienced better mood and less fatigue at bedtime (Sonnentag & Bayer, 2005). The association with fatigue was particularly prominent after days characterized by high time pressure at work. This finding suggests that particularly after very stressful days, it is important to switch off from work in order to protect one's well-being.

However, the association between lack of psychological detachment from work and indicators of poor well-being does not necessarily imply that thinking about one's job during off-job time is negative per se. Fritz and Sonnentag (2005) examined how ambulance workers experience their free weekends and how these experiences are related to well-being and performance during the next working week. Analyses showed that workers who engaged in *positive* work reflection during the weekend (i.e., who thought about aspects of their work they liked) reported a decrease in exhaustion and disengagement from work when returning back to their job. In addition, learning orientation on the job increased. These findings suggest that in order to recover it might not be necessary to refrain from all job-related thoughts. It rather seems that employees' well-being benefits from positive thoughts about work during off-job time.

Relaxation experiences during off-job time refer to experiences characterized by low activation and positive affect (Stone, Kennedy-Moore, & Neale, 1995). Such experiences can occur during specific relaxation exercises such as progressive muscle relaxation (Jacobson, 1938), and also during other activities that relax the mind and body (Hartig, Evans, Jamner, Davis, & Gärling, 2003; Pelletier, 2004). From Sonnentag and Fritz's (2007) cross-sectional study, there is evidence that relaxation during off-job time is associated with good health, low emotional exhaustion, good sleep quality, and a high degree of life satisfaction.

Mastery experiences stem from off-job activities that provide challenging experiences and the opportunity to learn new skills and to experience competence in domains outside the job. Typical examples include taking a language class or learning a new hobby (Fritz & Sonnentag, 2006). Also many kinds of sport activities and volunteer work (Ruderman et al., 2002) can include mastery experiences. In contrast to relaxation, the initiation and pursuit of mastery experiences may require a certain degree of effort. However, it can result in recovery if it taxes other functional systems than those required during one's work on the job (cf. Meijman & Mulder, 1998). In empirical research, mastery experiences were found to be negatively related to emotional exhaustion, depressive symptoms, and positively to life satisfaction (Sonnentag & Fritz, 2007).

Control during off-job time refers to a person's experienced discretion about which activity to pursue during off-job time and when to engage in the activity. Although the experience of control over one's time might be seen as an essential aspect of leisure time, it might be hampered by other tasks and obligations to be followed through during off-job time (Mardberg, Lundberg, & Frankenhaeuser, 1991). There is empirical evidence that control experienced off the job is related to indicators of well-being such as good health, low emotional exhaustion, sleep quality, and life satisfaction (Sonnentag & Fritz, 2007).

Sonnentag and Fritz (2007) have argued that not only psychological detachment, relaxation, mastery, or control are important for recovery. It might be that experiencing one's leisure time in a positive way also fosters recovery processes. A study with health service workers showed that just perceiving the activities pursued during off-job time as a *positive experience* contributed to the prediction of well-being (Sonnentag & Zijlstra, 2006). Study participants reported lower levels of tensions at bedtime after they engaged in activities that they experienced as positive — above and beyond the effects of specific types of activities. This finding fits nicely with the broaden-and-build-view of positive emotions (Fredrickson, 1998, 2000). It seems that positive experiences during off-job time can undo the negative effects of unfavorable experiences at work. During leisure time employees do not pursue activities all the time, but they spent a lot of time in sleeping. In the following section we describe research on the role of sleep for individuals' recovery.

12.4.   The Role of Sleep in the Recovery Process

Sleep is assumed to be highly important for recovery as sleep ensures an individual's physiological functioning and health (Zijlstra & Cropley, 2006). Numerous studies showed that even moderate sleep deprivation or sleep disturbances can lead to various negative consequences, such as impaired health (indicated for example by depression, cardiovascular disease, or high blood pressure), decreased performance, an increased risk of occupational or driving accidents, and an increased risk of mortality (Akerstedt, 2006; Van Dongen, Maislin, Mullington, & Dinges, 2003). Furthermore, several studies established a relationship between high work demands and impaired sleep (Akerstedt, 2006; Cropley, Dijk, & Stanley, 2006). However, research on recovery from work-related stress has rarely examined the role of sleep in the recovery process and the processes by which high job demands are related to impaired sleep are still not fully understood. One assumption is that individuals experiencing stress at work are more physically aroused at work and even at bedtime and therefore suffer from sleep disturbances. A study of Steptoe and Cropley (2000), however, failed to find support for this assumption. Another idea is that individuals with high job demands have more difficulties to detach from work, ruminate about work in the evening, and therefore suffer from impaired sleep. Although the relationships between high job demands and increased rumination (Cropley et al., 2006; Cropley & Purvis, 2003; Sonnentag & Bayer, 2005) and between rumination and impaired sleep (Gross & Borkovec, 1982) have been established, a recent study failed to show rumination as a mediator between high job demands and impaired sleep (Cropley et al., 2006). Instead, Cropley et al. (2006) found that high job demands and rumination both independently contributed to impaired sleep. In sum, sleep is an important mechanism of the recovery process, but future research should pay more attention to the interplay between high job demands.

12.5.   Predictors of Recovery

In the previous sections, we described how specific recovery activities and experiences are related to subsequent well-being. In this section, we address the question if there are specific factors that are related to the initiation of recovery activities and the enjoyment of recovery experiences as well as physiological indicators of recovery.

In a daily survey study conducted with police employees, Sonnentag and Jelden (2005) examined if stressors experienced at work are related to the amount of time these employees spend on activities during off-job time. Analyses showed that after working days on which police employees experienced a high level of situational constraints and hassles they spend more time on low-effort activities and less time on sport activities. These findings are intriguing because on a more general level, the same respondents indicated that they can recover best from job stress by engaging in sport activities. Thus, although these police employees were very inclined to engage in sport activities — maybe more than persons working in other jobs — they did not initiate sport activities after stressful days. By referring to the ego-depletion approach (Muraven & Baumeister, 2000), Sonnentag and Jelden (2005) argued that experiencing stressors at work exhausts a person's self-regulatory resources that would be needed to engage in sport activities. Probably, after having experienced a high level of stressors, resources are depleted and persons engage in low-effort activities that do not require much self-regulation. Support for this interpretation comes from a study with university staff members (van Hooff, Geurts, Kompier, & Taris, 2007). van Hooff et al. (2007) reported that persons who felt that their workday required a lot of effort engaged less in active leisure activities.

Another set of studies addressed the question if job stressors and job strain are related to recovery experiences, particularly psychological detachment from work. Cropley and Purvis (2003) found in their diary studies with teachers that the degree of rumination decreased over the course of the evening in all participants. However, teachers experiencing a high level of job strain (i.e., high workload and low job control) generally showed higher levels of rumination and a less pronounced decrease over the course of time than teachers not experiencing high levels of job control. These findings (except for the interaction effect) were replicated in a more recent study (Cropley et al., 2006).

The daily survey study conducted by Sonnentag and Bayer (2005) referred to earlier in this chapter points into a similar direction. Study participants who held a job with a high level of chronic time pressure experienced less psychological detachment from work during off-job time than respondents not experiencing this type of stressor. In addition, on days when participants worked long hours (e.g., stayed longer in the office) they detached less easily from their job while being at home. This effect was not due to the fact that leisure time per se was shorted on these days. It rather seems that working for a long period of time makes it particularly difficult to switch off mentally from one's work.

A recent study also showed that job stressors are negatively related to recovery experiences (Sonnentag & Fritz, 2007). Analyses showed that stressors including time pressure, role ambiguity, situational constraints, and hours of overtime were negatively related to psychology detachment from work. Time pressure and hours of overtime were also negatively related to experienced relaxation and control during leisure time. Job stressors, however, were not related to mastery experiences during leisure time. In this study, it was also tested whether personality dimensions were related to recovery experiences. Overall, most of the correlations between personality dimensions and recovery experiences were low and non-significant.

It seems that workplace factors such as job stressors are not only related to subjectively reported recovery activities and experiences but also to physiological indicators of recovery. On the physiological level, recovery becomes evident when physiological parameters (e.g., heart rate, blood pressure, cortisol) return to their pre-stressor levels after a stressful working day. For example, Rau and Triemer (2004) reported that women working overtime had higher diastolic blood pressure during leisure time and at night than women working regular hours. With respect to endocrine responses, studies showed that employees working overtime or under stressful conditions have elevated adrenaline levels during non-work time (Meijman, Mulder, Van Dormolen, & Cremer, 1992; Rissler, 1976). With respect to cortisol levels during non-work time a combination of a high level of demands and low level of control seems to be the most problematic (Fox, Dwyer, & Ganster, 1993). Overall, these findings suggest that stressful working conditions do not only impact recovery activities and subjective recovery experiences but are also reflected in physiological processes (Linden et al., 1997; Sonnentag & Fritz, 2006).

12.6. Implications for Individuals and Organizations

So far we outlined that recovery is an important process that can reverse the negative consequences of work-related stressors and is associated with increased health and well-being. Recovery has also been shown to be related to a reduced risk of early death (Gump & Matthews, 2000; Kivimäki et al., 2006) and to performance-related outcomes at work (Fritz & Sonnentag, 2005; Sonnentag, 2003; Trougakos et al., 2008). Consequently, individuals and organizations should be interested in fostering and maintaining successful recovery. In the following we point out implications for individuals and organizations that result from research on recovery after work.

First, we address the question how employees themselves can promote recovery after work. Regarding leisure time activities, engaging in physical activities, and social activities contributes to successful recovery. Thus, employees should try to increase engagement in such activities if possible. However, it is important to note that for employees, such as flight attendants and others who have to perform emotional labor social activities do not seem to benefit recovery. Working during leisure time should be prevented if possible, because it is associated with impaired recovery. Time-management techniques (Claessens, van Eerde, Rutte, & Roe, 2007; Green & Skinner, 2005) can help employees to accomplish their tasks more efficiently and might to some extent prevent that employees have to work during leisure time.

With respect to specific experiences during leisure time, detaching from work has been shown as an important factor for successful recovery. If employees cannot stop thinking about work or ruminate about work-related problems during leisure, strategies to actively separate the work and non-work domain (Ashforth, Kreiner, & Fugate, 2000; Nippert-Eng, 1996) might help to foster psychological detachment and thus successful recovery. In addition, the experience of relaxation, mastery, and control during leisure time is associated with improved recovery and health

(Sonnentag & Fritz, 2007) and should therefore be encouraged. For example, relaxation may be experienced by actively engaging in relaxation techniques, such as progressive muscle relaxation (Jacobson, 1938) or meditation (Grossman, Niemann, Schmidt, & Walach, 2004). Furthermore, activities such as taking a walk in nature or listening to music may also be experienced as relaxing by individuals (Sonnentag & Fritz, 2007).

On the one hand, fostering specific activities and experiences during leisure time can be achieved by making individuals aware of successful recovery activities and experiences. On the other hand, training interventions that strengthen and build up individuals' resources to recover from work-related stress and that help individuals identify efficient recovery strategies for themselves can be developed (see, e.g., Weh, 2006). Such training interventions could also become part of organizations' personal development programs in order to promote their employees' recovery, well-being, and performance.

With regard to organizations' possibilities to support their employees' recovery, organizations should aim at reducing work-related stressors. First, work-related stressors are directly related to a higher need for recovery and poor health (deCroon et al., 2004; Sluiter et al., 2001; Sonnentag & Zijlstra, 2006). Furthermore, work-related stressors also impair the recovery process itself and thereby additionally reduce individuals' health and well-being (Geurts & Sonnentag, 2006). In addition to reducing work-related stressors, organizations can also support employees' opportunities to recover, for example by providing sport facilities. Moreover, organizations should offer working time arrangements that enable employees to organize their leisure time in a way that promotes recovery. As recovery after work has been shown to be related to health- and performance-related outcomes on the same or following day (Binnewies et al., in press; Rook & Zijlstra, 2006; Sonnentag, 2003; Sonnentag & Zijlstra, 2006) employees should take care of their recovery every day and not delay recovery until the weekend or until next vacation.

Taken together, employees and organizations alike should pay attention to recovery after work, because it is an important process that benefits health and job performance in the short and in the long run. Taking sufficient time for recovery after work is therefore not only a hedonistic experience but can be seen as an efficient strategy to unwind from work-related stressors and to maintain individuals' well-being and effectiveness from day-to-day.

References

Akerstedt, T. (2006). Psychosocial stress and impaired sleep. *Scandinavian Journal of Work, Environment and Health, 32,* 493–501.

Aronsson, G., Svensson, L., & Gustafsson, K. (2003). Unwinding, recuperation, and health among compulsory school and high school teachers in Sweden. *International Journal of Stress Management, 10,* 217–234.

Ashforth, B. E., Kreiner, G. E., & Fugate, M. (2000). All in a day's work: Boundaries and micro role transitions. *Academy of Management Review, 25*, 472–491.

Binnewies, C., Sonnentag, S., & Mojza, E. J. (in press). Daily performance at work: Feeling recovered in the morning as a predictor of day-level job performance. *Journal of Organizational Behavior.*

Bolger, N., Davis, A., & Rafaeli, E. (2003). Diary methods: Capturing life as it is lived. *Annual Review of Psychology, 54*, 579–616.

Burke, R. J., & Ng, E. (2006). The changing nature of work and organizations: Implications for human resource management. *Human Resource Management Review, 16*, 86–94.

Claessens, B. J. C., van Eerde, W., Rutte, C. G., & Roe, R. A. (2007). A review of the time management literature. *Personnel Review, 36*, 255–276.

Craig, A., & Cooper, R. E. (1992). Symptoms of acute and chronic fatigue. In: A. P. Smith & D. M. Jones (Eds), *Handbook of human performance, Vol 3: State and trait* (pp. 289–339). San Diego, CA: Academic Press Inc.

Cropley, M., Dijk, D.-J., & Stanley, N. (2006). Job strain, work rumination, and sleep in school teachers. *European Journal of Work and Organizational Psychology, 15*, 181–196.

Cropley, M., & Purvis, L. J. M. (2003). Job strain and rumination about work issues during leisure time: A diary study. *European Journal of Work and Organizational Psychology, 12*, 195–207.

De Lange, A. H., Taris, T. W., Kompier, M. A. J., Houtman, I. L. D., & Bongers, P. M. (2003). "The very best of the millennium": Longitudinal research and the demand-control-(support) model. *Journal of Occupational Health Psychology, 8*, 282–305.

deCroon, E. M., Sluiter, J. K., & Blonk, R. W. B. (2004). Stressful work, psychological job strain, and turnover: A 2-year prospective cohort study of truck drivers. *Journal of Applied Psychology, 89*, 442–454.

Demerouti, E., Taris, T. W., & Bakker, A. B. (2007). Need for recovery, home-work interference and performance: Is lack of concentration the link? *Journal of Vocational Behavior, 71*, 204–220.

Etzion, D. (2003). Annual vacation: Duration of relief from job stessors and burnout. *Anxiety, Stress & Coping: An International Journal, 16*, 213–226.

Fox, M. L., Dwyer, D. J., & Ganster, D. C. (1993). Effects of stressful job demands and control on physiological and attitudinal outcomes in a hospital setting. *Academy of Management Journal, 36*, 289–318.

Frankenhaeuser, M., & Johansson, G. (1986). Stress at work: Psychobiological and psychosocial aspects. *International Review of Applied Psychology, 35*, 287–299.

Fredrickson, B. L. (1998). What good are positive emotions? *Journal of General Psychology, 2*, 300–319.

Fredrickson, B. L. (2000). The undoing effect of positive emotions. *Motivation and Emotion, 24*, 237–258.

Fritz, C., & Sonnentag, S. (2005). Recovery, health and job performance: Effects of weekend experiences. *Journal of Occupational Health Psychology, 10*, 187–199.

Fritz, C., & Sonnentag, S. (2006). Recovery, well-being and performance-related outcomes: The role of work load and vacation experiences. *Journal of Applied Psychology, 91*, 936–945.

Fuller, J. A., Fisher, G. G., Stanton, J. M., Spitzmueller, C., Russell, S. S., & Smith, P. C. (2003). A lengthy look at the daily grind: Time series analysis of events, mood, stress, and satisfaction. *Journal of Applied Psychology, 88*, 1019–1033.

Gerkovich, P. R. (Ed.) (2006). *Work–life policy and practice in the USA: Gendered premise, radical potential?* New York, NY: Psychology Press.

Geurts, S. A. E., & Sonnentag, S. (2006). Recovery as an explanatory mechanism in the relation between acute stress reactions and chronic health impairment. *Scandinavian Journal of Work, Environment & Health, 32*, 482–492.

Grandey, A. A. (2000). Emotional regulation in the workplace: A new way to conceptualize emotional labor. *Journal of Occupational Health Psychology, 5*, 95–110.

Green, P., & Skinner, D. (2005). Does time management training work? An evaluation. *International Journal of Training and Development, 9*, 124–139.

Gross, R. T., & Borkovec, T. D. (1982). Effects of a cognitive intrusion manipulation on the sleep-onset latency of good sleepers. *Behavior Therapy, 13*, 112–116.

Grossman, P., Niemann, L., Schmidt, S., & Walach, H. (2004). Mindfulness-based stress reduction and health benefits: A meta-analysis. *Journal of Psychosomatic Research, 57*, 35–43.

Gump, B. B., & Matthews, K. A. (2000). Are vacations good for your health? The 9-year mortality experience after the multiple risk factor intervention trial. *Psychosomatic Medicine, 62*, 608–612.

Hansen, C. J., Stevens, L. C., & Coast, J. R. (2001). Exercise duration and mood state: How much is enough to feel better? *Health Psychology, 20*, 267–275.

Hartig, T., Böök, A., Garvill, J., Olsson, T., & Gärling, T. (1996). Environmental influences on psychological restoration. *Scandinavian Journal of Psychology, 37*, 378–393.

Hartig, T., Evans, G. W., Jamner, L. D., Davis, D. S., & Gärling, T. (2003). Tracking restoration in natural and urban field settings. *Journal of Environmental Psychology, 23*, 109–123.

Haworth, J., & Lewis, S. (2005). Work, leisure and well-being. *British Journal of Guidance & Counselling, 33*, 67–78.

Heuven, E., & Bakker, A. B. (2003). Emotional dissonance and burnout among cabin attendants. *European Journal of Work and Organizational Psychology, 12*, 81–100.

Hobfoll, S. E. (1989). Conservation of resources: A new attempt at conceptualizing stress. *American Psychologist, 44*, 513–524.

Hobfoll, S. E. (1998). *Stress, culture and community: The psychology and philosophy of stress.* New York: Plenum Press.

Hochschild, A. R. (1983). *The managed heart: Commercialization of human feeling.* Berkeley, CA: University of California Press.

Iso-Ahola, S. E., & Mannell, R. C. (Eds). (2004). *Leisure and health.* New York, NY: Routledge.

Jacobson, E. (1938). *Progressive relaxation.* Chicago: University of Chicago Press.

Jansen, N. W. H., Kant, I., Van Amelsvoort, L. G. P. M., Nijhuis, F. J. N., & Van Den Brandt, P. A. (2003). Need for recovery from work: Evaluating short-term effects of working hours, patterns and schedules. *Ergonomics, 46*, 664–680.

Jansen, N. W. H., Kant, I., & van den Brandt, P. A. (2002). Need for recovery in the working population: Description and associations with fatigue and psychological distress. *International Journal of Behavioral Medicine, 9*, 322–340.

Jones, F., & Fletcher, B. (1996). Taking work home: A study of daily fluctuations in work stressors, effects on moods and impacts on marital partners. *Journal of Occupational and Organizational Psychology, 69*, 89–106.

Kivimäki, M., Leino-Arjas, P., Kaila-Kangas, L., Luukkonen, R., Vahtera, J., Elovainio, M. Härmä, M., & Kirjonen, J. (2006). Is incomplete recovery from work a risk marker of cardiovascular death? Prosprective evidence from industrial employees. *Psychosomatic Medicine, 68,* 402–407.

Klumb, P. L., & Perrez, M. (2004). Why time-sampling studies can enrich work–leisure research. *Social Indicators Research, 67,* 1–10.

Linden, W., Earle, T. L., Gerin, W., & Christenfeld, N. (1997). Physiological stress reactivity and recovery: Conceptual siblings separated at birth? *Journal of Psychosomatic Research, 42,* 117–135.

Mardberg, B., Lundberg, U., & Frankenhaeuser, M. (1991). The total workload of parents employed in white-collar jobs: Construction of a questionnaire and a scoring system. *Scandinavian Journal of Psychology, 32,* 233–239.

McEwen, B. S. (1998). Stress, adaptation, and disease. Allostasis and allostatic load. In: S. M. McCann, J. M. Lipton, E. M. Sternberg, G. P. Chrousos, P. W. Gold & C. C. Smith (Eds), *Annals of the New York Academy of Sciences. Neuroimmunomodulation: Molecular aspects, integrative systems, and clinical advances* (Vol. 840, pp. 33–44). New York: New York Academy of Sciences.

McEwen, B. S. (2004). Protective and damaging effects of the mediators of stress and adaptation: Allostasis and allostatic load. In: J. Schulkin (Ed.), *Allostasis, homeostasis, and the costs of physiological adaptation* (pp. 65–98). New York: Cambridge University Press.

Meijman, T. F., & Mulder, G. (1998). Psychological aspects of workload. In: P. J. D. Drenth & H. Thierry (Eds), *Handbook of work and organizational, Vol 2: Work psychology* (2nd ed., pp. 5–33). Hove, England: Psychology Press/Erlbaum (UK) Taylor & Francis.

Meijman, T. F., Mulder, G., Van Dormolen, M., & Cremer, R. (1992). Workload of driving examiners: A psychophysiological field study. In: H. Kragt (Ed.), *Enhancing industrial performances* (pp. 245–260). London: Taylor & Francis.

Muraven, M., & Baumeister, R. F. (2000). Self-regulation and depletion of limited resources: Does self-control resemble a muscle? *Psychological Bulletin, 126,* 247–259.

Nippert-Eng, C. (1996). Calendars and keys: The classification of 'home' and 'work'. *Sociological Forum, 11,* 563–582.

Pelletier, C. L. (2004). The effect of music on decreasing arousal due to stress: A meta-analysis. *Journal of Music Therapy, 41,* 192–214.

Rau, R. (2006). Learning opportunities at work as predictor for recovery and health. *European Journal of Work and Organizational Psychology, 15,* 158–180.

Rau, R., & Triemer, A. (2004). Overtime in relation to blood pressure and mood during work, leisure, and night time. *Social Indicators Research, 67,* 51–73.

Rissler, A. (1976). Stress reactions at work and after work during a period of quantitative overload. *Ergonomics, 20,* 577–580.

Rook, J. W., & Zijlstra, F. R. H. (2006). The contribution of various types of activities to recovery. *European Journal of Work and Organizational Psychology, 15,* 218–240.

Ruderman, M. N., Ohlott, P. J., Panzer, K., & King, S. N. (2002). Benefits of multiple roles for managerial women. *Academy of Management Journal, 45,* 369–386.

Schabracq, M. J., & Cooper, C. L. (2000). The changing nature of work and stress. *Journal of Managerial Psychology, 15,* 227–241.

Semmer, N. K. (2003). Job stress interventions and organization of work. In: J. C. Quick & L. E. Tetrick (Eds), *Handbook of occupational health psychology* (pp. 325–353). Washington, DC: American Psychological Association.

Sluiter, J. K., De Croon, E. M., Meijman, T. F., & Frings-Dresen, M. H. W. (2003). Need for recovery from work related fatigue and its role in the development and prediction of subjective health complaints. *Occupational and Environmental Medicine, 60,* 62–70.

Sluiter, J. K., Frings-Dresen, M. H. W., van der Beek, A. J., & Meijman, T. F. (2001). The relation between work-induced neuroendocrine reactivity and recovery, subjective need for recovery, and health status. *Journal of Psychosomatic Research, 50,* 29–37.

Sluiter, J. K., van der Beek, A. J., & Frings-Dresen, M. H. W. (1999). The influence of work characteristics on the need for recovery and experienced health: A study on coach drivers. *Ergonomics, 42,* 573–583.

Sonnentag, S. (2001). Work, recovery activities, and individual well-being: A diary study. *Journal of Occupational Health Psychology, 6,* 196–210.

Sonnentag, S. (2003). Recovery, work engagement, and proactive behavior: A new look at the interface between nonwork and work. *Journal of Applied Psychology, 88,* 518–528.

Sonnentag, S., & Bayer, U.-V. (2005). Switching off mentally: Predictors and consequences of psychological detachment from work during off-job time. *Journal of Occupational Health Psychology, 10,* 393–414.

Sonnentag, S., & Frese, M. (2003). Stress in organizations. In: W. C. Borman, D. R. Ilgen, R. J. Klimoski & I. B. Weiner (Eds), *Handbook of psychology: Industrial and organizational psychology* (Vol. 12, pp. 453–491). Hoboken, NJ: Wiley.

Sonnentag, S., & Fritz, C. (2006). Endocrinological processes associated with job stress: Catecholamine and cortisol responses to acute and chronic stressors. In: P. L. Perrewé & D. C. Ganster (Eds), *Research in organizational stress and well-being: Employee health, coping and methodologies* (pp. 1–59). Amsterdam: Elsevier.

Sonnentag, S., & Fritz, C. (2007). The recovery experience questionnaire: Development and validation of a measure for assessing recuperation and unwinding from work. *Journal of Occupational Health Psychology, 12,* 204–221.

Sonnentag, S., & Jelden, S. (2005). The recovery paradox: Why we don't exercise after stressful days. Poster presented at the conference of the Society for Industrial and Organizational Psychology, Los Angeles, CA.

Sonnentag, S., & Kruel, U. (2006). Psychological detachment from work during off-job time: The role of job stressors, job involvement, and recovery-related self-efficacy. *European Journal of Work and Organizational Psychology, 15,* 197–217.

Sonnentag, S., & Natter, E. (2004). Flight attendants' daily recovery from work: Is there no place like home? *International Journal of Stress Management, 11,* 366–391.

Sonnentag, S., & Zijlstra, F. R. H. (2006). Job characteristics and off-job activities as predictors of need for recovery and well-being. *Journal of Applied Psychology, 91,* 330–350.

Steptoe, A., & Cropley, M. (2000). Persistent high job demands and reactivity to mental stress predict future ambulatory blood pressure. *Journal of Hypertension, 18,* 581–586.

Steptoe, A., Lundwall, K., & Cropley, M. (2000). Gender, family structure and cardiovascular activity during the working day and evening. *Social Science & Medicine, 50,* 531–539.

Stone, A. A., Kennedy-Moore, E., & Neale, J. M. (1995). Association between daily coping and end-of-day mood. *Health Psychology, 14,* 341–349.

Strauss-Blasche, G., Ekmekcioglu, C., & Marktl, W. (2002). Moderating effects of vacation on reactions to work and domestic stress. *Leisure Sciences, 24,* 237–249.

Taris, T. W., Beckers, D., Verhoeven, L. C., Geurts, S. A. E., Kompier, M. A. J., & van der Linden, D. (2006). Recovery opportunities, work–home interference, and well-being among managers. *European Journal of Work and Organizational Psychology, 15,* 139–157.

Tiedje, L. B., Wortman, C. B., Downey, G., Emmons, C., Biernat, M., & Lang, E. (1990). Women with multiple roles: Role-compatibility perceptions, satisfaction, and mental health. *Journal of Marriage and the Family, 52,* 63–72.

Trougakos, J. P., Beal, D. J., Green, S. G., & Weiss, H. M. (2008). Making the break count: An episodic examination of recovery activities, emotional experiences, and affective delivery. *Academy of Management Journal, 51,* 131–146.

Van Dongen, H. P. A., Maislin, G., Mullington, J. M., & Dinges, D. F. (2003). The cumulative cost of additional wakefulness: Dose-response effects on neurobehavioral functions and sleep physiology from chronic sleep restriction and total sleep deprivation. *Sleep: Journal of Sleep and Sleep Disorders Research, 26,* 117–126.

van Hooff, M. L. M., Geurts, S. A. E., Kompier, M. A. J., & Taris, T. W. (2007). Workdays, in-between workdays and the weekend: A diary study on effort and recovery. *International Archives of Occupational and Environmental Health, 80,* 599–613.

Weh, S. M. (2006). *Förderung individueller Erholungsprozesse: Ergebnisse einer Trainingseva-luation [Promoting individual recovery processes: Results from a training evaluation].* Marburg: Tectum Verlag.

Westman, M., & Eden, D. (1997). Effects of a respite from work on burnout: Vacation relief and fade-out. *Journal of Applied Psychology, 82,* 516–527.

Westman, M., & Etzion, D. (2001). The impact of vacation and job stress on burnout and absenteeism. *Psychology & Health, 16,* 595–606.

Zijlstra, F., & Cropley, M. (2006). Recovery after work. In: F. Jones, R. J. Burke & M. Westman (Eds), *Work–life balance: A psychological perspective* (pp. 219–234). New York, NY: Psychology Press.

Zohar, D. (1999). When things go wrong: The effect of daily work hassles on effort, exertion and negative mood. *Journal of Occupational and Organizational Psychology, 72,* 265–283.

Zohar, D., Tzischinski, O., & Epstein, R. (2003). Effects of energy availability on immediate and delayed emotional reactions to work events. *Journal of Applied Psychology, 88,* 1082–1093.

Chapter 13

Positive Psychology for Work-Life Balance: A New Approach in Treating Workaholism

Rebecca Burwell and Charles P. Chen

13.1. Introduction

Although it is not an easy task to identify the exact number of individuals who suffer from work addition or workaholism, empirical evidence suggests that workaholic-related experiences have become a more common phenomenon than ever before among the working adults. According to a 2007 study released by Statistics Canada, 31 per cent of Canadian workers identified themselves as workaholics (Yang, 2007). While workaholism has received increasing attention both in the popular and academic literature, very little has been written on how to treat it. Indeed, there is not a consensus on whether work addiction should even be treated: a result of differing opinions on whether workaholism is defined as a positive quality or as a harmful disorder (Berglas, 2004). The fact that an unknown number of individuals suffer from high levels of job stress and perfectionism (Spence & Robbins, 1992), and spend long hours working and significantly fewer hours with families or engaging in leisure activities, signifies to the authors of this chapter that more discussion of how workaholism can be treated is not only warranted, but that it is also probably long overdue. The fact that workaholism impacts not only individuals and families, but often co-workers and employers as well (Porter, 2004), provides even more reason to begin having a dialogue regarding possible treatment strategies.

Such a dialogue would first attempt to answer the following questions: (a) what does it mean to be addicted to one's work, and (b) do all workaholics need to be treated? With no generally accepted definition of workaholism, these questions are not readily answered. Burke (2004) is of the same mind, asking, "Is working hard always problematic? The answer is a definitive NO! It seems to make a difference why the person is working hard (low self-esteem) and how the person is working hard (perfectionistic, obsessive-compulsive, high levels of stress)" (p. 422).

The Long Work Hours Culture
Copyright © 2008 by Emerald Group Publishing Limited
All rights of reproduction in any form reserved
DOI:10.1016/B978-1-84855-038-4.00013-0

In one of the most significant contributions to the study of workaholism to date, Spence and Robbins (1992) developed the concept of a workaholic triad, consisting of work involvement, driveness, and enjoyment of work. Their research led to the identification of three types of workaholics based on this triad: the workaholic (WA), the enthusiastic workaholic (EW), and the work enthusiast (WE). WAs get high ratings in all three dimensions: work involvement, driveness, and enjoyment of work. EWs and WEs score high in both work involvement and enjoyment, with EWs scoring lower on the degree of driveness. Research has shown that the first two types (WAs and EWs) experience greater job stress and perfectionism anxiety than WEs (Burke, Oberklaid, & Burgess, 2004; Spence & Robbins, 1992). WAs also tend to have more problems with their physical well-being (Buelens & Poelmans, 2004; Spence & Robbins, 1992). In other research, Burke (2000) found that managers reporting greater feelings of being driven also exhibited poorer emotional and physical well-being, while managers reporting higher levels of work enjoyment indicated more positive emotional and physical well-being. These studies reinforce the idea that work involvement (or number of hours worked) alone does not indicate the existence of a disorder or problem, and that there are indeed different types of workaholics, some of whom are much more likely to need treatment than others.

This chapter explores some psychological helping methods for treating workaholic symptoms. In particular, it considers positive psychology as a viable means to help individuals who suffer from workaholism to tackle the problem. The chapter will first take a look at the antecedents of workaholism, examining some of the main internal and external factors that have originated and reinforced the existence of workaholism in individuals' lives. It will then elaborate the rationale of adopting positive psychology in the treatment of workaholism. Two therapeutic approaches derived from the positive psychology framework, namely, positive psychotherapy (PPT) and quality of life therapy (QOLT), will be incorporated as viable options into the treatment effort. The notion of workaholism in this chapter refers to a broad, inclusive, and overarching phenomenon that covers an array of workaholic-related behaviours, indicators, and issues. Thus, terms such as workaholism, workaholic(s), work addiction, and work addict(s), will be used interchangeably throughout the discussion. To address these workaholic and work addition behaviours in a general manner, the central focus of this chapter is on proposing the applicability of positive psychology-based therapies.

13.2.   Antecedents to Workaholism

13.2.1.   *Personal Factors*

The exact precipitates of work addiction are unknown, though we do know that personal demographics, including age and gender, do not appear to be related (Burke, Matthiesen, & Pallesen, 2006; Spence & Robbins, 1992). Many have speculated that one's upbringing plays a major role in the development of workaholism. Killinger (1991) argues that workaholics typically come from dysfunctional families where children receive the message that what they do and how well they perform is more important than who they are. One result of this message is that such children feel constant pressure to perform, and they experience great anxiety as a result; they nonetheless continually strive for more, a pattern that often ultimately leads to workaholism. Similarly, Robinson (1998) notes that workaholics somehow feel they must earn the right to be, and use work as a way to try to prove their human value, as well as to numb the pain that stems from unfulfilled needs. Berglas (2004) suggests that workaholism is caused by an individual's attempt to cope with the failure to establish and maintain close relationships with family and community, a process known as psychosocial integration. Erikson postulated that psychosocial integration is essential for every person in every type of society; it is what makes life bearable, or even joyful (Alexander, 2004). Berglas suggests that failing to achieve psychosocial integration is usually the result of one of two extreme child-rearing patterns; either parental abuse that makes a child cower from human contact, or parental overindulgence that instills a naïve sense of superiority in a child. He states:

> I often hear workaholics report that the seed of their disordered lifestyle was something one or both parents told them was a "gift" — superior intellect, a skill, or both. Unfortunately, making a child the focus of inordinate attention because he has the ability to secure materialistic rewards causes two forms of damage: (1) the belief that the child is loved only for *what he does* and cannot secure love for *who he is* and (2) the derivative conclusion that the only sort of love or approval one need seek in life derives from achievement. (p. 396)

Regardless of the cause, the idea that workaholism is derived from feelings of inadequacy and/or a need to prove oneself is clearly prevalent in the literature.

13.2.2. Work Factors

Some suggest that the workplace often plays a role in the incidence of workaholism. Fassel (1990) is one proponent of the notion that organizations themselves can be workaholic in nature, and suggests that this is brought on by an organization's obsession with higher profits. She states that there are "several technologies that facilitate the invasion of the corporate in the private" (p. 99). On the contrary, Robinson (1998) suggests that the notion that work addiction actually originates in high-pressure jobs is nothing more than a myth, and that while a fast-paced environment and modern technology may indeed enable workaholism, they are not the *cause*.

13.2.3. Societal Factors

Some also suggest that society may play a role in the incidence of workaholism. Killinger (1991) uses the term "workaholic society", and states that "the work ethic encourages the attitude that it is respectable to work hard and put in long hours" (p. 14). Similarly, Diane Fassel, in her book *Working Ourselves to Death* (1990), dedicates the work to "those who know that facing the reality of work addiction is to meet the wrath of society. It is for all who long for life-giving workplaces and a saner society" (dedication page). This book dedication underscores the author's belief that organizations and society as a whole should shoulder some of the responsibility for the incidence of workaholism. Further, she states later in her study: "I am increasingly uneasy with our tacit acceptance of our organizations' and our society's right to work us to death" (p. 53). In spite of her ultimate conclusion that workaholism is an individualistic disease, Fassel continues to contend that "to keep our focus pointed solely at the individual and not turn a laser light at the society is blindness approaching stupidity. Addictions are individual, family, institutional, and societal diseases" (p. 53). Robinson (1998), while agreeing that work addiction is mainly a psychological problem and less a sociological problem, does argue that workaholism enablers can include cultural/societal beliefs, including the Puritan work ethic. Indeed, it is the authors' perspective that our society's near obsession with productivity, time management, and goal-setting could certainly enable workaholism.

13.2.4. Theoretical Explications

McMillan, O'Driscoll, Marsh, and Brady (2001) reflected in depth on three possible theoretical explications for workaholism, including addiction, learning, and trait theories. In spite of fairly widespread support for the addiction theory, their research concluded that it is premature to suggest that a formal addiction paradigm best explains workaholism. The authors suggest that they present a feasible basis for using learning theory to explain workaholism, which would suggest that workaholism is gradually conditioned into people over time, though that theory has not yet been studied in depth. To date, the most widely accepted is trait theory, in which workaholism would be explained as the result of an underlying trait (such as obsessiveness or conscientiousness) that appears in late adolescence and is exacerbated by an environmental stimuli such as stress. One study, conducted by Burke, Matthiesen, and Pallesen (2006), examined the role of personality factors with regards to workaholism. They concluded that several personality factors, including extraversion, self-efficacy, neuroticism, openness, and conscientiousness, are indeed correlated to the three workaholism components identified by Spence and Robbins (1992). They state that "the findings of this investigation suggest that workaholism is best explained as a personal trait that *may* be activated and supported by experiences and events in one's environment, the workplace likely being the most important setting" (???Burke, Matthiesen, & Pallesen, 2006, p. 1231). Workaholism treatment suggestions to date can be delineated as either individual or workplace interventions.

13.3. Overview of Treatment Strategies to Date

As stated earlier, the treatment of workaholism has received significantly less attention than the syndrome as a whole, and what has been written to date is largely speculative. Porter (2004) suggests that one of the things that makes discussion regarding treatment difficult is that "society supports workaholism, as it does no other addiction. One might question to what extent workaholism has become the new norm, making it even more difficult to determine whether anything in today's model can be labeled excess work" (p. 436). Indeed, workaholism has been frequently referred to as "the best dressed mental health and family problem of the 21st century" (Robinson, 2000, p. 34), thus negating treatment of this non-issue.

13.3.1. Individual Interventions

The fact that many workaholics are in denial about their work addiction (Robinson, 1998) presents an irrefutable challenge to its treatment; and as a result, workaholics tend not to enter into individual psychotherapy (Berglas, 2004). Berglas suggests that most workaholics "find their way into marital therapy [rather than individual therapy] because of the disruptive consequences that workaholism has on spousal relationships" (p. 388). Killinger believes that "denial is the ultimate defence that protects this addiction, and it is the workaholic's real enemy. Workaholics need help and courage to recognize their addiction" (p. 7).

When clients do enter therapy, Robinson (1998) makes it clear that simply cutting back on the number of hours worked will not by itself lead to recovery. Similarly, Berglas (2004) states that it is never appropriate to demand that a workaholic withdraw from his or her professional life; to do so may cause "hostile termination" of psychotherapy. Robinson (1998) reassures his clients that decreasing their working hours is not the focus of therapy, and that they will remain "the architect of any and all changes in their lives" (p. 39). This, he states, relieves his clients and allows them to focus on therapy.

Therapeutic strategies take one of two forms: some strategies attempt to deal with the underlying, internal cause of the work addiction, while others attempt to change the behaviours associated with workaholism, which can include working excessive hours, perfectionism, and non-delegation. Berglas (2004) advocates for the former type of strategy, suggesting that failure to address what is behind the disorder can render any balance-seeking exercise useless. Berglas believes that "a person who lacks the capacity to form authentic intimate ties with others is drawn to workaholism as a lifestyle because it enables him to block out the emotional pain caused by this lack of connectedness" (p. 386). Thus, he suggests psychotherapeutic approaches that "focus primarily on addressing the emotional consequences (disturbances) of the failure to achieve psychosocial integration and secondarily on the symptoms of workaholism" (p. 388). With regards to therapy, he suggests that therapist and client "must ultimately agree on an unambiguous cost-benefit analysis of the gains accrued from a compulsive devotion to work or the rewards it provides, relative to the interpersonal and spiritual losses this concern causes" (p. 388).

Robinson (1998) suggests that the cognitive psychotherapies of Drs. Aaron Beck and David Burns are useful approaches when treating workaholism because they help clients get to the core of the workaholic cycle and ultimately change incorrect beliefs about themselves such as "I must be thoroughly competent in all tasks that I undertake or else I am worthless", or "I should be loved by everyone", and "if only things were perfect, then I could be happy" (p. 114). By changing these rigid beliefs, he contends, workaholics will "develop a more flexible, balanced perspective of themselves that automatically translates into a healthier, more balanced, and more flexible lifestyle" (p. 114).

With respect to changing workaholic behaviours, Robinson (1998) suggests that therapists help their clients to set boundaries, manage their time, and learn to take work more lightly and play more seriously. To this end, he recommends helping clients develop a self-care plan. In such an exercise, therapists have their clients imagine their lives as a circle made up of four parts, including self, family, play, and work. Clients consider what portion of their time is currently spent in each area, then consider what portion of their time they would prefer to spend in each. The client then sets several goals regarding each area that allow them to make the necessary changes to achieve greater balance. Fassel (1990) suggests a similar strategy. She asks her clients to develop daily programs, or agendas, consisting of the number of hours spent at work, rest, play-leisure, and time spent with family and alone. She stresses, however, that time management is not recovery, suggesting that it can be a helpful supplement to recovery, but that the therapist must be careful not to generate the illusion that one can control the disease through time management alone. Fassel also suggests that work addicts need to determine their triggers and bottom-line behaviours. Triggers are situations that tend to bring on workaholism, while bottom-line behaviours are activities that invariably move people back into their addiction. An example of a trigger might be working on the weekend, while a bottom-line behaviour might be agreeing to participate in a large new project at work.

A discussion of current treatment strategies would be remiss if Workaholics Anonymous were not mentioned. This organization has chapters around the world and states that they are "a fellowship of individuals who share their experience, strength, and hope with each other that they may solve their common problems and help others to recover from workaholism" (Workaholics Anonymous, 2005). They subscribe to a similar 12-step approach as is used in the treatment of a variety of addictions. Fassel (1990) recommends Workaholics Anonymous as the most effective process for treating work addiction, contending that "to face ... the addictive disease process you need to experience that you are powerless over your work addiction and that everything you've tried has failed" (p. 147).

13.3.2. Workplace Interventions

It is unlikely that an organization can, by itself, cause workaholism, but an organization can certainly enable work addiction. As Fassel (1990) states, "managers would do well to ask themselves if they are contributing to workaholism by unrealistic expectations, impossible job descriptions, and a corporate culture that pursues profit above everything else" (p. 140). Fortunately, companies can take measures to reduce the incidence of workaholism or to help those employees who may already be work addicts. Workplace interventions range from work/life balance initiatives to training managers to recognize and handle work addiction.

Work-life balance programs are perhaps the most obvious means to encourage employees who may be prone to overwork to seek out non-work activities. However, these programs must be genuine in nature; organizations that present a concern for work/life balance can often do so even as they promote a "go-hard or go-home" attitude, thus sending mixed messages to employees and doing nothing to help the workaholic (O'Connor, 2006). Vodanovich and Piotrowski (2006) suggest that employees' efforts that aspire to achieve work/life balance must be recognized and rewarded. Porter (2004) suggests that companies must begin to "look below the surface of that romanticized vision that good work ethic means always at work or on-call" (p. 437). She believes that organizations should require employees to have a balance of non-work interests, and that those employees who resist this request may identify themselves by working in an addictive manner.

Providing training for managers regarding how to identify and assist workaholics is another way to reduce the incidence of workaholism (Vodanovich & Piotrowski, 2006). A manager who can spot workaholism can then help the affected employee to reestablish work priorities, alter job schedules, or assure that he/she leaves work at a designated time. Identifying the workaholic pattern, however, may be easier said than done. Porter (2004) states that "the idea of excessive work is hard to pin down, until the point at which workers are falling over in exhaustion or emotional collapse" (p. 436). Still, "forums that allow honest conversations about the perils of excessive work, and how we are responsible for glorifying it, may be the best way to start creating healthier norms" (O'Connor, 2006, p. 75).

13.4. Positive Psychology: Towards a New Intervention Rationale

Positive psychology, while it has gained extensive coverage in both the popular press and in academic literature for much of the past decade, has rarely been linked to the treatment of workaholism. Berglas (2004) does recommend *Flow: The Psychology of Optimal Experience* to his readers, which is the work of Mihaly Csikszentmihalyi, one of the world's leading researchers in the area of positive psychology. Berglas suggests that this book is an "ideal place to start if you want to understand the ultimate treatment goal for workaholics" (p. 406).

Positive psychology was officially launched in 1998 by Martin Seligman, another of positive psychology's founders, during his presidency of the American Psychological Association (Wong, 2006). Despite being a comparatively new field, the study of positive psychology has grown quickly. Since the year 2000, hundreds of articles have been written on the topic, and a positive psychology network along with an annual positive psychology summit were developed. Positive psychology courses now exist at the undergraduate and graduate level at universities around the world, and the University of Pennsylvania instituted a Master of Applied Positive Psychology degree in 2005 (Seligman, Steen, Park, & Peterson, 2005).

It is the aim of positive psychology to "correct mainstream psychology's preoccupation with human weaknesses and diseases by promoting a greater emphasis on positive human qualities" (Wong, 2006, p. 133). After World War II, psychology began focusing disproportionately on pathology and repair (Seligman & Csikszentmihalyi, 2000). Seligman (2002) writes that "this almost exclusive attention to pathology neglected the idea of a fulfilled individual and a thriving community, and it neglected the possibility that building strength is the most potent weapon in the arsenal of therapy" (p. 3). Indeed, as Clark (2006) states, "as psychotherapists, we have ignored the 'half-full' side of the equation. That is, we rarely address issues of happiness, contentment, and quality of life" (p. ix). It is predicted, however, that positive psychology in the next century will have evolved into a science and profession that understands and builds the foundations to allow individuals, communities, and societies to flourish (Seligman & Csikszentmihalyi, 2000).

13.5. Linking Positive Psychology to the Treatment of Workaholism

In treating workaholism to date, therapists have tended to focus on the more traditional therapies that place their focus on problems and pathologies rather than on quality of life. However, there are several reasons to believe that a positive approach may have something better, or at a minimum, something additional, to offer the workaholic.

It is well understood that many workaholics seek and experience little pleasure in life; "The key indicator of workaholism is the choice to neglect other life interests" (Porter, 2004, p. 436). Berglas (2004) uses the term "anhedonia" to describe his workaholic clients' dominant mood, anhedonia being the absence of pleasure or the ability to experience it. Killinger (1991) concurs: "As the workaholic breakdown progresses, life becomes overly serious and empty of meaning and fulfillment. The workaholic becomes intense, joyless, and pessimistic" (p. 130). She goes on to state that "pleasure for its own sake is alien to their [the workaholic's] thinking" (p. 131).

The role of leisure has long been considered one of the essential components comprising a healthy and integral self in an individual's total life-career journey and vocational and work-life well-being (McDaniels, 1989; Super, 1990). While play is an integral part of adult life (Snyder & Lopez, 2007), the workaholic's play is rarely done for pleasure alone, but is instead motivated by obligation or purpose (Killinger, 1991). Martin (2005) believes the distinction between intrinsic motivation and extrinsic motivation is very important. When a person is intrinsically motivated, he or she will take on a task for the sake of enjoyment or satisfaction alone. When a person is extrinsically motivated, he or she will take on a task for reward (such as money or social status) or to avoid punishment. A workaholic is rarely intrinsically motivated and is much more likely to perform a task for external reward. Similarly, Csikszentmihalyi (2003) distinguishes between autotelic and exotelic activities. Autotelic activities are those done for something other than an external reward; the "reward" is simply the enjoyment, whether one is playing a musical instrument or enjoying a sunset. Conversely, exotelic activities are done only for the expectation of some type of gain. Again, the very nature of workaholism will lead the work-addicted individual to exotelic rather than autotelic activities. Workaholics are performance and goal-directed; they want everything they do to have a purpose or some tangible outcome (Killinger, 1991).

In addition to not seeking pleasure in life, the workaholic also tends to avoid or spend little time on relationships (Berglas, 2004). "Too often workaholics allow their perfectionistic work ethic to overpower their weaker love ethic" (Killinger, 1991, p. 171). One of the central themes of Martin's book *Making Happy People* is that relationships are the single most important contribution to happiness (2005). Berscheid (2003) concurs, stating "people who have formed and maintain satisfying relationships with others do in fact appear to be happier than those who have not succeeded in doing so" (p. 42).

While workaholics tend to work to the exclusion of play and relationships, positive psychology stresses the importance of work, love, and play to mental health (Snyder & Lopez, 2007). Seligman (1998) refers to these as the three great realms of life. The workaholic, however, has a "single-minded pursuit of professional success" (Berglas, 2004, p. 387). Killinger (1991) describes how anything outside of the realm of work is unusual for the workaholic:

> The workaholic's world is one of power, control, success, and prestige; of complexity, responsibility, ambition, and drive. The ideals of simplicity, freedom, spontaneity, humility, love, and delight ... are foreign to the workaholic's thinking and to his or her current way of life. (p. 3)

Apparently, positive psychology's focus on connections, meaning, and pleasure provides an ideal model to help the workaholic break free from his or her exclusive focus on work.

Several positive psychology therapies have recently been developed to enhance human happiness and quality of life, including PPT, QOLT, strength-centred therapy, and well-being therapy. Despite the likely relevance of these therapeutic approaches to workaholism, it is beyond the scope of this chapter to include all of them for discussion. The next section examines the potential application of two of these new therapies to the treatment of workaholism: PPT and QOLT, with an emphasis on the latter.

13.5.1. Positive Psychotherapy

PPT emerged from the field of positive psychology and theorizes that many mental health issues can be improved by increasing positive emotion, engagement, and meaning within the client's life, rather than exclusively focusing on negative symptoms during therapy (Seligman, Rashid, & Parks, 2006). Its founders suggest that lack of positive emotion, lack of engagement, and lack of felt meaning are not simply symptoms or consequences of depression, but that they actually cause depression — suggesting that the development of positive emotion, engagement, and meaning could alleviate or prevent depression (Seligman et al., 2006). Whether PPT is an effective method for treating workaholism is unknown, but it is certainly true that many workaholics are working to the exclusion of performing activities that provide them with the opportunity to experience positive emotion or engagement. Seligman et al. (2006) state, "we doubt that the effects of PPT are specific to depression, and we expect that increasing positive emotion, engagement, and meaning promote highly general ways of buffering against a variety of disorders and troubles" (p. 785).

Two face-to-face studies were conducted to determine the utility of positive interventions, one with a group of mild to moderately depressed young adults and the other with a group of more severely depressed young adults. The former group experienced greater symptom reduction and more increases in life satisfaction than did the control group that received no treatment. The latter group had more symptomatic improvement and more remission from depression than the control groups (Seligman et al., 2006). It is postulated that PPT works by refocusing attention, memory, and expectations away from the negative and towards the positive (Seligman et al., 2006). The authors of the study warn that their sample sizes were small and that participants in both studies were university or professional students, thus raising the question of whether their findings are generalizable to other populations.

Numerous PPT interventions have been developed, but three popular ones include: using signature strengths in a new way, three good things in life, and the gratitude visit. In the first exercise, participants take an inventory to determine their top five "signature strengths". They are then asked to use one of these five strengths in a new way everyday for a week. In the second exercise, for seven nights, clients write down three things that went well in their day and suggest the causes for these positive occurrences. The third exercise involves having a client write and deliver a letter of gratitude to someone important to them who they felt had never been properly thanked (Seligman et al., 2005). Each of these exercises works by helping clients focus on the positive rather than the negative. Again, the efficacy of these exercises has not been tested with workaholics, but we postulate that such interventions might slowly engage workaholic clients in more positive dialogue with themselves. As many believe that low self-esteem is at the heart of work addiction (Fassel, 1990; Killinger, 1991; Porter, 2004; Robinson, 1998), these could prove to be valuable exercises.

To use the method of signature strengths in a new way, the workaholic client could be asked to use one of their personal strengths in a new way everyday for a certain length of period. For example, the high level of attention they give to their work-life could be practiced to exercise their deliberate effort in nurturing family relationships and fostering a healthy personal hobby for relaxation. Similarly, the three good things in life intervention could be of particular relevance to workaholics. Clients could write down three things that went well in their day when they successfully avoided the excessive attention on their own performance. As the clients are invited to suggest the causes for these positive occurrences, they come to realize that there are more relaxed and healthier ways in achieving equally satisfactory results in their work-life. Moreover, the gratitude visit technique could involve having a workaholic client write and deliver a letter of gratitude to someone important to them who they felt had never been properly thanked. The receiver of the letter could be a family member whom the workaholic had neglected for a long time due to the work addition. The letter recipient might also be a colleague to whom the workaholic was finally able to delegate some tasks. In both scenarios, the workaholic client increases the awareness of important dynamics and possibilities such as relationship, liberty of choice, and collaboration that breakdown the obsession of work addition.

13.5.2.   Quality of Life Therapy

QOLT will be the central focus of this part of the discussion on workaholism treatment interventions. QOLT is a new therapeutic approach that combines the works of a number of authors. Among these works, our analyses will use the work of Frisch (2006) as a major reference in elaborating the essential frame and features of QOLT. Thus, unless otherwise noted, the reader is referred to the work of Frisch (2006) for assertions made in the following discussion.

13.5.3.   Essential Framework and Premises

Although QOLT, like PPT, "adheres strongly to the positive psychology movement's concern with human happiness, strengths, and a better quality of life for all" (Clark, 2006, p. x), QOLT also integrates cognitive therapy (a more traditional therapy) into its practice, thus its dual focus may make it the ideal match for work addiction. The cognitive therapy portion may serve to challenge the underlying thought patterns that originally caused the disease, while the positive psychology facet could work to address some of the behaviours that are associated with work addiction, including, but not limited to, excessive time spent in work-related activities and a lack of time spent in leisure activities.

QOLT can be used with both clinical and non-clinical clients much the same as PPT interventions can be used with both groups. For clinical clients, cognitive therapy is the first stage of treatment, followed by quality of life interventions. For non-clinical clients, QOLT interventions can be used on their own. Although workaholism is not officially listed in the American Psychiatric Association's (1994) *Diagnostic and Statistical Manual of Mental Disorders*, it would be logical for workaholic clients to go through the cognitive therapy stage in an attempt to understand whether and/or how the presence of negative schemas might have contributed to their work addiction. This chapter does not cover specific strategies used in cognitive therapy; for this discussion, readers are encouraged to consult texts by Drs David A. Clark and Aaron T. Beck (1999).

QOLT teaches a life satisfaction approach in which clients are "taught a theory, tenets, and skills aimed at helping them to identify, pursue, and fulfill their most cherished needs, goals, and wishes in valued areas of life" (Frisch, 2006, p. 5). Frisch maintains that there are 16 life areas that may contribute to a person's overall quality of life, including health, self-esteem, goals-and-values/spiritual life, money (or standard of living), work, play, learning, creativity, helping, love, friends (or friendships), children, relatives, home, neighbourhood, and community. Not every person will place equal (or even any) value on all areas. According to quality of life theory, happiness stems from fulfilling our goals in each of the areas that we care about, not necessarily in all of them. Workaholics would be encouraged by a quality of life therapist to identify those areas outside of work that are important to them, be they friendship and creativity, or love and children. Exposure to this model may at least remind workaholic clients that "there is life outside of work".

Such therapy begins with having the client determine from among the 16 areas of life those that are most important to him/her. This is assessed through the quality of life inventory (QOLI), which, in addition to helping a client determine which areas of life may or may not be important to them, produces an overall score, or measure, of life satisfaction. The inventory consists of respondents first rating how important each of the 16 items is to their overall happiness and life satisfaction, then rating how satisfied they are in each area identified as being important. The importance and satisfaction ratings for each item are multiplied to give weighted satisfaction ratings ranging from -6 to $+6$. The results generated suggest areas for intervention (any area with a negative rating) and intervention priorities (areas receiving a score of -6 to -4). Results also provide an overall rating of the client's quality of life compared to nationwide norms. Frisch suggests that "client feedback can be very motivating as in those cases in which clients acclimated to misery in a high-stress job deny their misery only to find themselves in the low or very low range on a test like the QOLI that puts them at risk for a host of physical and psychological maladies" (p. 52). Since workaholics may be reluctant to admit to experiencing problems with their work behaviour, this assessment provides a clear picture of which life areas may require attention or intervention.

The CASIO model of life satisfaction is at the heart of quality of life theory. It is a linear, additive model of life satisfaction based on the 1976 work of Campbell, Converse, and Rogers; one that "assumes that happiness comes largely from achieving goals and gaining fulfillment in the areas of life that we value" (p. 90). The CASIO model of life satisfaction forms the basis for many of the QOLT interventions, as intervention in any CASIO element may lead to greater happiness in a life area. The CASIO model asserts that an individual's level of satisfaction within any area of life is composed of four elements: (1) the objective characteristics or circumstances of an area, (2) the individual's attitude towards these circumstances, (3) the individual's evaluation of fulfillment in an area based on the application of standards of accomplishment or fulfillment, and (4) the individual's acknowledged importance of the area for overall life satisfaction. The "O" in the CASIO acronym stems from the belief that an individual may increase his/her overall life satisfaction by increasing satisfaction in an area. Other than those that are of immediate concern, based on the idea that an individual's overall satisfaction in life is comprised, in part, of the sum of satisfactions experience in all valued areas.

13.6. QOLT Principles

13.6.1. Core Principles

QOLT consists of three core principles, or pillars, known as the "tenets of contentment". Frisch states that these are essential to the approach and that they should be conveyed to all clients at the beginning of therapy. He explains that these tenets "will often be 'the answer' or an answer to clients' unhappiness, stuckness or resistance to intervention, or life problem/challenge" (p. 78). He also suggests that these principles be reviewed on a daily basis, as practices that become routine appear to have the greatest effect on happiness. The first of the tenets is the inner abundance principle. It suggests that through self-care (e.g., rest, exercise, and meditation), individuals are able to be more available for others, as well as becoming better able to avoid overwhelming themselves with too many responsibilities. The second tenet is the quality time principle, which suggests clients allow themselves approximately 30 min of strictly alone time per day to relax and centre on feelings and goals. The third is the find a meaning/find a goal tenet which advocates that clients develop a "guiding vision" of what matters most in their lives, including personal and career goals for the future. Each of these tenets clearly conforms to the thinking and needs of the workaholic client.

13.6.2. Area-Specific Principles

In addition to these three core principles, QOLT offers over 30 tenets specific to particular areas of life (i.e., health, work, learning, love, etc.). The three area-specific principles most relevant to the workaholic include: the balanced lifestyle principle, the flow it principle, and the leisurely pace and lifestyle principle.

The balanced lifestyle principle stems from the assumption that all valued areas of life contribute to one's overall life satisfaction, thus time must be given to each of these valued areas in order to feel happier. While this may simply be commonsensical, the workaholic often has a life that is out of balance, spending the majority of his/her time and energy on work. In spite of this, the workaholic client will normally acknowledge that there are areas outside of work that are important to him/her. The balanced lifestyle principle serves as a reminder to the client that happiness comes from a balance of areas, not from any one area (i.e., work) exclusively.

The flow it principle is based on the concept of flow, an important term in positive psychology. A flow activity is one in which the individual becomes so engrossed that he/she loses track of time and has the sense that nothing else matters (Csikszentmihalyi, 1990). Flow activities are a major source of joy and fulfillment. What is important about flow activities in the sense of workaholism is that they are activities done for their own sake, in other words, they are intrinsically rewarding. Workaholics generally choose activities that have a clear purpose or outcome — extrinsically motivated activities. The flow it principle of QOLT encourages activities that produce happiness and are done for their own sake, an important reminder for workaholics.

The basis of the leisurely pace and lifestyle principle is that individuals experience greater happiness, contentment, and wisdom when they reduce the number of outside responsibilities they have. While workaholics will undoubtedly experience distress and will resist giving up work responsibilities, this principle reminds them that there is value in letting go of work tasks.

13.6.3. QOLT Interventions

While such principles or tenets may prove useful to the workaholic client, they still remain as the general guidelines and theoretical premises to form the basis of intervention. QOLT offers both general interventions that increase happiness in all areas of one's life and area-specific interventions designed to focus on those areas that cause dissatisfaction (e.g., health, work, self-esteem, etc.). The client and therapist work together to determine all potential areas for improvement and then choose the most appropriate general and area-specific interventions.

13.6.4. General Interventions

The five paths to happiness intervention incorporates all five CASIO factors (unlike other QOLT interventions, which may target only one). In this exercise, happiness is explained to the client as the extent to which their most important needs, goals, and wishes have been fulfilled. Five strategies for boosting satisfaction are then presented to the client, each relating directly to one of the five CASIO factors. In the first strategy, clients are presented with the idea that they can change their circumstances. Most workaholics will not respond to the idea of changing their work-related circumstances, but they may be open to problem-solving other areas of their lives. The second strategy involves changing one's attitude, and is based on the concept of reality testing. At this stage, workaholic clients might be challenged to critically think about the impact of their workaholism on the rest of their life, or on their family. The third strategy involves changing goals and standards, where a client is encouraged to experiment with raising or lowering his or her standards. Given that workaholics often demonstrate perfectionist tendencies, the goal would be to help them lower their expectations of themselves. The fourth strategy is changing priorities; clients are urged to reevaluate and consider what is most important to them. The workaholic clients would be encouraged to look at areas outside of work that are most important to them. In the fifth strategy of the five paths to happiness intervention, clients are encouraged to pick any area of life and increase their satisfaction within it, in order to gain an overall boost to happiness. Here, the therapist might encourage the client to pursue a favourite hobby, without discussing any possible changes to the work situation.

Another general intervention that might be useful for workaholic clients is the Happiness Pie exercise. This activity is not unlike the Robinson (1998) self-care plan exercise described earlier. It specifically addresses the fourth element of the CASIO model, changing priorities. In this activity, clients draw a circle and divide this circle into "slices", each slice denoting an area of their life. Larger life "slices" are delineated for aspects that take more time and energy, and smaller "slices" for those requiring less time and energy. This first circle is a snapshot of their current life and affords the client the opportunity to view the reality of his or her current life. A workaholic's circle will more than likely show work to be the most time-consuming area of life. Just this visual depiction may have a significant impact on workaholic clients. The clients then draw a second circle to depict how they would ideally like their life to be. A workaholic would be encouraged to lessen the work "slice" and consider other areas of life important to them, be that play, love, creativity, and so on.

13.6.5. *Area-Specific Interventions*

While QOLT offers area-specific interventions for all 16 areas, some areas are more likely to be problematic for the workaholic, and thus more helpful to consider. The areas looked at specifically will obviously depend on the individual client, but the areas of self-esteem, relationships, and play may prove most relevant to the largest number of workaholics.

13.6.5.1. Self-esteem In QOLT, self-esteem is defined as "liking and respecting yourself in light of your strengths and weaknesses, successes and failures, and ability to handle problems" (Frisch, 2006, p. 187). Low self-esteem is very often at the core of a workaholic's disorder. Frisch suggests that clients can improve their self-esteem by acting in agreement with the standards of behaviour they have set for themselves in valued areas of life. One suggested exercise for boosting one's self-esteem in QOLT is the BAT (blessings, accomplishments, and traits) exercise, designed to increase clients' self-esteem by helping them become more aware of the positive features about themselves and their lives. In this activity, clients first recall and then chart their blessings (things they are thankful for), accomplishments (whether small or significant, past or present), and talents or traits (things they excel at, or that others appreciate about them). This exercise provides a good opportunity for the workaholic clients to spend time thinking about those things beyond work for which they are thankful — perhaps family, relatives, or community. With respect to considering accomplishments or traits, the therapist may prompt the workaholic client to consider those that are unrelated to work, to encourage the client to place value on other aspects of his or her life.

13.6.5.2. Relationships According to Frisch, positive relationships may be the most important component of the "happiness stew". Workaholics, however, commonly place more emphasis on work than on relationships. Numerous QOLT relationship-related interventions are available. The most useful would, of course, depend on which specific relationship issues are being experienced by the workaholic and on whether the relationship is with a spouse, friend, or other family member. Frisch provides a list of QOLT relationship skills that include complimenting, constructive criticism, feeling statements, and problem-solving. Any or all of the suggestions may be pertinent to workaholic clients as they try to improve their interpersonal relationships.

13.6.5.3. Play The importance of play, or recreation, is emphasized in QOLT. "Choosing not to recreate risks destroying your quality of life" (Frisch, 2006, p. 250). In a study on the effect of play in adults' lives, researchers found that when play is a notable part of an individual's identity, he or she tends to be more aware of and accepting of his/her emotions, more skilful in expressing feelings, more likely to pursue intellectual stimulation, to avoid exposure to harmful chemicals and drugs, and to engage in behaviours that promote the health and welfare of their wider social community (Doster, Mielke, Riley, Toledo, & Goven, 2006). Unfortunately, many workaholics ignore play for their more favoured "purposeful" activities. Recreation is so important that Frisch believes the question "I wonder if I'll have time to play today"? should be replaced with "How and when shall I choose to play today"? QOLT offers a step-by-step approach to play that works to create a routine or habit for recreation — a substantial and necessary act leading to positive change for workaholic clients.

The first step involves building motivation, as Frisch acknowledges that any client resistant to the idea of play will not benefit from the intervention. Indeed, the workaholic may have a difficult time accepting the need to infuse pleasure into his or her daily life. Frisch suggests several means that might be used to increase motivation to play, including the use of a pro versus con technique in which the client lists and then challenges reasons to maintain the *status quo*. The second step involves identifying interests to pursue recreationally. Workaholic clients who have put outside interests aside may have difficulty even identifying leisure activities that would engage them. These clients could be encouraged to remember past activities they have enjoyed, or to think of interests that intrigue them in the present. Frisch's book presents a list of over 200 potential play activities. The third step involves problem-solving about the inevitable list of potential obstacles to play. Workaholics have naturally let other, more "purposeful", activities take precedence in their life, so this is an important step. They are apt to believe that play is an "unnecessary luxury". Frisch states, "Often negative core beliefs are an obstacle to play satisfaction, as in the case of people who define their self-worth strictly in terms of how well they perform in their work" (p. 262). In these cases, changing the workaholics' attitude towards play and their belief that they do not have time to play will be crucial. Therapists will need to be careful that clients do not take on play as "one more thing to do" and try to turn it into an exotelic activity. Over time, the workaholic client may begin to understand that play is necessary for its own sake and not try to attach purpose to it beyond this. Step four involves implementing the leisure plan, while step five involves evaluating the plan for recreation and whether it increased satisfaction. Therapists may need to be patient in waiting to hear from their workaholic client that he/she experienced satisfaction from recreation, but should not give up on this pursuit.

The importance of relationships and recreation cannot be over-emphasized as an issue in workaholism, and for this reason, positive psychology, and perhaps QOLT in particular, have much to offer as a potential new treatment for those caught up in the cycle. QOLT, like the field of positive psychology, is very new, and as a result little research has been performed to test its efficacy. Frisch states that QOLT "showed clinically significant gains in quality of life and life satisfaction at posttreatment and follow-up assessments" (p. 7), though he readily acknowledges that the method requires further studies to prove its effectiveness. It does, however, provide numerous suggestions for interventions that may prove to be highly effective with the workaholic client.

13.7. Conclusion

This chapter summarizes what it means to be a workaholic, outlines the factors believed to contribute to the syndrome, describes the range of strategies currently used to treat/reduce workaholism, and suggests a new approach that might help this client group — that of positive psychology. Within the general theoretical and philosophical frame of positive psychology, the usefulness of the two specific therapeutic approaches, i.e., PPT and QOLT are explored. Both promote positive cognitive and behavioural changes by encouraging the client to focus on areas outside of work in order to produce greater happiness and, in the process, reduce the extent, or incidence of, workaholism. Similar to its utilization in other psychological helping contexts, positive psychology in the treatment of workaholism and work addiction is at the onset of its trial. More evidence based on empirical research and clinical intervention remains to be generated to enrich the rationale and consolidate the efficacy of this new approach in the helping process. Notwithstanding its novelty, positive psychology appears to have great potential to provide a beneficial addition for the treatment of workaholism.

References

Alexander, B. K. (2004). Finding the roots of addiction. *Transition Magazine, 34*. Retrieved on March 21, 2007, from www.vifamily.ca/library/transition/342/342.html

American Psychiatric Association. (1994). *Diagnostic and statistical manual of mental disorders* (4th ed.). Washington, DC: American Psychiatric Association.

Berglas, S. (2004). Treating workaholism. In: R. H. Coombs (Ed.), *Handbook of addictive disorders: A practical guide to diagnosis and treatment* (pp. 383–407). Hoboken, NJ: Wiley.

Berscheid, E. (2003). The human's greatest strength: Other humans. In: L. G. Aspinwall & U. M. Staudinger (Eds), *A psychology of human strengths: Fundamental questions and future directions for a positive psychology* (pp. 37–47). Washington, DC: American Psychological Association.

Buelens, M., & Poelmans, S. A. Y. (2004). Enriching the Spence and Robbins' typology of workaholism: Demographic, motivational and organizational correlates. *Journal of Organizational Change Management, 17*, 440–458.

Burke, R. J. (2000). Workaholism in organizations: Psychological and physical well-being consequences. *Stress Medicine, 16*, 11–16.

Burke, R. J. (2004). Introduction: Workaholism in organizations. *Journal of Organizational Change Management, 17*, 420–423.

Burke, R. J., Matthiesen, S. B., & Pallesen, S. (2006). Personality correlates of workaholism. *Personality and Individual Differences, 40*, 1223–1233.

Burke, R. J., Oberklaid, F., & Burgess, Z. (2004). Workaholism among Australian women psychologists: Antecedents and consequences. *Women in Management Review, 19*, 252–259.

Clark, D. A. (2006). Foreword. In: M. B. Frisch (Ed.), *Quality of life therapy: Applying a life satisfaction approach to positive psychology and cognitive therapy* (pp. ix–x). Hoboken, NJ: Wiley.

Clark, D. A., & Beck, A. T. (1999). *Scientific foundations of cognitive theory and therapy of depression*. New York: Wiley.

Csikszentmihalyi, M. (1990). *Flow: The psychology of optimal experience*. New York: Harper Collins.

Csikszentmihalyi, M. (2003). *Good business: Leadership, flow and the making of meaning*. London: Hodder & Stoughton.

Doster, J. A., Mielke, R. K., Riley, C. A., Toledo, J. R., & Goven, A. J. (2006). Play and health among a group of adult business executives. *Social Behavior and Personality, 34*, 1071–1080.

Fassel, D. (1990). *Working ourselves to death: The high cost of workaholism & the rewards of recovery.* San Francisco: Harper Collins.

Frisch, M. B. (2006). *Quality of life therapy: Applying a life satisfaction approach to positive psychology and cognitive therapy.* Hoboken, NJ: Wiley.

Killinger, B. (1991). *Workaholics: The respectable addicts.* Toronto, Ontario, Canada: Key Porter.

Martin, P. (2005). *Making happy people: The nature of happiness and its origins in childhood.* London: Harper Collins.

McDaniels, C. (1989). *The changing workplace: Career counseling strategies for the 1990s and beyond.* San Francisco: Jossey-Bass.

McMillan, L. H. W., O'Driscoll, M. P., Marsh, N. V., & Brady, E. C. (2001). Understanding workaholism: Data synthesis, theoretical critique, and future design strategies. *International Journal of Stress Management, 8,* 69–91.

O'Connor, T. (2006). When work becomes your fix. *In the Black, 76,* 74–76.

Porter, G. (2004). Work, work ethic, work excess. *Journal of Organizational Change Management, 17,* 424–439.

Robinson, B. E. (1998). *Chained to the desk: A guidebook for workaholics, their partners and children, and the clinicians who treat them.* New York: University Press.

Robinson, B. E. (2000). A typology of workaholics with implications for counselors. *Journal of Addictions & Offender Counseling, 21,* 34–48.

Seligman, M. E. P. (1998). Work, love, and play. *APA Monitor, 29.* Retrieved on May 29, 2007, from www.apa.org/monitor/aug98/pc.html.

Seligman, M. E. P. (2002). Positive psychology, positive prevention, and positive therapy. In: C. R. Snyder & S. J. Lopez (Eds), *Handbook of addictive disorders: A practical guide to diagnosis and treatment* (pp. 3–9). New York: Oxford University Press.

Seligman, M. E. P., & Csikszentmihalyi, M. (2000). Positive psychology: An introduction. *American Psychologist, 55,* 5–14.

Seligman, M. E. P., Rashid, T., & Parks, A. (2006). Positive psychotherapy. *American Psychologist, 61,* 774–788.

Seligman, M. E. P., Steen, T. A., Park, N., & Peterson, C. (2005). Positive psychology progress: Empirical validation of interventions. *American Psychologist, 60,* 410–421.

Snyder, C. R., & Lopez, S. J. (2007). *Positive psychology: The scientific and practical explorations of human strengths.* Thousand Oaks, CA: Sage.

Spence, J. T., & Robbins, A. S. (1992). Workaholism: Definition, measurement, and preliminary results. *Journal of Personality Assessment, 58,* 160–178.

Super, D. E. (1990). A life-span, life space approach career development. In: D. Brown & L. Brooks (Eds), *Career choice and development: Applying contemporary theories to practice* (2nd ed, pp. 197–261). San Francisco: Jossey-Bass.

Vodanovich, S. J., & Piotrowski, C. (2006). Workaholism: A critical but neglected factor in O.D. *Organization Development Journal, 24,* 55–60.

Wong, Y. J. (2006). Strength-centered therapy: A social constructionist, virtues-based psychotherapy. *Psychotherapy: Theory, Research, Practice, Training, 43,* 133–146.

Workaholics Anonymous. (2005). Retrieved on May 28, 2007, from http://www.workaholics-anonymous.org.

Yang, J. (2007). Workaholism can harm your health. *Metro Toronto,* May 30, p. 27.

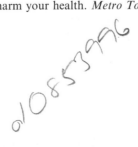

010853996 (RH)